Transformational grammar as a theory of language acquisition

CAMBRIDGE STUDIES IN LINGUISTICS

General Editors · W. SIDNEY ALLEN · EUGENIE J. A. HENDERSON
FRED W. HOUSEHOLDER · JOHN LYONS · R. B. LE PAGE
F. R. PALMER · J. L. M. TRIM

TRANSFORMATIONAL GRAMMAR AS A THEORY OF LANGUAGE ACQUISITION

A STUDY IN THE EMPIRICAL, CONCEPTUAL AND METHODOLOGICAL FOUNDATIONS OF CONTEMPORARY LINGUISTICS

BRUCE L. DERWING

Assistant Professor of Linguistics
University of Alberta

CAMBRIDGE

at the University Press · 1973

Published by the Syndics of the Cambridge University Press
Bentley House, 200 Euston Road, London NW1 2DB
American Branch: 32 East 57th Street, New York, N.Y. 10022

© Cambridge University Press 1973

Library of Congress Catalogue Card Number: 72–88620

ISBNs: 0 521 08737 6   hard covers

0 521 09798 3   paperback

Type set in Great Britain
by Alden & Mowbray Ltd
at the Alden Press, Oxford

Printed in the United States of America

Contents

To my parents
Henry C. and Clara L. Derwing

Preface

This book is an extensively revised and enlarged version of my 1970 Indiana University Ph.D. dissertation, originally written between January 1969 and May 1970, while I served as Visiting Professor of Slavic Languages at the University of Alberta. As with most books, the main contribution of the fellow whose name appears on the title page is one of persistence in collating the ideas of others in some systematic way and in pounding out the text. Every author must build on the work of his predecessors; in this present work, however, the debt owed to numerous collaborators, both witting and unwitting, surely exceeds the average by a considerable margin. I have tried to acknowledge most of the unwitting ones in my bibliography. The witting ones deserve mention here.

My first and greatest debt of gratitude goes to Dr Carleton T. Hodge, Professor of Linguistics and Anthropology at Indiana University and my dissertation supervisor. Without his constant help and encouragement at each of several critical branch-points throughout my graduate career, I simply could never have made it through school; hence this work would never have been contemplated. My fondest wish is to be remembered by some of my own students with but a fraction of the affection, gratitude and esteem I hold for this man.

I also owe a special debt to Dr Fred W. Householder, Jr, Research Professor of Linguistics and Classics at Indiana University, for numerous helpful suggestions, both as a member of my original dissertation committee and afterwards on a purely voluntary basis. Scarcely a page of either version of this book escaped his all-seeing eye unscathed. I should never dare suggest that this book represents an accurate reflection of Dr Householder's philosophical position; nevertheless, whenever I think of the term 'mentor', it is always his name which comes first to mind. It was also at Dr Householder's suggestion that my manuscript was submitted to Cambridge University Press.

A third individual has also had a particularly important role to play in this whole affair. This is Dr Gary D. Prideaux, Associate Professor of Linguistics at the University of Alberta. He has taught me, by personal example, everything that the word 'colleague' ought to imply. Initially he provided me with much-needed moral support to get a lonesome work of this sort off the ground; thereafter he served, in effect, as a kind of one-man 'committee in absentia' while the original version of this book was being constructed, and he has continued to serve as my closest confidant and collaborator throughout the revision phase. I can no longer estimate how many ideas of his have become mingled with my own and made their way into these pages unacknowledged; I only know that there are many and that the role which they played in the development of this work has been a significant one.

Another colleague has made his influence very much felt as well. This is Dr William J. Baker, Associate Professor and our 'friendly neighborhood psychologist', who joined the Department with me in 1970. From him I received my first real inkling of the mysterious but fascinating world of the psychologist and learned the value of having an 'enemy' in the camp. There are few substantive improvements introduced in this revised version of my book which did not have their origin in one confrontation or another which I have had with Dr Baker. I hope he does not resent the fact that I gained far more from these exchanges than he did.

I am also grateful to Professor C. I. J. M. Stuart, Head of the Department, not only for many stimulating ideas and suggestions, but also for many practical favors which made the task of preparing the manuscript much easier for me. Among the many students who kept me well-supplied with both counterargument and encouragement, Mr Peter R. Harris was especially helpful as critic and discussant, as well as in providing much valuable bibliographic assistance, particularly in connection with chapters 1, 7 and 8. Special thanks are also due to Mrs Pearl Dahlberg for her cheerful, patient and efficient handling of the typing duties on several successive versions of the same old manuscript, and to Miss Barbara Hoey for her help with the proofs and index.

If this final version is at all comprehensible and reasonably compact, this is due far more to the superb and extensive editorial assistance provided by John Lyons and staff of the Cambridge University Press than it is to me. I also gratefully acknowledge the support provided me by the American Council of Learned Societies during my last year on the Indiana campus, when the ideas realized in this work were first beginning to take shape.

Finally, I owe a very special thanks to my wife and family for long-suffering consideration and understanding throughout a 'crisis' situation which somehow managed to stretch out into three full years.

B.L.D.

Edmonton, Alberta,
Canada
August 1972

There can be asked respecting language no other question of a more elementary and at the same time of a more fundamentally important character than this: how is language obtained by us? how does each speaking individual become possessed of his speech? Its true answer involves and determines well-nigh the whole of linguistic philosophy.

William Dwight Whitney
The Life and Growth of Language, 1876

Part I

BACKGROUND

1 Introduction

1.1 Purpose of the study

This book is primarily a contribution to a relatively new branch of linguistic inquiry, 'foundational analysis'. The term and much of the inspiration for this book come from Stuart (1969), the leading study in this area to date. Like Stuart in that more compact statement, I am mainly interested in seeking answers to such fundamental questions as the following:

(1) What *metatheoretical and methodological assumptions* underly the currently dominant paradigm of linguistic investigation, namely transformational-generative grammar (henceforth TGG)? To what extent are these assumptions tenable and viable?

(2) What is *the status of a linguistic description* (or, as the notion is most commonly construed, of a transformational-generative grammar)? What kind of reality does such a description represent, and to what extent are its claims to a specific ontological status justified?

(3) In sum, to what extent is linguistics, as defined primarily by the paradigm of the generative grammarian, concerned with *establishing knowledge* about some aspect of the real world? Where does this knowledge end and supposition and speculation begin? In other words, to what extent is linguistics as understood today to be taken seriously as a scientific discipline?

Such questions are fundamental to linguistics, as they would be to any field which claimed allegiance (as linguistics does) to the aims and methods of empirical science. Nevertheless, these questions have had surprisingly little attention. One reason for the oversight may be that, until recently, no one really cared much, as the answers to such questions mattered only to a small group of specialists (linguists) whose influence on the world outside their own circumscribed domain of interests was negligible. Today, however, chiefly through the influence of Noam Chomsky, this picture has changed. The influence of current work in linguistic theory is now felt in other disciplines, especially in

3

psychology (beginning with the Chomsky and Miller papers in Luce, *et al.*, 1963) and in philosophy (as indicated by the appearance of such books as Hook, 1969). Moreover, the number of scholars now directly involved in the development and dissemination of linguistic information has grown substantially during the past decade. As a consequence of this rapid growth of influence, linguistics suddenly finds itself far more familiar and popular than before, with news of some of its basic controversies even reaching the popular press (as in the *Time* article of 16 February 1968 on 'The Scholarly Dispute Over the Meaning of Linguistics', the Sklar interview and commentary on 'Chomsky's Revolution in Linguistics', which appeared in volume 207 of *The Nation* that same year, and Mehta's perceptive interview with Chomsky, Hockett and Jakobson in 8 May 1971 issue of *The New Yorker*.) Increasingly, it is coming to matter more and more whether or not linguistics is indeed intent upon the establishment and dissemination of knowledge about some aspect of the real world or whether it is merely playing at science, surrounding itself with much form but little substance.

Considering the substantial investment in time, effort, people and money devoted to research in linguistics today (and especially under the banner of transformationalism), there is another reason for serious exploration of the questions which concern us here. For the linguist, like his fellow researchers in other fields, has to carry out his work in a world beset by serious problems whose resolution may involve the survival of the human species – everything from overpopulation, to environmental pollution, to the inequitable distribution of wealth and resources to the problems of the arms race and war itself. It is all the more obvious that the linguist will have to compete for the dwindling research dollar with agencies and individuals involved in projects of great social, economic and political import. Unless he can demonstrate that the goals he pursues are worthwhile and his methods adequate to the task and likely to bear fruit in real understanding of the nature of human learning or human cognition (for example), he won't get the money.

To illustrate: for the past several years linguistics departments all over North America have been turning out what can be described as a generation of professional grammar writers. This has been primarily because the dominant paradigm (that of TGG) sets great store by the construction of such grammars, in the enunciation and explication of the general principles underlying their construction and in the implications of such work for other disciplines (notably psychology). Yet the empirical status of these grammars has not been analyzed (cf. question 2 above), nor has the basic soundness of the underlying principles (question 1). A central thesis of this book is that the empirical status of such grammars is sufficiently obscure and the viability of the basic assumptions sufficiently in doubt to warrant a fundamental shift in the attitude of linguists both to the nature of the work they do or ought to be doing and of the results they achieve or ought to be achieving. It is characteristic of foundations that they support the superstructure, and linguistics is no exception. It will be a chief contention of this book that current work in linguistics along transformational-generative lines is yielding little in the way of substantive accomplishments of any empirical significance, while offering much in the way of unsupported (and, given present methods of research, unsupportable) speculative assertion, with the larger portion of current metatheoretical discussion being devoted to marginal or irrelevant 'smoke screen' issues which hide deep conceptual and methodological difficulties.[1]

1.2 Rationale for the study

The reader will gather that this book is an attempt to develop a unified and reasonably thorough critique of the theoretical foundations of TGG. Of necessity, therefore, it takes on more of a philosophical flavor (focused primarily at the level of methodology) than a strongly data-oriented one. The problem of language acquisition in children has been a serious study for centuries, but I allude here only briefly to small and isolated parts of the vast (though relatively uncontrolled) literature, making no attempt to survey the whole. That work still begs to be done, of course, but my purpose here is different. My point of departure is not the laboratory, but linguistic theory. I justify my title by arguing (particularly in chapter 3) that all linguistic theorizing is, at base, theorizing about the nature of language acquisition, just as Whitney said a century ago (see epigraph). In the final analysis, therefore, I am concerned here with developing and testing what might be called alterna-

---

[1] I would contend, for instance, that it makes little sense to argue at great length whether or not a level of 'autonomous phonemics' fits naturally into a generative grammar so long as the notion of a generative grammar itself, construed as a model of 'linguistic competence', remains as confused and ill-defined as it is at present. (See 6.1 and chapter 8 below for detailed treatments of these particular issues.)

tive *linguistic theories of language acquisition*, and with attendant questions related to their essential tenability (Are they the right *kind* of theories? Do they make sense?) and viability (Are they appropriate heuristic devices for increasing our knowledge of the phenomenon of language acquisition? Can they be generalized to account for other kinds of learning?).

My primary audience, then, is my fellow linguists. Non-linguists, as a consequence, may have difficulty coming to grips with the decidedly in-group orientation adopted here. I have tried to avoid using too much linguistic jargon and its formalisms in the hope of making this book accessible to as large and heterogeneous an audience as possible, but the problem goes far deeper than that. For one thing, the outsider (and many an insider, for that matter) may fail to see the point of my excursions into areas of seemingly dubious relevance, while others may think that I appear at times to be belaboring the obvious.

Indeed, I find myself torn between two conflicing interpretations of what it is that I am doing here. On the one hand, I worry that an embarrassingly large portion of what I say is so obvious that it borders on the trite, or even trivial. At other times, however (and particularly when a new book in linguistics or language acquisition or a new issue of a major linguistic journal appears), I find myself in a different frame of mind: I begin to wonder whether the whole field of linguistics has not lost its senses. Yet one continues to read the same kind of thing so often (and in larger and more expensive books all the time – some of which are major incursions into other fields of study[1]) that one gets the definite impression that these statements are intended to be taken seriously and even thought by many to be solid advances in our knowledge of the nature of language and the process of language acquisition, despite the seemingly obvious and fundamental considerations which by now strongly indicate to me the opposite. Even when it comes to the issues at present most heatedly debated within linguistics, it is often the case that the basic questions involved in these discussions are ones which other disciplines have debated to the point of exhaustion and have resolved by reaching a set of generally accepted conclusions.[2] Yet these conclusions,

[1] Cf. the recent outpouring of new books on psycholinguistics and language acquisition with a strong transformational-generative orientation (e.g., Brown, 1970; Deese, 1970; Hayes, 1970; McNeill, 1970a; Slobin, 1971c; and Dale, 1972).

[2] To give three illustrations which I shall refer to again later, consider the old notion in biology (and psychology) that 'ontogeny recapitulates phylogeny' (cf. 4.5.2), as well as the truly ancient 'nature vs. nurture' and 'induction vs. deduction' controversies (cf. 3.5 and 7.1 respectively).

sound as they appear to be, remain unknown to, or have been forgotten by, or have failed to make an impression on linguists, long isolated from other branches of science. It is necessary to inject (or reinject) some of these fundamentals into current linguistic meta-discussion, if only to spare linguists having to go over again ground which has already been well surveyed for us by others. True enough, what is 'obvious' or 'generally accepted' by researchers in other fields may not be appropriate or right for linguists (or even for the other disciplines), but neither should such matters be neglected or ignored.

My dilemma is very much the one described by Koestler (1967, p. 4):

If one attacks the dominant school in [some field]...one is up against two opposite types of criticism. The first is the natural reaction of the defenders of orthodoxy, who believe that they are in the right and that you are in the wrong – which is only fair and to be expected. The second category of critics belongs to the opposite camp. They argue that, since the pillars of the citadel are already cracked and revealing themselves as hollow, one ought to ignore them and dispense with polemics. Or, to put it more bluntly, why flog a dead horse?

I suspect that the number of scholars in the second of these two categories with respect to Chomsky's views is larger than the average transformational-generative grammarian might like to think (especially if he feeds his mind mainly on unpublished papers circulated privately among a closed circle of like-minded colleagues and friends). There are some people (and not all of them ill-informed or irrational), who find little or nothing which is compelling enough in Chomsky's work to be worth the trouble of criticizing. Yet here I am producing a book which, from that point of view, is simply an overindulgent exercise in 'overkill'. So why do I bother?

Having been trained as a linguist, I naturally feel a close affinity, if not identification, with linguistics over and above any which could possibly be felt for any other discipline, at least for the time being. Consequently, I feel concerned about the sort of image which linguistics presents to the world. To enlightened and severe critics this image is very tarnished: to them, linguistics isn't even worth discussing. But, oddly enough, the impression one gets from within the field is that this image is not the one which *most* outsiders see. To the contrary, the general feeling among linguists seems to be that scholars in other fields have more to learn from linguistics than vice versa and, moreover, that most of these outsiders are becoming more and more aware of this.[1] But in selling one field to another one does have certain inherent advantages, does he not? For one thing, most outsiders are too busy with their own work to have time to analyze the claims which linguists make; if these ambassadors from linguistics talk easily and confidently about their subject, they are likely to be given the benefit of the doubt, particularly if there is a good deal of obvious enthusiasm thrown in for good measure. (After all, a whole discipline cannot be in error, can it?) The self-confidence and apparent unanimity of transformational-generative grammarians has thus proven successful even to the point of persuading the occasional well-known psychologist to hop onto the Chomsky bandwagon, often with little awareness of what it is he is selling.[2] It is to be expected that enthusiasts are going to advocate their own point of view, and I agree with P. Harris that this can be tolerated up to a point (1970, p. 4). But without guidelines to help us determine when that point is reached, there is danger of advocating ideas which are merely very popular, though still open to considerable doubt, as if they were well-established truths. As Seuren says:

There is no denying that transformational grammar is, broadly speaking, well-established. That is precisely the reason why it must be taught. But it is not well enough established to teach it as a corpus of doctrine in the same way as natural sciences are taught. The pedagogical difficulty in teaching generative grammar is mainly that we want our students to become aware of the debatable and tentative nature of most, if not all, grammatical descriptions given in transformational terms (1969, p. 188).

If this is true in the training of linguists, then it ought all the more to be kept in mind in our dealings with other disciplines. There is an important professional responsibility here, namely, that we must be careful to

---

[1] So McNeill, in his contribution to Mussen (1970), shuns a literature survey of the sort his predecessor undertook (McCarthy, 1954) on the grounds that 'recent developments in linguistics pose important issues *for psychology*, and examination of them takes priority within the limits of space over comprehensive citation' (p. 1062; italics added).

[2] Cf. Deese, 1970, for example: 'The most significant function [TGG] has had in the past decade...has been to provide our ideas about language with a firm theoretical foundation...Generative theory gives us the means of characterizing those things that are really essential to language in a precise and detailed way...One of the consequences of the development of generative theory has been to show that learning theory, when it is carefully and strictly interpreted,...cannot apply to the way in which people acquire, use, and understand ordinary human languages. Those who have tried to apply learning theory to the problem of how people use languages do not really understand what language really is' (pp. 2–3).

offer people not in a position to verify our claims for themselves a clear differentiation between the speculative assertion and the well-established fact; otherwise, we risk doing our discipline a disservice. One reason, therefore, for an extended critique of Chomsky's views is the very fact that these views have been so widely disseminated and popularly accepted, and that Chomsky's reputation and influence extend across the borders of linguistics itself.

Chomsky's reputation and influence are such that he is accepted as a spokesman for the entire field of linguistics. It is all the more important that workers in other fields be made aware that Chomsky does not, by any means, speak for *all* of us and that, if the truth were known, all is by no means as well within linguistics as they might be led to believe. By this time a subtle, yet quite perceptible, undercurrent of unease is felt within linguistics, even among generative grammarians, though few are aware of the full extent of the difficulties which confront them. To be sure, there is talk of 'real problems with the theory', but usually in the context of 'hope for developments and modifications in Chomsky's theorizing that will eventually take care of the limitations that seem apparent now' (G. Faust, 1970, p. 47). Another reason for this book, therefore, is to convey to the public at large that many linguists are worried about a great many things; to illustrate some of the particular problems which cause this concern; and to develop the thesis that far more radical measures than mere 'developments and modifications in Chomsky's theorizing' are going to have to be adopted in order to bring about any satisfactory solution.

1.3 Some problems of strategy

1.3.1 On Kuhn's notion of the paradigm. Although there are indications that a thoroughgoing critique of the sort I propose is likely to get more attention and acceptance within linguistics today than it could have even five years ago, it would still be a serious mistake to underestimate the difficulties. For the frame of reference under attack here has no doubt achieved the status of a full-fledged 'paradigm' in Kuhn's sense. That is to say, TGG is today the most widely accepted body of theory in linguistics, is taught almost universally as part of initiation into the field, and serves thereafter 'to define the legitimate problems and methods of research' for most of its professional practitioners (cf. Kuhn, 1962, p. 10). Moreover, linguists on the whole seem quite convinced that it is altogether proper (and even advisable) that one particular frame of reference should predominate in this way in their discipline. Quite possibly it was Kuhn who inculcated this particular attitude. He argues persuasively that without a governing paradigm, any science remains 'immature' in the sense that data-collection at that stage is essentially random, often yielding confusion (pp. 15–18). Hempel makes the same point that 'tentative hypotheses are needed to give direction to a scientific investigation' (1966, p. 13). And, indeed, it does seem that if one is ever to have any hope of finding anything, he must have in advance some idea just what he is looking for, lest he remain buried forever in a morass of heterogeneous 'facts'. It is the function of the paradigm to give us this idea.

Having adopted a particular paradigm, then (such as the paradigm of TGG in linguistics), there are advantages in sticking with it, through thick and thin, at least until all its logical possibilities have been fully explored. Kuhn outlines some of these advantages:

Just because he is working only for an audience of colleagues, an audience that shares his own values and beliefs, the scientist can take a single set of standards for granted. He need not worry about what some other group or school will think and can therefore dispose of one problem and get on to the next more quickly than those who work for a more heterodox group. Even more important, the insulation of the scientific community from society permits the individual scientist to concentrate his attention upon problems that he has good reason to believe he will be able to solve. Unlike the engineer, and many doctors, and most theologians, the scientist need not choose problems because they urgently need solution and without regard for the tools available to solve them (1962, p. 163).[1]

The paradigm-oriented scientist, in short, need not necessarily be involved in the solution of important or significant problems (from the standpoint of value to society at large), but only with what Kuhn calls those particular 'puzzles' which the dominating paradigm defines as legitimate and to which solutions are more or less assured (p. 37). In this way a whole universe of potential distractions is conveniently avoided, a great concentration of effort permitted on a small range of specific problems, and continued progress guaranteed towards their solution. As Kuhn puts it, 'By focusing attention upon a small range of

---

[1] Cf. Jungk, citing Franck: 'It is a custom in science – and perhaps a principle – to select from the infinite reservoir of unsolved problems only those simple ones the solution of which seems possible in terms of available knowledge and skills' (1958, p. 34).

relatively esoteric problems, the paradigm forces scientists to investigate some part of nature in a detail and depth that would otherwise be un-imaginable' (p. 24).

Yet there is another side to this picture. There are distinct dis-advantages, as well as advantages, in the adoption of a particular strict paradigmatic orientation in any field. Kuhn hints at this when he re-marks that what he calls 'normal' (or paradigm-oriented) science

seems an attempt to force nature into the preformed and relatively inflexible box that the paradigm supplies. No part of the aim of normal science is to call forth new sorts of phenomena; indeed those that will not fit the box are often not seen at all. Nor do scientists normally aim to invent new theories, and they are often intolerant of those invented by others. Instead, normal-scientific research is directed to the articulation of those phenomena and theories that the paradigm already supplies (1962, p. 24).

In other words, whereas pre- or non-paradigmatic research adopts, of necessity, an essentially 'fox' orientation, normal science involves instead a distinctly 'hedgehog' approach, and each has its weak points; in particular, while the former is disoriented, the latter is 'loaded'.[1] The fact that beliefs (or paradigms) can stand in the way of crucial discoveries and distinctions (cf. Toulmin, 1963, p. 95) and even distort reality to suit one's own ends or expectations is so familiar that it has been given a name: it is the phenomenon of 'mental set'.[2] We all have an insidious natural tendency to see only what we want or expect to see, and this can seriously interfere with the objectivity with which we draw many of our conclusions.[3] It is one thing to *think* one has solved a problem (i.e., to get that exhilarating 'Eureka feeling' of which Koestler speaks (1964, pp. 107ff)), but quite another to have *actually* solved it: 'The trouble with "Eureka"', Caws observes, 'is that the temptation to shout it is a very poor index of success in the enterprise at hand' (1969, p. 1375). Thus errors of honest miscalculation or premature conviction, being more subtle in their effects than prejudice, ignorance or outright

---

[1] The fox knows many things; the hedgehog knows one big thing. For a clear and concise comparison of these two orientations and the effects each can have on re-search, see M. Maddocks' two book reviews under the caption 'Could Things Be Worse?' in the 11 September 1970 Canadian issue of *Time* magazine, p. 88.

[2] Hyman (1964, pp. 33–5) and Kuhn (1962, pp. 62–4) both provide excellent illustra-tions involving the use of playing cards to demonstrate the effects of this familiar, but important, limitation in the capacity of the human being as an observer.

[3] As Kuhn puts it, 'In science, as in the playing card experiment [cf. n. 2 above], novelty emerges only with difficulty, manifested by resistance, against a background provided by expectation' (p. 64).

falsification, may be the more dangerous. So, while theories are indispensable as heuristic tools, they also represent biases, in a very literal sense (cf. Agnew & Pyke, 1969, p. 70). Thus particular theories (or paradigms) can be a very great help to research, or, contrariwise, a very great hindrance — and one never knows in advance which they will be.[1]

1.3.2.   On the role of criticism in science. It seems clear nonetheless that the prevailing attitude among linguists today is that the strict transformational-generative orientation has more advantages than disadvantages; hence the continued willingness of most linguists to continue working within the framework of TGG without raising serious questions about it. Part of the reason for this attitude is the widespread conviction that TGG has already proven itself so highly resistant to critical attack that further attempts would be fruitless. One even detects a certain impatience with argument. And, to be sure, much of the criticism of TGG which has so far appeared can fairly be described as ineffectual. In many cases, this has been because the intended criticism has often involved a misconception or misrepresentation of TGG itself. Still other would-be critics have expressed little more than a vague discontent with the 'new linguistics', or have simply dismissed TGG as 'absurd' or 'unscientific', without getting down even to specifics, much less to fundamentals. Others have attempted to damn the entire transformationalist movement in the manner of a religious crusade, employing arguments and tactics which are more emotional than rational (and in this way not unlike many of the familiar anti-structuralist diatribes). Not surprisingly, few such attacks have caused the Chomskyan juggernaut the slightest inconvenience; in fact, most have actually backfired (cf. Botha, 1968, p. 14), leaving TGG with greater prestige and popularity than before.

Nevertheless, it is my conviction that the image of essential invulnerability engendered by this pattern of events is more apparent than real, the fault lying both in the kind of attack and the kind of defense which transformationalists have typically put up in response. A good, deal of the criticism of Chomsky's work has been either misdirected or,

---

[1] Toulmin observes that 'though Nature must of course be left to answer to our interrogations for herself, it is always *we* who frame the questions. And the questions we ask inevitably depend on prior theoretical considerations' (1963, p. 101). So while he agrees that preconceptions are 'both inevitable and proper', Toulmin also argues that care must always be taken to ensure that they remain always 'suitably tentative and subject to reshaping in the light of our experience' (p. 101).

at best, superficial. We also find a tendency on the part of many transformationalists to try to make a great deal of hay out of selected attacks
of the inferior sorts, while virtually ignoring a substantial body of
penetrating criticism. Part of my task will be to attempt to bring together in one place a representative sample of this more substantial
criticism which, widely scattered in the literature, has not been given
the publicity it deserves, and has failed to make its full impact.

Even if the impression that TGG has already successfully survived
critical attack were true, and that all previous attempts to probe the
foundations of the theory for weaknesses had failed, the essential
rationale for new or continued attempts to find flaws in the theory would
not be nullified. Hockett states well the basic methodological principle
involved here when he remarks that 'Hypotheses...are by definition
proposals to be knocked down, not beliefs to be defended' (1963, p. 6;
see 7.2.1 below for a brief discussion of the logical considerations which
justify this principle). In this same vein, Caws observes that philosophy
involves not one, but two mutually beneficial sorts of activities:

on the one hand, it *constructs theories* about man and the universe, and offers
them as grounds for belief and action; on the other, it *examines critically*
everything that may be offered as a ground for belief or action, including its
own theories, with a view to the elimination of inconsistency and error (1965,
p. 5; italics added).

It is generally true, as Caws goes on to point out, that there is usually
far more 'analytic' (critical) work to be done than 'metaphysical'
(theoretical), since 'novelists, poets, politicians, and religious men [to
name but a few] are [all] amateur metaphysicians who do not hesitate
to inundate the world with their theories' (p. 6). Therefore,

although there could never be a sound defense for a policy of doing only
metaphysics, there may sometimes be such a defense for a policy of doing only
analysis, namely at times when a great deal of unanalyzed and conflicting
metaphysics has been inherited, some of which must be wrong and may be
harmful (p. 6).

Popper puts all these remarks in their proper broad perspective by
noting that this basic 'method of philosophy' is not an approach characteristic of philosophy alone, but is rather

the one method of all *rational discussion*, and therefore of the...sciences as
well as of philosophy. The method I have in mind is that of stating one's
problem clearly and of examining its various proposed solutions *critically*.
    I have italicized the words *'rational discussion'* and *'critically'* in order to
stress that I equate the rational attitude and the critical attitude. The point is

that whenever we try to propose a solution to a problem, we ought to try as hard as we can to overthrow our solution, rather than defend it (1965, p. 16).

I conclude that there is ample justification for a work of the sort proposed here. However much one may tire of having to deal with criticism, or even believe that most of it is doomed to failure, he must still allow that the door should always remain open for more. This is simply the price one has to pay for constructing theories in the first place.

1.3.3   Some special problems in dealing with paradigms. It is one thing, however, to advocate an attitude of open-mindedness and cautious skepticism in the average linguist, and quite another to attempt to express such an attitude in the form of a concerted attack on the foundations of a theory which has acquired virtual paradigmatic status. The immediate special problem which must be faced in any such endeavor is that one can attack a given paradigm effectively only by going outside that paradigm for one's basic arguments and data,[1] a move which immediately exposes the critic to criticism for dealing in matters outside the concern of his discipline. In particular, the question of values (as in asking whether the problems being studied in great detail under the influence of some particular paradigm are *significant* and *worth* the attention devoted to them) 'can be answered only in terms of criteria that lie outside of normal science altogether' (Kuhn, 1962, p. 109), and it is a moot point whether a discipline may be ready to broach questions of this sort at any particular time in its history. If people are content with the goods they possess, there is little reason to expect that they will be inclined to attach significance to the remarks of neighbors denigrating them, much less to consider trading them in for new goods of unknown quality. On the other hand, if the goods appear to be turning to dust in their hands, they might be receptive to suggestions which would otherwise have made no impact. The issue is essentially one of proper timing, and on such matters one can only test the wind and then take his chances.

In short, once a paradigm is in, there is no easy way to get rid of it until the time is ripe (which ought to give pause to anyone wishing to see a paradigm imposed on some discipline prematurely). We find it

[1] Cf. Hjelmslev: 'If the linguist wishes to make clear to himself the object of his own science he sees himself forced into spheres which according to the traditional view are not his' (1961, pp. 101–2).

comforting, no doubt, to think that bad theories or paradigms will be quickly weeded out by their failure to square with the facts, their failure to be predictive or to uncover new kinds of useful facts (cf. Caws, 1969, p. 1378), but 'it is not easy to expose the fundamental intellectual frameworks of an age to the bare mercy of the facts' (Toulmin, 1963, p. 97). For not only are factual statements 'conceptually contaminated' to begin with (Turner, 1967, p. 192) but, as Caws emphasizes, the problem is compounded by the fact that

certain social factors tend to interfere with the evolutionary pattern, just as they do in the biological case. Just as the children of rich families may, under a less than equitable social system, be comparatively better protected against the hostility of the environment . . . so some theories produced under powerful sponsorship may have a longer run than they deserve (1969, p. 1378).

I foresee two kinds of special problems in store for my attempt to develop a unified critique of the transformational-generative paradigm in contemporary linguistics, both of which relate directly to the fact that we must go outside the paradigm itself in order to bring effective criticism to bear. The first of these is that a good deal of recent linguistic controversy has been highly charged emotionally, leading me to expect that people on both sides have lost sight of Caws' wise dictum 'to be wary of emotional commitments to their hypotheses' (1969, p. 1376). To the extent that such commitments have developed, one runs the risk of having criticism of *ideas* interpreted as criticism of those *personalities* who are most closely associated with them. On this point I declare that I have no bones to pick or grudges to bear (as yet) against anyone in the field, and most especially not with Chomsky. I was at one time an advocate of TGG myself (and not so very long ago, at that). The chief reason why I feel I understand the extent of the difficulties is precisely because I once went through the conversion-to-TGG experience and can therefore appreciate the intellectual and emotional commitment which the experience can engender. I have myself looked through transformationalist eyes at the era of structuralism out of which TGG has grown and have found it seriously wanting, and for all the standard reasons. Even more, I have shared with my former fellow transformationalists the feeling that linguistics was, before Chomsky, a dull and unexciting discipline, in great measure a data-cataloguing enterprise of the most stultifying sort. Though I shall argue in the pages to come that Chomsky's 'revolution' in linguistics has been nowhere near as revolutionary as it may once have appeared, I fully allow with G. Faust (1970,

p. 47) Chomsky's undeniable success in 're-energizing linguistics' at a point in its history when it seemed much in need of it. Few (if any) of the ideas in this book would have been possible (i.e. coming from this pen) but for my close familiarity with Chomsky's work, which was ultimately responsible for attracting my interest to the particular questions explored here. No criticism, good or bad, is possible without a set of original ideas to criticize.

A second problem is that, in dealing with arguments not normally considered by linguists as part of their familiar everyday research, I may well end by developing points which seem clear and indisputable, perhaps even devastating, from my perspective, but which may strike many readers as incomprehensible, problematical or quite irrelevant, from theirs – and to the extent that my readers and I may disagree about fundamentals, we may end up talking through one another in the classic Kuhnian style (cf. Kuhn, 1962, pp. 108–9). I have adopted two strategies to minimize this danger. The first of these relates to overall organization. Throughout this book I try to develop first those ideas which I feel are likely to be shared by a major portion of my primary audience (as, for example, with a restatement of some of Chomsky's more familiar views), to introduce new or alternative views only in close conjunction or juxtaposition with these, and then slowly and deliberately to attempt to build a case for clearly differentiating the two, both conceptually and empirically. On matters which I consider especially important for my case, I adopt the additional tactic of re-introducing what is essentially the same argument a number of times, but each time either in a slightly different form or in a new context, hoping that at least one statement of the argument will manage to come through, despite the difficulties. I have made no effort to avoid detailed documentation of positions which might have been clear to many readers in a more condensed form, or to spare redundancy, wherever I felt that a further restatement might increase the probability of my getting my major points across. Many readers will find the redundancy bothersome, but I have thought it better to be diffuse than obscure.

1.3.4 The method of alternative hypotheses. The last, and probably most difficult, strategic problem in attacking a well-established theoretical framework, is the stubborn fact that no paradigm is ever abandoned unless there is an alternative candidate to take its place. Kuhn reasons as follows:

Once a first paradigm through which to view nature has been found, there is no such thing as research in the absence of any paradigm. To reject one paradigm without simultaneously substituting another is to reject science itself (1962, p. 79).

Thus, though one might argue (as I do) that in the case of TGG the accepted paradigm is so anomaly-ridden and methodologically unsound that it is not viable even in its own right, there is the nagging suspicion that we may still expect to be confronted with that ultimate defense that, whatever its faults, TGG remains nevertheless 'the best theory we've got'. There is only one effective response, and that is to try to develop, at least in general outline, a potential alternative frame of reference which shows sufficient promise of overcoming at least some of the difficulties inherent in the frame of reference under attack.[1] Consequently, as an integral part of my critique of TGG, I have attempted to formulate, first, a reasonably clear and distinct *alternative theory of language acquisition* to the one propounded by Chomsky which underlies virtually all of his major theoretical work, and to suggest in some detail what effects an alternative theory of this kind is likely to have upon the character of linguistic descriptions. As my argument develops, I suggest that these linguistic descriptions will differ not only in detail, but also must be fundamentally *different in kind and in interpretation* from those familiar to transformational-generative grammarians today, and, finally, that an entirely *different research strategy* will be required in order to provide substantive answers to a host of crucial questions which the transformational-generative paradigm seems incapable of resolving in any non-arbitrary way. In brief, the basic strategy of this work may be described as *the method of alternative hypotheses*.

In adopting this basic strategy, I have found that a number of important, though originally unexpected, advantages have accrued. In particular, the proposed alternatives, I find, provide an ideal vehicle

---

[1] This ingredient of 'future promise' seems to be the crucial one, at least for Kuhn, who remarks that 'paradigm debates are not really about relative problem-solving ability, though for good reasons they are usually couched in those terms. Instead, the issue is which paradigm should in the future guide research on problems many of which *neither* competitor can yet claim to resolve completely. A decision between alternate ways of practicing science is called for, and in the circumstances that decision must be based *less on past achievement than on future promise*. The man who embraces a new paradigm at an early stage must...have faith that the new paradigm will succeed with the many large problems that confront it, knowing only that the older paradigm has failed with a few' (1962, pp. 156–7; italics added).

for helping to decide which aspects of the transformational-generative paradigm should be the main focus of attention in the development of my critique, as well as serving as a principled guide to the outside criteria and arguments which most need to be brought into play. In more general terms, the method of alternatives appears to be the ideal solution to the methodological dilemma encountered in 1.3.1: that while paradigm-free data collection is at best inefficient and essentially unproductive (if not an outright contradiction in terms; cf. Lees, 1965b, p. 22), the presuppositions associated with the adoption of any paradigm also have the disturbing propensity to bias our judgment – as though with too poor an idea of what we are looking for, we never find it, but with too good an idea, we invariably find it – whether it is really there or not. Only the technique of maintaining alternative hypotheses at each stage of the research effort seems capable of being both psychologically safe and methodologically sound, that is, of providing us with pre-conceived ideas and conceptual flexibility simultaneously.[1]

For the ultimate defense of the method of alternative hypotheses, however, I must defer to Feyerabend. He argues that this method is not merely useful or advantageous, but is an *essential* ingredient of any empirical inquiry which has the remotest hope of being objective. 'You can be a good empiricist,' he says, 'only if you are prepared to work with many alternative theories rather than with a single point of view' (1968, p. 14). What is more, he continues,

This plurality of theories must not be regarded as a preliminary stage of knowledge which will at some time in the future be replaced by the One True Theory. Theoretical pluralism is assumed to be an *essential feature* of all knowledge that claims to be objective. Nor can one rest content with a plurality which is merely abstract and which is created by denying now this and now that component of the dominant point of view. Alternatives must rather be developed in such detail that problems already 'solved' by the accepted theory can again be treated in a new and perhaps also more detailed manner. Such development will of course take time... *It takes time to build a good theory* (a triviality that seems to have been forgotten by some...); and it also takes time to develop an alternative to a good theory. The *function* of such concrete alternatives is, however, this: They provide means of criticizing the accepted theory in a manner which goes *beyond* the criticism provided by a comparison of that theory 'with the facts'...[and therefore] allows for a much sharper criticism of accepted ideas (1968, pp. 14–15).

[1] I owe a great debt of gratitude especially to B. Spolsky for first introducing me to this particular mode of thinking, which has served as the basis for virtually everything I shall have to say in this book.

These remarks lead to the issue which Feyerabend calls the question of the 'relative autonomy of facts', i.e. the question whether or not facts even exist, or are 'available independently of whether or not one considers alternatives to the theory to be tested' (p. 27). For although most discussions of the problem of theory validation appear to present a model in which 'a *single* theory is compared with a class of facts (or observation statements) which are assumed to be "given" somehow' (p. 27), Feyerabend submits instead (and the history of the development of TGG in linguistics confirms this) that such a view offers

much too simple a picture of the actual situation. Facts and theories are much more intimately connected than is admitted by the autonomy principle. Not only is the description of every single fact dependent on *some* theory (which may, of course, be very different from the theory to be tested). There exist also facts which cannot [even] be unearthed except with the help of alternatives to the theory to be tested, and which become unavailable as soon as such alternatives are excluded (p. 27).

Feyerabend then sets up a hypothetical case in which some investigator has decided to adopt a particular theory (or paradigm) in his field and has refused to consider alternatives at this level.[1] He further allows that the pursuit of the particular theory which this investigator has selected has led to a reasonable degree of success in the sense that it has served to explain (at least to the satisfaction of the original investigator and his colleagues) a number of circumstances which had hitherto been regarded as unintelligible:

This gives empirical support to an idea which to start with seemed to possess only this advantage: It was interesting and intriguing. The concentration upon the theory will now be reinforced, the attitude towards alternatives will become less tolerant. Now if it is true, as has been argued in the last section, that many facts become available only with the help of such alternatives, then the refusal to consider them *will result in the elimination of potentially refuting facts*. More especially, it will eliminate facts whose discovery would show the complete and irreparable inadequacy of the theory. Such facts having been made inaccessible, the theory will appear to be free from blemish and it will seem that 'all the evidence points with merciless definiteness [to the essential correctness of the accepted theory]'. This will further reinforce the belief in the uniqueness of the current theory and in the complete futility of any account that proceeds in a different manner... Popular science books (and this includes... books on the philosophy of science) will spread the basic

---

[1] It is not at all surprising that he should do this since, after all, as Feyerabend points out, 'a man can do only so many things at a time and it is better when he pursues a theory in which he is interested rather than a theory he finds boring' (1968, p. 30).

postulates of the theory; applications will be made in distant fields. More than ever the theory will appear to possess tremendous empirical support. The chances for the consideration of alternatives are now very slight indeed. The final success of the fundamental assumptions...will seem to be assured.

At the same time it is evident...that this appearance of success *cannot in the least be regarded as a sign of truth and correspondence with nature.* Quite the contrary, the suspicion arises that the absence of major difficulties is a result of the decrease of empirical content brought about by the elimination of alternatives, and of facts that can be discovered with the help of these alternatives only...Such a system will of course be very 'successful' not, however, because it agrees so well with the facts, but because no facts have been specified that would constitute a test and because some facts have even been removed. Its 'success' *is entirely man-made.* It was decided to stick to some ideas and the result was, quite naturally, the survival of these ideas. If now the initial decision is forgotten, or made only implicitly, then the survival will seem to constitute independent support, it will reinforce the decision, or turn it into an explicit one, and in this way close the circle. This is how empirical 'evidence' may be *created* by a procedure which quotes as its justification the very same evidence it has produced in the first place.

At this point an 'empirical' theory of the kind described...becomes almost indistinguishable from a myth (pp. 30–1).

So he concludes:

This, I think, is the most decisive argument against any method that encourages uniformity, be it now empirical or not. Any such method is in the last resort a method of deception. If enforces an unenlightened conformism, and speaks of truth; it leads to a deterioration of intellectual capabilities, of the power of imagination, and speaks of deep insight; it destroys the most precious gift of the young, their tremendous power of imagination, and speaks of education.

To sum up: *Unanimity of opinion may be fitting for a church, for the frightened victims of some (ancient, or modern) myth, or for the weak and willing followers of some tyrant; variety of opinion is a feature necessary for objective knowledge; and a method that encourages variety is also the only method that is compatible with a humanitarian outlook* (p. 33; all italics are Feyerabend's).

1.4 Overview

The chapters which follow are arranged in this way: To begin with (in chapter 2), I play the role of devil's advocate in order to read into the record a set of basic methodological and metatheoretical assumptions which (so it would seem) must be regarded as absolutely central to the transformational-generative paradigm as understood today, and which (it has been claimed) distinguish this paradigm from previous approaches to the study of language (and, most specifically, from those of the immediately preceding post-Bloomfieldian or 'structuralist' era). In short, I attempt to reconstruct the kinds of issues and arguments which appear to have led to the adoption of the transformational-generative paradigm in the first place, i.e. which have been responsible for the so-called 'Chomskyan revolution' in American linguistics.

In chapter 3 I introduce the argument that underlying virtually all the basic metatheoretical tenets of TGG is a smaller set of more fundamental assumptions which turn out, upon analysis, to represent pre-suppositions about *the nature of language acquisition*, and these I develop in some detail. At this point in the discussion, I suggest that we must not 'rest content with the theory that is in the centre of attention', but should instead bring to bear 'the most fundamental and the most general [form of] criticism [which] is the criticism produced with the help of alternatives' (Feyerabend, 1968, p. 38). For I also introduce (or, more accurately, resurrect) and develop in this chapter *an alternative theory of language acquisition* diametrically opposed to Chomsky's (as well as allude to the possible existence of any number of additional 'hybrid' alternatives).

In chapters 4 through 6 I endeavor to pit these two alternative theories against one another in terms of the kinds of *linguistic analyses* which may be directly associated with each, in the attempt to isolate a corpus of *specific problems* or difficulties, conceptual and empirical, to which each seems particularly liable, given the perspective provided by consideration of the other. As the result of this analysis, quite contrary to what might have been expected, given the great popularity, influence and appeal of Chomsky's work at the present time, I suggest that not only does his theory of language acquisition have very little plausibility, but, more significantly, has virtually no empirical evidence in support of it, either.

In fact, we encounter so many conceptual and empirical difficulties with Chomsky's basic theory that we are driven by curiosity (in chapters 7 and 8) to look back upon some of the other specific assumptions (now methodological, as well as metatheoretical) of Chomsky's entire general approach to the study of language in order to ascertain what more *general problems* may lie at the base of those very specific ones uncovered in Part II and to determine whether some more promising alternatives might be conceived in these broader areas, as well. In particular, I explore in these chapters the legitimacy of the view, at present widely accepted in linguistics, that 'generative grammar is very much in keeping with contemporary views on the philosophy of science' (Langacker, 1967, p. 10), and conclude as the result of that study that, in almost every detail, precisely the opposite is true. I then attempt to conceive of an alternative approach to the study of language which seems to be more in keeping with well-established views of theory construction and theory justification as generally understood in other sciences and proceed to explore whether or not transformational-generative grammarians are asking the right kinds of questions for the scientific study of language, whether the theories which they have been proposing are of the kind likely to be useful in finding answers to these questions, and, finally, whether the kinds of data now being considered are sufficient for (or even appropriate to) the serious evaluation of such theories. In all three respects, I conclude that TGG has gone far astray, and that a radical methodological, conceptual and empirical reorientation will be needed in linguistics if any significant knowledge is ever to be gained either about the nature of language as a natural phenomenon or about the process of language acquisition.

In the final chapter I attempt, first, to assay what residue can be salvaged from the transformational-generative era which might help provide a useful starting point for such a proposed reorientation of future linguistic research, and to develop in broad outline the essential nature of the *basic reconceptualization* called for. I also attempt to explicate this discussion by outlining a fundamentally new *research strategy* which might be adopted as an essential part of such a redefinition of the goals and methods of linguistic inquiry, and which seems to show promise of advancing our knowledge and understanding of the phenomena of language use and acquisition in ways not possible for the transformational-generative paradigm. To illustrate the basic character of this proposed new research strategy, I then conclude with the description of a few *specific experimental studies* which are already either in the advanced planning or pilot stage at the University of Alberta.

In sum, I argue in this book that while it may well be true, as Lyons says (1970, p. 9), that 'linguistics has established its credentials as a mature academic discipline with its own methodology and criteria of relevance' (i.e. that it has adopted a paradigm), there are nevertheless numerous sufficient and even compelling grounds for thinking that the bases upon which this paradigm has been established are insecure, that the particular methodology and criteria of relevance implied by this theoretical orientation are insufficient and often inappropriate to the empirical tasks assigned to them, and, consequently, that a drastic reorientation (or counter-revolution, if you like) is required if any substantial progress is to be made along the kind of lines which our appetites have already been well-whetted to pursue. My argument thus boils down to a recommendation that the essential features of the currently dominant transformational-generative paradigm ought to be abandoned and that a new approach be adopted which shows some promise of achieving the sort of goals which Chomsky, as clearly as anyone else, has outlined for us. In reality I do not opt for the adoption of a new 'paradigm', in the strict Kuhnian sense, since it seems obvious to me that it is still far too early in the game to adopt any tight theoretical commitment of the sort which many linguists are already accustomed to. Given our continued state of near-complete ignorance of anything substantial about our subject matter, I argue instead that it would be better rather to 'hang loose' from any very constraining paradigmatic affiliation in linguistics for some time, and to continue (or re-initiate) instead the search for a useful all-embracing theoretical orientation along a number of different lines of inquiry, all of which seem equally promising, and only one of which I attempt to outline here.

I realize that it may be asking too much of the present highly committed generation of linguists to take such a drastic step. My arguments may be faulty, in part or in whole, and even in the unlikely circumstance that they should prove essentially inviolate, they may still be premature or too limited. For, as Kuhn says, 'The transfer of allegiance f[r]om paradigm to paradigm is a conversion experience that cannot be forced' (1962, p. 150). I also concede with Kuhn that 'as in political revolutions, so in paradigm choice – there is no standard higher than the assent of the relevant community' (p. 93). For me, the relevant community must be that contemporary body of fellow linguists, and I am perfectly content to leave the judgment in their hands. I simply present to that community a set of personal observations and convictions for their consideration. Some of these will, no doubt, be demolished by criticism more adept than my own, while others may be marginally influential in helping to bring about the kind of re-orientation urgently required. Whatever the result, the effort will have been worthwhile. As Toulmin has said, 'We are *justified* in placing the trust in [our theories] that we do, only because – and to the extent that – they have proved their worth in competition with alternatives' (1963, pp. 101–2).[1] I pro-

---

[1] Cf. also his remarks on p. 110 of this same volume to the effect that 'progress can be

pose here a few such alternatives and suggest that it might be interesting to see whether or not TGG can continue to exist alongside them, or should the theory prove more resilient than I can presently conceive of its being, to see at least how much better it may become for having been required to make the effort.

made in science only if men apply their intellects *critically* to the problems which arise in their own times, in the light of the evidence and the ideas which are then open to consideration...In the evolution of scientific ideas, as in the evolution of species, change results from the selective perpetuation of *variants*' (italics added).

2 Some central aspects of the 'Chomskyan revolution' in American linguistics

2.1 Some signs of revolutionary struggle

Chomsky's impact on American linguistics is commonly described as revolutionary. The metaphor (like the concept of 'paradigm') is borrowed from Kuhn (1962), a little book which appears to have made a similar impact on the linguistic community, although it was not written with linguistics in mind at all. (I have been able to find only one passing reference to linguistics in the entire book, on p. 120.) Nevertheless, many linguists are convinced that Kuhn's analysis of the revolutionary nature of scientific advance is an especially clear and accurate reflection of the recent history of their own study; as Sklar says: 'What has happened in linguistics since Chomsky appeared on the scene almost perfectly fits Kuhn's description of how a scientific revolution works' (1968, p. 213).

Recent controversies in linguistics have characteristically been both ineffectual, for the most part, and also bitter. For much of the past decade and a half, the entire discipline has given the appearance of being racked with disputes, lack of communication, even downright hostility – almost as though it were organized into armed camps. Part of the attractiveness of Kuhn's analysis, I suspect, is that it provides a plausible explanation for these facts: this is the sort of confrontation to be expected whenever the basic paradigm of a discipline is at stake, i.e. whenever there is a scientific revolution in the making. On the failure of Chomsky and many of his antagonists to communicate, for example, Thorne (1965) writes:

The student who learns linguistics from *Syntactic Structures* is, in effect, learning a different subject from the student who learns linguistics from, say,

25

Zellig Harris's *Structural Linguistics*. This explains why at the moment so many discussions appear inconclusive, so many misunderstandings fundamental. Kuhn points out that scientists working within different paradigms consistently 'talk through' each other[1] (p. 74).

The rancor and bitterness is readily explainable as a natural by-product of the heavy-handed propaganda and black-and-white sloganeering which seems to be part of any revolutionary movement. More specifically, in a latter-day re-emergence of the old he-who-is-not-with-me-is-against-me philosophy, linguists seem to have been under some pressure in recent years to swear allegiance to one or the other of two sub-societies: either to join forces with the *revolutionaries* (young, vigorous, enthusiastic and as proud of their new insights and successes as they are scornful of the misguided ignorance and intransigence of their feeble – and feeble-minded – opponents) or to remain behind with the *reactionaries* (old, paralyzed with the heavy burden of a hoary but largely useless tradition and now lashing out irrationally in a desperate, though futile, struggle for survival): in an age of revolution, clearly, there can be no room for compromise. It has been very much a fight to the finish with (thank God!) one inevitable outcome: sooner or later the reactionaries will all die off and all this needless controversy will disappear with them.[2] Sklar sums the situation up this way: 'The new and old paradigms compete against each other for adherents, but the new paradigm is fated to win, because it provides possibilities for normal scientific research that the anomaly-ridden old paradigm no longer can' (1968, p. 213).

Events of the last few years do appear to be bearing such predictions out. At present the Chomskyan (or transformationalist) orientation clearly dominates the field, especially in North America, being more than simply well represented on the editorial boards of the major linguistics journals and publishing houses, and with Chomsky himself regarded as unofficial spokesman for the entire discipline. In this chapter I attempt to trace those particular issues which seem to have brought the Chom-

[1] Cf. Toulmin (1963, p. 57): 'Men who accept different ideals and paradigms have really no common theoretical terms in which to discuss their problems fruitfully. They will not even *have* the same problem: events which are "phenomena" in one man's eyes will be passed over by the other as "perfectly natural".'

[2] Cf. Max Planck's remark that 'a new scientific truth does not triumph by convincing its opponents and making them see the light, but rather because its opponents eventually die, and a new generation grows up that is familiar with it' (cited by Kuhn, 1962, p. 150, who also relates some remarks from Darwin's *Origin of Species* along this same line; cf. also Holton & Roller, 1958, p. 135).

skyan paradigm to the attention of the linguistic community in the first place and caused its rapid rise to virtually unchallenged dominance thereafter. I shall refer to the two main camps as the 'transformationalist' (Chomskyan) and the 'structuralist' (pre-Chomskyan), respectively, and I shall discuss the chief issues which reputedly divide them in terms of these three categories: (1) on the nature of language, (2) on the purpose of linguistic description, and (3) on the data of linguistics, with a brief concluding section.

2.2 On the nature of language

The first (and most fundamental) tenet of the Chomskyan era is that language itself is no longer seen in the old way. In a literal sense, language itself may be said to have been redefined. Consider, for example, this typical old-school definition: 'The totality of utterances that can be made in a speech-community is the *language* of that speech-community' (Bloomfield, 1926, p. 26). This definition can easily be shown to be useless or incorrect, or both. It is useless, first of all, in that it is non-rigorous, i.e. inexplicit, since the primitive terms on which it is based are too ambiguous to be of any real utility without further interpretation by a trained investigator (who would presumably be in a position, by virtue of his training, to 'feel' what is meant by the statement). 'Utterance', for example, is, by Definition 1 in Bloomfield's schema, 'an act of speech'. But what is that? Is it any signal *whatsoever* which emanates from the organs of speech, or do we not wish to exclude such things as whistles, coughs, humming, musical notes, etc.? (cf. Halle, 1959, p. 13). And what about the 'instinctive cries'? (Sapir, 1921, p. 5). Are they to be included, because a certain communicative function might be associated with them? (And if they are, what consequences would this have on the possibility of producing any sort of simple, reasonable, and homogeneous description?) And what about hesitation phenomena, for surely they constitute part of 'speech'? In short, unless we know what is meant by 'an act of speech' to begin with, Bloomfield's definition leaves us quite in the dark as to what language is, as well. Very much the same can be said of the other primitive term, 'speech-community'. This, we are told (Bloomfield's 'Assumption 1'), is a community in which 'successive utterances are alike or partly alike'. Is it even possible to conceive of *any* random set of utterances which will not be at least 'partly alike'? On the other hand, if we view the matter in strictly physical terms, we find that in no communities anywhere are any two utterances ever *completely* alike at *any* time, in which case we are faced with chaos. So how are we to interpret the term 'alike'? Then, too, there is that infelicitous phrase 'can be made'. Obviously (within the broad constraints imposed by human physiology) virtually *any* utterance (i.e. any sequence of syllables or words, say) *can* (and even *may*) be produced by speakers, either intentionally (as in jokes) or inadvertently (as in lapses). The only reasonably clear aspect of Bloomfield's definition thus appears to be his decision to regard a language as a 'totality' of something (namely, 'utterances'). Therefore, if we may be allowed certain minimal liberties of interpretation to smooth out the ambiguities already discussed, we might quickly conclude that Bloomfield wished to regard language as a mass (or corpus) of speech acts, presumably in some sort of regularized transcription (since speech acts are in themselves very fleeting and messy things). In short, *a language is a mass of regularized speech data*. And it is on this very point that we come across the first major bone of contention between our two schools of thought.

To the transformationalist, it is untenable to view language as merely a collection of utterances. The argument is simple, but devastatingly effective. All one need do is ask one simple question:[1] 'What, then, does it mean to *learn* a language?' (or, by the same token, just what is it that is *lost* when one chances to suffer from any of the various types of aphasic disorder?) For no old-school advocate may casually answer that 'to learn a language means, of course, to learn a collection of utterances' and expect to get away with it. The reason for this is obvious: for to say that to learn a language means to learn a set of utterances *per se* is to fail to consider what Chomsky and Miller refer to as the 'fundamental fact that must be faced in any investigation of language and linguistic behavior', that 'a native speaker of a language has the ability to comprehend an immense number of sentences that he has never previously heard and to produce, on the appropriate occasion, novel utterances that are similarly understandable to other native speakers' (1963, p. 271). In brief, so the transformationalist argument goes, the structuralist position

---

[1] As Chomsky has observed, 'Most people come into the social and behavioral sciences and they're immediately faced with a fixed range of questions and a format of problems that you're supposed to look at, and it's very hard to challenge it, I suppose, because you go through and then you repeat it to your students and the same sort of nonsense gets repeated for fifty years. *Finally somebody asks a simple question and the whole field collapses*' (quoted in Sklar, 1968, p. 215; italics added).

cannot stand up in face of the undeniable fact that normal language behavior is characteristically *innovative*.[1] In fact, the structuralist position
is vitiated the moment it is recognized that every child learning English
sooner or later comes up with forms like 'goed' or 'foots'. Such errors are
sufficient to convince even non-linguists (uncommitted to either of the
linguistic schools under discussion) that what the child acquires is a set
of '*general principles* independent of vocabulary . . . not ready-made formulations – although he picks up some of these, too – but *a way of constructing formulations, a set of schemata*' (Church, 1961, p. 65; italics added).

This pinpoints the sort of 'redefinition' of language which the transformationalists have advocated, namely, to cease looking upon language
as a conglomeration of speech acts and to see it instead as an abstract
system of organizing principles which *underlies* these acts.[2] Yet all that
is actually being suggested, we are told, is a return to the 'traditional
view' prevalent before (as the transformationalists like to put it) that
anomalous aberration, the era of structuralism, diverted the attention of
linguists to less productive paths (cf. Chomsky, 1968a). For the distinction to be made between language as a *system* and the data which *manifest*
that system is very much the same as the familiar distinction made by
Saussure between *langue* and *parole*: for him, the essence of language
was *langue*, 'a well-defined object', which was to be contrasted with 'the
heterogeneous mass of speech facts' which characterized *parole* (1959,
p. 14). To put the issue in the terms of contemporary psychology, the
distinction between *language* and *speech* is essentially the same sort of
distinction which is to be made between *learning* (the underlying
reality) and *performance* (its surface manifestation): only confusion
results if the two are not distinguished (Hilgard & Bower, 1966, p. 5).
Thus Chomsky remarks:

Psychologists have long realized that a description of what an organism does
and a description of what it knows can be very different things . . . *Langue*,

---

[1] Cf. the following particularly elegant formulation of this principle by Roberts:
'It is obvious that we don't learn our language by hearing sentences, storing them,
and then speaking them when the occasion arises. The number of sentences that
any speaker of a language is capable of using is enormously greater than could
conceivably be learned and stored. Most of the sentences that we speak and write
are new sentences, ones that never occurred before [as far as we know]. Yet we use
them with the confidence that they will be understood and accepted as English
sentences' (1964, pp. 411–12).

[2] Actually, the qualification 'abstract' is unnecessary here for the reason which Bloch
and Trager stated as clearly as anyone: 'A system cannot be observed directly'
(1942, p. 5). Lamb adds that it is only the 'manifestations of linguistic structure'
which can be observed (1966a, p. 3).

the system represented in the brain, is the basic object of psychological and linguistic study, although we can determine its nature and properties only by study of *parole* (1963, pp. 326–27).

In Saussure's terms, therefore, 'the American descriptive linguists studied only utterance, and did not concern themselves with language at all' (Chomsky in Sklar, 1968, p. 213).

The first major aspect of the Chomskyan revolution may thus be summarized as follows: 'Henceforth language shall no longer be regarded as a corpus of utterances *per se*, but rather as the abstract system of rules which *underlies* these utterances.'[1]

2.3   On the purpose of linguistic description

Accompanying this radical change in the way in which language is viewed by the younger generation of linguists is an accompanying and equally radical change in interpretation regarding the ultimate purpose

---

[1] Actually, it is not difficult to find statements in the structuralist literature which appear to reflect this same general point of view. Bloch and Trager for example, defined language as 'a system of arbitrary vocal symbols by means of which a social group cooperates' (1942, p. 5), Gleason followed with his own characterization as 'an organized system or structure [by means of which information is conveyed]' (1961, p. 2), and in Chao's latest formulation a language is defined as 'the system of habits as embodied in the brains of its speakers' (1968, p. 11). Now while it may be true that these attempts leave room for terminological (if not conceptual) attack, it is nevertheless also clear that all these attempts share the general notion that a language is a system, not just a stock of utterances.

On the opposite side of the ledger, it ought also to be acknowledged that wherever Chomsky uses the term 'language' in a technical sense, he, too, much like Bloomfield, defines it as a 'set of sentences' (1957b, p. 13; 1964, p. 51; etc.), rather than as 'the abstract system of rules which underlies them', as I have put it above (a thing which Chomsky refers to instead as the 'grammar' of the language). This usage reflects, I would think, not only the strong influence of the Bloomfieldian tradition on Chomsky's work (especially his early work), but also, and probably more significantly, Chomsky's familiarity with automata theory, which no doubt has been responsible for suggesting to him that an analogy might usefully be established between a formal language (in mathematics) and a natural language (see pp. 284–5 below). Despite this usage, however, it is abundantly clear that Chomsky is not so much interested in the set of sentences *per se* which may constitute a language, but rather in the generative algorithm or 'system of rules' which *defines* this set, i.e. the grammar, since he has argued that to learn a language means to learn (or 'internalize') its grammar, to speak or understand a language means to make use of the rules in it, etc. (see especially chapter 1 of Chomsky, 1965a). I feel secure in arguing, therefore, that, for the transformationalist, the essence of a language is held to *be* its grammar, in some very important sense. Consequently, although there appears to be considerable overlap between the structuralist and transformationalist views on the issue of the nature (or definition) of language, there is at least a decided shift in emphasis involved which serves to differentiate the two rather sharply.

of linguistic description or analysis. Although even the crustiest of the Old Believers indulged in analysis from time to time, we are hard put to ascertain what essential reason could have lain behind such activity, given the prevailing view that language consisted of nothing but a corpus of utterances: under such a definition it would seem that the discipline of linguistics should, by direct implication, consist simply of the collection (and, perhaps, cataloguing – though purely for reasons of convenience) of as many of these utterances as possible. Yet few (if any) linguists have been content to limit their activities in this way (despite the obvious open-ended character of the proposed task). What was proposed instead (or in addition) was that the linguist, as 'a scientist whose subject-matter is language', adopt as his basic task 'to analyze and classify the facts of speech...in such a way as to account for all the utterances used by the members of a social group' and in this way to compile a so-called *linguistic description* which is 'what we call the system or the grammar of the language' (Bloch & Trager, 1942, p. 8). Further, it was generally understood from the beginning that the main goal of linguistic analysis was to achieve a categorization and simplification of linguistic utterances by a process of identifying and 'factoring out' recurrent entities so as to yield an abstract set of utterance-types into which all the utterances of a language could conveniently be classified. It was further understood that an important accompanying feature of any attempted 'simplification' of this sort would be the maintenance of objectivity, such that all trained investigators would arrive at an identical or equivalent analysis for any given body of data, in which case each distinct body of data (or language) could legitimately be said to have been described in its 'own terms' (see Lamb, 1966a, pp. 3–5). Thus attention became focused primarily on the development of explicit data-analytical procedures (or 'ways of arranging the original data') which would guarantee this requisite degree of objectivity by dealing only with the formal distinctions extant in languages (as opposed to the 'intuitive' or 'semantic' distinctions so commonly employed by earlier 'traditional' grammarians) and which would accurately reflect the range of variation of linguistic structures from language to language in terms of 'differences in how the data [of various languages] responded to identical methods of arrangement' (Harris, 1951, p. 3). If the desired degree of objectivity could be achieved, the resulting linguistic description of each language so analyzed might then be regarded as a reliable 'summary of the behavior of native speakers', a whole language reduced to a more manageable 'concentrated form', yet still free from any distortions imposed by the whim of the analyst (cf. Twaddell, 1935, p. 58).

Laudable though this goal might seem (especially by comparison with the mostly empty philosophical speculations about language of the pre-structuralist era), the transformationalist would argue that this whole effort was misguided from the very beginning. As Lees put it:

> It would seem that our conception [heretofore] of what the grammar of a language is like is all too often of the purely taxonomic, data-cataloging sort. When we compare a modern descriptive ['structuralist'] grammar with an old-fashioned prescriptive grammar of a century ago, we are accustomed to dismiss the latter as unscientific, especially to the extent that it slavishly reproduces Latin and Greek grammatical categories in an effort to order the data of a non-classical language. But what more is our descriptive grammar than another reordering of the data – now, to be sure, according to a less traditional scheme of categories, but nonetheless according to an arbitrary set of descriptive labels which has become fossilized within linguistic tradition? (1957, p. 377).

In other words, of what significance is a simple re-arrangement, codification or other arbitrary systematization of a corpus of data, however large? For clearly, 'a set of empirical "facts" can be analyzed and classified in many different ways, most of which will be unilluminating for the purposes of a given inquiry' (Hempel, 1966, p. 13). The essential difficulty with the structuralist era, therefore, was that its activities were 'pre-scientific' in the important sense that everything boiled down, in the final analysis, to the collection, collation, and classification of primary data. A structural linguistic description was nothing more than a taxonomic classification. And no such classification can be 'right or wrong, valid or invalid, true or false' for the simple reason that it is inevitably 'nothing more than an arrangement of the data which makes no claims whatever about the nature of the data' (Rosenbaum, 1966, pp. 180, 182), and no amount of argument about the 'logical consistency', 'simplicity', or 'elegance' of any proposed classificatory scheme can change this fact one iota.[1] This was the inherent and fatal flaw in the activities of the structuralist era.

What, then, do the transformationalists propose instead? They propose that we look to the natural sciences (or, better still, to the philosophy of science, which tells us what the sciences are up to). What we discover if we do this is that science 'is typically concerned with data not for itself but as evidence for deeper, hidden organizing principles that

[1] For an interesting illustrative discussion of this point, see Botha, 1968, pp. 53–6.

cannot be detected "in the phenomena" nor derived from them by taxonomic data-processing operations' (Chomsky, 1968a, p. 14). Or, as Lees put it, 'a scientific discipline is characterized essentially by the introduction of abstract constructs in theories and the validation of those theories by testing their predictive power' (1957, p. 376). That is, 'the work of the scientist consists in putting forward and testing theories' (Popper, 1965, p. 31).

But what is there to theorize *about* in linguistics? The answer is, the nature of language itself. After all, it seems clear that 'the person who has acquired knowledge of a language has internalized a system of rules that relate sound and meaning in a particular way' (Chomsky, 1968a, p. 23). It is this very intricate and highly organized system, then, which makes linguistic 'creativity' possible (Chomsky, 1964, pp. 50–1 and elsewhere). Therefore, when Chomsky proposes that linguists regard a grammar (or linguistic description) not as a classification of utterances, but rather as *theory* of a language (1957b, p. 49), he is proposing that a grammar should be regarded as 'a hypothesis concerning this internalized system' (1968a, p. 23).[1]

This view, presumed correct in its essentials, is nevertheless subject to certain qualifications. Chomsky insists that a fundamental distinction must be made, first of all, between linguistic *competence* ('the speaker–hearer's knowledge of his language') and linguistic *performance* ('the actual use of language in concrete situations') (1965a, p. 4), and that it is only the former with which the linguist must seriously concern himself (1968a, p. 4). But this, the transformationalists suggest, is merely to say that the linguist must abstract away from such extraneous factors as lapses, hesitation phenomena, false starts and other such uncontrolled variables in the actual performance of speech which are irrelevant to the underlying system of competence. Furthermore, since we regard the grammar as a whole as, ultimately, a complex device whose function is to pair semantic representations with phonetic ones (Chomsky, 1964, p. 52 and elsewhere), we assume that we need not be concerned with separate grammars for the speaker and for the hearer in the communication process, since speaking and hearing are but two different 'manifestations of the same underlying capacity, the same generative principle, mastery of which provides the speaker–hearer with the ability to use and

---

[1] Thus one inherent defect in the structuralist approach, which centered its attention on the speech act itself, was that it was capable of leading only to the very limited aim of 'the classification of the OUTPUT of performance, i.e. the utterances, and...to no theory about the dynamic process of performance itself' (Fromkin, 1968, p. 47).

understand all of the infinite range of linguistic items' (Chomsky, 1964, p. 57). Chomsky's position is therefore as follows:

Linguistic theory is concerned primarily with an ideal speaker–listener, in a completely homogeneous speech-community, who knows its language perfectly and is unaffected by such grammatically irrelevant conditions as memory limitations, distractions, shifts of attention and interest, and errors (random or characteristic) in applying his knowledge of the language in actual performance ... The problem for the linguist, as well as for the child learning the language [therefore], is to determine from the [defective] data of performance the underlying system of rules that has been mastered by the speaker–hearer and that he puts to use in actual performance (1965a, pp. 3–4).[1]

Thus the suggestion is made that the main shortcoming of the structuralist era in American linguistics was that it 'failed totally to come to grips with the "creative" aspect of language use, that is, the ability to form and understand previously unheard sentences' (Chomsky, 1964, p. 113). Rather than trying to advance hypotheses to account for this ability, it contented itself with the formulation of 'procedures of segmentation and classification' which might serve to reduce a (hopefully) representative set of sentences in a language to manageable proportions (same page). Despite this characteristic failing of the age, however, there were isolated voices who seemed at least to recognize the existence of the problem. Bloomfield, for example, noted that 'it is obvious that most speech-forms are regular, in the sense that the speaker who knows the constituents and the grammatical pattern, can utter them without ever having heard them' (1933, p. 275); but as Chomsky says, 'he has nothing further to say about the problem beyond the remark that the speaker utters new forms "*on the analogy* of similar forms which he has heard" ' (1966a, p. 12). Other analysts attempt to treat the problem by defining language as a 'system of habits' (e.g. Chao, 1968, p. 11). But, again, Chomsky argues, attributing the creative aspect of language use to such

[1] The transformationalist would also emphasize here that idealization of this sort is highly characteristic of the hard sciences. As Fodor and Garrett put it, 'The prepositivist [i.e. correct] view of science...held that science is primarily concerned to understand the laws that determine the behavior of ideal objects...and the character of ideal events' (1966, p. 135). Thus Lees is disposed to observe that 'once a grammar has been acknowledged to be the THEORY of some language, all grammatical units which appear in it may be accorded the same [ideal] status as the notions in any physical or chemical theory. For instance, the volume which appears, symbolized by the letter V, in the gas law $pV = nRT$ is not an actual gas volume, nor even a class of gas volumes, it represents volumes in *a theory of ideal gas behavior*' (1957, p. 391; italics added). Thus, properly speaking, 'a grammar of a language purports to be a description [i.e. is a theory] of the ideal speaker–hearer's intrinsic competence' (Chomsky, 1965a, p. 4).

concepts as 'analogy' or 'habit' is empty, as it involves using these terms 'in a completely metaphorical way, with no clear sense and with no relation to the technical usage of linguistic theory' (1966a, p. 12). Nor is it any help to interpret the notion of 'analogy' as something akin to a 'grammatical pattern' (as in Bloomfield, 1933, p. 275), since it is easy to find innumerable 'patterns' in linguistic data, but difficult to decide which are the relevant ones (cf. Chomsky & Halle, 1965, p. 103). Furthermore, upon inspection, these proposed 'grammatical patterns' turn out to be, once again, merely sets of utterance classifications, or lists (see Harris, 1951, pp. 376ff), which treat all aspects of linguistic structure as if they were exceptions. To overcome these difficulties, the transformationalists have therefore proposed to substitute for the notion of *list* (or 'inventory of elements') a new concept of grammatical *rule*, in terms of which the real regularities of a language might be explicitly formulated (Postal in Woodworth & DiPietro, 1963, pp. 4–5). It is these rules which incorporate the 'systematic principles' which are 'immanent' in the utterances of a language and according to which children eventually come to learn to speak the language,[1] and therefore the formulation of these rules must be of primary concern to the linguist (Lyons, 1968, p. 48). As Halle has put it, 'A complete scientific description of a language must pursue one aim above all: to make *precise* and *explicit* the ability of a native speaker to produce utterances in that language' (Halle, 1962, p. 344; italics added), and to do this we must state *precisely* what particular system of rules is required correctly to characterize an indefinite number of sentences in a language (Chomsky, 1962b, p. 213).

This new criterion of explicitness brings to light one further fatal shortcoming of the structuralist age: the one most forcefully put forward by Chao under the rubric of 'non-uniqueness' and enunciated in the dictum that linguists must accept that 'different systems or solutions are not simply correct or incorrect, but may be regarded only as being good or bad for various purposes' (1934, p. 38). In other words, no linguist of the structuralist period could suppose that he had written a 'God's Truth' grammar: just as the purpose of writing a linguistic description might vary, 'it is certain that our grammars will vary also' (Sledd, 1962, p. 177).[2] However much we may be inclined to attribute such remarks as these to the 'humanistic impulses' of the investigator

---

[1] If this were not so, the child would be unable to do more than 'repeat, parrot-wise, utterances of the language which he has previously heard around him' (Lyons, 1968, p. 36).
[2] See also the exchange between Sledd and Smith on p. 116 of the same volume.

(Teeter, 1966, p. 475), it is clear that this permissive attitude is intolerable in serious scientific work. In particular, if we agree to regard a language as some particular psychological system of principles or rules which relates meanings and sounds, surely to hold the view that 'two inconsistent and irreconcilable descriptions of a language may each convey some important "intuition" about the language which cannot be conveyed by the other, nor both by any third' (Householder, 1965, p. 16) would be as absurd as if a physicist, say, were to set forth a new mathematical law of the universe as simply 'one possible way' of looking at the phenomena. In science it is *truth* which is at issue, not convenience (cf. Chomsky & Halle, 1965, pp. 105–6). If, on the other hand, one takes the opposite view (like Householder, presumably), that there simply 'is no truth to be discovered' and is willing to accept the premise that 'the optimal description of a language consists of two mutually inconsistent parts', it is clear that

this description cannot be proposed as a significant and verifiable assumption concerning the language – that is, no claim to empirical truth can be made for the description that is presented, and no evidence can conceivably be relevant for or against what the linguist does...[Such a person] has simply given up the attempt to find out the facts about a particular language or about language in general. His work is immune to criticism...as an automatic consequence of his tolerance of inconsistency (p. 106).

Once again, the source of this structuralist error is not difficult to track down. In the first place, in line with the general consensus of the times that the main purpose of all work in descriptive (structural) linguistics was 'to obtain a compact one–one representation of the stock of utterances in the corpus' (Harris, 1951, p. 366), linguistic theory eventually became equated with 'the set of techniques used by the field linguist to arrive at a description of a language...[and] justification of a given analysis came to mean the specifying of the procedures used to arrive at the given result from the data' (Teeter, 1964, p. 203). But the transformationalists recognized that

there is an endless number of procedures which can be applied to linguistic data to turn classifications into units. Hence, we cannot, in principle, justify linguistic description by showing that it follows from some procedure [for the simple and obvious reason that to do so]...ignores the crucial question of how one justifies one's choice of procedure (Postal in Woodworth & DiPietro, 1963, p. 6).

Yet this situation has remained virtually unchanged among structuralists until now: 'An analysis is justified if one can specify procedures, but the justification of the procedures themselves is given no attention' (Teeter, 1964, p. 204). The end result has been a gradual reconciliation to the fact that 'any clearly specified procedure of analysis is [so far as we can tell] as good as any other' (Chomsky, 1966a, p. 107) and thus to the eventual acceptance of the permissiveness I have been speaking of.[1]

To sum up, the principles of structural analysis are *arbitrary* and 'there are radical inadequacies in the formulation of the goals of a field whose methods are arbitrary' (Postal in Woodworth & DiPietro, 1963, p. 5). The time has come to abandon the view that linguistics is 'primarily a set of operations serving to organize into a structure a set of otherwise disparate data ("hocus-pocus" linguistics)' and adopt instead the view that linguistics is 'a cognitive science, whose aim is to gain knowledge of an existing structure which manifests itself in the data ("God's Truth" linguistics)' (Garvin, 1953, p. 472; cf. Householder, 1952, p. 260).[2] To accomplish this, however, it will become necessary not only to begin thinking seriously about the explicit *specification* of grammars, but also about the problem of the *justification* of grammars and of the criteria which are to be brought to bear in preferring one analysis over another. We must, in short, seek to provide 'a principled basis for choosing among particular linguistic descriptions and forms of linguistic description' (Rosenbaum, 1966, p. 184).

But how is this to be done? Postal points the way: 'The question of justification of grammars is handled in generative grammar as in other sciences. We justify a grammar by showing that it is the *simplest* theory, capable of explaining all the facts' (in Woodworth & DiPietro, 1963, p. 8). This statement introduces two more important new notions into linguistic meta-discussion: *simplicity*, on the one hand, and *explana-*

---

[1] Thus Z. Harris admits in his Introduction that 'the methods described here do not eliminate non-uniqueness in linguistic descriptions. It is possible for different linguists, working on the same material, to set up different phonemic and morphemic elements, to break phonemes into simultaneous components or not to do so. The only result of such differences will be a correlative difference in the final statement as to what the utterances consist of' (1951, p. 2).

[2] The real issue involved here is thus between viewing linguistics as a *game* and viewing it as a *science*, though the terms 'hocus-pocus' and 'God's truth' have been bandied about in a number of other senses, as well. Chomsky himself has interpreted the distinction as between what is *true* of language (or what is 'inherent in the structure of language') and what is most *convenient* for the analyst to think true (or what 'can most profitably be imposed upon the linguistic code'), a distinction which he rejects on the grounds that the two represent 'just two ways of describing the same thing' (1957a, p. 240).

tion, on the other. To consider the latter one first, the search for explanations in linguistics is easily understood as part of the transformationalists' efforts to make a true science of the discipline. For as Nagel has observed, 'To explain, to establish some relation of dependence between propositions superficially unrelated, to exhibit systematically connections between apparently miscellaneous items of information are distinctive marks of scientific inquiry' (1961, p. 5). Caws defines scientific explanation as 'accounting for particular events by reference to general laws...or accounting for laws by reference to principles still more general' (1965, p. 91). In short, a particular fact or event is construed to be *explained*, in the scientific sense, if it can be shown to be subsumed under a *broader generalization*, i.e. if it can be proved to be a special case of, or a logical consequence of, some more general statement which accounts for a great number of other apparently heterogeneous facts, as well (cf. Nagel, 1961, pp. 37ff). The classic case in physics, of course, is Newton's theory of universal gravitation, from which not only Kepler's three laws of planetary motion could be derived, but also Galileo's laws of terrestial mechanics (not to mention a host of other empirical generalizations pertaining to phenomena as widely diverse as the action of the tides and the precession of the equinoxes). By the same token, therefore, Chomsky remarks that 'certain features of given languages can be reduced to *universal properties of language*, and explained in terms of these deeper aspects of linguistic form' (1965a, p. 35; italics added).[1] So the linguist must be brought to realize that the question of specifying the precise nature of any speaker's ability to innovate in language is ultimately a question about the nature of language itself, and in order to answer it, 'we must make explicit the underlying structure inherent in all natural languages' (Chomsky & Miller, 1963, p. 271). Chomsky and Halle thus interpret a major goal of general linguistics to be 'to develop a theory of natural language as such', or, in other words, to propose 'a system of hypotheses concerning the essential properties of any human language...[which] determine the class of possible natural languages and the class of potential grammars for some human language' (1968, p. 4). Nor is there anything strikingly novel or controversial in this approach, which is a revival and elaboration of traditional views outlined in the seventeenth and eighteenth centuries

---

[1] For some examples of this, see especially chapter 8 of Chomsky (1957b) on 'The Explanatory Power of Linguistic Theory', pp. 85–91. I deal at some length with the notion of explanation in TGG in 5.1 and 7.2.2 below.

which held that 'the general features of grammatical structure are common to all languages and reflect certain fundamental properties of the human mind' (Chomsky, 1966a, p. 59; see also pp. 72–3).[1] All that is involved in this proposal, so it is said, is that linguists ought to begin searching for a set of common concepts and principles which may serve not only to define language, but also to delineate the domain of linguistics as a discipline.

The role of explanation in the justification of grammars is thus clear: we accept a grammar which *explains* some complex of linguistic phenomena in preference to one which simply restates the facts. As Chomsky has put it:

If someone says of my description that this doesn't fit, and this, and this, I would say that it is not a very interesting comment. If on the other hand he says that the exceptions can fit into a different pattern [without sacrificing a corresponding degree of coverage elsewhere in the system], that is of the highest importance (in Hill, 1962, p. 32).

For it is clear enough that whether or not a phenomenon is 'messy' or 'irregular' 'often depends on the way it is described' (Postal in Woodworth & DiPietro, 1963, p. 24). What the transformationalist seeks, therefore, is a description of the highest possible generality. This leads us directly to the transformationalist's notion of *simplicity*, which is defined, within the theory itself, as a measure of the degree of 'linguistically significant generalization' achieved by a grammar (see Chomsky, 1965a, pp. 37–47).

To sum up, the problem of non-uniqueness in linguistic description which plagued linguists throughout the structuralist era is the direct result of the fact that 'choice of a grammar for a particular language L will always be much underdetermined by the data drawn from L alone' (Chomsky, 1965a, p. 41). Justification of a *particular* grammar of L will only be possible, under these circumstances, if the investigator has at his disposal an explanatory theory of language. This entails both an explicit characterization of *the form of (possible) grammars*, on the one hand, and the development of *an evaluation (or simplicity) measure*, on the other, which will permit the analyst to choose between grammars all of which are of the prescribed form (Chomsky, 1957b, p. 54, and 1964, p. 104).

[1] This view is, however, to be sharply contrasted with the prevailing view of the structuralist interregnum which held that there was practically no way in which languages could *not* differ from one another (cf. Householder, 1968, p. 10, and Joos, 1963, p. 96), i.e. that there were virtually 'no linguistic universals' whatsoever (Teeter, 1964, p. 200).

Such a theory would limit the choice of grammars in two ways: by imposing universal formal conditions on *all* linguistic descriptions and by providing an evaluation procedure which could be utilized in selecting some *specific* linguistic description for any particular language (Chomsky, 1965a, p. 41), where the *ultimate* criterion in evaluation is the simplicity of the whole system (Chomsky, 1957b, pp. 55–6). So Postal concludes:

> An adequate scientific description of language thus involves, as a minimum, an account of the possible types of linguistic rule, an account of the way these rules enumerate both sentences and their structural descriptions, and an account of the way simplicity of grammars may be determined (in Woodworth & DiPietro, 1963, p. 8).

We might therefore characterize the second main aspect of the Chomskyan revolution briefly as follows: 'Henceforth linguistics shall no longer be considered a "classificatory" science but an "explanatory" one in the sense that the linguist's main task shall not be to collect and classify utterances, but rather to attempt to formulate a universal theory of language which might, in turn, be utilized to yield a unique, explicit and explanatory theory of the structure of the (idealized) system which underlies the linguistic behavior of the speaker of any particular language.'[1]

2.4   On the data of linguistics

The data with which the structuralist linguist was concerned were simply 'speech-forms' (Bloomfield, 1933), by which is meant actual physical utterances. To this must be added, as a practical matter, such supplementary data as whether or not two successive utterances are the same or different and whether or not they belong to the same language. (This is implicit even in Bloomfield's 'Postulates', 1926.) But little beyond this was ever allowed. In particular, introspective judgments of native speakers – particularly about meaning – were not consciously admitted as relevant for purposes of linguistic analysis.[2] This restriction,

---

[1] Thereby, Lees suggests, transforming linguists from 'dull catalogers of data' into 'brilliant scientists' (1957, p. 380).

[2] Nevertheless, some such judgments inevitably crept in surreptitiously now and again. Consider, for example, Bloomfield's discussion of the status of the sequence *book on*: he rejects it as a linguistic form on the grounds that it is 'meaningless' (1926, p. 27). Today the modern transformationalist would simply say that *book on* is not a constituent on the basis of his intuitive knowledge of English and insist, therefore, that one requirement of a descriptively adequate grammar of English would be that it account for the fact in an explicit and natural way.

like the earlier ones pertaining to analysis as outlined in the preceding section, was also imposed in the name of objectivity and in a more-or-less conscious reaction against the profoundly meaning-oriented approach to linguistic description which had dominated the earlier traditional era – as well as against the principles and methods of introspective psychology in general, which had been coming under increasingly devastating critical attack, particularly by the behaviorists. By the transformationalists, however, such attempts to achieve objectivity were regarded as self-defeating in that they had the effect of imposing such narrow constraints on the discipline that any possibility of developing a general theory of language was virtually precluded (see Teeter, 1964, p. 201). In Chomsky's view, therefore, all the behaviorist era ever proved was that 'objectivity can be pursued with little consequent gain in insight and understanding' (1965a, p. 20).[1]

But, beyond such profound methodological considerations, it seems clear that 'there are all sorts of things that speakers know about their utterances that do not emerge as features of a corpus', such as, for example, whether a given utterance is grammatical or not (i.e. whether or not it belongs to the language), or is ambiguous, or synonymous with some other utterance, or related grammatically to others which might be superficially different, or even anomalous (see Postal in Woodworth & DiPietro, 1963, pp. 6–8; Chomsky 1962b, pp. 233–40; Katz & Fodor, 1963, p. 175, and Chomsky, 1965a, pp. 63–4, for numerous examples); yet so long as the linguist limited himself to the study of a corpus, there was no way for him to avail himself of these data. If, on the other hand, as Fodor and Garrett suggest, the linguist were to think of his corpus 'as merely a *clue* to the informant's competence, which *latter* is the primary object of scientific scrutiny, there would seem to be no good reason why he should not also avail himself of *whatever other clues he can find*' (1966b, p. 137; italics added). Furthermore, it is also clear that by including the introspective judgments of native speakers into the body of data which must be explained by the grammar (or theory) of any language, we are imposing additional requirements on the theory in the form of greatly tightened 'external conditions of adequacy' (Chomsky, 1957b, p. 49) which the theory must meet in order to be acceptable, so providing additional criteria for purposes of evaluation or justification.[2]

[1] Thus Chomsky insists that 'the behaviorist position is not an arguable matter. It is simply an expression of lack of interest in theory and explanation' (1965a, p. 193, n. 1).
[2] This consideration has given rise to a new distinction relating to the 'adequacy'

So it becomes obvious that in order to accomplish the ambitious goals outlined in the preceding section, the empirical base of the discipline of linguistics will have to be dramatically broadened in the way indicated. This will make theory-construction more difficult, but theory-rejection much easier. And, in the final analysis, a far more comprehensive and useful theory will result, since it cannot be denied that the 'best kind of theory is [the] one which systematizes the widest range of facts' (Katz, 1964, p. 127; see also Botha, 1968, p. 76). Consequently, it is not only desirable to allow introspective evidence in linguistics, but absolutely *essential* to do so if there is to be any hope of achieving the ambitious goals outlined in the preceding section. This is because:

All linguistic work is, obviously, guided by certain assumptions about the nature of linguistic structure and linguistic patterns; and such assumptions, which are the heart of linguistic theory, can be tested for adequacy in *only one way*, namely, by determining whether the descriptions to which they lead are in accord with [the native speaker's] tacit knowledge concerning the language (Chomsky & Halle, 1968, p. 103; italics added).

The third, and for our purposes final aspect of the Chomskyan revolution can thus be paraphrased as follows: 'Henceforth the empirical data with which linguistics must be concerned will consist not only of speech-forms, but will also include, as an essential supplementary component, various judgments which native speakers can make about these forms.'

2.5 Summary and conclusions

It has been argued that the effects of the Chomskyan revolution on American linguistics have been far-reaching and cataclysmic. Language has been redefined as a *psychological phenomenon* and the goals and priorities of linguistic research have undergone a dramatic about-face: where once data-collection and cataloging was the fashion, the new imperative is for formal *theory construction*; where once a linguistic

or 'degree of success' which a given linguistic description may be said to achieve. At the 'lowest level' we find mere *observational adequacy*, which is the level of success achieved if the grammar simply manages to give a correct account of the observed primary data (such as the physical make-up of utterances with which the structuralists were so preoccupied), whereas a 'second and higher level of success', called *descriptive adequacy*, may be achieved if the grammar provides, in addition, 'a correct account of the linguistic intuition of the native speaker, and specifies the observed data (in particular) in terms of significant generalizations that express underlying regularities in the language' (Chomsky, 1964, pp. 62–3).

'description' might have been construed as satisfactory if it merely managed to incorporate an objective and concise recapitulation of the facts of speech, any description worthy of the name must now incorporate a proposed *explanation* for the body of data with which it is concerned; where once a linguist might have aspired to spend years collecting curious anecdotes about the ways in which languages could differ from one another, he is now driven to seek those *universal properties* of human language which tie the field together and reflect the inherent organizing principles of the intellect. For arbitrariness is gone forever from the discipline of linguistics; in its place we find the serious quest for *truth*. And just over the horizon lies that one breakthrough which will unlock the door to the secrets of the human mind.[1]

In view of the extent, inevitability and apparent irreversibility of this profound sociological development, I shall devote the remainder of this work to a general evaluation of this assessment and its implications for the future development of linguistics.

[1] Since, as Chomsky puts it, 'language, after all, nas no existence apart from its mental representation', it is quite natural to expect 'a close relation between innate properties of the mind and features of linguistic structure' (1968a, p. 81). Consequently, 'it is fair to suppose that the major contribution of the study of language will lie in the understanding it can provide as to the character of mental processes and the structures they form and manipulate' (p. 59).

3 On the nature of language acquisition

3.1 An inductive requirement on grammars

It is clear from the preceding chapter that two main characteristics of the transformational movement in American linguistics have been (1) emphasis upon the 'creative' or 'innovative' aspect of language use as *the* fundamental fact of language and, associated with this, (2) the conviction that the main task of the linguist is to formulate an explicit characterization of 'the precise nature of this ability' (Chomsky & Miller, 1963, p. 271). Combining these two basic methodological directives with the fundamental (and traditional) notion that language itself can be most productively regarded as a formal structure or system whose task is, ultimately, to relate meanings to sounds (cf. 2.2 above), we come to the conclusion that 'the correct goal for synchronic linguistic description is the formulation of explicit, precise, formalized, in short, generative grammars' (Postal in Woodworth & DiPietro, 1963, p. 43). And, to be sure, this 'dazzling Chomskyan vision of a generative grammar – a grammar, that is, whose formulae are truly productive in the strictest sense' (Weinreich, Foreword to Zimmer, 1964) is the most notable and characteristic feature of the transformationalist approach (cf. Lyons, 1966, p. 393).

The magnitude of the task is not to be underestimated. For one thing, it seems clear that some of the structures to be related by such a grammar must, by their very nature, exhibit vastly different properties. As Lamb has aptly and concisely described the situation:

Phonological systems must be adapted to the articulatory and auditory organs, while semological [semantic] systems must be adapted . . . to the phenomena, events, and relationships about which people think and talk. Moreover, phonological systems must conform to the fact that speech takes place in time, which is linear; . . . [whereas] the things to which semological systems must relate. . . are often multidimensional (1966a, p. 2).

Thus it is to be expected that the mediating system, or grammar, is going to be rather complex. Moreover, this system, as a system, cannot be directly observed (cf. p. 29, n. 2). So Chafe says: 'Language is an elephant, and we are all blind men trying to discover what the elephant is like' (1968b, p. 594). It is no simple matter even to know where to start looking (or feeling).

Chomsky, however, has dared to advance a fourfold first step: he suggests that the linguist should begin by advancing hypotheses about each of the following: (1) the conditions that the phonetic and semantic representations of all natural languages should meet, (2) the conditions that the 'syntactic descriptions' of all natural languages should meet, (3) the class of potential, i.e. possible, grammars, and (4) the ways in which these grammars function, i.e. how they go about pairing phonetic representations with semantic ones (see Chomsky, 1966b, p. 8, and Botha, 1968, p. 22). Chomsky advocates, therefore, that the linguist begin his search by focusing attention on the discovery of *linguistic universals*, those 'essential' or 'defining' properties of language which make it explicit just how languages may be said to be, in some important sense, 'cut from the same mold' (cf. 2.3 above).

The nature of this issue may be clarified by brief reference to a few of the specific universals which have already been proposed by transformationalists in response to methodological directives of this sort. These proposals can conveniently be grouped into three (more-or-less) distinct categories. First of all, a certain number of ORGANIZATIONAL UNIVERSALS have been proposed. These are intended to specify 'the abstract structure of the subcomponents of a grammar, as well as the relations between subcomponents' (Botha, 1968, p. 22). A relatively succinct (but already somewhat dated) summary statement of Chomsky's along these lines is the following:

The *grammar* of a language is a system of rules that determine a certain pairing of sound and meaning. It consists of a *syntactic component*, a *semantic component*, and a *phonological component*. The syntactic component defines a certain (infinite) class of abstract objects (D, S), where D is a *deep structure* and S a *surface structure*. The deep structure contains all information relevant to semantic interpretation; the surface structure, all information relevant to phonetic interpretation. The semantic and phonological components are purely interpretive. The former assigns semantic interpretations to deep structures; the latter assigns phonetic interpretations to surface structures. Thus the grammar as a whole relates semantic and phonetic interpretations, the association being mediated by the rules of the syntactic component that define paired deep and surface structures (1967a, pp. 406–7).

Secondly, a number of FORMAL UNIVERSALS have also been proposed.[1] These are intended to specify 'the abstract formal structure of the types of rules of each subcomponent of...a grammar' (Botha, 1968, p. 23). In this connection we read in Chomsky's *Aspects* (1965a), for example, that a very specific general condition ought to be imposed on strict subcategorization rules (within the syntactic component of the grammar), namely, that they be 'strictly local', i.e. that 'each such rule must be of the form...$A \rightarrow CS/\alpha$—β, where $\alpha A\beta$ is a δ, [and] *where, furthermore, δ is the category symbol that appears on the left in the rule $\delta \rightarrow ...A...that introduces* A' (p. 99), and in Chomsky (1967d) that (certain) rules of the phonological component should apply 'cyclically', i.e. that each rule in a sequence is applied in turn first 'to a string bounded by paired brackets of the surface structure and containing no internal brackets; after the last rule of the sequence has applied in this way, innermost brackets are ceased and the sequence of rules re-applies as before' (p. 115).[2]

Finally, certain SUBSTANTIVE UNIVERSALS have also been proposed which are intended to specify 'the theoretical vocabulary that provides the constructs for the formulation of particular rules exhibiting the formal structure required by the formal universals' (Botha, 1968, p. 23), or, as Chomsky and Halle have more concisely put it, which 'define the sets of elements that may figure in particular grammars' (1968, p. 4). Thus in Chomsky (1965a), for instance, we find repeated reference to such concepts as those of 'sentence', 'phrase-marker', 'noun phrase', 'complex symbol', 'formative', etc., and in Chomsky and Halle (1968) such concepts as 'phonetic feature', 'formative boundary', 'diacritic feature', 'segment', 'variable', and many others. Putting this all together, the net result is a vast, complex, highly structured and admirably explicit (and ingenious) general theory of language structure.

A vital question which arises at this point (at least in my own mind), however, is what reason we have for assuming that any of these very specific and detailed 'universal' properties (or of any other set which might be proposed), upon which any given 'linguist's grammar' of some language is to be based, may be said to correspond in any significant

---

[1] Chomsky himself, of course, does not normally distinguish between what I (after Botha) have called the 'organizational' and the 'formal' universals, but uses the term 'formal universals' to include both those which determine either 'the structure of grammars' or 'the form and organization of rules' (Chomsky & Halle, 1968, p. 4). The labels are, of course, arbitrary and are employed here (and elsewhere) merely for convenience of reference.

[2] This latter principle, we are told, 'is quite intuitive, in fact almost obvious' (Chomsky, 1967d, p. 115).

way to the properties of the 'real' or 'mental' grammars (cf. Watt, 1970, pp. 137ff) which are presumed to be internalized by native speakers.[1] That it is the stated intent of transformational grammarians (and the implicit intent of virtually every other brand of grammarian) that such a correspondence must be assumed, is hardly open to question. Katz puts it most boldly: 'The theoretical constructions used by a mentalist linguist in building his theories are intended by him to have psychological reality' (1964, p. 129). But, in any case, apart from some such assumption, it would hardly make any sense to characterize linguistics as 'the subfield of psychology that deals with...aspects of mind' (Chomsky, 1968a, p. 24). The goal of linguistics, we are reminded, is not simply to analyze linguistic data for their own sake, or in some arbitrary way, but rather to establish something of general psychological significance. Unless, therefore, some rational basis can be established for making us think that some very close relation holds between the linguist's (ultimate) grammar of any language L and the native speaker's own internalized 'mental' grammar for this same L, all the linguist's grammar-writing activity must surely degenerate into a kind of highly intellectualized and complex game, the results of which can seemingly have no relevance to anything in the real world and hence can be of no interest to anyone (except, perhaps, to that special type of individual who is simply drawn by natural inclination to crosswords, cryptograms, chess and other such intellectual puzzles for the pleasure of the mental stimulation which they afford). We can clarify this question, I think, by taking a preliminary look at the phenomenon of language acquisition.

Strictly speaking, the activities of the language-learner and those of the linguist are very different. The former is *acquiring* competence (in Chomsky's terms), whereas the latter is trying to describe, characterize or otherwise *give an account* of this competence (see Donaldson's discussion of McNeill, 1966a, p. 121). From a 'formal' point of view, however, as Chomsky has argued, the activities of both parties can be looked upon as very much the same in the sense that both the child and the linguist may be thought of as being engaged in a complex task of

---

[1] As Saussure put it, 'All these things [may] exist in language...as *abstract entities*; [but] their study is difficult because we never know exactly whether or not the awareness [explicit or implicit] of speakers goes as far as the analyses of the grammarian' (1959, p. 138). This is to be contrasted with Chomsky and Halle's casual assertion that we may, with no further ado, simply 'use the term "grammar" to refer both to the system of rules represented in the mind of the speaker–hearer...and to the theory that the linguist constructs as a hypothesis concerning the actual internalized grammar' (1968, p. 4).

'theory construction'.[1] For just as the linguist does not simply *list* the utterances which he encounters in the language he is analyzing, but strives instead to formulate a (linguist's) grammar (or theory) of the language which will both account for the observed utterances (plus certain native speaker's judgments about them) and predict new ones, the child, likewise, does not simply memorize or catalog the utterances he hears but rather 'somehow utilizes these utterances to construct for himself a [real] grammar' on the basis of which he will be able to create new sentences upon demand (Chomsky & Halle, 1968, p. 249). So the question raised in the preceding paragraph may be restated simply as 'How can we be reasonably confident, then, that both come to the same conclusions?'

The first, and most obvious, factor which ties together the notion of the 'hypothetical' grammar of the linguist with the 'real' grammar of the native speaker, is that both are presumed to be based on a roughly equivalent set of primary linguistic data, in each case a representative sample of actual utterances of the particular language being analyzed (by the linguist) or learned (by the child). It seems clear, however, that this consideration is insufficient to lend much credibility to the supposition that the grammar internalized by a child learning some language L must necessarily conform in every (or even partial) detail to the rather rigid set of proposed universal constraints which the linguist imposes on his own grammar of L. For one thing, while the linguist is in a position to make use of many different kinds of evidence in determining what *he* considers to be the best form of grammar, including (1) similarities among the languages of the world and (2) facts about language history, we have no obvious reason to believe that the monolingual child has access to (1), or that *any* child has access to (2).[2] The only data we can be sure are at the child's disposal, in fact, are the highly uncontrolled and defective sampling of primary data (utterances) which happen to come his way (plus, of course, the cultural situations coincident with their use). Yet 'the grammar of a language must be discovered by the child

---

[1] 'When we learn our native language we make some very complicated inductions' (Chomsky in Hill, 1962, p. 181). For, clearly, 'a child who has learned a language has developed an internal representation of a system of rules that determine how sentences are to be formed, used, and understood' (Chomsky, 1965a, p. 25). Thus 'it seems plain that language acquisition is based on the child's discovery of what from a formal point of view is a deep and abstract theory – a generative grammar of his language' (p. 58).

[2] See also McNeill (1966a, p. 100) for some additional considerations along this line.

from the data presented to him' (Chomsky, 1968a, p. 74). So while the basic task facing both the linguist and the language-learner may conveniently be looked upon as analogous in some sense, the former is in a position to bring a much greater range of facts to bear on his solution than the latter is. And under these circumstances one tends to question the 'logic' behind Menyuk's (1969) assertion that 'it would be logical [plausible?] to suppose that a child, in understanding and producing a language, uses the structural aspects of the language which the linguist might use to characterize it' (see her Preface).

Faced with the apparent fact that the linguist and the child are operating in two very different ball parks, so to speak, what I propose here is the imposition of what I shall call an *inductive requirement* on grammars. By this I mean that some reasonable provision must be made for the 'learnability' of a (linguist's) grammar by a child *solely on the basis of the data which is available to him* before we elevate such a grammar from the domain of 'scholastic fiction' (Jakobson, 1961a, p. 250) to that of a plausible model of the 'real', 'internalized', or 'psychologically valid' grammar of some language.[1] Broadly speaking, we can envision two different ways of accomplishing this. The first might be for the linguist to limit the range of data which he will consider in formulating his theories to those which he can feel reasonably certain are also available to the child. This, clearly, was the alternative selected by the structuralists, but which the transformationalists have found unacceptable (cf. 2.4 above). The transformationalists have therefore opted for a second approach, namely to attempt to set forth some satisfying hypothesis as to how both the child and the linguist *might* come to the same conclusions *despite* the apparent asymmetry in the range of data which each is in a position to bring to bear. This attempt is found in the transformationalist literature under the rubric of Chomsky's 'learning' (1964,

[1] What I propose is obviously a modest requirement. Without it, surely, we would have no reason to think that the linguist would ever chance to prefer precisely what the child prefers. But even with it, we should have little reason to be overconfident. To give some idea of the wide range of issues which would ultimately have to be considered in comparing a linguist's grammar-writing activities to the child's grammar-learning ones, I quote briefly from Matthews (1967, p. 123): 'A linguist would normally require, for instance, that a grammar should be self-consistent and non-redundant; but is there any reason to suppose that the internalized "grammar" would meet this condition? Indeed could the brain develop such a "grammar"? A linguist can eliminate redundancy or inconsistency simply by wielding a red pencil or throwing cards into the wastepaper basket; but is it likely, from what is known of human remembering and forgetting, that the brain can discard "rules" in an equivalent fashion?'

p. 62 and elsewhere) or 'acquisition' (1967a, p. 401 and elsewhere) model for language, which I shall now examine in some detail.

3.2   Chomsky's model of language acquisition

The model of language acquisition which Chomsky associates with his theory of TGG has been schematically represented as shown in fig. 3.1,

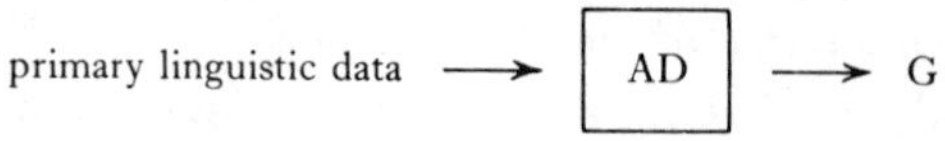

primary linguistic data ⟶ | AD | ⟶ G

FIG. 3.1

where AD represents a 'hypothetical language-acquisition device' which 'can provide as "output" a descriptively adequate grammar G for [some] language L on the basis of certain primary linguistic data from L as an input' (1966b, p. 10). In order for this model to pertain to any language-learning situation whatsoever, Chomsky adds that:

We naturally want the device AD to be language-independent – that is, capable of learning any human language and only these. We want it, in other words, to provide an implicit definition of the notion 'human language'. Were we able to develop the specifications for a language-acquisition device of this sort, we could realistically claim to be able to provide an explanation for the linguistic intuition – the tacit competence – of the speaker of a language. This explanation would be based on the assumption that the specifications of the device AD provide the basis for language-acquisition, primary linguistic data from some language providing the empirical conditions under which the development of a generative grammar takes place (p. 10).

What is clearly at issue, therefore, in Chomsky's own view, is the question of the *internal structure* of the device AD, which is presumed to constitute the sum total of the relevant *innate equipment* which the child brings to the language-learning situation.[1] In the final analysis, therefore, 'We can think of general linguistic theory as an attempt to specify the character of the device [AD]' (Chomsky, 1964, p. 62).[2]

[1] In Chomsky's words, a description of the child's language-acquisition device represents 'a hypothesis about the innate intellectual equipment that a child brings to bear in language learning' (1962a, p. 530) and the way in which this device selects a grammar 'will be determined by its internal structure' (1967a, p. 401).

[2] Given this characterization, it follows that we would be wrong to follow Matthews' advice and consider that the 'two parts' of Chomsky's *Aspects*, namely, the 'speculative and wide-ranging' arguments of chapter 1 and the remainder of the book on 'the virtues and limitations of specific forms of grammatical rule' are 'conceptually independent' to the extent that 'one may accept the concept of a generative grammar

Obviously *some* relevant innate endowment exists in human beings; this point is not open to serious question. It is sufficient support for this general assertion that genuine 'language' is an apparent species-specific trait of the human race alone: no other species appears capable of mastering a communication system which approaches human language in internal complexity or external flexibility.[1] We all agree that in order to learn a (human) language one must first be a human being – which is another way of saying that the human being has innate characteristics of *some* sort which he alone can bring to bear in a language-learning situation. (In fact, without innate equipment of some sort, how could we learn *anything*? (cf. Putnam, 1967, p. 16).) The issue here is, therefore, not whether some sort of innate endowment for language exists, but rather its precise nature (or, in terms of Chomsky's acquisition model, the nature of the internal structure of the device AD above).[2] It is obviously improper to confuse these two issues, as, for example, Langacker appears to have done.

Specifically, Langacker, following Chomsky's (1966a) lead, interprets the issue of innateness in terms of the age-old rationalist-empiricist philosophical controversy, which he greatly oversimplifies in the process.

(and hence take a sympathetic interest in the later chapters) while assenting to none of the more controversial suggestions in chapter 1 [on language acquisition, competence, etc.]' (1967, p. 119). Though each specific proposal in the later chapters would, of course, have to be examined individually as to the extent it depends upon the theoretical framework within which it is presented, it would seem that almost all of the formulations which have appeared as products of the theory of TGG rest, to a very great extent, on those very 'speculative' considerations which are presented in chapter 1, for these are the considerations which attempt to give the very abstract *linguistic* theory which Chomsky presents some measure of plausibility as a *psychological* theory; they are the considerations, in short, which attempt to justify the sort of 'systematic ambiguity' in the use of the term 'grammar' which Chomsky indulges in so freely and which Matthews criticizes so strenuously. For obviously, if Chomsky's 'content' interpretation of the innate language-acquisition device could be shown to be incorrect, the impact on the basic theory of TGG would be catastrophic: the shambles would consist mainly of a vast proliferation of putative linguistic universals (and the rules which follow from them) but with no basis for thinking that any of them could conceivably be acquired by the child. A theory is only as sound as its basic presuppositions, and the basic presuppositions of TGG clearly include presuppositions about the nature of language acquisition (see 3.6 below for further discussion of this important point).

[1] Moreover, as Lenneberg has observed, language appears to be species-specific even in its 'most primitive stages' (1964, p. 67).

[2] As McNeill has put it, 'the view that children are endowed with a capacity for language is not a particularly interesting hypothesis. It merely repeats the observation, apparently true, that man is alone among all animals in possessing language. To make the hypothesis interesting, it is necessary to show what some of the specific features of this capacity might be' (1966a, p. 99).

The 'empiricist view' he characterizes (1967, p. 235), as the view that '*no* linguistic structure is innately specified, that language is learned *entirely* through experience'. Next he presents what is presumably the only alternative, the so-called 'rationalist view', which states that 'language is innately specified *almost in its entirety*' (italics are added in both citations). He then presents a number of arguments (such as the species-specific argument I have just given above) in support of the obvious conclusion that some sort of innate endowment must exist which makes it possible for human beings (alone) to learn language. But from this Langacker then concludes (p. 237) that 'evidence for the rationalist claim [in the very explicit sense defined by him] is very strong'. The false dichotomy he thus sets up is between (1) an innate neural specification which provides the 'blueprints for any possible linguistic system' in such great detail that the child 'has only to learn those details of structure that differentiate the language spoken around him from other possible human languages' and (2) an initial 'blank slate' from which the linguistic system which is eventually learned 'is somehow built up from scratch, its structure being determined by experience alone' (pp. 235–6).[1] It is, however, quite obvious, is it not, that no amount of evidence in favor of the existence of some sort of innate capacity in general can have any bearing on the question of its specific nature, for the simple reason that this argument fails to take into consideration the limitless number of logically possible gradations between the two extreme positions with which Langacker actually deals?

The source of Langacker's error on this point is not at all difficult to track down, since the specific interpretation of his notion of 'innate capacity for language' is clearly that of Chomsky himself. In his 1966b article, for example, although he makes passing reference to the 'difficulties of developing an empirically adequate language-independent

---

[1] Chomsky seems to admit that this is a simplification of the classical 'empiricist' position when he observes that 'empiricist speculation has characteristically assumed that only the *procedures* and *mechanisms* for the acquisition of knowledge constitute an *innate* property of the mind', whereas 'rationalist speculation has assumed that the *general form* of a system of knowledge is fixed in advance' (1965a, p. 51; italics added). Thus the empiricist–rationalist controversy cannot involve a distinction between an initial 'blank slate' as opposed to an initial detailed 'blueprint' for knowledge, but rather one which revolves instead around the question of the specific *nature* of man's innate endowments, since innate propensities or dispositions of some sort are conceded to exist by proponents of *both* sides of the debate. Langacker makes essentially this same admission himself (1967, p. 236), which really makes one wonder what all the empiricist–rationalist fuss is therefore about.

specification of AD', Chomsky immediately moves on boldly to propose what seems to him the most promising course of action, namely, to proceed in the 'two parallel ways' already touched upon in 2.3. To recapitulate, in Chomsky's own words:

First, we must...develop as rich a hypothesis concerning linguistic universals as can be supported by available evidence. This specification can then be attributed to the system AD [and thus to the child] as an intrinsic property. Second, we may attempt to develop a general evaluation procedure, as [another] intrinsic property of AD, which will enable it to select a particular member of the class of grammars that meet the specifications [of the theory] ...on the basis of the presented primary linguistic data. This procedure will then enable the device to select one of the *a priori* possible hypotheses – one of the permitted grammars – that is compatible with the empirically given data from a given language (p. 11).

Remarks like these (which have been restated in one form or another in almost all of Chomsky's major works) seem to justify Matthews' contention that

Chomsky believes that a 'long-range task for general linguistics' is that of characterizing an 'innate linguistic theory' which enables a child to construct some sort of 'grammar' for the language of its speech-community...Such a 'theory', he believes, must provide both a definition of the class of possible 'grammars' and a procedure for deciding which of these 'grammars' is the most appropriate; that is to say, a hypothesis about the innate 'theory' will correspond quite closely to a theory of generative grammar as it is normally understood...Accordingly Chomsky feels entitled, by a 'systematic ambiguity'..., to argue from one to the other interchangeably. In particular, he argues that a theory of generative grammar must incorporate every possible [essential] language universal... Otherwise, one gathers, it would be insufficiently 'rich, detailed and specific' to account for the 'fact of language acquisition'...In this way, the whole problem of restricting the form of grammar...and of evaluating the grammars which are permitted by such restrictions...is discussed more or less consistently within the language-learning context (1967, pp. 120–1).

3.3 An alternative model of the AD

The theory of language acquisition which Chomsky sets forth is the one which Slobin (1966, pp. 87–8) has referred to as a 'content' view of the AD, that is, the view that 'a child is held to be born with the entire set of linguistic universals [plus evaluation procedures, built-in] and that he somehow uses this set as a grid through which he filters the particular language he happens to hear around him' (cf. Chomsky, 1968a, p. 76).

Slobin himself favors what he calls a 'process' approach, in terms of which 'the child is born not with a set of linguistic categories but with some sort of process mechanism – a set of procedures and inference rules, if you will – that he uses to process linguistic data'. Under such an interpretation as this, then, any linguistic universals would be 'the *result* of an innate cognitive competence rather than the content of such a competence' (p. 88).[1]

We are confronted here with what appears to be an interesting empirical question fraught with important implications for the study of language: does the child come equipped with a full set of linguistic universals plus evaluation procedures or, instead, with an algorithm or special technique for performing linguistic analysis – or perhaps with a little of both (or maybe with something entirely different which has yet even to be imagined)?[2] Whatever the answer to these questions, at least three things seem certain: (1) not all of these alternatives can be correct (i.e. true), (2) the matter is empirical in nature (hence the stipulation about 'truth' has some teeth in it),[3] and (3) the correct answer, whatever it is, is not going to be an easy one to discover.

It seems curious, therefore, that Chomsky should have continued to be so boldly explicit in adhering to the 'content' approach in preference to the logically possible alternatives. This persistent inflexibility is the more surprising when we consider that he does explicitly recognize that both the algorithm (process) and formal universals (content) approaches are compatible with his model of language acquisition and thus, presumably, that the question remains for him not only an empirical one but also one which is still very much open. One of his most straightforward remarks to this effect is the following:

[1] Fodor sets forth a parallel dichotomy in another article in this same volume. It is self-evident, he says, that 'the child must bring to the language-learning situation some amount of intrinsic structure. This structure may take the form of *general learning principles* or it may take the form of relatively *detailed...information* about the kind of grammatical systems that underlies natural languages' (1966, p. 106; italics added).

[2] Consider, for example, Fodor's quite plausible additional proposal that the learning principles in terms of which the child organizes his linguistic experience may *themselves* be learned, i.e. that what the child may be born with is 'a very general capacity to *learn learning principles* and that it is such *learned* principles that the child brings to the problem of mastering his language' (1966, p. 106; italics added). It is along the lines of Fodor's more 'extreme' suggestion here that my own proposals for a viable alternative model of language acquisition will eventually develop (see 6.2 below, especially pp. 200–1).

[3] Cf. Chomsky & Halle (1965, p. 101): 'There is, in particular, a right answer to the question: what is the basis for the acquisition of linguistic competence?'

Just how the [language acquisition] device...selects a grammar will be determined by its internal structure, by the *methods of analysis* available to it, and
the *initial constraints* that it imposes on any possible grammar...Although
these are not the terms that have been used, linguistics has always been concerned with this question. Thus modern structural linguistics has attempted to
develop methods of analysis of a general nature, independent of any particular
language, and an older and now largely forgotten tradition attempted to
develop a system of universal constraints that any grammar must meet. We
might describe both these attempts as concerned with the internal structure of
the [language acquisition] device,...with the innate conception of 'human
language' that makes language acquisition possible (1967a, p. 401; italics
added).

What is more, Chomsky's position would actually appear to be the
least preferable imaginable alternative. Consider, first of all, what is
involved in comparing only the two extreme alternatives outlined above.
In the first place, 'the empiricist holds that very little of psychological
structure is innately specified, while the rationalist claims that a great
deal of it is' (Langacker, 1967, p. 237): in fact, that 'the bulk of language
is genetically transmitted' (p. 236). Moreover, Chomsky's 'content' or
'rationalist' position also involves the assumption that there exists 'a
special inborn capacity for language' (Langacker, 1967, p. 237), that is,
a special set of psychological predispositions which are *specifically
linguistic* and which consequently have no other (known or as yet
imagined) function other than to insure that the child learns one or more
languages. Once again, this view contrasts sharply with that of the
'empiricist' who holds that 'the human child is born with no *special*
capacity for language, only *a general ability to learn*' (Langacker, 1967,
p. 237; italics added). The inherent advantages of the 'process' or
'empiricist' position are thus twofold: (1) this is the position which
makes the *fewer assumptions* about the child's innate capacity for language
and hence is to be preferred on conceptual grounds, all other things
being equal; the burden of proof rests on Chomsky's 'content' or
'rationalist' hypothesis to demonstrate that the additional innate structure which it invokes is actually required to account for the facts of
language acquisition; and (2) it is only this less complex and less
restricted 'learning algorithm' approach which offers any hope of
actually *explaining* language acquisition as a special case of some more
general theory of human learning (see 7.2.2 below). Chomsky's approach,
to posit a particular set of innate *linguistic* universals to account specifically for the acquisition of *language*, is an *ad hoc* maneuver which '*only*

postpones the problem of [language] *learning; it does not solve it'* (Putnam, 1967, p. 21). Chomsky's reply that 'invoking an innate representation of universal grammar *does* solve the problem of learning, *if it is true that this is the basis for language acquisition,* as it well may be' (1968a, p. 75; italics added; see also Chomsky, 1969, p. 80) is not an adequate defense of his position because (as we shall see in 3.5 below) it appears to be methodologically *impossible to establish* whether or not any proposed behavioral traits are innate – hence it is impossible to demonstrate empirically whether any proposals along 'content' or 'innate universals' lines do constitute the actual 'basis for language acquisition'. A conclusion of this sort could thus only be arrived at by *default*, i.e. by demonstrating conclusively that *no other hypothesis* could account for the phenomenon. The student of language acquisition therefore needs to determine whether 'the empiricist position has possibilities that have not yet been explored' (Brown, 1968, p. 290) before abandoning hope of explaining language acquisition and falling back on the 'Humboldtian' position that 'language is not really learned [at all]...but rather develops "from within", in an essentially predetermined way, when the appropriate environmental conditions exist' (Chomsky, 1968a, p. 67).[1] I suppose it has been for such good reasons, then, that the 'learning algorithm' interpretation of language acquisition has traditionally been regarded as preferable, more plausible and 'most obvious' (cf. Householder, 1968, p. 7).

3.4 Some background considerations

In order to understand Chomsky's curious inflexibility on this point, it is necessary to regard the issue in its historical context. As I suggested in chapter 2, transformational generative grammar has developed mostly as a reaction to the 'structuralist' era (just as that developed essentially as a reaction to an earlier 'traditional' one) and, like most reactions before it (in science no less than in society in general), it has tended to overstatement. The point can be illustrated most effectively here, I think, by referring to what is perhaps one of the best-known and most influential chapters in the transformationalist literature, chapter 6 of *Syntactic Structures*, the work which is generally conceded to constitute the demarcation line between the structuralist and transformational eras in American linguistics. The chapter is entitled 'On the Goals of Linguistic

[1] See also Campbell & Wales (1970, pp. 248–9).

Theory', and it is here that we find the basic metatheoretical proposition which has underlain all work in transformational generative grammar since that time: 'A grammar of the language L is essentially a theory of L' (p. 49). Virtually everything stems from that.

Of more specific interest to us here is Chomsky's influential presentation of what he called the 'external conditions of adequacy' (i.e. that the sentences generated by a grammar would have to be acceptable to a native speaker) and the 'conditions of generality' which he felt would have to be imposed on grammars. By this Chomsky meant 'that the grammar of a given language [should] be constructed in accordance with a specific theory of linguistic structure in which such terms as "phoneme" and "phrase" [i.e. the linguistic universals] are defined independently of any particular language'. This discussion led immediately to what ultimately proved the major consideration of the chapter: the crucial question of the relation 'between the general theory [of language] and the particular grammars [i.e. theories of particular languages] that follow from it'; or, in other words, what the appropriate criteria should be 'for selecting the correct grammar for each language' (pp. 49–50). In his lucid attempt to answer this question, long a bugaboo to linguistics of all persuasions (cf. 2.3 above), Chomsky outlined three conceivable alternatives. The first was that the general theory might provide the analyst with what he called a 'discovery procedure' for grammars, i.e. the general theory might be so complete and detailed as to 'provide a practical and mechanical method for actually constructing the grammar, given a corpus of utterances' (p. 50). He then presented a somewhat weaker requirement which might be imposed, called a 'decision procedure' for grammars, in terms of which the general theory would need only to 'provide a practical and mechanical method for determining whether or not a grammar proposed for a given corpus [was], in fact, the best grammar of the language from which this corpus [was] drawn'. And finally he set forth an even weaker requirement, what he called an 'evaluation procedure' for grammars, in terms of which the general theory, given two proposed grammars, would be required only to select which of the two was 'the better grammar of the language from which the corpus [was] drawn'. Chomsky also presented here the familiar graphic representations for each of these possibilities. Chomsky's conclusion was that he found it 'unreasonable to demand of linguistic theory that it provide anything more than a practical evaluation procedure for grammars' (p. 52). This position received strong support from Lees

(1957, pp. 378ff) and has apparently remained a fundamental tenet of TGG since (cf. Bach, 1964, p. 181; McCawley, 1968c, pp. 24–5; etc). For this reason alone, the basis of Chomsky's argument in this chapter deserves our most careful attention.

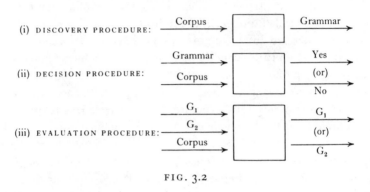

FIG. 3.2

Of particular interest is Chomsky's treatment of alternatives (i) and (iii) above (fig. 3.2). First, Chomsky unabashedly interprets 'the more careful proposals for the development of linguistic theory' of the structuralist era (such as, for example, Bloch's 'A set of postulates for phonemic analysis' and other similar attempts 'to state methods of analysis that an investigator might actually use, if he had the time, to construct a grammar of a language directly from the raw data') as, in fact, attempts to satisfy the strongest of his three requirements, i.e. as attempts to incorporate into linguistic theory metacriteria sufficient to establish a discovery procedure for grammars. Chomsky's contention, on the other hand, was (and is) that only 'by lowering our sights to the more modest goal of developing an evaluation procedure for grammars [can] we...focus attention more clearly on really crucial problems of linguistic structure and...arrive at more satisfying answers to them' – though he admits, at the same time, that 'the correctness of this judgment can only be determined by the actual development and comparison of theories of these various sorts' (1957b, p. 53). Apart from Chomsky's own disillusionment with the results achieved by certain of the methods and techniques adopted during the structuralist era (notably invariant-biunique phonemics – see 6.1 below), the main strength of Chomsky's argument has rested on the establishment of an analogy between the search for 'a discovery procedure for grammars' in linguistics and a search for 'a discovery procedure for theories' in science in general. For if the reader accepts the validity of the analogy (made possible by Chomsky's proposition that a grammar of a language is essentially a 'theory' of that language), he is, to be sure, already set up for the real crusher: 'No one in the physical sciences ever dreamed of asking for a precise characterization of how the discoverer gets from the observations to the theory which enables him to predict' (Chomsky in Hill, 1962, p. 175).[1] To make a long story short, the argument is: (1) no science requires a step-by-step mechanical procedure by which its theories are 'discovered', (2) structural linguistics attempted to do precisely that for language (see Chomsky, 1959a, p. 210), (3) the 'process' approach is simply the structural approach all over again, and therefore, (4) the process approach is doomed to failure. It is short, sweet, cut-and-dried and, *in toto*, fallacious.

In the first place, the argument hinges, as I have already suggested, on a very fuzzy analogy.[2] Part of the difficulty stems from another of Chomsky's now-famous 'systematic ambiguities', involving, in this instance, the term 'theory'. On the one hand, as noted above, Chomsky chooses to construe a grammar of any given language as a 'theory' of that language. On the other hand, he also speaks of 'the general theory' or of 'linguistic theory' (or, simply, 'the theory') as, for example, in the question, 'What is the relation between the general theory and the particular grammars [theories] that follow from it?' (1957b, p. 50). It is apparent that if we are to accept the term 'theory' as synonymous with the notion of 'a grammar of some language L', then in order to keep our terminological sidewalks clean we are going to have to assign some different designation to the notion of 'the general theory', i.e. something akin to 'metatheory', perhaps. The next question is, to which of *these* (quite disparate) senses of the term 'theory' are Hempel, Nagel and others referring in note 1 below? It is by no means obvious to me that this thing of which they speak (that is, that thing for which no 'step-by-step algorithm' can be expected) is not the thing which we have just called

---

[1] Cf. Hempel: 'There are...no generally applicable "rules of induction", by which hypotheses or theories can be mechanically derived or inferred from empirical data. The transition from data to theory requires creative imagination. Scientific hypotheses and theories are not *derived* from observed facts, but *invented* in order to account for them' (1966, p. 15) and Nagel: 'There are no rules of discovery and invention in science, any more than there are such rules in the arts' (1961, p. 12).

[2] Not to mention the fact that recent developments in the philosophy of science have called into serious question earlier oversimplified accounts of the nature of scientific discovery, as represented by the remarks cited in the note above, for example (see 7.1.1 for discussion).

the 'metatheory' in linguistics, i.e. the *general* theory. Chafe, at least, appears to be of much the same mind on this point:

There is more to this question than simply the idea that earlier American linguists labored under the benighted notion that a theory could be arrived at by the application of mechanical procedures to data, that there is an algorithm for the construction of a theory. There is a difference, first of all, between a general theory of language and theories (or grammars) of particular languages. The post-Bloomfieldian belief was not that the contemporary general theory of language (phonemes, morphemes, IC structure, and the rest) had been mechanically arrived at, but that this theory should constitute, or at least include, a discovery procedure for particular grammars. If there had in fact been thought to exist a recipe for the formulation of a general theory, this recipe itself would have belonged to a nonmechanically arrived-at metatheory. It strikes me that Bloomfield's and Bloch's postulates show well what the situation was. The postulates themselves were not the result of any discovery procedure; rather, they were simply 'thought to be true'. But in the presence of any particular language they were thought to form a theoretical basis for the mechanical recognition of the entities which they postulated (1965, p. 642).

In these terms, then, just what it is in science in general that is akin to the notion of 'theory' in Chomsky's sense of a 'grammar' in linguistics becomes obscure – and with it the sense of Chomsky's whole argument.

But I think the most effective way to demonstrate the vacuousness of Chomsky's campaign against the 'discovery procedure' (to the point where this phrase has now become taboo in some linguistic circles) will be to show that Chomsky clearly (though not explicitly) refutes it himself in his own work. For if we compare Chomsky's graphic representation of the much-maligned 'discovery procedure for grammars' (diagram (i) of fig. 3.2 on p. 58 above) with Chomsky's schematic model for language acquisition (fig. 3.1 on p. 50 above), we discover that the two are both reducible to the form shown in fig. 3.3. In other words, implicit

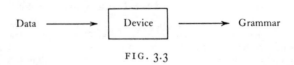

FIG. 3.3

in Chomsky's own definitions of the two notions 'language-acquisition device' and 'discovery procedure for grammars' is the claim that they are *equivalent*: LANGUAGE ACQUISITION IS A DISCOVERY PROCEDURE FOR GRAMMARS (in Chomsky's own technical senses of both terms). Furthermore, since Chomsky also tells us that, 'formally speaking', the task of the child in learning a language is essentially the same as that which faces the linguist in analyzing it, namely the task of constructing a unique grammar on the basis of a finite corpus of primary linguistic data; LINGUISTIC DESCRIPTION (i.e. grammar- or theory-construction for language by the linguist) likewise constitutes a discovery procedure for grammars.

This point can be further clarified, I think, by reference to Chomsky's notion of 'explanatory adequacy', one of the clearest accounts of which appears in Chomsky and Halle (1965), where we read that:

A linguistic theory meets the level of explanatory adequacy insofar as it succeeds in describing the internal structure of [the language-acquisition device] and thus shows how the descriptively adequate grammar arises from the primary linguistic data. Such a linguistic theory is explanatory in that it accounts for the linguistic intuition...of the speaker on the basis of a certain assumption about the form of language...and about the data that was available to the speaker (p. 100).

In other words:

a linguistic theory that aims for explanatory adequacy is concerned with the internal structure of the [language-acquisition] device...; that is, it aims to provide a principled basis, independent of any particular language, for the selection of the descriptively adequate grammar of each language (Chomsky, 1964, p. 63);

or, it attempts 'to account for the child's construction of a grammar and to determine what preconditions on the form of language make it possible' (Chomsky & Halle, 1968, p. 331). Chomsky's contends that a 'two-pronged attack' on this problem offers some hope of success. First, 'we attempt to enrich the structure of linguistic theory so as to restrict the class of grammars compatible with the data given' and, secondly, 'we attempt to construct an evaluation procedure for selecting *one* among the various grammars permitted by the proposed linguistic theory and compatible with the given data' (Chomsky & Halle, 1965, p. 107; italics added). As neatly summed up by McNeill, 'Explanatory adequacy is obtained when linguistic theory gives a PRINCIPLED basis for accepting *one* way of representing the competence of the speakers of a language over other possible ways' (1966a, p. 100; italics added).[1]

---

[1] Similarly, for the child, to *acquire* a language means to 'select from the store of potential grammars a specific *one* that is appropriate to the data available to him' (Chomsky, 1965a, p. 36; italics added).

But what is a 'discovery procedure for grammars', after all? It is, as indicated by Chomsky's diagram (i) reproduced in fig. 3.1 on p. 50 above, the imposition on linguistic theory of the *strongest* of Chomsky's three requirements that, given the (meta)theory (represented in the diagram by the box) and some corpus of primary data as input, the output will be a *unique* grammar of the language from which the corpus was drawn. Clearly, this is precisely the goal which Chomsky set for his own work under the guise of 'explanatory adequacy'.[1] The original dream of 'lowering our sights to the more modest goal of developing an evaluation procedure for grammars' (Chomsky, 1957b, p. 53) evaporates into thin air once it is realized that the evaluation procedure constitutes but one aspect (or 'prong') of a total attack which *also* involves the specification of a full set of linguistic universals.

Chomsky's language-acquisition device AD, in short, is structurally complex in the sense that it contains *two* distinct subcomponents, each of which has a specific function to perform. The first of these is *the full set of linguistic universals* (the component LU) which takes the primary data as input and 'specifies the form of the grammar of a possible human language', thereby yielding as output a *set of possible grammars* of the language in question. Then the second component, the so-called *evaluation measure or metric* (EM), takes over and completes the task of discovery by 'selecting a [unique or particular] grammar of the appropriate form that is compatible with the primary linguistic data' (Chomsky, 1965a, p. 25). A more careful and complete schematic representation of Chomsky's model of language acquisition (or of grammar-construction)

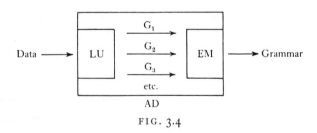

FIG. 3.4

would therefore look something like fig. 3.4. Obviously, therefore, to attempt to specify *both* an evaluation procedure *and* the full set of

---

[1] As he says, 'The problem of internal justification – of explanatory adequacy – is essentially *the problem of constructing a theory of language acquisition*' (Chomsky, 1965a, p. 27; italics added).

linguistic universals in this way constitutes as much an attempt to provide a 'discovery procedure for grammars' as did any of the earlier more 'mechanical' approaches of the structuralist era. The only differences, clearly, lie in the number (two versus one) and the nature (content versus process) of the components utilized in the attack on the problem, whereas what makes a discovery procedure a discovery procedure (in Chomsky's own terms) is not the kind or number of 'prongs' which are used, but simply whether or not the ultimate goal is to achieve *uniqueness in linguistic description*. Therefore, assuming that uniqueness is the ultimate goal sought by all, the discovery-procedure versus evaluation-procedure controversy in linguistics, for all the publicity which has been given to it, is a *pseudo-issue*, since it involves the comparison of things which are not commensurable (i.e. the *whole* of a language acquisition model with one of its *parts*). The only substantive issue, once again, is the question *what sort* of discovery procedure (or language-acquisition device) is appropriate for language: is it simple or complex, process or content, a blend of the two, or something else altogether?

3.5 Are innate linguistic universals really necessary?

We may now move to the question of what *other* possible grounds might be adduced for preferring one of these interpretations over the other. Before we actually attempt to do so, however, we ought perhaps first try to establish whether or not a content-process distinction of the sort we have been discussing is conceptually and empirically meaningful.[1] This very topic occupied much of the discussion which followed Fodor's (1966) paper and among the conclusions reached there was the one that since a 'content' child (of the sort described in McNeill, 1966b, for example) would have a lot of structural information 'wired in' *per se*, a 'process' child (such as Fodor's) would be equipped with no structures at all, but rather with 'rules for processing the information in his corpus'; so superficially, at least, the two proposals would seem to be conceptually distinct in the sense that 'the innate information was available in a rather different form' in the two cases (Smith & Miller,

---

[1] Otherwise, of course, despite all the attention which many transformationalists, and Chomsky in particular, have paid to a distinction of this sort, one might nevertheless run the risk of having the proposed distinction dismissed out-of-hand as merely terminological, in much the same way as Chomsky has recently attempted to dismiss the current interpretive versus generative semantics controversy as an essentially empty one involving 'mere notational variants' (Chomsky, 1970a; cf. p. 64, n. 1).

1966, p. 123).[1] The question whether or not a requisite 'empirical distinction' can be established to differentiate these two views is, however, quite another matter.[2] The major difficulty which arises here is that both alternatives are formulated as hypotheses about the specific nature of certain of man's innate predispositions and so are incapable of being submitted to any kind of direct empirical test. This is by now a commonplace among psychologists, who, after decades of fruitless debate on the matter, now realize that it is virtually impossible to demonstrate experimentally whether or not any given characteristic is innate (using the term synonymously with 'hereditary' or 'genetically determined'), the chief reason being that there is an essential interdependence or interaction between the factors of heredity and environment which makes it a practical impossibility to sort out the two influences in virtually all cases. As Anastasi puts it, 'It is now recognized that every trait of the individual and every reaction that he manifests depend *both* upon his heredity and upon his environment' (1958, p. 68; italics added).[3] In consequence, English & English (1958) recommend that the term 'innate' (if used at all) should be restricted only to refer

to the differences in structure or behavior of two members of the same species that have been reared in the same environment. Note that it is not a CHARACTERISTIC that is said to be INNATE, but only *differences* in characteristics. Walking is not an innate trait, but differences in ability to walk may (or may

[1] The distinction, in short, is between innate *knowledge*, on the one hand, and innate *capacities*, on the other. Stated in these terms, it is quite obvious which of these two notions is the more suspect.

[2] An old positivist (non-rationalist) principle recently revived and introduced into linguistics by Chomsky insists that in order for alternative hypotheses to be 'significantly different', there must exist an 'empirical distinction' between them, i.e. they must differ at least in some of their 'empirical consequences' (Chomsky, 1970a, pp. 56–8). As I attempt to demonstrate in 8.1.3 below, though Chomsky invokes this principle in an effort to defend some of his views, he ends by refuting himself.

[3] Even the genes themselves, she notes (p. 71) 'operate within a specific environment', thereby making it impossible even to 'speak of certain structural characteristics as being "normal" for a given species and fixed by hereditary constitution. If the environment in which the organisms develop were to undergo a change of a more or less permanent nature, a different set of characteristics would come to be considered normal. Similarities of development are attributable to common exposure to an essentially similar environment as much as to the possession of common genes' (p. 66). Thus the number and location of the eyes of some species of fish have been shown to vary as a function of the proportion of magnesium chloride in the sea water in which the minnow eggs are allowed to develop (pp. 65–6) and the number of facets in the eyes of the fruit fly *Drosophila* has been shown not only 'to vary widely in several types which differ in their gene constitution', but also to vary for a *given* type as a function of the 'temperature at which the larvae are kept' (p. 69).

not) be wholly or partly innate. Innate does not mean the same as UNLEARNED or as SPECIES-SPECIFIC...Though a clear meaning can be given to this term, it has been badly abused and is probably best avoided (pp. 263–4).

Consider now in this connection the 'Humboldtian' view, endorsed by Chomsky (1968a, p. 67) and to which I have already referred (p. 56 above), that language itself represents an example of 'unlearned behavior' which somehow develops 'from within' (cf. also Lenneberg, 1964). Anastasi observes:

Truly unlearned behavior can only mean behavior that is determined wholly by the structural characteristics of the organism, such that the mere presence of the necessary structures at a certain stage of development ensures the appearance of the behavior in question. Merely to say that a certain type of behavior is unlearned, however, is no answer to the question of how it develops. Such a statement only reformulates the problem, so that the question still remains to be answered. The answer now calls for knowledge of what structural factors determine such behavior and how they operate. To prove that behavior is unlearned, i.e. *not* learned, is a negative finding, which furnishes no positive information. It does not in itself tell us how the behavior develops. To call such unlearned behavior 'instinctive', 'innate', or 'hereditary' simply obfuscates the problem, because these terms seem to suggest positive explanations or active processes, whereas *in this case they are being used only as synonyms for the negative term 'unlearned'*.

Moreover, it is incorrect to regard unlearned behavior as hereditary. In the first place, behavior cannot be inherited as such. It is only structural characteristics which can be directly influenced by the genes. In the second place, the structural conditions that determine such unlearned behavior may themselves result from either hereditary or environmental factors, or varying combinations of the two (p. 80).

Consequently, to invoke 'innateness' is useless as an explanatory device – one might just as well invoke 'revelation' (cf. Schlesinger, 1971, p. 100).[1] It is also clear from the above account that the whole language acquisition problem as formulated in 3.2 and 3.3 is couched in the wrong kind of language for this very same reason. For though the question of the essential nature of man's innate predisposition for language certainly appears to be empirical in *principle*, no specific proposals along such lines constitute legitimate 'empirical hypotheses' in *practice*, because there is no practical way of experimentally evaluating such claims. I shall nevertheless continue to treat the alternative

---

[1] Cf. Wiest's apt use of the phrase 'pseudoexplanations by mere naming' (1967, p. 214) and Chomsky's own admonition in his Skinner review to avoid talk of explanation in terms of some familiar but vague or meaningless label which merely 'perpetuates the mystery under a new title' (1959b, p. 42).

proposals already outlined regarding the internal structure of some hypothetical 'language-acquisition device' *as if* they constituted potentially meaningful hypotheses which might be distinguishable at least in terms of some of their more remote empirical consequences, since this is the frame of reference which I have been forced by circumstances to adopt for the moment (cf. 1.3.3).

One such possibility, outlined in Smith & Miller (1966), involves recognition that implicit in the 'process' view of the language acquisition device, but *not* in the 'content' view, is what Smith and Miller call the potential existence of 'counterfactual possibilities' (p. 128). That is, an essential corollary of Chomsky's 'innate universals' hypothesis is the proposal that 'the child approaches the data with the presumption that they are drawn from a language of a certain antecedently well-defined type' (Chomsky, 1965a, p. 27), so that a 'content' child must therefore be presumed to be capable of learning *only* languages (or rules) which conform to the very limited range of possibilities defined by his posited innate set of universal constraints.[1] Hence only the 'process' child would be in a position to learn something quite different from real human language if he were to be placed in an appropriate artificial environment (cf. Fodor, 1966, p. 128). To be sure, there are numerous new practical difficulties which immediately arise in any practical attempt to exploit this potential distinction between the two hypotheses (see especially Matthews, 1967, pp. 122–3), but the point remains that this suggestion opens at least one potential avenue towards establishing some crucial empirical distinction between these two competing and 'logically independent' (Peizer & Olmsted, 1969, p. 60) point of view.[2] Moreover, it also seems reasonably clear that there must be certain restrictions of a parallel sort imposed upon the 'process' child, as well. More specifically, assuming that a 'learning' or 'data-analysis' algorithm is meant essentially to perform the task of simply 'extracting regularity' from the primary linguistic data to which he is exposed (which is a

---

[1] Chomsky states this position clearly in *Aspects*: 'A theory that attributes possession of certain linguistic universals to a language-acquisition system, as a property to be realized under appropriate external conditions, implies that *only certain kinds of symbolic systems can be acquired and used as languages by the device*' (1965a, p. 55; italics added).

[2] Moreover, this possibility does not favor the 'content' hypothesis. Consider, for example, Halle's own discussion of Pig Latin (1962). Is it conceivable that any viable scheme of universal constraints on phonological rules making any appeal to 'naturalness' (see 4.3 and 5.2 below) can allow for the incorporation of such a rule as 'shift initial consonant cluster to end of word and add /ē/'? (p. 342). Yet it seems that such rules are learned effortlessly and applied productively by children.

reasonably appropriate way of defining what might be meant by a 'process' mechanism of the sort we have been discussing), it seems reasonably clear that the child who comes to the language learning situation equipped solely with a data-processing device of some such sort will also be highly restricted (although in quite a different way) in the kinds of 'languages' (or, better, descriptive systems for linguistic data) which he is, in principle, capable of learning. From both points of view, therefore, it appears that the two hypotheses under consideration here might prove to be differentiable in terms of the kinds of linguistic descriptions (or grammars) which may reasonably be described as 'learnable' or 'non-learnable' from the standpoint of each, given some reasonable interpretation as to what each of these hypotheses might actually involve.

As a matter of fact, it is along these lines that Chomsky himself has developed his own main-line defense of his particular views about innateness. He and Halle, for example, argue that it is 'fairly obvious' that 'there must be a rich system of *a priori* properties' (i.e. what they call the 'essential linguistic universals') to account for the fact that 'every normal child acquires an extremely intricate and abstract grammar, the properties of which are much underdetermined by the available data', and, furthermore, this acquisition process 'takes place with great speed, under conditions that are far from ideal, and. . . [with] little significant variation among children who may differ greatly in intelligence and experience' (1968, p. 4). In sum, Chomsky's main argument (which is restated in a number of his works) is the following:

We have a certain amount of evidence about the character of the generative grammars that must be the 'output' of an acquisition model for language. This evidence shows clearly that taxonomic views of linguistic structure are inadequate and that knowledge of grammatical structure cannot arise by application of step-by-step inductive operations (segmentation, classification, substitution procedures, filling of slots in frames, association, etc.) of any sort that have yet been developed within linguistics, psychology, or philosophy. Further empiricist speculations contribute nothing that even faintly suggests a way of overcoming the intrinsic limitations of the methods that have so far been proposed and elaborated. In particular, such speculations have not provided any way to account for or even to express the fundamental fact about the normal use of language, namely the speaker's ability to produce and understand instantly new sentences that are not similar to those previously heard in any physically defined sense or in terms of any notion of frames or classes of elements, nor associated with those previously heard by conditioning, nor obtainable from them by any sort of 'generalization' known to psychology or philosophy. It seems plain that language acquisition is based on the child's discovery of what from a formal point of view is a deep and abstract theory – a generative grammar of his language – many of the concepts and principles of which are only remotely related to experience by long and intricate chains of unconscious quasi-inferential steps. A consideration of the character of the grammar that is acquired, the degenerate quality and narrowly limited extent of the available data, the striking uniformity of the resulting grammars, and their independence of intelligence, motivation, and emotional state, over wide ranges of variation, leave little hope that much of the structure of the language can be learned by an organism initially uninformed as to its general character (1965a, pp. 57–8).

All these arguments beg the question. First, it is precisely the nature (or character) of the internalized 'grammar' which the linguist is (purportedly) trying to discover; and it is clear that there will be a wide range of opinions on this score, depending on the particular theory of language (or of language acquisition) to which the analyst may subscribe. Chomsky, nonetheless, seems to believe that (1) to a great extent these properties are already known, or, in any event, that (2) the certain knowledge now available is already sufficient to rule out any and all conceivable process mechanisms which might be devised to account for these properties, and, therefore, that (3) the content interpretation (or, more specifically, his own particular version of it) must be true. Now these are fairly strong claims and I shall devote the whole of the following chapter to the attempt to come to grips with some of them. The crucial questions are obviously, first, what are these specific properties of language which invalidate, in advance, all theories but Chomsky's and, secondly, what kind of evidence and arguments support the claim that languages must have essentially 'unlearnable' properties of this sort. For the present I must simply say that though it seems true that some of the specific properties which Chomsky ascribes to language must be unlearnable in terms of a process mechanism of any sort heretofore conceived or imagined, there is, on the other hand, no compelling evidence that languages must have anything like those properties which Chomsky insists that they must have.

As to the first point – that many of the essential properties of transformational-generative grammars (the linguistic universals) would seem to be, from our present perspective, quite 'unlearnable' in any familiar sense – Chomsky may be right; and he argued this point most cogently, perhaps, in his 1967b paper, illustrating it with a number of clear and concise examples. I will not repeat all the examples which he cites there. Let us concentrate on his key-example, namely, the convention of the transformational cycle. As he explained once to an audience of philosophers,

it is misleading to speak of the innate schematism that has been proposed as merely providing 'limitations' for acquisition of language. Rather, what has been proposed is that this schematism *makes possible* the acquisition of a rich and highly specific system on the basis of limited data. To take one example, the problem is to explain how the data available to a language learner (first or second) suffices to establish that the phonological rules (the rules that assign phonetic representations to surface structures) apply cyclically, first to innermost phrases of the surface structure, then to larger phrases, etc., until the maximal domain of phonological processes – in simple cases, the full sentence – is reached. There is in fact good evidence that the rules do apply cyclically, but this evidence is not of a sort that can be used as the basis for induction from phonetic data to the principle of cyclic application, by any procedure of induction that has general validity. In particular, much of this evidence is derived from an analysis of percepts, that is, from investigation of the way in which someone who has already mastered the language interprets speech signals. It seems that this interpretation imposes a certain structure that is not indicated directly in the speech signal, for example, in the determination of stress contours. Obviously the child cannot acquire the knowledge that phonological rules apply cyclically from data that are available to him only after he knows and makes use of this principle (1969, p. 67).

Chomsky admits this is 'an extreme example', but one which nevertheless 'illustrates quite well the basic problem: to explain how *a rich and highly specific grammar* is developed on the basis of *limited data* that is consistent with a vast number of other conflicting grammars' (pp. 67–8, italics added). Suppose we grant the first premise here and argue, with Chomsky, that transformational-generative grammars (and the associated universal conventions which go with them) are incapable of being 'learned' in any presently understood sense of the term. What conclusions are to be drawn from this? To my mind the answer is straightforward: if grammars of the Chomskyan sort cannot be learned by any means presently known, such grammars simply *cannot be accepted* as plausible or realistic models of any actual psychological entity or process. We must, therefore, abandon the unpromising abstract transformational-generative framework and devote our efforts instead towards the articulation of an alternative descriptive system for language which does not make such unrealistic demands of the language learner nor demand, in principle, essential recourse to innate linguistic structures. To assume instead, as Chomsky has done, that the child must come to the language learning situation fully equipped with *a priori* knowledge of some specific set of innate 'linguistic universals' which 'makes possible' the acquisition of such 'a rich and highly specific system' as he proposes for grammar is counterproductive, since this amounts to defining the problem away. I conclude, therefore, that despite the number and range of claims advanced for linguistic descriptions cast within the abstract transformational-generative framework, these descriptions are inappropriate to the output of the process of language acquisition, and that serious metatheoretical and methodological difficulties must be inherent in the whole Chomskyan approach to the study of language. I explore these particular questions in detail in the chapters to follows and come to precisely these same conclusions on independent grounds.

This is not to say that everything which Chomsky and Halle have said in defense of their position is nonsense. There is no argument, for example, on the matter of whether or not it is appropriate to characterize language as either 'intricate' or 'abstract', as Chomsky and Halle have put it; there is, however, considerable argument (as I shall demonstrate in Part II) as to what interpretation and weight is to be placed on the word 'extremely' which Chomsky and Halle also employ (to them, obviously, it means something very much like 'as in a transformational-generative description'). Some transformationalist-oriented investigators, for example, have argued for the innateness of 'deep' structures in syntax on the ground that such structures raise 'profound difficulties for any theory of language-learning', since, 'by definition, the base structures of a language are not themselves possible utterances in the language' and are hence not available to the child as models for either imitation or selective reinforcement (Fodor, 1966, p. 112; cf. also Bever, Fodor & Weksel, 1965a, pp. 260ff). But are such extremely abstract 'deep' structures really necessary? I argue in 5.3 below that the main linguistic arguments which have been offered by transformationalists in support of such structures are highly suspect, at best. Furthermore, Schlesinger presents an alternative conception of underlying or semantic structure which circumvents these objections and which does not seem in any way 'beyond the capacity of learning theory' (1971, p. 69; see also p. 85). The need to posit certain kinds of 'abstract' structures, therefore, does not necessarily imply that language acquisition is impossible apart from some highly specific, innate systems of linguistic universals. Lyons states, in fact, that he is a little disturbed by the readiness with which some psychologists [not to mention linguists – BLD] have interpreted Chomsky's arguments...about the formal and substantive 'universals' of syntactic theory as evidence in support of this...By the time that the child arrives at the age of eighteen months or so, he is already in possession of the ability to distinguish 'things' and 'properties' in the 'situations' in which he is learning and uses language. And this ability seems to me quite adequate as a basis for the learning of [for example] the principal deep structure relationship between lexical items (the subject-predicate relationship), provided that the child is presented with a sufficient amount of 'primary linguistic data' in real 'situations' of language-use...As for the 'grammatical features', which vary considerably from language to language, the acquisition of these would seem to depend, not only upon such general notions as 'number', 'sex', 'animacy', and so on, but more particularly upon what might be called the 'deictic co-ordinates' of the spatio-temporal situations of utterances. Briefly then, what linguistic evidence there is does not seem to me to lend any support whatsoever to the view that a knowledge of the 'substantive universals' of syntactic theory is genetically transmitted as part of an innate 'faculté de langage' (in Lyons and Wales, 1966, pp. 131–2).

Slobin offers independent but parallel remarks on this issue:

Indeed, as McNeill has pointed out, the child has to notice rather than invent classes. But this noticing is not necessarily based only on criteria available to him at birth. For example, human languages distinguish animate from inanimate because of objective facts of referents; may not the child come to notice this distinction as a result of experience with these same objective facts? According to McNeill's [content] model, the child searches the 'local language' for embodiments of a subset of the substantive universals he carries about with him....It seems to me more reasonable to suppose that it is language that plays a role in drawing the child's attention to the possibility of dividing nouns on the basis of animation; or verbs on the basis of duration, or determinacy, or validity; or pronouns on the basis of social status, and the like.

Perhaps all that is needed is an ability to learn certain types of semantic or conceptual categories, the knowledge that learnable semantic criteria can be the basis for grammatical categories, and, along with this substantive knowledge, the formal knowledge that such categories can be expressed by such morphological devices as affixing, sound alternation, and so on. The child's 'preprogramming' for substantive universals is probably not for specific categories like past, animate, plural, and the like, but consists rather of the ability to learn categories of a certain as-yet-unspecified type (1966, p. 89).

Slobin also presents evidence that cognitive or semantic development (learning) may even be the real 'pacesetter' in language acquisition, such that 'the appearance in child speech of a new formal device serves only to code a function which the child has already understood and expressed implicitly' (1971a, pp. 319-20), and Schlesinger outlines a theory of grammatical development along these same general lines (1971, especially pp. 72ff; see also Macnamara, 1972). I conclude that there is still considerable room left for manipulation and maneuver with respect to the 'abstractness' issue, anyway.

Let us now move to the matter of the 'great speed', etc. with which language acquisition is said to take place and which Chomsky and Halle also use as an argument in favor of their position. Here, once again, we find that the impressions of different investigators vary widely, depending on the particular school of thought to which each subscribes. To McNeill (who is obviously sympathetic to Chomsky's point of view) the rate at which a child masters a language is 'astonishing': he tells us that the child of four is already 'able to produce sentences of almost every conceivable type' and that, for all practical purposes, the process of language acquisition is accomplished in the short span of 'approximately thirty months' (1966a, p. 99). In Rivers (1964), however, we read instead of 'the slow and tortuous acquisition of words', 'inaccurate pronunciations repeated over many weeks' (p. 103) and of the 'many mistakes' and the 'long time' it takes a child to perfect his utterances (p. 129). The hard facts of the matter are that we have very little systematic knowledge about the relative competence of, say, the four-year-old child *vis-à-vis* the adult. Therefore, for the time being, at least Fraser's rebuttal of McNeill is, I think, sufficient to eliminate this factor, too, as a serious argument in favor of innate universals:

How long is it before we can say that a child has mastered his native language? We do not know with any precision. McNeill suggests that, thinking particularly of syntax, we could say it takes approximately thirty months, from the age of one and a half to the age of four. But this seems like a considerable underestimate, even for syntax...Menyuk's...work, for example, provides some evidence of gaps up to the age of about six and a half and one suspects that a finer analysis than hers would reveal much more room for development.

Perhaps more interesting is the question of where syntax begins. McNeill, like a number of other writers and researchers, suggests eighteen months, when the child starts to produce two- and three-word utterances. But it may be important to remember that the child has been responding, apparently appropriately, to speech for some six months prior to this. It seems quite conceivable that there are definite regularities in what the child is responding to, that these regularities might make up a passive grammar or a grammar of comprehension and this might be predictive of the elementary grammar of production which the child reveals when he starts to speak for himself. Thus, by taking one year as our starting point and insisting on development past the age of six, we have, with very little effort, more than doubled the time a child is supposed to take to acquire language. Clearly further extensions could be argued for at either end.[1]

Even if the speed of acquisition was known, on what grounds would one be justified in describing it as 'astonishing'? Is it so astonishing, if one is convinced that, for five or more years, the child is working very hard and for long hours on mastering language? After all, what else is there for a young child to do with his time! I think recent research has demonstrated that some children, at least, do tackle the job most assiduously. Again, is it so astonishing, if one feels that the absence of interference from prior learning or development is relevant?

But perhaps the real basis of astonishment lies in the assumption that, in mastering what is unquestionably an extremely intricate and complex task, exposure, 'mere exposure' [McNeill], is enough... If a child were kept in a darkened room, fed by machine and hit over the head at five-minute intervals would he acquire English even if normal adult conversation were provided twenty-four hours a day? Perhaps not. Perhaps one needs 'normal' exposure. But if this involves a normal mother–child relationship, then the door is wide open for primary and secondary reinforcement as an invariable part of acquisition by exposure (in Lyons & Wales, 1966, pp. 117–18).

I might also develop counterarguments to Chomsky's other points related to the 'degenerate' and 'limited' nature of the data available to the child, the 'striking uniformity' of what each child ultimately learns, and its 'independence of intelligence, motivation and emotional state'; but, to prevent this discussion from becoming tedious, suffice it to say that none of these arguments are any less problematical and anecdotal than the two main ones already discussed; hence they are insufficient to lend any significant degree of additional support to Chomsky's claims regarding the necessity of innate linguistic universals.[2] In sum, then, I think it can already safely be said that there is virtually nothing substantive (from the standpoint of objective evidence) or compelling (from that of inherent plausibility or inevitability) to tilt the balance in favor of Chomsky's innate-universals interpretation of language acquisition over and against the traditional learning-algorithm approach; if anything, the opposite is true. Yet few arguments about this are offered any more within linguistics, as though most observers were convinced that the old data-processing approach has had its day and failed – truly

---

[1] Cf. C. Chomsky's conclusions to her own study on the matter of the 'surprisingly late' acquisition of certain syntactic structures and that 'contrary to the commonly held view that a child has mastered the structures of his native language by the time he reaches the age of six, we find that active syntactic acquisition is taking place up to the age of nine and perhaps even beyond' (1969, pp. 120–1).

[2] See Campbell & Wales (1970) for further discussion.

a tribute to Chomsky's skill in polemic (cf. Leech, 1968, p. 93). Things have come to the point where the very idea that a language might be learned in accordance with some set of data-analytical procedures can be quickly dismissed with a few words of the following sort:

A common suggestion is that children have a specific capacity to process data in wonderful ways, one outcome of which is linguistic competence...The assumption implicit in these suggestions is that a capacity not specific to language will be simpler than one specific to language. The assumption is probably false and certainly it is unjustified (McNeill, 1966a, p. 114).

But what is it about such an assumption which is 'probably false' and 'certainly unjustified'? How can an *ad hoc* approach which posits linguistic universals which are useful only for acquiring language be preferred over an alternative approach which seeks to explain language acquisition as a special case of learning in general? Is it not generally the case that 'the wider the range of phenomena to which an explanation can be shown to apply, the more satisfactory as an explanation we may take it to be'? (Donaldson in Lyons & Wales, 1966, p. 126).[1] For certainly the most obvious and least disputed of the linguistic universals proposed so far appear to fit very well with a fairly clear-cut set of general learning principles of much broader application than language alone. Take, for instance, the fundamental assumption of phonetics to which Halle (1954, pp. 197–8) devotes so much attention – that human beings interpret speech as a sequence of discrete sounds, though, physically (acoustically) it is an unbroken continuum of sound having no such clear-cut internal structure. Furthermore, from a realm of what is, strictly speaking, an infinite variety of speech sounds, the vast majority of such 'new' sounds are interpreted as repetitions of old ones. Thus we might say that the human mind imparts a pattern of DISCRETE TOKENIZA-TION onto the domain of phonetics (cf. Lyons, 1968, p. 68). Moreover, this sort of patterning is by no means restricted to the realm of speech sound alone, but appears to be part of the human cognitive process in general,[2] as evidenced by the equally infinitely variable and physically non-discrete character of the universe in general and such a typical

---

[1] Cf. Holton & Roller: 'What makes certain concepts important...is their recurrence in a great many successful descriptions and laws, often in areas very far removed from the context of their initial formulation' (1958, p. 233).

[2] Nor is it by any means limited to 'human cognitive processes', or even to human beings; there is evidence that many animals (including all mammals) perform this same kind of activity.

discretely tokenized general cognitive concept as that of 'tree'.[1] In this case, surely, it is much more reasonable (at least as a starting point) to assume that man is not born into this world equipped with a rich 'content' structure which provides him with a basis for every possible conceptualization,[2] but rather that he comes equipped instead with some sort of a discretizer-plus-generalizer[3] which searches through the ebb and flow of continuous events for potentially useful discrete repetitions.[4] From this perspective we might extend the domain of our theory to the point where people in general could be regarded as 'machines whose input [linguistic and otherwise] consists of miscellaneous and apparently unrelated data and whose output is a [more-or-less] coherent account of a world' (Caws, 1965, p. 24), in which case language

[1] Similarly, the well-attested 'holophrastic' stage in the linguistic development of the child is apparently paralleled by a considerably more far-reaching 'Gestalt' stage in his general cognitive development (see Dunkel, 1948, p. 24, and Caws, 1965, p. 20).

[2] Would it be reasonable to assume, for example, that semantic concepts such as 'banana' or 'rime ice' are innate? Or how about some now-extinct bird – or some new machine to be invented in the mid-twenty-first century? Content-style innateness is dubious because it cannot be a general solution to the problem of learning; process mechanisms will be required for some situations, in any case. On the other hand, it is conceivable that process might be shown to be a general solution, given merely a general innate capacity to 'extract regularity from the environment' or something of the sort. It thus seems to me that this is the only approach worth serious consideration (see Putnam, 1967, p. 20, and 6.2 below).

[3] Householder (1968) proposes 'an automatic generalizer' and 'a similarity-seeking drive', as well as a 'discriminator' or 'difference-seeking drive', none of which are specifically linguistic, but which serve rather to regulate 'the way we acquire all our opinions about the world' (p. 8). Surely this is a better place to start, i.e. with a set of fundamental concepts (in this case, *generalization* and *discrimination*) already *known* to play an important role in learning in general, and to determine how far they will take us in accounting for language acquisition as well. The role of the former is clear enough (to identify similarities and to extrapolate on the basis of past experiences), while the latter seems required to allow the child to take the immense undifferentiated mass of data which faces him and to learn to make more and finer useful distinctions within it until a measure of intellectual maturity is achieved (cf. the common characterization of the unenlightened and/or dogmatic individual as easily and quickly drawn to 'oversimplifications'.) From this point of view, 'competence' in language is no different in principle from 'expertise' in any other human intellectual endeavor, in that it, too, necessarily involves both 'being able to observe differences that the non-expert fails to note' and knowing 'which differences to ignore – which differences do not make any difference' (Postman & Weingartner, 1966, pp. 34–5).

[4] It must, of course, also be admitted that we are innately predisposed to notice certain distinctions and not others. This is clearest in those cases where we are not biologically equipped even to perceive certain distinctions (as among sound beyond the threshold of hearing or among electromagnetic waves as short as the ultraviolet or as long as the infrared).

acquisition would be but *a special case of learning in general*. (This, of course, is the traditional view.)

A corollary is the notion that 'language is not unique by virtue of its structure, this structure in fact being rather just one manifestation of more general logical systems' (Morton in Lyons & Wales, 1966, p. 132). This, too, is counter to Chomsky's beliefs (cf. especially chapter 3 of Chomsky, 1968a); Chomsky's approach is that (1) human language *is* unique in its structural properties, and (2) since it is also species-specific to man, then (3) man is in possession of some collection of unique cognitive structures which we can best get at by studying language. The two processes discussed above, however, namely discrimination and generalization (see n. 3 on p. 75), are by no means unique to man. How, then, can we reconcile the analysis or process view with the fact that only man learns language (given that more is involved than mere articulatory deficiencies on the part of the lower species)? This is not as ponderous a conceptual difficulty as it may seem. White, for instance, has suggested that man is unique in the extent of his ability to *symbolize*, i.e. to create at will new vocal (and other) symbols which stand for something else. So while many species may yawn, stretch, cough, scratch themselves, cry out in pain, shrink with fear, 'bristle' with anger and so on, only man 'communicates with his fellows with articulate speech, uses amulets, confesses sins, makes laws, observes codes of etiquette, explains his dreams, classifies his relatives in designated categories and so on' (1949, p. 34). Clearly, the ability to symbolize is essential to the creation of language and, consequently, any serious disability in the lower species to do this could, in and of itself, explain why they do not have comparable languages.

Morton has an alternative (and even more prosaic) possible explanation: that it all might depend on *memory*. In other words, it is certainly possible 'to conceive of a species which has a well formed language, but has an organizational memory which is no more complex than that of a chimpanzee. The members of such a species would not be able to remember who said what to them, or what they said to whom' (in Lyons and Wales, 1966, p. 132) and this alone would preclude the development of language within this species (or even to make use of whatever powers of 'symbolization' it might possess). In such a case, clearly, Householder's similarity- or difference-seeking drives, at least, would be useless for language-learning purposes and the whole effort would consequently fall through.

In short, there are not only numerous logical alternatives to Chomsky's content hypothesis of innateness which might explain the species-specific character of language, but also a number of far more plausible approaches, all of which indicate that it is by no means impossible to imagine that a species-specific phenomenon (such as language) might exist totally independent of any species-specific innate features which are *specifically related* to the phenomenon in question (cf. Lackowski, 1968, p. 612).[1]

3.6 Some implicit dangers

A main point made earlier in this chapter was that the question of the innate endowment which the child brings to the language-learning situation is open to a wide spectrum of possible interpretations, none of which seem to be decisively excluded by the data now at our disposal. (This follows from the condition of general untestability associated with any such hypothesis about innateness.) Though in certain places in his published works Chomsky appears to admit this,[2] he does not generally argue as though he really thought that this were so, as is demonstrated by his continued insistence that only some extreme version of what we have been calling the innate-universals or 'content' interpretation is adequate to the challenge. And yet Chomsky also takes the position that this issue is an empirical one. Nowhere is his inconsistency in this matter more clearly illustrated than in the following section from *Aspects*, where he first remarks that 'there are no grounds for any specific assumptions...about the internal structure of this [language-acquisi-

---

[1] It is interesting to consider some of the positions to which a *reductio ad absurdum* argument might lead if Chomsky's approach to the species-specific character of language were carried over to other domains of activity. For there are *many* things which man can do which the other species cannot. Are we to posit 'a full set of innate universals' to account for each of these, as well? To consider only one extreme example: since only man can 'do' science, are we therefore to assume that he is born with a full set of innate 'scientific universals'? I think not. On the other hand, it is just as preposterous to think that an animal species as restricted in time and space as the human race could have 'succeeded in discovering the principles according to which the cosmos operates' in so short a span as a few centuries (Caws, 1965, p. 265), were he not especially equipped with *some* innate advantages to help him. As in the case of language, we must assume an innate predisposition of *some* sort (say to discriminate, to generalize, to form analogies, etc.), but to think that what is innate is the very form or content of these theories *themselves* seems not only absurd, but also useless and unnecessary.

[2] See Chomsky, 1965a, p. 52; 1965b, p. 19; and 1967a, p. 401; for example.

tion] device' (a statement with which I whole-heartedly agree), but then goes on *in the very next sentence* to say:

Continuing with no preconceptions, we would naturally turn to the study of uniformities in the output (formal and substantive universals), *which we then must attribute to the structure of the device*...This, in effect, has been the rationalist approach, and *it is difficult to see what alternative there can be to it if dogmatic presuppositions as to the nature of mental processes are eliminated* (p. 207, n. 33; italics added).

Clearly, in thus negating his own assertion that there is no sound basis at present for any specific preconceptions regarding the nature of the internal structure of the language-acquisition device, Chomsky is open not only to the venial charge of self-contradiction but also to the more grave charge of OVER-AXIOMATIZATION, as well. He has, both in his theory and in his attempted rationale for it, *axiomatized away* what is not only an empirical issue in principle but one which in addition, and by his own admission, still remains very much an open one (as it probably always will). It follows that everything in his theory which is predicated upon this dubious assumption is itself made equally suspect. In other words (as I shall attempt to show in the next chapter), should the content hypothesis of innateness prove to be incorrect, much of the work which has gone into the development of the theory of transformational-generative grammar will have been wasted (except, of course, for any new information which might have been uncovered in the process. In this respect, to be sure, the transformationalists have made a lasting contribution, not so much because of the theory *per se*, but because of requirements associated with it that much greater attention be paid to new kinds of evidence, such as, for example, ungrammatical sentences). In other words, Lakoff's claim (1969, p. 121) that the methodological assumptions of transformational grammar may only be undone 'point by point' is highly exaggerated and misleading: a theory is only as good as its premises. As Chomsky and Halle themselves have put it, 'To the extent that [the basic] assumptions [of TGG] are false to fact, the conclusions that follow from them may also be false to fact' (1968, p. 332). And a fundamental premiss of transformational-generative grammar is that the essential properties of language, the putative linguistic universals, are innate. If they are not, we would have no reason to believe that the grammars which transformationalists have constructed on the basis of these properties could ever be learned – and the 'real' or internalized grammars which native speakers are presumed to have could not be anything like what the transformationalists say they are. It is as simple as that.[1]

Although this seems obvious, I find it striking that many linguists – including some of Chomsky's critics – do not appear to be cognizant of it nor concerned with its implications. Part of this apparent lack of concern can be traced to that general lack of interest in theoretical foundations so characteristic of most linguistic work today (so that certain quite fundamental metatheoretical positions are either adopted or rejected uncritically and almost willy-nilly); even less comprehensible, however, is the view expressed by Matthews (1967) that Chomsky's formal investigations (into the nature of grammar) can – and even should – be dissociated from his proposed psychological interpretations for them (in terms of the role of competence in linguistic performance, of innate linguistic universals in language acquisition, etc.), for the only basis which Chomsky suggests for preferring his grammatical model over any other arbitrary descriptive system for primary linguistic data is expressed in terms of certain 'posited relationships among a grammar, a language-acquisition device, and a production-perception model' (P. Harris, 1971; cf. Chomsky, 1966b, pp. 11–12, n. 8).[2] Moreover, it is abundantly clear that it has been Chomsky's claims for the essential 'psychological content' to be associated with his linguistic formalisms which has had most to do with the popularity of his views today, especially outside linguistics itself. In any event, no matter how other linguists may choose to view the matter, the main point is that, as P. Harris put it, 'Chomsky [himself] considers his work in these areas to be

---

[1] No matter 'how well that theory accounts for *real linguistic data* in syntax and phonology' (Lakoff, 1969, p. 120). It is, in fact, quite easy to conceive of many ways a good deal of this 'real linguistic data' (based as it is primarily on introspective evidence) may be very much in error either as to fact or interpretation. (See 5.3 for discussion.)

[2] I therefore find it impossible to disagree with the point of view which P. Harris has adopted on this issue: 'There seem to be two attitudes current among those linguists who accept the generative framework. The first is characteristic of those among Chomsky's partisans who passively accept his ideas about linguistics and psychology and their interrelationship. Their position is at least understandable. The second attitude is that of people like Lyons (1966) who remarks, in a review of Chomsky's *Aspects*, that there is 'a good deal of irrelevant and tendentious argument about "mentalism", "innate ideas", and "intuition"'. Tendentious it certainly is, but I would hardly consider it irrelevant unless that simply implies leading to confusion rather than enlightenment. For it is just these concepts that form (along with others like 'competence') the very basis of *the attempt to make generative grammar something more than a purely formal exercise*. Thus they are part of the theory's foundations, and foundations are simply not superfluous (1970, pp. 4–5; italics added).

inseparable from his purely linguistic endeavors' and that, indeed, 'over the last few years his attention has been increasingly directed towards these problems' (1970, p. 24); so no in-depth criticism of Chomsky's views is possible that does not give much attention to those psychological interpretations which he insists are integrally associated with his grammatical model.

One further aspect of Chomsky's language-acquisition model should be touched upon. This is the fact that 'models, like all analogies, while often helpful as guides to the imagination, can also lead it into dangerous traps' (Holton & Roller, 1958, p. 130). The principal reason for this is that all hypothesized models tend to be, by their very nature, over-simplifications. Thus the particular danger in dealing with models is, as Nagel puts it, 'that adventitious features of a model may mislead us concerning the actual content of the theory' (1961, pp. 96–7).

Not only is transformational grammar predicated upon an unwarranted (and implausible) set of specific assumptions about the nature of the innate language-learning mechanism (ultimately an empirical question); it is also predicated upon two further (and false) assumptions that (1) language acquisition is instantaneous (Chomsky & Halle, 1968, p. 332) and, as alluded to earlier, that (2) language acquisition by the child and grammar-construction by the linguist are equivalent sorts of activities (cf. 3.1). Both assumptions are implicit in Chomsky's schematic representation of his language-acquisition model (p. 50 above).

As McCawley has observed (1968a),[1] this model 'treats the acquisition of language as if it could be divided into two phases, the recording of data and the construction of a grammar, which were separate in time', i.e. much like a special (and impractical) kind of linguistic analysis in which, first of all, the relevant data are collected and, then and only then, a complete grammar produced to account for it all.

However [McCawley continues], it is clear that language acquisition does not work like that: at any stage of the game the child has a grammar of some sort and probably remembers relatively little of the data which he was presented with in formulating that grammar. Each stage of language acquisition consists of modifying the grammar which the child has already acquired by making it cover facts which the child has been presented with and which his grammar does not yet cover. Consequently, a much more plausible theory of language acquisition would seem to be expressed by the diagram:

---

[1] Though I cite here from a widely circulated unpublished paper, McCawley has expressed much the same views in published form (McCawley, 1968d), though with interesting details omitted.

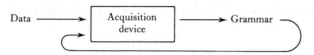

The input to the acquisition device will not be simply a body of data but rather a grammar and a [new] fact, and the output of the device will not be a grammar constructed from scratch but rather a modification of the input grammar.[1]

Assuming that McCawley's model does provide a more accurate picture of the facts, the question is whether this makes any important difference as far as linguistic theory is concerned, or is Chomsky on the right track with his less realistic but more practical 'first approximation' (Chomsky, 1967a, p. 441, n. 41, and Chomsky & Halle, 1968, p. 331)? McCawley suggests that the answer is no, since his model has, for one thing, important implications regarding the nature of the evaluation measure which Chomsky's model entirely overlooks. In particular, what McCawley's revised model of language acquisition suggests is

that if *any* kind of evaluation measure is relevant to language acquisition, it will not be one which evaluates entire grammars but one which evaluates possible changes which can be made in a grammar, given a fact which it is to be made consistent with. Thus, a theory of language acquisition must solve the following problems:

(1) Given a grammar and a fact, what are the possible revisions of the grammar to make it consistent with that fact?...

(2) Under what conditions does a fact which a child is presented with stimulate him to modify his grammar in order to make it consistent with that fact?...

(3) Of the possible revisions in his grammar which a child can make upon being presented with a fact, which one does he in fact make?...Finally,

(4) if in fact some notion of an evaluation measure of changes in grammars makes sense, is there any relation of such an evaluation measure to the notion of evaluation measure for grammars which Chomsky originally proposed?... Only by demonstrating that such is the case could one show that an evaluation measure for grammars had any relevance to linguistic competence (McCawley, 1968a; italics added).

A recent article in *Language* illustrates another danger involved in ignoring the step-by-step character of language acquisition. For from

---

[1] Readers familiar with the work of Piaget will note a striking similarity here between McCawley's proposed revised model of language acquisition and Piaget's 'adaptation' mechanism, which involves the cyclical interaction of the two complementary processes of 'assimilation' of new environmental data by the child and a later 'accommodation' of his conceptual structures in response to them (see, e.g. Ginsburg & Opper, 1969, pp. 18–19).

the perspective provided by his oversimplified 'instantaneous' model of language acquisition:

Chomsky has argued with much justice that a comparison between a haphazard sample of speech and the grammar itself (presumably the way language is ultimately organized in the mind) leaves little doubt that the task in inferring the latter from the former is difficult to the point of improbability. On such grounds, it is argued that the child must bring a great deal of apparatus into the learning situation (Shipley *et al.*, 1969, pp. 337–8).

But the results of the authors' own study seem to suggest, among other things, that 'the child seems to have ways of biasing his linguistic input [at each stage] so that the flow of new information can be controlled' (p. 338; see also Smith, 1970, pp. 125ff), thus taking much of the bite out of Chomsky's original argument and leaving open, once again, the basic question 'whether what the child brings to the situation is knowledge about language [*per se*], or certain general methods for organizing various kinds of sensory input' (p. 338).[1]

I now return to the last question, 'how far one can reasonably go in drawing parallels between the problems faced by linguists when they construct a grammar and the problem faced by a child when he begins to acquire his native language' (Donaldson in Lyons & Wales, 1966, p. 120). In Chomsky's view, the problem which faces the linguist is fundamentally that which faces the language learner, as well, namely, 'to determine from the data of performance the underlying system of rules that has been mastered by the speaker–hearer and that he puts to use in actual performance' (1965a, p. 4). Chomsky thus makes no formal distinction between the child's process of learning a language (or 'internalizing' a grammar) and the linguist's process of describing one; as I have already said in 3.1, this is not a realistic assumption, to say the least: the linguist has a broader and more diverse range of data and skills to bring to bear in performing his task than we are free to assume that the child has in his. So the implicit danger here is that it is easy for the linguist to forget this and to incorporate into his own analyses certain evidence, professional opinions, theoretical biases or other considerations which there is no reason to assume the child can take similar

[1] Cf. also McCawley's arguments for omitting the words 'primary linguistic' from before 'data' in Chomsky's schematic model (McCawley, 1968d, p. 560, n. 4) and the discussion in Campbell and Wales (1970, pp. 254ff) of a number of heretofore neglected sources of information which the child may be presumed to have available to him, all of which greatly complicate the 'limited data' issue which Chomsky emphasizes in the citation given on p. 67 above.

advantage of, and this detracts significantly from the plausibility of the resulting description as a psychological model.

3.7 Summary and conclusions

In this chapter I have examined some potential shortcomings in Chomsky's stated views on the question of language acquisition, focusing particularly on his conception of the innate 'knowledge' which the child is presumed to bring to language learning. I contrasted this 'content' (innate-universals-plus-evaluation-measures) view with the more traditional 'process' (learning-algorithm or data-analysis) view, and concluded that apart from a widely accepted but quite empty philosophical argument against the notion of a 'discovery procedure' for grammars (presumed to be implicit in the second position but not in the first) most of the arguments in favor of the content view are question-begging: no such data-analysis mechanism is presumed to be possible because of intrinsic limitations in the nature of the input to the device AD, because of the vast complexity and abstractness of the final output, and because of the consistent speed and accuracy achieved in establishing the input–output relation, i.e. in learning languages. My position is, however, that very little of substance is known in any of these areas and that, furthermore, there are a number of very powerful counter-arguments (some of them deployed in this chapter) which give the advantage, in terms of both sound methodology and essential plausibility, to the (admittedly old-fashioned) process view.

Nonetheless, I find that transformational-generative grammarians, either by overt uncritical assent or covert unmindful default, have committed themselves as a group to a very specific version of the content position; thus the plausibility of their model of linguistic competence as a viable psychological model of language is critically dependent on these specific and doubtful assumptions about innateness. The transformationalists have therefore exposed themselves to a number of implicit dangers, some of which have been explicitly noted here. In the following two chapters I shall look at some specific examples of linguists' grammars which have flowed from the content position and investigate the extent to which any of these potential dangers may have been realized. Then in chapter 6 I shall explore certain counterproposals which might be formulated from the competing process point of view.

Part II

LINGUISTIC METATHEORY

4 Some problems in phonological description

4.1 Selecting the problem

In the preceding chapter I discussed two extreme views about man's innate capacity for language acquisition: first, that intrinsic *knowledge* of the full set of linguistic universals (including evaluation measures) was involved, second, that it took the form of a set of general *learning principles*. My general conclusion was that on the evidence presently available about language acquisition, we cannot make a definitive non-arbitrary choice even between these alternatives (not to mention the vast number of conceivable 'hybrid' possibilities in between), except insofar as certain methodological and plausibility considerations favor the learning algorithm approach (see 3.5). Nevertheless, I noted that the theory of TGG (or, better, *each* theory of TGG, as several radically different versions have, in fact, appeared over the last decade or so) has opted for the innate-universals view, despite certain 'implicit dangers' which were also noted (3.6). In this chapter I try to investigate some of the consequences of this choice as far as the details of linguistic description are concerned. What specific kinds of linguistic analyses have been linked to the innate universals hypothesis and, conversely, what other possibilities might be suggested from the point of view of the alternative data-analysis interpretation? Can we find in linguistic description compelling grounds for choosing between the two positions, or can we at least find clues which support or dispel our suspicions that the innate universals approach leads up those blind alleys envisioned in chapter 1? I shall look at some of the solutions which have been proposed to specific problems of linguistic analysis and see what we can learn from them which might help us in evaluating these two conflicting theories of the nature of language acquisition.

The first task is obviously one of selection: which particular analyses of which particular problems will be most useful? Since it is the very basis of language acquisition or language learning[1] which is at issue here, it seems appropriate to isolate for examination some aspect of linguistic behavior which we can agree is actually *learned*, whichever interpretation of the innate mechanism we accept. Only in this way will we be able to pit the two approaches against each other. It would not be interesting to ask how some such notion as 'noun phrase' (or any other putative 'essential linguistic universal' which we might choose) is learned from these two points of view, since in all such cases the innate-universals view wins in a runaway: the concept is simply presumed to be there to begin with. Yet a presumption of this sort gets us nowhere if the question is precisely whether or not such universals really *are* there to begin with, since we have at present no independent (non-linguistic) means of testing the empirical validity of such an assertion. We must therefore isolate some feature of linguistic competence which we may all agree is *not* included as part of the innate language-acquisition mechanism under *either* interpretation, and which must presumably be learned by means of whichever mechanism *is* present; this will give us an opportunity to compare the effectiveness of the two models on some stretch of neutral territory. The particular feature must, therefore, be language-specific.

Given our discussion of the problem of learning deep (or semantic) structure in 3.5 above, we might think this aspect a likely candidate, as it seems (as was apparently supposed in some earlier versions of trans-formational generative grammar) that, since these deep representations are not present in the primary linguistic data *per se*, they presumably have to be abstracted from it, i.e. learned. The difficulty is that more recent proposals within the content (transformational) framework have included versions of the theory which incorporate a form of the so-called 'universal base hypothesis', which assumes, in effect, that 'the actual rules of the base are the same for every language' (Bach, 1968, p. 114). This implies that it is not the deep structures which have to be learned at all (as these may now simply be added to a growing list of innate universals of various types), but rather the transformations which map them onto surface structures (cf. McNeill, 1966a, p. 101). That is,

---

[1] Obviously, the first of these terms ('language acquisition') would be more properly associated with the content view (where choosing between a highly constrained initial set of alternatives is involved) and the second ('language learning') with the competing process (data-analysis) approach, but, in order to maintain some neutrality between the two views, I shall continue to use these terms interchangeably.

under this interpretation, given initially the full list of possible base structures, and presented with a representative set of sentences (from which, with the help of other innate universals, a set of surface structures may conveniently be derived), the child has merely to put the two sets together (no doubt with the help of a few additional restrictions on the notion of 'transformational rule') by positing a set of rules which pair these off in a way which works (and is consistent with all the other universals in his inborn mechanism). So deep structures are 'out', since linguists can simply say: 'No, content wins again. The deep structures are there to begin with.'[1]

How about the transformations, then? We might try, of course, but with all the recent talk about 'constraints' on transformations (see especially Ross, 1967, and Chomsky, 1971) it is no longer clear what is presumed to be universal (and thus innate) about them and what is not. Besides, every time the theory changes the transformations change with them, and it is very hard to hit a moving target. Then, too, there is a lingering suspicion that, even if we were to attempt to discuss the transformations in this context on one day (and a monumental and speculative task this would surely be!), it might all be undone the next by the sudden appearance of yet another version of transformational grammar (perhaps even formally – and surely 'empirically' – equivalent to one or more of the universal base versions) in which it turned out that it was the *transformations* which were innate, after all, and the base forms which were learned (that is, by pairing surface structures with rules in some way).[2]

In any case, it seems clear that we have both a more reliable and a far more manageable candidate in the *lexical* component of the grammar.

[1] Cf. Chomsky (1967b, pp. 80–1): 'It seems to be true that the underlying deep structures vary very slightly, at most, from language to language. That is quite reasonable, because it seems impossible to learn them, since they are not signaled in the sentence and are not recoverable from the signal in any nontrivial way by any inductive or analytical operation, so far as I can see. Since it is hard to imagine how anyone could learn them, it is pleasant to discover that they do not vary much from language to language. That fact [*sic*] enables us to postulate that they form part of the technic which a person uses for acquiring language; that is, they are part of the conceptual apparatus he uses to specify the form of the language to which he is exposed, and not something to be acquired. It is fortunate that this postulate is tenable, since it is difficult to imagine an alternative.'

[2] See especially Bach, 1965a and 1971a, for some hints of this. Chomsky himself has remarked that 'so far as evidence is available, it seems that very heavy conditions on the form of grammar are universal. Deep structures seem to be very similar from language to language, and the rules which manipulate and interpret them also seem to be drawn from a very narrow class of conceivable formal operations' (1967c, p. 7).

For here, as Bach points out, is one place where the famous 'arbitrariness' of the linguistic sign is presumed (by all concerned, so far as I can tell) to reside. For not only do the phonological representations of morphemes differ widely from language to language (thus satisfying our language-specific criterion), but also the particular sets of semantic (and/or syntactic) representations which are paired with them in each specific case.[1] Thus it would seem that we have in the lexical representations of morphemes[2] a clear case of precisely the sort of entity we are searching for: an aspect of the grammar which (apart from similarities due to historical factors and other fortuitous similarities of no consequence to the child learning the language) is agreed to be idiosyncratic to each particular language and which therefore must be learned (i.e. the hard way) in each and every case.[3] In the critical testing of our two hypothetical models of language acquisition, we can start from linguistic descriptions which differ in their apparent capacity to be unambiguously associated with one or the other of the two approaches to language acquisition under consideration, but which are alike in that they both hold that the lexical representation of each morpheme should be expressed as a single 'basic' or 'underlying' phonological shape. On the one hand, there is generative phonology, i.e. the approach to phonological description associated with the theory of TGG, and clearly predicated upon the *content* or *innate universals* interpretation of the language

[1] Though not, as Bach points out, 'without limit' (1968, p. 117). Presumably this limitation will be expressed in terms of a set of universal constraints on phonetic representation, on the one hand, and on semanto-syntactic representation on the other – but *not*, however, having very much to do with any natural or intrinsic relationship which must exist between the two (cf. Hockett, 1963, p. 8). Thus [šu] can be paired with 'cabbage' in French and 'shoe' in English, while the phonological representations for 'cabbage' and 'shoe' in English have little similarity to their corresponding representations for these concepts in French (Chao, 1968, p. 2).

[2] Or, more precisely, in the *phonological portion* of the lexical representation of morphemes, assuming that the lexicon is the respository of *all* the idiosyncratic information about morphemes, phonological and otherwise (see Lakoff, 1970, p. 21). Since I shall be dealing almost exclusively with phonological representation in this booĸ, I shall continue to use the term 'lexical representation' in this very restricted sense throughout.

[3] While one hesitates to dismiss any conceptual scheme out of hand, it seems clear that there are immense obstacles (from the point of view of plausibility) to the satisfactory formulation of any hypothesis which assumes that these lexical representations might also be innate. Among these obstacles are the considerations that (1) the full set of base forms of every possible language would have to be there (since we assume that no individual is predestined to learn any *particular* language), and (2) each of these representations would presumably have to vary in time and in phase with the lexical restructuring going on in each language

acquisition device, and in which each morpheme is presumed to have a single 'base form' or 'underlying representation'. On the other, in striking contrast, we have the markedly different analytical approach exemplified by Jakobson's now-classic article on 'Russian Conjugation', in which a clearly analogous concept of the 'basic stem' (or 'basic alternate') appears and is utilized within a theoretical framework clearly predicated upon a specific version of the second of our two language-acquisition models, i.e. the *learning algorithm* or *process* approach – judging from the data-analytical character of the procedure which Jakobson proposes for *finding* basic forms: 'we take as basic the alternant which appears in a position where the other alternant too would be admissible' (1948, p. 156).[1] Comparison is further assisted in that we have available a transformational (content-motivated) treatment of many of the very same linguistic problems which Jakobson deals with in his (process-motivated) analysis: specifically, in the recent work of Lightner (see especially 1965). Let us now proceed to compare some aspects of the work of Jakobson and of Lightner on Russian conjugation, asking what implications this has for our two competing models of language acquisition.

4.2 The ov ~ uj alternation in Russian

Of particular interest are the treatments which Jakobson and Lightner give to the problem of the ov ~ uj alternation in Russian. The relevant facts are that Russian verbs whose infinitives end in the sequence -ovat' (which we may tentatively analyze as a suffix -ova plus the infinitive ending -t'), all of which contain the sequence -oval in their past-

[1] The concept of a single, or basic, lexical representation is implicit in virtually all pre-generative work in phonological theory, not just in that of Jakobson; cf., for example, Whitney's concept of 'representative forms' for roots and stems (1889, pp. 34–7); Sapir's 'phonologic orthography' (1933, pp. 50–1); Bloomfield's 'basic alternants' (1933, pp. 164 and 209), 'artificial underlying forms' (p. 219) or 'theoretical basic forms' (1939, p. 105); Nida's 'basic allomorphs' (1949, p. 45); Francis' 'normal forms' (1958, p. 210); Harris' 'one-spelling morphophonemic writing' (1951, p. 226, n. 18); etc. The main reason for choosing Jakobson here is that apparently only he refined his analytical procedure to the point that it automatically selected his basic alternants for him; the others appear to have resorted to a less rigorous *ad hoc* approach, where different criteria were applied in different cases (cf. Bloomfield's fluctuation between the criteria of 'range of distribution' and 'simplicity of statement' (1933, pp. 164 and 217) and Nida's three criteria of 'statistical 'predominance', 'productivity of new formations' and 'regularity of formation' (1949, p. 45)), or simply avoided the problem of selection altogether by resorting to special *ad hoc* morphophonemic cover symbols (as in Bloomfield, 1939, p. 109).

tense forms (-ova plus the past tense marker -l), exhibit the sequence -uj (rather than -ova) in their Imperative and Non-past forms (and, in general, before any vocalic suffix). That is, such forms occur as the following:[1]

Infin	torgovat'	'to bargain,	*Analysis:* torg + ova + t'
Past	torgoval	trade'	torg + ova + l
P Ger	torgovav		torg + ova + v
	etc., as opposed to		
Pres	torguju		torg + uj + u
Imper	torguj		torg + uj + ø
Pr Ger	torguja		torg + uj + a
	etc.		

Jakobson's (1948) treatment is as follows (with certain formalisms and extrapolations imposed to facilitate the comparison with Lightner's work):

(1) The longer of the two realizations of the stem (the so-called 'open full–stem') is chosen as the basic or underlying form. If we extrapolate on Jakobson's analysis so that each morpheme has its own basic form, this implies that the basic form of the root is °/torg°/ and of the thematic suffix °/ova°/. By the same reasoning we determine that the basic form of the Infinitive morpheme is °/t'i°/ (rather than °/t'/°/) and that that of the Imperative morpheme is °/i°/ (rather than ø). I also add the 'present tense' morpheme °/o°/. The basic forms of all of the other morphemes represented in the data are identical to the 'phonetic' (see note 1 below) transcriptions indicated.[2]

---

[1] For convenience I use a broad and regularized 'phonetic' transcription for Russian throughout this chapter, except where otherwise indicated. This transcription is 'regularized' primarily in the sense that the two phenomena of *vowel-reduction* in unstressed syllables and *voicing assimilation* within obstruent clusters are suppressed, as none of the phonetic details introduced as a result of taking these processes into consideration bear on the specific problems in question.

    Stress is indicated by a superscript ´, wherever relevant, and the apostrophe denotes *palatalization*. °/ °/ signifies a *morphophonemic* transcription. ø is null.

[2] I take some liberties with Jakobson's original analysis here in order to facilitate comparison with Lightner's. In particular, for reasons not at all clear to me, Jakobson chose to restrict his concept of 'basic variant' to (verb) stems only, and did not extend it to morphemes generally (as Bloomfield did; see his *Language*, p. 209, for example). My first departure from Jakobson, therefore, is to treat the 'basic stem' °/torgova°/ as a sequence of two 'basic morphemes' °/torg + ova°/. More drastically, I posit basic representations for all the other morphemes represented in the data as well, which Jakobson himself gave in terms of environmentally restricted 'allomorphic' statements of the traditional sort (though with certain apparent exceptions, such as the Preterite marker °/l°/ and some others – see pp. 157–8 of his article). The rationale behind my choice of °/i°/ and °/t'i°/ as basic representations for the Imperative and Infinitive markers, respectively, becomes apparent when the Imperative and Infinitive forms of some other verbs are also taken into consideration (such as *id'i* 'Go!' and *id't'i* 'to go'; *n'es'i* 'Carry!' and *n'es't'i* 'to carry'; etc.).

(2) The following three 'general rules' may then apply to produce the correct phonetic output in all cases:

(a) 'Open full-stem remain intact before a consonantal desinence and lose their final phoneme before a vocalic desinence' (p. 159). That is, if we adopt a familiar symbolic notation to replace Jakobson's prose:

$$V \rightarrow \emptyset \: / \: \underline{\hspace{2em}} + V$$

(b) 'Before dropped a- the group *ov* is regularly replaced by *uj-*' (p. 160).[1] Provided we formalize the notion 'before a dropped segment' by introducing the familiar convention of descriptive order to our rules, we can represent this rule symbolically as follows, where rule (b) follows rule (a):

$$ov \rightarrow uj \: / \: \underline{\hspace{2em}} + V$$

(c) Delete the unstressed *i* of the Infinitive or Imperative if the verb stem ends in no more than a single consonant,[2] that is:

$$\begin{array}{l} \breve{\imath} \\ \text{Infin} \\ \text{Imper} \end{array} \rightarrow \emptyset \: / \: VC_0^1 + C_0\underline{\hspace{2em}}$$

Given the analysis indicated above and base forms provided in step (1), the ordered application of the rules (a), (b) and (c) will yield the correct phonetic results in all cases, as illustrated by the following derivations:[3]

torgovát'	torgúju	torgúj
°/torg + ová + t'i°/	°/torg + óva + o + u°/	°/torg + óva + i°/
(a)	(a) torg + óv + u	(a) torg + óv + i
(b) . . . .[4]	(b) torg + új + u	(b) torg + új + i
(c) torg + ová + t'	(c)	(c) torg + új

Thus Jakobson's analysis accounts at least for the immediately apparent facts of the situation.[5]

---

[1] I ignore that portion of Jakobson's rule here which deals with stress, which is beyond the scope of the present discussion.

[2] Jakobson had no such rule (as indicated by the lack of quotation marks), but we require some rule of this sort here to accompany those decisions we have already made regarding the base forms of the Infinitive and Imperative morphemes (see p. 92, n. 2, above).

[3] I am not concerned with predicting stress in these examples and merely supply it in *ad hoc* fashion to the proper syllable of the underlying representations. Note that it is necessary to mark it in some way in order to insure the proper operation of rule (c), as formulated.

[4] Note that rule (b) does not apply here because of the *absence of a morpheme boundary* between the *v* and the *a* of the thematic suffix.

[5] Furthermore, this analysis extends to almost all other verbs of the -ovat' type, except for those in which the *ova* sequence cannot be regarded as an independent suffix, but must be considered as a suffix *a* attached to a root ending in the sequence *ov-* (as in the case of the verb *kovat'*, for instance). Given the analysis *kov + a + t'* for this form, for example, rule (b) now *will* apply, yielding the ungrammatical sequence **kujat'*. (Interestingly enough, Jakobson's own analysis – as originally formulated –

Lightner's analysis (1965) of these same facts is quite different. First of all, Lightner has no 'discovery algorithm' for his basic forms; rather, the metatheoretical framework within which he operates allows (in fact, requires) that he be free to posit virtually any base forms he chooses (within the constraints of a theory of universal phonetics), so long as he can utilize them to account for the phonetic facts in a 'natural' and 'insightful' way.[1] The only explicit guideline is that whatever underlying form is chosen for a particular morpheme, it must be constant for all occurrences of the morpheme in question (except in relatively rare cases of 'true suppletion', where lexical complexity is unavoidable). Thus the normal phonological shape of most morphemes can be given in a simple context-free 'lexical substitution' rule of the following general form:[2]

(set of syntacto-semantic features) → (sequence of phonological segments)

The specific base forms which Lightner posits for the morphemes which appear in this particular problem (with some minor adjustments for purposes of the exposition here) are as follows:

(trade)	→ °/torg°/	(Past)	→ °/l°/
(suffix)$_1$	→ °/ou°/	(1 SG)	→ °/ū°/[3]
(suffix)$_2$	→ °/ā°/	(Imper)	→ °/ī°/
(Infin)	→ °/tī°/	(Pres)	→ °/e°/

Lightner also includes in his grammar the following set of (ordered) rules (which are rewritten here in much the same *ad hoc* notation employed in presenting Jakobson's rules and with certain irrelevant details omitted. Lightner's own formulation of these rules in terms of phonetic feature notation may be examined by referring to the page references supplied after each rule below, all of which refer to his 1965 dissertation):[4]

---

will still work for such forms, but thanks only to the informal use of the convenient device 'before dropped a-' which he employs.)

[1] At present, of course, these notions of 'naturalness', etc. are mostly intuitive and remain very much underdetermined. I shall go into this in depth in 5.2.

[2] See, for example, Chomsky, 1965a, p. 84, and Sanders, 1967, pp. 80–1.

[3] Actually, Lightner ultimately posits a considerably more abstract representation for this particular morpheme (1965, pp. 59–62), but this has no bearing on the present problem, so I resort instead to this oversimplification which Lightner himself employed in his 1967 article and elsewhere.

[4] The superscripts ⁻ and ˘ over a vowel denote tenseness and laxness, respectively. A vowel not marked with a superscript of any sort is also to be interpreted as lax, except for the unmarked cover symbol V, which means 'any vowel'. The symbol V̇ denotes a *front* vowel.

$(\overline{V})$ $\bar{i} \rightarrow i \ / \ VC_0^1 \ (+t)\_\_\_\#$ (p. 211)

$(\overline{V}:j)$ $\overline{V} \rightarrow j \ / \ \_\_\_+\breve{V}$ (pp. 35, 210)

$(u:w)$ $\begin{bmatrix} i \\ u \end{bmatrix} \rightarrow \begin{bmatrix} j \\ w \end{bmatrix} \ / \ \begin{Bmatrix} \_\_\_V \\ \overline{V}\_\_\_ \end{Bmatrix}$ (pp. 38, 210)

$(C:C')$ $C \rightarrow C' \ /\_\_\_(\breve{V},j)$ (pp. 21, 212)

$(VV:\overline{V})$ $V_1V_2 \rightarrow \overline{V}_2{}^1$ (pp. 161, 212)

$(U\&I)$ $\begin{bmatrix} i \\ u \end{bmatrix} \rightarrow \begin{Bmatrix} \begin{bmatrix} \breve{e} \\ \breve{o} \end{bmatrix}/\_\_\_C_1 \ (\breve{i},\breve{u}) \\ \emptyset \end{Bmatrix}$ (pp. 28, 101, 213)

$(w:v)_2$ $w \rightarrow v$ (pp. 201, 213)

Now compare the following derivations with those of Jakobson's above:

	torgovat' $°/torg+ou+\bar{a}+t\bar{i}°/$	*torguju* $°/torg+ou+\bar{a}+e+\bar{u}°/$	*torguj* $°/torg+ou+\bar{a}+\bar{i}°/$
$(\overline{V})$	$torg+ou+\bar{a}+ti$	. . . .	$torg+ou+\bar{a}+i$
$(\overline{V}:j)$	. . . .	$torg+ou+j+e+\bar{u}$	$torg+ou+j+i$
$(u:w)$	$torg+ow+\bar{a}+ti$	. . . .	. . . .
$(C:C')$	$torg+ow+\bar{a}+t'i$	. . . .	. . . .
$(VV:\overline{V})$	. . . .	$torg+\bar{u}+j+\bar{u}$	$torg+\bar{u}+j+i$
$(U\&I)$	$torg+ow+\bar{a}+t'$	. . . .	$torg+\bar{u}+j$
$(w:v)_2$	$torg+ov+\bar{a}+t'$	. . . .	. . . .

Thus we find we have another 'single-base' solution to the problem which also yields the correct results.[2]

4.3 The case *for* the generative treatment

The question now is, how do we choose between these (or any other) two analyses? Or, to make the question more specific, why did Halle and Lightner feel the need to reformulate Jakobson's analysis, since Jakobson's obviously 'worked'?[3] I think some of the considerations

---

[1] Note that this rule incorporates Jakobson's rule (a), as one of its effects is to delete the first of two vowels which occur in succession.

[2] So negating Levin's argument that Jakobson's full-stem represents the 'ideal basic form of the verb from *the* linguistic point of view' (1969, p. 229), since it is 'the *only* system which makes it possible to derive all the forms of any regular verb from a single form, rather than from two or three forms' (p. 240) and 'since *any* system which makes it possible [to do this] is clearly the *best* system' (p. 241; italics added throughout).

[3] Especially since Lightner admits that Jakobson's 1948 article was one of the two works in the linguistic literature which 'made the deepest impression' on him during his pre-MIT days (1965, p. 260).

involved are reasonably clear in this case. First, it seems that Jakobson's proposed *ov* to *uj* rule (rule (b) in my presentation of his analysis above) is, phonologically speaking, very strange. One would have to look long among the languages of the world to find any close parallel (except, in closely related Slavic languages, such as Ukrainian, where the facts themselves are much the same). This rule (like most of the others in Jakobson's analysis – and a disturbing recalcitrant few in Lightner's analysis, as well) appears, in fact, to have *no reasonable phonological basis* whatsoever. Why should *ov* change to *uj*, of all things? And why only before a vocalic desinence? (Or, even more incredibly, why 'before dropped a-', as in Jakobson's original formulation?) In short, the things which bother the generative grammarian about Jakobson's analysis are, specifically, his *rules*. They do not seem to conform to any demonstrable scheme of natural universal constraints (whereas, as we noted in the previous chapter, it is a basic tenet of TGG that such constraints must exist in order to tie the field of linguistics together). Furthermore, Jakobson's solution is obviously *ad hoc*: the ov–uj rule is posited precisely to take care of the peculiar ov ∼ uj alternation manifested by a particular class of Russian verbs and is posited *only* for that purpose. The rule has no other function or usefulness within the grammar whatsoever. Jakobson's analysis thus appears to lack two presumably vital ingredients – specifically, *naturalness* and *generality* – and so it is not surprising that other linguists were disposed to go on searching for another solution which might not fall quite so short in these respects. To a great extent, Lightner seems to have found one.

First of all, consider Lightner's rules. Apart from rule ($\overline{V}$) (which, in effect, merely recapitulates our 'Jakobsonian' rule (c)), rule ($\overline{V}$:j) and possibly rule (U&I), all are not only phonologically (i.e. phonetically) plausible, but are statements of such familiar 'everyday' processes, which reappear in virtually every language family of the world, that they seem almost trivial (cf. chapter 21 of Bloomfield (1933) on 'types of phonetic change', for example). Even rules ($\overline{V}$:j) and (U&I), though themselves highly dubious on 'naturalness' grounds, do at least share with their more plausible partners the fact that each performs *multiple duty* in the grammar; that is, none of the rules listed in Lightner's analysis has been posited solely to take care of the particular alternation now under discussion (rule ($\overline{V}$) excepted, which seems decidedly *ad hoc* in both systems). Rule ($\overline{V}$:j), for instance, harks back to rule E of Halle's earlier paper (1963, p. 119), where it was posited not to take care of the ov–uj alternation at all, but rather as part of an early generative attempt to account for the apparently unrelated phenomenon of 'transitive softening' in Russian; similarly, rule (U&I) also plays a central role in Lightner's analysis of the Russian vowel–null alternations (see 4.4 below).

The apparently decisive argument in favor of Lightner's analysis comes, however, when one considers the additional mileage one can get out of it by appending very little supplementary machinery. (This is a direct consequence of its generality, as already mentioned.) First, without adding any extra machinery at all, Lightner can lexically unite a large number of noun and verb forms which Jakobson, by the nature of his neo-taxonomic approach, could not. In particular, verb roots ending in *ov-* or *ev-* (e.g. *kovat'* 'to forge', *kl'evat'* 'to peck, bite') present no special problems for Lightner (cf. p. 93, n. 5 above); moreover, Lightner can utilize these same rules and basic forms to account for the nominal derivatives of the -ovat' verbs, as well (such as *torgovl'a* 'trade' from *torgovat'*; *kl'ov* 'bite' from *kl'evat'*, etc.) by strict adherence to the convention of the transformational cycle (see Chomsky, 1967d, p. 115; and Lightner, 1965, pp. 38–9 and 173).

Secondly, by making only minor adjustments in his grammar, Lightner can also deal with a number of other hitherto completely baffling anomalies of Russian phonology. A particularly interesting and impressive case is the notoriously strange behavior of the voiced labial fricative segment *v* in Russian. For in addition to participating in the ov–uj alternation, this segment also behaves very oddly with respect to the phenomenon of voicing assimilation, the general rules for which, as formulated by Halle (1959, p. 64), appear to be as follows:

Rule P2. If an obstruent cluster is followed by a word boundary or by a phonemic phrase boundary, all segments in the cluster are voiceless.

Rule P3a. If an obstruent cluster is followed by a – (dash) boundary [as in abbreviated compound words such as *part-b'il'et* 'party card'] or by a sonorant, then with regard to voicing the cluster conforms to the last segment; if it is voiced, so are all other segments in the cluster; if it is voiceless, so is the entire cluster.

The behavior of *v* (also *v'*) is, however, exceptional. This segment, although it *de*voices in precisely the same environments as any other voiced obstruent in Russian, behaves quite differently from the other voiced obstruents in its role as a *conditioner* of voicing; in fact, in Halle's formulation, it can be regarded as playing no such role: 'Everything transpires as if /v/ or /v'/ had been absent; e.g. °/mog vo = jt'i°/ [mók vajt'í] "he could enter", [mókv'irnút'] "he could return", but [mógvzdaxnút'] "he could sigh"' (p. 64, with italics added and the diacritics reinterpreted to conform to the system in use here.) And within the general Jakobsonian framework, it appears that a statement to this effect (a 'mere summary of the facts', as the transformationalists would put it) is about all that could be said.[1]

Lightner offers instead a potential descriptive 'explanation' for this phenomenon. He proposes, first of all (as is evident from his treatment of the ov–uj problem discussed above), that all v's in Russian are derived from an underlying °/u°/ (as all observers are agreed was the case historically, with the likely exception of the prothetic v). He then adds to his grammar one additional rule, as follows:

$$(\text{w:v})_1 \quad \text{w} \rightarrow \text{v} \ / \ \underline{\quad} \begin{Bmatrix} \text{C} \\ \# \end{Bmatrix} \qquad \qquad (\text{p. 200})$$

If this rule is now ordered after the rule (U&I) but before the rule $(\text{w:v})_2$, and if Halle's voicing assimilation rules P2 and P3a from page 97 are also incorporated into the grammar (as they must be in any case, for Jakobson as well as for Lightner) and ordered between the two rules $(\text{w:v})_1$ and $(\text{w:v})_2$, the heretofore 'anomalous' behavior of the (phonetic) segment v as described by Halle can be predicted as an automatic consequence of the grammar (see Lightner, 1965, pp. 200–2). This can be shown by means of the following three sample derivations which illustrate (1) the devoicing of v before a voiceless obstruent (as in the first example below, *fsadáx* 'in the gardens'), (2) the failure of a voiceless obstruent to assimilate in voicing to a v immediately following it in a cluster (as in the second example, *kvólkam* 'towards the wolves') and (3) the effective assimilation of voicing from a v if the v is itself immediately followed by another voiced obstruent (as in the third example, *gvdovám* 'towards the widows'):

V SADAX[2]	k VOLKAM	k VDOVAM
°/uu + sād + āxu°/	°/k + uolk + āmu°/	°/k + uudou + āmu°/

[1] Halle's 1959 book is little more than a semi-formalization of Jakobson's earlier work, with a few new twists.

[2] A representation in small capitals here (as elsewhere) denotes a simple *transliteration* of the standard orthographic representation of the forms. The morphemic composition of each form is shown on the line immediately below in terms of the kind of *lexical representations* which Lightner would have to posit in each case in order for his rules to work (with certain irrelevant details omitted, once again).

(u:w)	wu + sād + āxu	k + wolk + āmu	k + wudow[1] + āmu
(U&I)	w + sād + āx	k + wolk + ām	k + wdow + ām
(w:v)₁	v + sād + āx	. . . .	k + vdow + ām
(P3a)	f + sād + āx	. . . .[2]	g + vdow + ām
(w:v)₂	. . . .	k + volk + ām	g + vdov + ām

But this is not all. In order to account for such alternations as *d'elaju ~ d'elat'* 'to do', *žívu ~ žít'* 'to live', *stanu ~ stat'* 'to become' and *žmu ~ žat'* 'to press, squeeze', Jakobson proposed the rule that 'full-stems in *j v n m* drop their terminal phoneme before a consonantal desinence' (1948, p. 159). This putative rule highlights yet another peculiar aspect of the behavior of the segment *v* in Russian, namely, that this segment seems clearly out of place as a member of the class upon which this rule is supposed to operate: it, and it alone, is not a resonant.[3] In other words, this class is not, as Halle would put it, a 'natural' one (see his 1962 and 1964 articles, pp. 337 and 328, respectively). In Lightner's reformulation along transformational-generative (innate-universal) lines, however, it is rather the patently 'natural' class *j, w, n,* and *m* (the non-liquid resonants or sonorants) which is subject to this rule, for at the stage in derivation at which this rule (Lightner's rule (S:ø)) applies, all of the *v*'s are still *w*'s, i.e. the rule is ordered in Lightner's grammar after rule (u:w) but before the rules (w:v)₁ and (w:v)₂, as indicated in the following (partial) derivation of the form *žít'* 'to live':

	žīu + tī
(V̄)	žīu + ti
(u:w)	žīw + ti
(C:C')	ž'īw + t'i
(S:ø)	ž'ī + t'i
(U&I)	ž'ī + t'[4]

From a number of viewpoints, therefore, it seems that Lightner has gone a long way towards his goal:[5] an analysis of Russian phonology

[1] Cf. the English 'widow'.

[2] Rule P3a does not apply here, since we have (as yet) no obstruent clusters in the string.

[3] As Townsend 'explains' it, '*v*, though it is paired with *f* phonetically, *functions as a resonant in conjugation*' (1968, p. 83; italics added).
The segment *ž'* is depalatalized here by Lightner's general rule (š':š) (1965, p. 214) and the vowel quality is modified by a low-level phonetic-detail rule, neither of which need concern us here.

[5] Much more could also be said in Lightner's favor. For example, among other fringe benefits associated with his analysis of Russian, he also achieves a great simplifica-

of much greater generality and naturalness than competing analyses which offers a set of attractive descriptive 'explanations' for phenomena which had previously to be regarded as anomalous and inexplicable. And since Lightner's approach is clearly predicated upon a set of basic assumptions associated with the general transformational-generative framework in which he operates (in particular, a set of specific explicit hypotheses as to a set of universal constraints on the notion of phonological description and phonological rule), Lightner's success lends an aura of credibility to the approach as a whole (including, fundamentally, the 'content' hypothesis of linguistic universals).

4.4 On learning abstract lexical representations

A first step in formulating a critical analysis of the viability of generative phonology (as an epitomization of TGG[1] and hence of the innate-universals hypothesis of language acquisition) is to ask how very abstract lexical representations of the sort posited by Lightner (1965) or by Chomsky and Halle (1968) might conceivably be learned. For it seems fairly obvious that many advantages of the transformational-generative approach to phonology as exemplified in these works – specifically the increase in generality and naturalness which Lightner seems to have achieved *via-à-vis* Jakobson's earlier proposals – are bought at a price. In this case the payment is in terms of a greatly *increased abstract-ness of underlying (lexical) representations*, i.e. of base forms. As Lightner has correctly observed, 'To explain the different phonetic shapes in which morphemes may appear, we were *obliged* to posit underlying representations which often bore no obvious relation to actual phonetic representations' (1966b, p. 21; italics added). That is, it can be demon-

---

tion in his lexicon in the sense that far fewer distinctive (or, in the latest terminology, 'marked') features need be specified for numerous entries, since he has eliminated the need of positing not only underlying palatalized segments, but also palatals (cf. the lexical representations in Lightner, 1965 with those in Halle, 1959 or Jakobson, 1948, for instance).

[1] Apart from the considerations already mentioned in 4.1 for the specific choice of topic in this chapter, a further argument for choosing generative phonological theory as the crucial section of the more general transformational-generative approach to language is supplied by Chomsky himself: 'I think we are at quite an advanced stage in our understanding of the phonological component; we have fairly substantial insight into the way surface structure is graphed onto sound, and we can formulate and order hundreds of phonological rules. We are still at a rudimentary stage in our understanding of the syntactic component, and we have practically no understanding of semantic component' (in Mehta, 1971, p. 58).

strated that an *essential* condition of most of the 'explanations' which follow from the application of transformational-generative theory to problems in (morpho-)phonology[1] is the postulation of lexical representations so 'abstract' as to violate the constraints of sound methodology. Before specifying the point at which such abstractness is reached, let me first try to give a better picture of the sort of lexical representations which can be associated with the typical transformational-generative analysis of a problem of phonological (or morphophonemic) alternation.

Consider, for example, Lightner's proposed 'explanation' of the vowel–null alternation in Russian. The essence of this problem is that Russian exhibits what might be called two parallel sets of vowels which, though indistinguishable from one another phonetically, exhibit markedly different behavior morphophonemically. In particular, while the members of one set persist in all environments in which the morphemes of which they form a part may occur, the members of the other set do not; more specifically, the members of the second set are predictably absent before (or within) open syllables. Taking the vowel *o* as a typical example, we find that some roots containing this vowel (such as *pot* 'sweat') retain it throughout the grammatical paradigm (cf. the G. Sg. *pota*), whereas other roots which ostensibly contain this same vowel (such as *son* 'sleep'), do not exhibit it overtly in any form of the paradigm which involves the presence of a vocalic ending (as in the G. Sg. *sna*). Furthermore, *o*'s of *both* types may also occur in roots immediately after soft (palatalized) consonants, as in the forms *t'os* 'boards' (G. Sg. *t'osa*) and *p'os* 'dog, hound' (G. Sg. *psa*). The problems posed by these facts are said by Lightner to be the following:

(1) What essential difference between the *o*'s which delete and those which do not accounts for their divergent behavior?

(2) What is the difference between those *o*'s which palatalize a preceding consonant and those which do not?[2]

---

[1] Cf. Chomsky (in Darley, 1967, p. 100): 'We can set up quite elegant theories of phonological structure that can explain quite a remarkable range of phenomena...I think rather striking explanations can be proposed for peculiar phenomena of phonetics.' (Here follows an admission, however, which is not at all typical of the kind of remarks Chomsky tends to make before professional linguistic audiences, but which the latter, I suggest, might benefit from taking more to heart: 'But [these explanations] are proposed on the basis of theories which, although I think they are intellectually quite satisfying, have no evidence for them other than the fact that they explain quite a lot of phonetic data. Here, certainly, one hopes it will be possible to go beyond that, and you cannot go on beyond that on the basis of linguistics alone.')

[2] The problem is so stated since Lightner has discovered that elsewhere in the language

An important clue to one possible set of answers is given when one considers the reconstructed etymons of the words *son* and *p'os* at an earlier stage in the history of the language. The historical facts appear to be that in place of the present 'fleeting' *o* in these words, there was apparently a high lax vowel, back in the case of *son*, but front in the case of *p'os* (i.e. the two famous 'jers' of Proto-Slavic). Furthermore, both words ended with a back jer, as well (cf. the Old Church Slavonic forms *sŭnŭ* and *pŭsŭ* cited in Lunt, 1959). The Modern Russian forms thus presumably developed by the lowering of the first ('strong') jer in each word and the deletion of the second ('weak') in each case, as well as by the backing of the preserved (now mid) vowel in the latter of the two words. Lightner then adapts these historical facts as part of his proposed 'synchronic' explanation of problems (1) and (2) above as follows (see especially his 1965, pp. 28–30 and 1966a, pp. 69–71):

(1) He posits the following set of base forms for the four words introduced above: (a) (sweat) → °/pot°/, (b) (sleep) → °/sun°/, (c) (boards) → °/tes°/, (d) (dog) → °/pis°/, plus (e) (N. Sg. masc.) → °/u°/ and (f) (G. Sg. masc.) → °/ā°/.

(2) He then incorporates the following rules into his grammar, ordered as indicated:

$$(U\&I) \quad \begin{bmatrix} \breve{\imath} \\ \breve{u} \end{bmatrix} \rightarrow \left\{ \begin{bmatrix} \breve{e} \\ \breve{o} \\ \varnothing \end{bmatrix} / \text{———} C_1 \, (\breve{\imath}, \breve{u}) \right\}$$

(e:o)   e → o/———[−sharp]

The derivations of the N. Sg. forms are therefore as follows:

	°/pot + u°/	°/sun + u°/	°/tes + u°/	°/pis + u°/
(C:C')	. . . .	. . . .	t'es + u	p'is + u
(U&I)	pot	son	t'es	p'es
(e:o)	. . . .	. . . .	t'os	p'os

In the G. Sg. forms, however, where the posited ending is the tense vowel °/ā°/, the vowel *u* of °/sun + ā°/ and *i* of °/pis + ā°/ will *not* lower by (U&I) but simply *delete*, thus accounting for the o ~ ø alternation.[1] Moreover, the palatalization in all these forms can be shown by this analysis to be still predictable by the same single and very general rule (C:C') introduced on p. 95.

palatalization can be predicted by general rule; hence he is loath to posit distinctive (marked) palatalized segments here unless absolutely necessary.

[1] The first segment of *psa* is predictably depalatalized before a hard consonant by general rule (see Halle, 1959, p. 67, rule P6c).

We might summarize the effects of Lightner's proposed set of rules here as follows: (1) an underlying (lexical) distinction between high vs. mid lax vowels has been effectively *neutralized* on the phonetic 'surface': where the high lax vowels are preserved, they are no longer distinguishable phonetically from the original mid lax vowels; where they are not preserved, the only manifestation of their 'deep' existence which remains is the vowel–null alternation which results from the action of the rules proposed above; and (2) what was lexically a distinction between front and back vowels is also *neutralized* here in favor of a surface contrast between hard and soft consonants. The analysis is very general, neat and tidy, and (in some sense) it can certainly be said to 'explain' the facts. The analysis is typical of the best work done within the framework of generative phonology. But Lightner's analysis, as I have pointed out, requires him to posit lexical representations which are exceedingly abstract.[1] When we call a representation 'abstract', we mean simply that it differs in some way from its overt 'surface' manifestation. In the case of phonological representations, this means that it differs from its *phonetic* realization; that is, with certain qualifications having to do with the theory of universal phonetics (which is essentially a matter of giving formal expression to our earlier decision that infinite variability is not to be recognized), an abstract phonological representation of a form is simply different from the linguist's way of representing how that form is 'actually pronounced'. An *exceedingly* abstract phonological representation is therefore *very* far removed from the phonetics, in this sense. But how is this notion to be formalized? Chafe offers one suggestion in terms of a notion of 'depth of ordering', which is defined in terms of 'the total number of [derivational] stages which are present between an underlying form and its phonetic realization' (1968a, p. 127). I do not think that we should wish to consider a measure of this sort here, however, for such a notion does not differentiate the two theoretical positions under discussion in a clear and unambiguous way. For it is not the number of rules which is crucial, but rather whether or not the link between these two levels of representation is *direct* or *indirect*. On this point we find a clear distinction between the two theories and one which is intimately related to the basic presuppositional distinction which distinguishes them, namely, the question of the nature of the language-

[1] For a detailed illustration of the close interplay which exists in TGG between the abstractness of lexical representations, on the one hand, and the apparent naturalness and generality of phonological rules, on the other, see pp. 119–23 of my dissertation (Derwing, 1970).

acquisition device. In particular, implicit in the work of Jakobson (not to mention Saussure, Whitney, Boas, Sapir, Bloomfield, Trager and most linguists of the pre-transformational era) is the assumption that the link between the lexical and phonetic levels in a synchronic grammar must be *direct*; that is, all these analysts apparently assumed (whether or not they ever considered the further possibility or desirability of positing unique base forms for morphemes) that the set of possible candidates for the lexical representations of particular morphemes was co-extensive with the set of phonetic (and thus phonemic) variants which actually appeared (cf. McCawley, 1967b, pp. 107–8). This assumption is fundamental to the data-analytical or 'process' hypothesis of language acquisition in general, and a corollary of the more general assumption which characterizes this approach, namely, that the process of language acquisition is reducible to the application of certain specifiable analytical procedures (or 'discovery algorithms') to the phonetic facts.[1] The transformationalist (or 'content') position, exemplified here in the work of Lightner, is that the link between the morphophonemic (lexical) and the phonetic levels of representation is *indirect*, i.e. that lexical representations may (and, in many cases, must) be posited by the linguist (as well as by the child) which are relatable to the phonetic level *only by means of the rules of the grammar*, without any requirement that they be derivable by application of any procedures applied directly to the phonetic data. An extreme, but apparently necessary and certainly typical statement of this basic transformationalist position is expressed in the remarks of Lightner cited on p. 100 above.

It might appear that the transformationalists have, in adopting this unprecedented position, abandoned the *inductive requirement* on grammars (see 3.1 above) so far as base forms are concerned. For if there is no direct connection between the phonetic facts (which are all the child has available to him as primary data) and the base forms (which the child must eventually learn), how is it possible that base forms could *ever* be learned? But we cannot dismiss this question quite so easily. For although the point has rarely, if ever, been made explicit before (surely there is little or nothing in the published literature which deals directly with the problem of learning base-forms within the framework of the theory of TGG), the mechanism presumed to operate in such

[1] This discussion presumes the operation of some sort of 'discretizer-plus-generalizer' which first ascertains what an appropriate phonetic representation might be, i.e. which serves to determine which speech sounds are genuinely different and which are to be considered mere repetitions of one another (cf. 3.5, especially p. 75).

cases seems to me to be roughly this: as always, the child is presumed to take maximum advantage of the intrinsic knowledge supplied to him by his innate language-acquisition device, which means that he is in a position to fall back on a store of knowledge about linguistic universals and evaluation procedures. So, while very little in the way of specific detail can be suggested (since even the most optimistic transforma-tionalist view overtly recognizes that there is a long way to go before the full set of putative universals can be specified), the intended picture seems generally clear. Although the child (in this view) has no direct way of deriving his *lexical representations* from their phonetic manifesta-tions he is presumed to come into the language-acquisition business well equipped in terms of knowing what potential (possible) *rules* to look for. What he presumably does (much like the linguist who is attempting to reduplicate his efforts) is to posit various base forms (perhaps at random) until he comes up with a set which will allow him to account for the observed facts (morpheme alternants in this case) in terms of a system of rules which conform to the innate specifications. It seems at least con-ceivable that the details of this process of 'backward abstraction' might eventually be worked out, so providing a particular 'content' model of the general character for the acquisition of base forms shown in fig. 4.1.

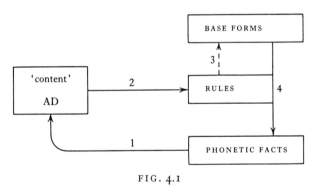

FIG. 4.1

In this model, (1) a phonetic input is supplied to a 'content' language-acquisition device which provides the child with (among other things) a relatively detailed specification of the notion 'possible phonological rule', thus enabling the child (2) to formulate (induce) a tentative set of 'natural' *rules* consistent both with this internal specification and the phonetic facts; on this basis he may (3) posit some arbitrary set of abstract underlying forms which, in conjunction with the postulated highly-constrained set of rules, can (4) fully account for the original set of phonetic facts, as well as predict new ones. The arbitrary, inexplicit or 'indirect' link in this chain, namely, the 'induction' of the *base forms* on the basis of the pre-linguistic knowledge supplied by the device AD about the form and nature of the rules, is indicated in the model by a dotted arrow (step 3).

I pass over in silence the matter of the utility and feasibility of an approach involving a set of 'content' assumptions about the device AD (already discussed in the preceding chapter); otherwise this model seems reasonably plausible. To the non-believer, however, the obvious 'looseness' of step 3 might seem overwhelming. If he is tempted to jump to unwarranted conclusions on this account, however, it should also be said that there seems to be a parallel indeterminacy in the competing 'process' view. In particular, while the structuralists appear to have been in agreement about the need to maintain some direct link between their proposed lexical representations and the phonetic 'facts', they had little to say about the kinds of *rules* which ought to be formulated in order to define the precise nature of the connection between these two levels within a grammar.[1] We might therefore schematize the traditional 'process' model for the acquisition of base forms in the manner shown in fig. 4.2. In this model, (1) the phonetic facts once

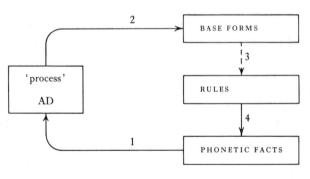

FIG. 4.2

---

[1] As Postal points out, many versions of 'structural' linguistics have 'no serious notion of linguistic rule...at all' (1966, p. 156). In some of the most extreme formulations of the post-Bloomfieldian era, for example, the notion of *phonological* rule is obviated altogether in favor of extremely complex – and heavily redundant – lexical representations, as illustrated in 6.1 below. Much the same can also be said of many of the so-called 'rules' formulated by Jakobson and some of his followers, for example (see especially Jakobson, 1948, and the discussion on pp. 93, 96 above, Levin, 1969, and Townsend, 1968, particularly pp. 86–7).

again provide the input, but this time to a 'process' language-acquisition device which supplies the child with the requisite analytical procedures for (2) selecting appropriate *base forms* in conjunction with which (3) any arbitrary workable set of phonological rules may now be formulated which will (4) relate these base forms back to the original set of phonetic facts, as well as extend to new forms. The guesswork within this framework lies not in coming up with a useful set of base forms (since the innate AD provides an algorithm for ascertaining these directly), but rather in formulating a set of *rules* which will work (step 3, as indicated by the dotted arrow). In both the 'content' and 'process' models, therefore there is an unmistakable 'gap' in the inductive chain: somewhere along the line in both accounts the child (like the linguist-analyst) must apparently resort to trial and error. And once again we find it difficult to choose between the two theories when they are formulated in this way as models of language acquisition.

We do appear, however, to have found one reasonable basis for preferring one of these alternatives over the other, for only within the 'content' framework adopted by Lightner did we find analyses which seemed in any way 'insightful' or 'explanatory'; we were particularly dismayed by the lack of phonetic plausibility and generality in the *rules* which Jakobson offered from the 'process' point of view. But it is precisely the rule-component of a process-oriented grammar which is bound to be most vulnerable to criticism, since there is little or no provision within this theoretical framework for any notion analogous to the generative grammarian's 'possible' or 'natural' *rule*. It is therefore clear that defects in the structuralist's model will be found in the relatively unconstrained system of rules. By the same token, the notion of 'possible lexical representation' is compatibly undefined within the competing 'content' model adopted by the transformationalists. If we were to submit this 'content' notion of 'base form' to the same sort of careful scrutiny, we might find corresponding difficulties within the transformationalist's model. In order to restore the balance, I shall now attempt to do just that.

4.5 The case *against* the generative treatment

4.5.1 Arguments of descriptive adequacy. Let us first consider some of Lightner's base forms. One sure way to get a look of incredulity (if not a belly laugh) from a native Russian is to tell him that his first

person singular morpheme is °/-m°/ (cf. Lightner, 1965, pp. 59–60).[1] Or that his second person singular morpheme is °/-xi°/. (He won't even recognize it; phonetically, it *always* appears as -š.) Equally bizarre are some of Lightner's proposed base forms for the case endings, a sample of which he provides on pp. 171–2 of his thesis (1965), as illustrated in the declension of the word OTEC 'father', given below:[2]

N. Sg.	OTEC-	°/ox°/	N. Pl.	OTC-Y	°/āx°/
G. Sg.	OTC-A	°/ā°/	G. Pl.	OTC-OV	°/ou+ox°/
D. Sg.	OTC-U	°/ou°/	D. Pl.	OTC-AM	°/āmu°/
A. Sg.	= G. Sg.		A. Pl.	= G. Pl.	
I. Sg.	OTC-OM	°/omu°/	I. Pl.	OTC-AMI	°/āmīx°/
P. Sg.	OTC-E	°/oi°/	P. Pl.	OTC-AX	°/āxu°/

Moreover, this is no solitary eccentricity of Lightner's. The same point could be made by turning to Chomsky and Halle (1968) for a few examples from English. Here we also find remarkable claims being made about base forms or underlying (lexical) representations. On p. 234, for example, we are told that the base form of the word 'righteous' is °/rixt+i+ɔs/,[3] on p. 222 that that of 'accede' is °/ab = kēd°/ (and not the historian's °/ad = kēd°/), on p. 220 that that of 'reduction' is °/re = duke = æt+iVn°/, etc., etc. Chomsky's own general conclusion is that:

A careful investigation of sound structure...shows that there are a number of examples of this sort, and that, in general, highly abstract underlying structures are related to phonetic representations by a long sequence of rules (1968a, p. 36).

As for the reactions of the native speaker to very abstract base forms of this sort, he has only this to say:

One cannot hope to determine *either* the underlying abstract forms *or* the processes that relate them to signals by introspection; there is, furthermore, no reason why one should find this consequence in any way surprising (1968a, p. 36; italics added).

[1] This form occurs phonetically with only two familiar roots, °/daj°/ (cf. dam ~ dat' 'to give') and °/jed°/ (cf. jem ~ jes't' 'to eat'), both of which are conceded by everyone but Lightner to be irregular in their conjugation. Elsewhere this morpheme is invariably realized phonetically as -*u*.

[2] The small capitals here, as before, represent a transliteration of the standard spelling of each form, with a hyphen added to separate the case-ending from the stem. Lightner's proposed base form for each case-ending is given immediately to the right in each instance (where my °/ā°/ = his °/ŏ°/).

[3] Chomsky presents a separate detailed argument in his little 1968a booklet to explain why 'the underlying phonological representation [of "right"] must be /rixt/ (in accord with the orthography and, of course, the history)' (p. 35.)

This is a remarkable statement in two respects. First, the issue is not one of 'determining' (i.e. discovering) base forms by introspection, but one of being able to accept them once they *are* proposed, by whatever means.[1] And secondly, if we find that we can't accept them, we are dismayed to learn that this should not be 'in any way surprising'. For is it not the essence of Chomsky's notion of a 'descriptively adequate grammar' that it should give a satisfactory account of the intuitions of the native speaker? (cf. p. 41, n. 2.) To be sure, intuition is a crude tool to begin with (cf. Chomsky in Hill, 1962, p. 177), but now, apparently, we are also being told that we are free to use it or not to use it as suits us. Look at syntax, for example. Here intuition takes us from 'surface structure' through 'grammatical relationships' and all the way to 'deep structure'. At each level the results of our investigations are presumed to be testable in terms of our native intuitions. Furthermore, it is our intuitions about grammaticality and meaning which provide the basic evidence upon which these hypothetical structures are built in the first place. Now, suddenly, when we come to such a fundamental notion as that of the lexicon or dictionary, all this is thrown to the wind: if we are told that the base form of some morpheme is such-and-such, we must accept it, no matter how outlandish it might seem – so long as it serves to 'explain' something. I cannot. Neither, apparently, can Teeter: he simply (and, I suspect, correctly) dismisses Chomsky and Halle's proposed lexical representations for English as 'psychologically absurd' (1969, p. 5; cf. also Maher, 1969). To the extent that this is true, Chomsky and Halle, to be consistent, would have to reject their own analyses (and, by the same token, Lightner his) on the grounds of 'descriptive inadequacy', i.e. by their failure to measure up to 'the standard provided by the tacit knowledge that [they presumably attempt] to specify and describe' (Chomsky, 1965a, p. 19).

There is a loophole, however. Like so many of Chomsky's basic concepts, the concept of 'descriptive adequacy' is defined and employed in a 'systematically ambiguous' way in his works. For instance, Chomsky has suggested, first of all, that a grammar may be considered to be descriptively adequate to the extent that it gives 'a correct account of the linguistic intuition of the native speaker' (1964, p. 63). We also learn that this intuition is rather 'elusive' in some areas (1965a, p. 24) and in

---

[1] No reputable linguist has yet claimed that native intuitions could be part of an effective *discovery* procedure for grammars (since, for one thing, no such intuitions are available in the pre-learning stage; see McNeill, 1966a, p. 100), but only that such intuitions might provide a valuable means of *evaluating* grammars already proposed.

others (as in the case of the actual *rules* of a grammar) virtually non-existent (p. 8). Yet, despite these assertions, Chomsky proceeds to justify a particular analysis of a problem of English morphophonemics (involving a newly proposed set of *rules* which give formal expression to a number of previously unexpressed or 'missing' generalizations) by arguing that

it is obvious that a grammar that accounts for this variety of phonetic facts by...rules...which are independently motivated, is much to be preferred, *on grounds of descriptive adequacy*, to one which contains in addition [certain other] rules (1964, p. 90; italics added).

The question which obviously arises here is, if descriptive adequacy has to do with the native speakers' intuitions and no such intuitions relate to actual rules of a grammar, how is it possible for any set of rules *ever* to be justified 'on grounds of descriptive adequacy'? The answer can only be that there must be some other criterion involved. And a search through Chomsky's remarks on this subject shows that this is so. My original quotation from Chomsky on this subject (1964, pp. 62–3) shows that descriptive adequacy involves not only the necessity of providing 'a correct account of the linguistic intuition of the native speaker', but, in addition, the specification of the observed data 'in terms of significant generalizations that express underlying regularities in the language'. In other places Chomsky restates this second criterion as a requirement that descriptive adequacy implies making specific the 'basic regularities' (1965a, p. 5) or, more commonly, the 'linguistically significant generalizations' (see Chomsky & Halle, 1968, p. 330) implicit in any given body of data. Yet this implies that it is known *in advance* which of any given set of possible generalizations are 'significant' (i.e. presumably, the ones which are psychologically valid), although the native speakers' intuitions are of little or no help in deciding this. In any case, it is clear that the notion of 'linguistically significant generalization' plays a central role in much current theoretical discussion and I shall explore this notion at length in 5.2.

One further point needs to be made here. To return to Lightner's work on Russian phonology, we find that one of the distinguishing features of his analysis is that he has managed[1] to devise a grammar in

---

[1] But not without resorting to a few *ad hoc* devices of his own in recalcitrant cases. Such is his use of the diacritic feature [-H], which triggers the (C:C') and (k:č) rules to make the final consonant of all roots marked with this feature automatically soft (palatalized) or palatal (as in *kos't'* from °/kost_н˘/ and *lož* from °/lug_н°/). For an improved analysis of such forms within the transformational-generative framework, see Lynkowsky, 1970, pp. 82–3.

which, first, palatalization is predictable in all its occurrences by general
rule (so that no underlying palatalized consonants need be postulated),
and, moreover, in which all palatals are also derivable by general rule,
either from underlying dentals (cf. the alternation in *plaču ~ plat'it'* 'to
pay') or from underlying velars (as in *plaču ~ plakat'* 'to cry'), so that
no underlying palatal consonants need be postulated either (see
Lightner, 1965, especially pp. 18 and 86–7). This achievement has the
advantage of reducing the underlying set of distinctive (or marked)
oppositions, provided the general rules for palatalization and for the
formation of palatals are extended to cover *all* cases where these segments appear – including those in which alternations of the types
illustrated do not manifestly occur. Thus Lightner proposes the underlying representations °/kēs°/, °/gēr°/ and °/xēg°/ for *čas* 'hour', *žar* 'heat'
and *šag* 'step', respectively (1965, p. 70), and °/kiln°/, °/gilt°/ and
°/xilk°/ for *čoln* 'canoe', *žolt* 'yellow' and *šolk* 'silk' (p. 126). Once
again, however, these proposals are counter-intuitive. I gather from
those native speakers with whom I have had contact that the palatals
and palatalized consonants are interpreted as every bit as 'distinctive'
(at least in these environments) from the corresponding velars and
plain consonants, respectively, as the labials are from the dentals, the
nasals from the orals, etc. And what experimental evidence as is available
in the area of discrimination-testing among native Russians supports
these intuitive judgments. In word-initial position, for example, the
voiced–voiceless pairs (such as *t-d*, *s-z*, etc.) are readily distinguished by
all Russian speakers, just as they are assumed to be distinctive by all
analysts. Difficulties crop up, however, in distinguishing such pairs as *c-з*,
č-ž and *x-ɣ* in obstruent clusters, where analysts, once again, agree that
the members of each pair are merely predictable variants of a single
underlying distinctive element. In the areas where the analysts (content
vs. process, or transformationalist vs. structuralist) are in serious disagreement, however, e.g. with respect to word-initial palatalized–non-
palatalized pairs (involving such words as *t'ok* 'flowed' and *tok* 'current')
or velar–palatal pairs (such as *k'em* 'with whom' vs. *čem* 'with what'),
the results of these discrimination-studies seem clearly to fall in line
with the first set, i.e. with the one involving the *distinctive* oppositions,
rather than the second, involving *predictable variants*.[1] In short, the

[1] Some of the experimental evidence leading to this conclusion is presented in chapter 2
of my M.A. thesis (Derwing, 1965, pp. 84–104), although the main focus of attention
in that work was rather the reactions of foreign-language (English) speakers to
Russian data; the native Russian interpretations provided merely the standard of

perceptual and intuitive evidence we do have on these matters all seems to suggest that (in some environments, i.e. at least where no alternations occur) the palatalized–plain and velar–palatal oppositions in Russian are virtually indistinguishable from any of the undisputed distinctive (lexical) oppositions which are manifested in the language, quite counter to Lightner's formal claim that the variation involved in all such cases is a predictable (non-lexical) one.[1]

4.5.2   Arguments of synchronic legitimacy. So far I have adumbrated discontent with certain ramifications of the theory of generative phonology (most notably, with the kinds of base forms which emerge when a reasonably comprehensive attempt at phonological description is attempted within this framework), but can hardly claim to have done more. In the first place, the experimental evidence on perception alluded to is both fragmentary and in need of replication and statistical analysis. In the second place, the results, even if confirmed (as experience with the language suggests they would be), would still be subject to alternative interpretations. As for intuition, this remains as unreliable an instrument as it ever was: certainly we can no more hope to tear down a theory on the basis of linguistic intuition alone than to build one up (cf. 7.3 below).

Nonetheless, I find it interesting that generative grammarians have so fully abandoned intuition as far as underlying representations in phonology are concerned. This is in striking contrast to the great bulk of work in generative syntax, where the desire to relate certain syntactic structures is generally directly traceable to specific intuitive feelings which the analyst (*qua* native speaker) has. Furthermore, it is clear (and admitted by all concerned) that the grammarian has, at best, only a fragmentary conception of what the most appropriate full set of putative 'content' universals might be. One asks, therefore: if generative grammarians so lack both intuitions and theoretical considerations to guide them, how do they ever manage to derive the base forms which they

comparison. Clearly, this work would have to be expanded and redone, and the results subjected to a careful statistical analysis, before anything very conclusive could be made of them. Nevertheless, those preliminary results still seem to me to be suggestive and interesting.

[1] Obviously, all the arguments offered in this section could be refuted by making certain assumptions of various sorts (such as an assumption to the effect that only *phonetic* representations actually describe any kind of 'perceptual reality' (cf. Chomsky & Halle, 1968, p. 25)). So I do not offer these arguments here as conclusive, but only as part of a longer chain of argument.

do? By trial and error? Hardly. By induction, like the child, from the full set of linguistic universals? Impossible at present. By intuition? Chomsky himself argues against this possibility. Then how? Despite repeated disclaimers,[1] the answer in many (if not most) instances seems to be that they do so by taking advantage of facts known about the *history* of the languages involved.[2]

4.5.2.1   On the use of diachronic information in synchronic description. Consider, for example, Lightner's treatment of the vowel–null alternation in Russian introduced in 4.4 above. His entire analysis revolves around the postulation of a pair of high lax vowels (one a front, or palatalizing vowel; the other a back, or nonpalatalizing one) which lower (and are thereby preserved as full vowels) in certain environments and otherwise delete (having completed their work), and which therefore never appear in the phonetic representation of *any* utterances in the language. The resulting analysis is neat and efficient. But is it not striking that Lightner posits these magical vocalic segments in precisely those places (so far as comparisons can be made) where it is supposed, on historical evidence, that the Proto-Slavic 'jers' (also presumed to have been a pair of high lax vowels, one front and one back) also occurred? Lightner claims that he was led to this solution (and this solution alone) by the primary linguistic data (and these data alone): the only legitimate source of the 'motivation for proposing underlying representations and phonological rules' (1967, p. 51). His dictum is (quite properly) that 'whether a particular synchronic description does or does not mirror diachronic description is not relevant to an evaluation of that synchronic description' (1966b, p. 24). But Lightner is well aware that the partial grammar which he has proposed for Old Church Slavonic, at least, is

also a reflection of the history of OCS: the underlying forms which we posit

---

[1] Lightner, for example, argues that his description of OCS phonology just 'happens' to reflect historical development (1966b, p. 25).

[2] Arguments to the effect that all 'item and process' or 'mutation' models represent mere carry-overs from historical linguistics or are inherently diachronic by nature (since they involve 'various processes of "change" taking place in a fictional time span' (Lamb, 1966a, p. 35)) are by no means new (cf. also Bloomfield, 1933, p. 213, and Hockett, 1954, pp. 386–7). Most of these previous arguments have been (rightly I think) dismissed by Chomsky and Halle as mere '*ex cathedra* pronouncement[s], for which no justification is offered' (1965, p. 111). The arguments presented here are therefore offered in dissociation from all such previous versions, and must stand or fall on their merits.

are similar to forms historical linguists postulate for Proto-Slavic, and the rules which we require mirror sound changes which occurred in the development of Proto-Slavic to OCS (1966b, pp. 23–4).

Presumably he also realizes that his similarity 'strictly synchronic' description of Modern Russian relates in much the same way to Proto-Slavic. So Lightner *knows* the history. The question is, can we accept that he was not influenced by this knowledge as he went about formulating his generative analysis, which so conveniently conforms to historical fact? In other words, would some other generative grammarian, unfamiliar with the history of Slavic (or even of Indo-European, let us say) have also posited *two high lax vowels* to take care of what is essentially an o ~ e ~ ø alternation in Modern Russian? I tend to doubt it.

This question is directly related to the one first introduced in 3.1 under the rubric of 'an inductive requirement on grammars'. Lightner himself states the main issue involved here:

In formulating (or evaluating) a synchronic description of a language, the only facts that can be brought to bear are the primary linguistic data of that language at one point in its history. . . A synchronic description must account for the facts of a single language at one point in the history of that language, with no reference to other languages or to historically earlier forms of the language under investigation. [This is because a synchronic grammar is supposed to be] a reflection of the native speaker's ability to produce and understand grammatical utterances, to distinguish between grammatical and ungrammatical utterances, to differentiate between more, and less, grammatical utterances and to place interpretations on some un-grammatical utterances. . . *Since native speakers normally know neither the Proto-forms of their language nor the corresponding forms in related languages, a grammar of a language which uses such diachronic/comparative information is not a true reflection of the native speaker's internalized knowledge of his language* (1967, p. 51; italics added).

Despite difficulties of this sort – all of which relate ultimately to the fact that 'the transmission of language is discontinuous, and a language is recreated [or, in Chomsky's terms, "reinvented" (1968a, p. 75)] by each child on the basis of the speech data it hears' (Kiparsky, 1968b, p. 175) – we still find the view expressed that 'there is every reason to believe that diachronic and synchronic studies in phonology have an intimate symbiotic relation with each other' (Wang, 1968, p. 705).[1]

[1] Wang also discusses, but dissociates himself from, an even stronger position involving what he calls 'the principle of historical realism', which literally 'requires us to choose that set of phonological rules which most faithfully recapitulates the historical events which actually occurred' (pp. 704–6), and Stankiewicz (a Jakobsonian) also expresses the view that the 'typological and diachronic *generality*' of a proposed set of synchronic rules is an important factor in its evaluation (1966, p. 501), though he does not say why.

Now this is obviously an important claim and directly relevant to the issue at hand for, clearly, if some close relation between synchrony and diachrony could be established – despite the discontinuity in the transmission of language from one generation to another (or even if some plausible case could be made for the *possibility* of such a close relation) – this would go a long way towards justifying the use of historical information by the linguist in formulating his synchronic linguistic descriptions, at least as a *temporary exigency* (something like the dictatorship of the proletariat, perhaps). The rationale might go like this: (1) the linguist's main problem (at present) is that he finds himself at a disadvantage in relation to his hypothetical ('content') child who 'knows' (in some sense of the term) all the linguistic universals, whereas the linguist is still in the process of discovering them; thus the linguist is forced to hypothesize; yet (2) if we are able to make the case that Wang's assertion is correct, so that, in consequence, the grammars which are internalized by children in learning a language will (despite compelling arguments against it) reflect far more of the historical development of that language than previously imagined; then (3) the linguist might reasonably inquire whether a synchronic grammar might not be written which was consistent both with the known facts of language change and the hypothesized set of linguistic universals with which the child is presumed to be operating. If such a grammar could be formulated, under such circumstances, this would be a distinct plus for the theory; in fact, provided the case made under step (2) was good, the possible development of such a grammar might be one means of confirming or refuting certain of the putative universals previously postulated.

Let us therefore look at the theory of language change as it has developed within the transformational-generative framework and inquire whether such a line of argument has any substance in it.

4.5.2.2 *The Chomsky–Halle–Kiparsky–Postal theory of language change.*

It has long been recognized that language change (and, in particular, sound change) is a slow, essentially imperceptible, apparently discrete ('sudden') and, most importantly, regular process. These factors have all posed serious problems for research, and all, notably the last two, have proved highly resistant to satisfactory explanation. That is, though historical linguists over the past 200 years have satisfactorily established many *facts* of sound change, there have appeared no equally satisfactory accounts of the underlying explanatory *mechanisms*.

One attempt was the neo-grammarian hypothesis, characterized by Bloomfield as involving 'merely the habits of articulating speech-sounds' (1933, p. 363), such that phonetic change could be pictured as 'a gradual favoring of some non-distinctive variants and a disfavoring of others' (p. 365). The proposed mechanism was thus one of phonetic 'drift' (Sapir, 1921, p. 150). But there was no explanatory principle involved here; for, while it was reasonable to assume that language change might have its origin in the range of individual variations, it was never clear how only those variations prevailed which moved in *certain directions*, i.e. how 'random phenomena,...moving backward and forward in purposeless flux' could reduce to a specific set of directed movements (Sapir, 1921, p. 155).[1] If language change arose from random variations, language change should itself be random – yet it is not. It is regular. The apparently discrete or 'sudden' characteristics of sound change is also left unexplained by the theory.

Halle's monumental 1962 paper, however, put the whole matter into an entirely new perspective. He supposed, first of all, that since such considerations as the innovative aspect of language use compel us to think that internalized grammars consist of ordered sets of statements called 'rules', then 'differences among grammars are due to one or both of the following: (a) different grammars may contain different rules; (b) different grammars may have differently ordered rules' (p. 343). In short, he supposed, first of all, that language change was *rule* change (see also Postal, 1968). This immediately accounted for the regularities. And as the theory developed, a notion of two fundamentally different *types* of rule change gradually emerged, one involving the simple addition, loss or reordering of rules, the second involving rather their restructuring or 'simplification' (Kiparsky, 1968b, p. 175). It was also suggested that this fundamental distinction might then be related to the one between adult and child language acquisition, respectively, under the assumption that the maturing adult loses the ability to re-structure his grammar in the most general way, and resorts to some less drastic procedure such as appending a few 'patch-up' rules to his grammar and/or re-ordering some of the rules he already has.[2] In short, the

---

[1] As Sapir readily admits, the general drift of language cannot be understood, but 'rather apprehended, for we do not, in sober fact, entirely understand it as yet' (1921, p. 155, n. 8).

[2] There is some evidence to suggest that the apparent deterioration of the capacity for language acquisition after puberty may have a psychological basis (see especially Lenneberg, 1966 and 1967).

adult becomes fixed in his linguistic ways and eventually loses the ability to restructure his grammar significantly, whereas the child, a generation later, is not so handicapped and proceeds to construct an optimal grammar to account for the utterances produced by his parents. Since the grammar which underlies the adult's utterances is thus somewhat more complex than the grammar induced by the child on the basis of these utterances, we would expect, in time, that the child would eventually produce some novel forms consistent with his own grammar but at odds with his parents'. And such an observed result is (according to the theory) precisely what has been called language change.[1] This is a *slow* process because the mechanism for change (the restructuring of the adult's grammar by the more efficient acquisition devices of the child) operates only across generations. It is an *imperceptible* one because neither the adult nor the child is consciously aware of the other's grammar, but only of the utterances which each produces – and these, for the most part, are compatible with the grammars of both. But most exciting of all, the theory at last affords some plausible explanation of the heretofore completely inexplicable phenomenon of sudden, yet regular, language change, for this is precisely the effect to be expected if a rule is present in some form at time T_1 but absent (or somehow reformulated) at time T_2. (Thus we find children saying *went* and *sang* one day, but *goed* and *singed* the next. See Ervin, 1964.)

Chomsky and Halle return to this theme in chapter 6 of *The Sound Pattern of English*, this time explicitly integrating it into their general theory of grammar, with special emphasis on the point that an 'essential feature' of their theory is that

it includes an evaluation measure which makes it possible to assign values to alternative grammars. It is on the basis of this evaluation measure that a child learning a language chooses one of the grammars...compatible with the fairly restricted body of linguistic data to which he has been exposed. The grammar that a child constructs in learning his native tongue will therefore always be the one that ranks highest in terms of this evaluation measure.

It is easy to see that the addition of a given rule to a grammar G_1 may result in a grammar G_2 that produces the same linguistic forms as some other grammar G_3 yet is ranked lower than G_3 by the evaluation measure. We shall assume that when the language of adults undergoes such a change, their grammar is modified only by the addition of the rule in question. When the children of these adults learn their native language from their parents, they will construct for themselves the highest ranking grammar G_3, which in

[1] See Halle (1962, pp. 344–5) for the original formulation of this theory and King (1969) for a detailed illustrative treatment of it.

principle may be quite different from G_2, the grammar of the parents. [Thus] children and parents may have quite different grammars though speaking all but identical idiolects... (p. 251)

Of special importance to our discussion here are the following remarks from this same section:

> In the traditional approach to sound change, a 'sound law' is an observed correspondence between two stages of a language, a formula expressing the relationship between the phonological representation of formatives before and after the change. The effects of a change, therefore, are incorporated directly into the lexical representations of individual formatives [or morphemes, in my terms – BLD]. In our approach, on the other hand, a rule that is added to the grammar may continue to function for many generations *without causing changes in the lexical representations* (Chomsky & Halle, 1968, pp. 250–1; italics added).

So here we have it: a theory of language change which, by implication, justifies the use of historical information by the linguist in formulating his analysis (and, in particular, in positing lexical representations for morphemes), since it is a prediction of the theory that certain aspects of the grammar (such as these base forms) are going to change very slowly (if at all) through time.[1] Thus if we assume that a theory of language change, formulated roughly along the lines indicated above, may be incorporated as an essential part of (transformational-generative) linguistic theory, it becomes clear how knowing the history of the language might allow one 'to formulate hypotheses concerning the nature of underlying forms and the types of phonological changes still operative in the contemporary language' (Schane, 1968, p. 141), so justifying the linguist's taking historical information into consideration in analysis, even though it is obvious that the child may not do so in acquisition.[2]

But all this is of no possible consequence to the child:

> The fact that the children of each generation in learning their language take a fresh look at the facts means that there is reason for underlying representations to be transmitted *only when the synchronic facts of the language warrant it* (Kiparsky, 1968b, p. 187; italics added).

[1] See Kiparsky (1968b, p. 175) for an illustration of how some language change might conceivably take place, given this theoretical framework, and yet all but a 'tiny corner' of the vocabulary be unaffected insofar as their underlying representations are concerned.

[2] So Chafe remarks: 'I believe we can say with some assurance that historical changes leave effects in a language which are most adequately described through rules that recapitulate those changes as well as (within limits) their order' (1968b, p. 596).

From the *child's* point of view, that is – despite the rationality of Halle's theory of language change – all that counts are the primary data and whatever guidelines for learning the child has; in itself, the historically more accurate analysis is of no consequence to him. So the linguist's use of such evidence in synchronic description can *only* be justified to the extent that it leads, fortuitously (through the cumulative effects of the mechanisms outlined in Halle's theory), to the correct description of the grammar presumed to be internalized by the child. I shall now attempt to show that the use of such evidence is *not* justified, because Halle's theory is itself no more compelling or plausible than the unusual practice which it serves to support.

4.5.2.3   Weinreich, Labov and Herzog's criticisms and counterproposals. The most telling criticism so far of the Chomsky–Halle–Kiparsky–Postal 'parent-to-child' model of linguistic change (or 'Halle's theory', for short) is presented in an important paper by Weinreich, Labov and Herzog (1968, p. 145), who uncover two important flaws in Halle's original argument. Their first main point develops as follows:

> The image of the parent-to-child relationship as a model for language change is a plausible one, in the context of a structural model based on the study of individuals (or of a 'homogeneous community', which is simply an individual under a group label). Furthermore, it seems clear that children do restructure their grammars not once, but many times, as they mature... *But the model depends upon the unexamined assumption that the children's grammars are formed upon the data provided by their parents' speech.* Yet there is a mounting body of evidence that the language of each child is continually being restructured during his preadolescent years *on the model of his peer group* [rather than of his parents]. Current studies of preadolescent peer groups show that the child normally acquires his particular dialect pattern...from children only slightly older than himself (p. 145, italics added).

This objection strikes at the heart of Halle's theory, which presumes that it is the restructuring of the *adult's* grammar by the more adept language-acquisition device of the child which is the chief mechanism of language change. This theory is strikingly modified if children actually do most of their learning from *one another*. Moreover:

> A further weakness of Halle's model is *the implication that a change is completed within a generation*, the product of a specific relation between parents' and children's grammars. But this implication is not borne out by the empirical evidence of change in progress...These investigations have described *changes that continue in the same direction over several generations* (p. 146, italics added).

According to Halle's theory, such a process would presumably be a product of pure chance (predicated upon the fortuitous presence or absence of certain kinds of utterances in adult speech) and would be expected to be far more the exception than the rule. Yet the phenomenon is quite common.

But Weinreich *et al.* go further. They also offer counterproposals which have important implications for other basic assumptions of trans-formational-generative theory. Their main point of attack is Chomsky's long-standing assumption that language is best seen in terms of 'an ideal speaker–listener, in a completely homogeneous speech-community' (1965a, p. 3). While agreeing with Chomsky that 'this seems...to have been the position of the founders of modern general linguistics', the authors disagree with his further statement that 'no cogent reason for modifying it has been offered' (1965a, pp. 3–4). For the picture which they find emerging as a result of their sociolinguistic investigations is that 'deviations from a homogeneous system are not all errorlike vagaries of performance, but are to a high degree coded and part of a realistic description, of the competence of a member of a speech community' (Weinreich *et al.*, 1968, p. 125). The authors thus build their theory directly on the once popular notion that any individual is simultaneously the master of several different dialects, styles, registers, etc.,[1] citing a now largely-forgotten article by Fries and Pike (1949) as one of the first which 'raised the possibility that systematicity and variability were not mutually exclusive' (Weinreich *et al.*, 1968, p. 160). Fundamental to their theory of language change, then, is the basic assumption that, contrary to Chomsky's presuppositions, language is best viewed as a 'differentiated' or 'heterogeneous' system (p. 150) and that 'the heterogeneous character of the linguistic systems...is the product of combinations, alternations, or mosaics of distinct, jointly available subsystems' (p. 165). As they see it, then, such a

multilayer conception of language, initiated by Mathesius and Jakobson in Prague, developed by Fries and Pike in America, and currently applied more systematically to sociolinguistic studies by Gumperz, has opened new horizons for the theory of language change. It replaced the concept of dialect borrowing – in principle a momentary and accidental event – with the concept of *style switching* – in principle a durative and recurrent phenomenon. It thus made unnecessary the abortive search (envisaged, e.g., by Paul and

---

[1] Cf. Bloomfield (1933, p. 476): 'At any moment, [the language of a given speaker] is a unique composite of habits acquired from various people.'

Bloomfield) after pure dialects undergoing change without interference (p. 164).

The mechanism of language change which they propose is therefore as follows:

It is suggested that a linguistic change begins when one of the many features characteristic of speech variation spreads throughout a specific subgroup of the speech community. This linguistic feature then assumes a certain social significance – symbolizing the social values associated with that group... Because the linguistic change is embedded in the linguistic structure, it is gradually generalized to other elements of the system. Such generalization is far from instantaneous, and change in the social structure of the community normally intervenes before the process is completed. New groups enter the speech community and re-interpret the on-going linguistic change in such a way that one of the secondary changes becomes primary... The advancement of the linguistic change to completion may be accompanied by a rise in the level of social awareness of the change and the establishment of a social stereotype. Eventually, the completion of the change and the shift of the variable to the status of a constant is accompanied by the loss of whatever social significance the feature possessed (pp. 186–7).

Thus 'linguistic change begins when the generalization of a particular alternation in a given subgroup of the speech community assumes direction and takes on the character of orderly differentiation' (p. 187).

To my mind, the theory outlined in this section gives a more plausible picture of what actually happens when a language changes – and without flying in the face of empirical evidence. But it does so at the expense of one of the most fundamental and cherished of all the assumptions of the transformational-generative framework: the assumption of a completely homogeneous speech community (cf. 2.3 above).[1] In exploring a side issue related to one potential defect in the methodology of transformational grammar (the use of historical information in synchronic description), we have inadvertently uncovered another example of the sort of trap into which over-axiomatization and oversimplification can lead. For the sort of theory of language change which Weinreich, Labov and Herzog propose would have been inconceivable from the standpoint of any strict transformational-generative orientation, since

---

[1] And in support of Householder's contention that it is neither 'possible nor wise' – and, what's more, 'counter-intuitive', as well – 'to put all the structural information there is about a given language into a single set of ordered rules' (1965, p. 18). It is strange that the idea of co-existent systems should ever have been abandoned in favor of any such 'all-in-one-blow' notion of generative grammar, since something like the old Fries–Pike co-existent-system concept must surely be maintained in *any* case in order to handle the phenomena of bilingualism and multilingualism.

the *basic mechanism* of change outlined in this proposal – specifically, that 'native command of [a] language includes the control of... heterogeneous structures' (Weinreich *et al.*, 1968, p. 188) – is *axiomatized away* in the Chomskyan approach as involving variables which are insignificant. Thus the rigid transformationalist could presumably *never* have been led to the conclusion that 'not all variability and heterogeneity in language structure involves change; but *all change involves variability and heterogeneity*' (Weinreich *et al.*, 1968, p. 188; italics added).

4.5.3   The problem of lexical identity. To return now to our main theme (the legitimacy of the use of historical information in synchronic analysis), we find there is another area in which historical considerations find their way into linguists' grammars, though in a more subtle manner; in this instance it is difficult to imagine how even a revised theory of language change might fill the breach. I am speaking of the unwarranted assumption that the facts of morpheme relatedness (or identity) are known in advance to the analyst and/or the child. For it must be recognized that more is involved in establishing base forms in a phonological analysis than the 'phonetic facts' alone, as the oversimplified models in 4.4 above suggest. In particular, as is evident from even a cursory examination of Chomsky and Halle (1968), for example, the analysis presented there is predicated upon the implicit and (virtually) unchallenged assumption that there is some synchronic relationship between forms like *reciprocal–reciprocity* (p. 168), *various–variety* (p. 179), *profane–profanity* (p. 184), *fable–fabulous* (p. 196), etc., and, as a consequence, the child must be presumed to go about relating them formally in terms of a single common lexical representation, supplemented by a Vowel Shift Rule (among others) of quite general application (and resulting ultimately in the so-called 'synchronic residue of the Great Vowel Shift of Early Modern English' (p. 184)). The synchronic justification for positing such a rule rests directly on the assumption that both the analyst (who has access to historical information which attests to such a set of relationships) and the child (who has no such information at his disposal but must rely solely on such things as *the facts of language use* and *the degree of phonetic similarity between forms* to guide him on the issue of 'relatedness') come to the same set of conclusions with respect to such forms. This is a remarkable assumption. In the first place, it is clear that any *particular* form could be learned as a separate and distinct lexical item; there is no *a priori* necessity that any given number or manner of forms be grammatically related (i.e. related lexically and by means of phonological rules) to any others. In fact, it is even conceivable that *all* words could be learned in this way.[1] Chomsky himself admits as much:

Phonology, as distinct from syntax, is a system that is essentially finite in scope. It would be possible, in principle, for the mapping from surface structure to phonetic representation to be simply memorized, case by case (in particular, each formative or word could be learned as an unstructured set of variants, each associated with its determining context) (1967d, pp. 126–7).

We know, however, that children learning English say such things as 'goed' and 'childs' and so we have good grounds for thinking that children must learn *some* morphological generalizations. But we don't know *which* ones. As a practical matter, we might (and do) assume, in those cases where both the semantic and phonetic similarities between forms are obvious, that we are justified in positing single base form plus one or more rules to associate them. Thus we assume that a child, confronted with a mass of forms which includes such tokens as *play, player, sing, singer, run, runner, dance, dancer, help, helper,* etc., will eventually abandon the attempt to learn each such form individually in favor of the straightforward generalization which runs through this whole list, i.e. a rule which might be symbolized in the following way: N → V + *er* (cf. Lyons, 1968, p. 196). This step both simplifies the child's (and the linguist's) lexicon considerably and provides a mechanism for the creation (prediction) of new forms on this same general pattern: *reader,* ?*studier,* *liker. In this way the creative aspect of language use is involved. But without additional evidence from language acquisition or adult competence (which in this particular case is easily found) we are not justified *a priori* in assuming that this is what must happen on grounds of the obvious transparency of the putative relationships *alone.* And if this is true in the case of transparent relationships, it is all the more true when we move into the fuzzier areas, i.e. when we consider what might be going on in the case of forms where the semantic and/or phonetic similarities between the putative 'variants' are not obvious, and where even adult intuitions, as I have discovered, may vary radically from speaker to speaker and case to case. Consider the structured set of forms in table 1, for example, in which pairs of words

[1] Some assumption of this sort is clearly implicit in those 'heavily redundant' systems of phonological analysis which abandoned the notion of phonological rule altogether (cf. p. 106n above) and which regarded biunique phonemics as the level of representation appropriate to the lexicon (see 6.1 below).

TABLE I

Semantics			
III. OBSCURE	ear–irrigate four–formation wine–whine cold₁–cold₂	idiot–ideology labor–laboratory reside–residue month–menstrual	circle–Ku Klux Klan lead–plumber holy–Halloween moon–menstrual
II. INTERMEDIATE	crypt-cryptic search–research hand–handle fond–fondle ray–radiate	moon–month louse–lousy tame–timid fable–fabulous wild–wilderness	candle–incandescent hand–handkerchief guise–beguile royal–regalia sister–sorority
I. CLEAR	friend–befriend happy–happiness joy–joyous ride–rider sad–sadly	residue–residual save–salvation royal–regal various–variety joke–jocular	milk–lactate brain–cerebral brother–fraternity father–paternalism devil–diabolical
Phonetics	A. CLEAR B. INTERMEDIATE C. OBSCURE		

are graded into blocks according to my own feelings about the relative degree of phonetic similarity (horizontal axis) and semantic similarity (vertical axis) between them.[1]

Notice, first of all, that the problem of determining morphological relationships has both its *qualitative* and *quantitative* aspects. Qualitatively there is, first, the serious problem of having to know *how similar* (semantically and phonetically) two forms have to be before they become potential candidates for analysis within the grammar. The extreme cases seem reasonably clear: class IA above, where everything is transparent all across the board, is 'in' (by assumption);[2] class IIIC, on the other hand, is 'out' (except, perhaps, for the scholar or dilettante who specializes in obscure etymologies). But elsewhere we are not so sure. Class IIIA is especially interesting, as this is where the most glaring (and hence documented) errors of children occur (cf. Sturtevant's well-known 'nosigated' and 'two-mation' examples (1947, pp. 97–8)) and is also the domain of the pun.[3]

[1] No necessary derivational or historical relationships are implied to exist between any of the word-pairs indicated.

[2] Though my daughter Elizabeth, for example, was nearly four years old before she noted (to her delighted surprise) that even 'oranges' and 'orange juice' had anything in common! Also see Engel (1970, p. 18).

[3] Many of the pairs in classes IIC and IC, it is worth noting, might not be learned until quite late. I myself did not know the etymology of many of these words before I

Even if the qualitative difficulty could be quantified in some non-arbitrary way (i.e. even if sharp boundaries could be set up on the basis of the degree of semantic and phonetic similarity in a pair of forms), we would still be left with an equally imposing quantitative difficulty. How *many* forms, we must now ask, of the requisite degree of semantic-phonetic correspondence, are required in order to establish a pattern (for the child) or justify (for the linguist) the restructuring of the lexicon in favor of a new rule? Two forms (one pair) would presumably not be enough, as a rule in this case would seemingly only complicate the grammar (since two lexical entries would be necessary in either case).[1] How about three? (e.g. *play, player, mayor*). Two pairs would seem to be about the minimum (*play–player, run–runner*). But what if the child hears these forms several days apart? Will he still make the association? Will he even remember the earlier forms? We no more know the answers to these questions than to any of the others. Yet, strangely enough, we still presume to perform morphological analysis.[2]

So when we read that one important reason for preferring the abstract generative analysis such as Chomsky and Halle's of English or Lightner's of Russian is that only such analyses can 'show the correct relationships between the forms' (Lightner, 1967, p. 53), implying that alternative neo-taxonomic analyses fail in that they obscure certain (synchronic) morphological relationships (cf. Lightner, 1966b, pp. 23ff, and Foster, 1966, pp. 142, 182), we may take such remarks with a

started college, e.g. *sorority, lactate, cerebral, fraternity, paternalism*, etc. If they are related with their more familiar counterparts for me now, it is only because my early years in college forced this awareness upon me.

This has some interesting implications for the compatibility of Halle's proposed theory of language change (see 4.5.2.2 above) with the theory of phonological description set forth in Chomsky & Halle (1968). On the one hand, Chomsky and Halle admit that many of the linguistic forms which they use to justify the postulation of various of their rules (in particular, the Vowel Shift Rule) 'belong to a more learned stratum of vocabulary' and, as a consequence, 'are, in general, available to the child [*sic*] only at a fairly late stage in his language acquisition' (1968, p. 332). But, according to Halle's theory of language change, if such forms come along *too* late in this development, they will be of no use for the purposes for which Chomsky and Halle use them, namely, to construct an *optimal* grammar of English; for according to Halle, once puberty is reached the child loses the ability to construct such a grammar and the forms would presumably have to be tacked on as exceptions, as in an adult's grammar. We are not very far from a contradiction here.

[1] Taking *play* and *player* as an example, the competing solutions contrast a lexicon having both words entered as single unanalyzed items as opposed to a second lexicon which contains the morphemes *play* and *-er* and which is further supplemented by a rule of the sort $N \rightarrow V +$ Derivational Affix.

[2] See Bolinger (1948 and 1950) for other interesting examples and comments.

grain of salt. For who is to say that, synchronically speaking, such morphological relationships are *not* obscure to begin with? The very existence of folk etymologies is proof enough (if any proof were needed) that such is often the case.[1] Furthermore, we know that false or 'unsuccessful' analogies are formulated by children in the process of language acquisition itself, i.e. many morphological relationships tentatively established by the child are not 'correct' from the adult's standpoint (see Hockett, 1968b, pp. 89ff, for examples in English and Čukovskij, 1961, for examples in Russian). Failure to recognize true (diachronic) morphological relationships is thus part and parcel of (synchronic) language acquisition and contributes to the process of language change itself. The cart of theory, it seems, is tending to get progressively farther and farther ahead of the horse of relevant data.

4.5.4   Other anomalies of generative phonology. A related, and equally disturbing, development in current phonological theory is that underlying representations for morphemes appear to be getting more and more like their conventional orthographic ones (especially in English and French, as in Chomsky and Halle, 1968, and Schane, 1968, respectively). This is justified by Chomsky and Halle (1968) as follows:

There is...nothing particularly surprising about the fact that conventional orthography is...a near optimal system for the lexical representation of English words. The fundamental principle of orthography is that phonetic variation is not indicated where it is predictable by general rule. Thus, stress placement and regular vowel or consonant alternations are generally not reflected. Orthography is a system designed for readers who know the language...[and who therefore] can produce the correct phonetic forms, given the orthographic representation and the surface structure, by means of the rules that they employ in producing and interpreting speech. It would be quite pointless for the orthography to indicate these predictable variants. Except for unpredictable variants (e.g. *man–men, buy–bought*), an optimal orthography

---

[1] In fact, what *is* (legitimate) synchronic morphemic analysis, after all, if it is not 'folk analysis'? (cf. Malone, 1970, p. 333). As Hocket has argued, '*ALL* morphemic analysis is in a sense folk-analysis, and one might suspect that the identifications thus arrived at [by the "folk", not by the linguist – *BLD*] would be *as valid as any the modern analyst might discover*' (1950, p. 84; italics added). This is not to say that a good morphemic analysis can be arrived at simply by *asking* naive native speakers what the facts of morpheme relatedness are; such an approach, as Bloomfield pointed out, will yield only 'inconsistent or silly answers' (1933, p. 208), as in syntax, phonology and all the rest. For like so much else in language, morphemic (folk) analysis is typically performed by the language learner at a subconscious level, and experimental techniques and controls would have to be devised to draw out any such grammatical 'knowledge' (see 9.2.2 for further discussion).

would have one representation for each lexical entry...[Conventional orthographic systems] are designed for the use of speakers of the language. It is therefore noteworthy, but not too surprising, that English orthography, despite its often cited inconsistencies, comes remarkably close to being *an optimal orthographic system for English* (p. 49, italics added).

The orthographies of Russian and Old Church Slavonic are interesting and notable exceptions, if Lightner's work (1965 and 1966a) is authoritative.[1] In these cases, the trend is for base forms to turn away from the traditional orthography and towards some more ancient pseudo-orthography which antedates even Old Church Slavonic (OCS). Consider the following examples (given first in transliterated Russian orthography, next in transliteration from OCS and finally in terms of Lightner's proposed *underlying* representations for Russian):

Russ ŽIT'   OCS ŽITI   Russ base form $°/g\bar{\imath}u + t\bar{\imath}°/$
Russ MOLČAT'   OCS MILČATI   Russ base form $°/milk + \bar{e} + t\bar{\imath}°/$
Russ LOVLJU   OCS LOVLJǪ   Russ base form $°/lou + \bar{\imath} + \bar{\imath} + m°/$
Russ SLYŠAT'   OCS SLYŠĘTU   Russ base form $°/sl\bar{u}x + \bar{e} + \bar{\imath} + n + tu°/$

Thus the conventional orthographies for neither of these languages are conservative enough for Lightner (although the OCS orthography dates from the tenth century) in that both, first of all, specify certain consonantal segments (such as the palatals *č*, *š*, *ž* from underlying velars and *v* from an underlying $°/u°/$) and vowel segments (such as *a* from underlying $°/\bar{e}°/$ and *y* from underlying $°/\bar{u}°/$) which Lightner finds predictable by general rule from some more abstract basic representations and, secondly, they specify certain other segments (such as the nasals in the last two forms and the high lax vowels $°/\check{\imath}°/$ and $°/\check{u}°/$ – see pp. 102, 108 above) which Lightner argues are deleted by general rule once they have introduced certain concomitant phonetic affects. In short, these orthographies fail in that they specify 'predictable' phonetic information in many forms, rather than the 'correct' underlying segments from which this information can be predicted.

From the generative grammarian's point of view, therefore, while English orthography presents a 'near optimal system' for the lexical representation of English words, Russian orthography is less efficient in this regard for Russian. But if this is so, we are faced with a strange anomaly: why do the problems encountered by English-speaking children in learning their own 'near optimal' spelling system (in which the

[1] Lightner's analysis of the Russian vowel system is cited by Chomsky and Halle (1968, p. 379), and presumably has their approval.

orthographic representation of morphemes *corresponds very closely* to their abstract lexical representations in a generative grammar) *far* outweigh the minimal difficulties which the typical Russian child appears to have in learning to spell Russian (where the orthography *diverges greatly* from Lightner's level of lexical representation, and parallels instead the less abstract morphophonemic representation of the sort proposed by Jakobson)? For there is no question, really, that spelling (*pravopisanie*) is of marginal, even peripheral, interest in the Soviet school system, whereas it constitutes an area of considerable difficulty in our own schools. Are we to presume that Russians are vastly superior intellectually to their English-speaking counterparts? For English speakers seem to have more difficulty when it comes to 'spelling pronunciations', as well – a marginal problem for the Russian, an almost insurmountable problem for some of my English-speaking acquaintances. Furthermore, if stress is predictable in English to the extent which Chomsky and Halle (1968) claim it is (see especially chapter 3 of their book), and if it is also true for native speakers of English that they 'can produce the correct phonetic forms, given the orthographic representation and the surface structure' (p. 49), why have I had so much difficulty all my life in learning the proper stress of new English words, given *both* the spelling (and hence a close approximation to their ideal lexical representation) and the syntactic context – and even knowing the meaning – of these words? Does this make me a non-native speaker – or are Chomsky and Halle perhaps wrong?

We encounter parallel anomalies when we look at the claims which Lightner's grammar makes about Russian. One of the more important is that all palatals are predictably derived from underlying velars (except those which participate in a palatal–dental alternation) before front vowels or jod (Lightner, 1965, pp. 18ff). Thus we have the implied claim that the velar–palatal alternation constitutes a general, active, or (to use traditional terms) 'living' and perfectly 'productive' process in the language. But if this is so, why does this rule *never* apply to foreign loan-words (nor has it for centuries past). Kennedy, for example, is *kenned'i* in Russian, not *čennei̯ž* (as in some other languages), just as 'kino' came out *k'ino*, 'quinine' as *x'in'in*, etc. In order to handle such forms, Lightner is forced to mark them all with some such diacritic feature as [− Slavic] and so treat them as exceptional (see Chomsky and Halle, 1968, pp. 373–4). But why do *all* such words behave in this 'exceptional' manner? Why are these general, predictable and presumably 'living' processes not also 'productive' to new words which appear in the language? We have here either a contradiction in terms, or else an error. It is distinctly possible that these processes are dead, as traditionally supposed.[1]

---

[1] Since this section was written, an interesting article has appeared in *Language* (L. M. Hyman, 1970) which emphasizes the point merely suggested here: that the study of borrowed forms might be of considerable value in assessing the productivity of proposed phonological rules. In particular, Hyman, dealing with a different language for which the facts about borrowings are unlike Russian, reaches conclusions on more general theoretical issues which are diametrically opposed to mine, and the resulting controversy therefore deserves attention. Some basic issues require discussion before the more important ramifications of such a debate can fruitfully be discussed, so I defer this until pp. 150–1 below.

5 'Explanation' and 'naturalness' in TGG

5.1 On 'explanation' and 'regularity' in generative phonology

In his interview with Sklar, Chomsky remarks at one point that 'really the only innovation I think I introduced into the field [of linguistics] basically was to try to give descriptive explanations – to try to give a theory of the synchronic structure of the language which would actually explain the distribution of phenomena' (Sklar, 1968, p. 215), and, to be sure, this was the great initial attraction of the theory.

But before one can claim to have *explained* something, he must first have some idea what it is incumbent on him to explain.[1] As Caws puts it:

Only the individual can decide which elements of nature as given he chooses to render in the observation language of science, and thus to constitute as candidates for scientific explanation. The public and shared aspects of science and of the philosophy of science are the collective outcome of individual decisions of this sort, and not the other way around (1965, pp. 329–30).

The most straightforward statement along these lines by Chomsky is perhaps found in Hill (1962): 'The empirical data that I want to explain are the native speaker's intuitions' (p. 158) which 'I believe...are what everyone studies' (p. 167). This early methodological decision led directly to interpreting linguistic competence as what a native speaker (in some obscure sense) 'knows' about his language (cf. 7.4 below), and most work in transformational-generative syntax is consistent with this approach. But it is not so clear that this is the case in generative phonology, for this is an area where few intuitions are presumed to exist (certainly both 'base forms' and 'rules' are out, and there really isn't much left; cf. pp. 109–10 above). What has evolved instead is the notion

---

[1] This point is emphasized by Postal, who takes Martinet and his followers to task for failing 'to perceive those aspects of language which are truly fundamental and most in need of an explanation' (1966, p. 155).

that it is *forms* (i.e. the phonetic representations of utterances), together with certain of their presumed interrelationships, which the phonological component of the grammar must explain. This is apparently supposed to be obvious, for little explicit mention is made of it, though we do have this unequivocal statement of Lightner's:

De Saussure's conclusion ([that various forms of a word] 'can be explained only historically, by relative chronology') is *wrong*; the forms *must* be explained historically (as De Saussure explained them) *and also synchronically* (1966b, p. 25, n. 42; italics added).

Well, why?

First, it is obvious that any given utterance (from word to phrase to sentence to poem to song to narrative) can simply be memorized and (from the linguist's point of view) stored as a distinct and unanalyzed separate lexical item.[1] And for any such form no kind of 'synchronic explanation' is required or appropriate (except in the broad psychological sense of explaining how people memorize things in general). On the other hand, we have reason to believe that not all utterances are learned in this way – or, better, that they do not remain *stored* in this way, i.e. as individual items – since it seems clear that language behavior is (to some extent, at least) innovative. But the crux of the matter is that we really have very little idea of *just what this extent is*. Various linguistic schools have implied a variety of claims about this – there is, in fact, a fundamental distinction between TGG and all earlier models with regard to what each claims to be 'true suppletion' as opposed to the 'general', the 'regular' or the 'rule-governed' – but there are almost no empirical studies which give a clear idea of where the lexicon ends and the rules begin (see 9.2.1 below). Yet from any rational point of view, it is only this (unknown) proportion of words which are *not* learned as separate lexical items which *must* (or even *should*) be explained in terms of a synchronic grammar.

The generative approach seems to be quite different. I infer from reading Chomsky and Halle (1968) and Lightner (1965) something more like this: 'The forms which must be explained in a synchronic grammar are precisely those which are *demonstrably related historically* and which *can be related in a grammar*, given some initial set of metatheoretical

---

[1] My daughter Elizabeth could recite an enormous repertoire of songs by the age of two, though she obviously understood hardly a word (she could sing one French and one Russian song with equal facility, not knowing another word in either language). And, in general, children do appear to have a remarkable facility for rote memorization or lexical storage.

assumptions.'[1] Having accomplished this, one is in a position to say that he has a more 'descriptively adequate' (or 'empirically supported') grammar than his competitors on the ground that he has managed to 'explain' a greater number of variety of forms. Meanwhile, the essential empirical question involved has been shoved under the rug. For it is not the *number* or *variety* of forms 'explained' which is important, but rather which forms are actually learned as unanalyzed wholes (as part of a 'lexicon' or 'list') and which are reconstituted instead on the basis of some particular set of learned general principles (or 'rules'). Chomsky has axiomatized away this empirical issue and substituted in its place an arbitrary principle of evaluation which might be called *the principle of maximum regularity*, which states that the 'best' grammar or linguistic description is the one which involves or 'captures' the greatest degree of regularity (or, conversely, which leaves behind the fewest 'exceptions', i.e. distinct lexical entries).[2] By the same token, the best system of metatheoretical constraints is that which *allows* the analyst to capture the greatest amount of such regularity.[3] But if any interesting sense is to be made of the notion 'amount of regularity' in language, we must surely be speaking of something like the proportion of rule-governed activity in the native speaker, relative to that of rote recall – and no such proportion can be established by the adoption of any arbitrary principle. We are dealing with an *empirical* question, a matter of *fact* – and hence a matter for *discovery*, not fiat. Chomsky's stated preference for maximum regularity or generality, therefore, is inappropriate as a criterion in this context.

We now have to reconsider some arguments advanced in the previous

---

[1] Since the metatheoretical assumptions are subject to revision, this directive boils down to a simple condition of exclusion: 'Explain all those forms you possibly can – except those which we know (though the child doesn't know) are *not* historically related.' The fewer 'exceptions' (distinct lexical entries) in a grammar, the better – and the more psychologically valid it is! This is very strange, especially in the light of n. 1, on p. 131 above.

[2] Chomsky stated his intentions clearly enough in 1958, but has never, to my knowledge, been seriously challenged on this point: 'What you expect when you describe a language is a *large* area of very systematic behavior, and a certain residue around the edges. If someone says of my description that this doesn't fit, and this, and this, I would say that it is not a very interesting comment. If on the other hand he says that the exceptions *can fit* into a different pattern, *that is of the highest importance* (in Hill, 1962, p. 32; italics added).

[3] Cf. Lakoff, who argues that once rules are formulated which enable the analyst 'to explain deep facts about language' (whatever *they* are!), then 'there is every reason to believe whatever methodological assumptions are necessary in order *to permit one to state such rules*' (1969, p. 120; italics added).

chapter in favor of Lightner's generative analysis of Russian phonology over and above Jakobson's more traditional 'neo-taxonomic' approach. I argued on p. 97, for example, that Lightner's analysis of the Russian verb seemed superior to Jakobson's on the grounds that Lightner could 'lexically unite a large number of noun and verb forms which Jakobson ...could not' (cf. Lightner, 1967, p. 54). Now we recognize that this point is not *necessarily* significant, for to be significant it would have to be demonstrated that the forms which Lightner's grammar *claims* are lexically united are *in fact* (psychologically) so identified in the minds of native speakers.[1] In the absence of any such demonstration, Lightner simply has no empirical basis for preferring his 'abstract form of grammar' on the ground that it allows him 'to make explicit the correct [*sic*] relationships existing among forms which within other theoretical frameworks could be related only by *ad hoc*, unmotivated rules' (1967, p. 54).

But, surely, the reader might argue, Chomsky, Halle, Lightner, and the other generative phonologists do at least provide 'a kind of "explanation"' (Schachter, 1969, p. 342), do they not? No doubt. The *logical* framework, at any rate, is all there: the forms involved *are* subsumed under a set of broader generalizations. But *descriptive* explanations (like those found in the physical sciences) and *genetic* explanations (like those of history) – not to mention *pseudo*-explanations – are all statable in essentially the same *deductive-nomological* form (see Hempel, 1968). To determine the true nature of any proposed set of 'explanations', more is required than simply to note the *logical structure* of the line of argument presented. In particular, before one can expect his proposed explanatory system to be accepted, he must supply good reasons for believing that the underlying hypotheses (or generalizations) are *true* (cf. Hempel, 1966, pp. 55ff).[2] And, from a synchronic (or psychological) point of view, the so-called 'descriptive explanations' of generative phonology (which involve the postulation of 'underlying forms' which seem unreal and 'general processes' which seem dead) must be considered mere *pseudo-explanations*, for there is no reason to suppose that they reflect psychological reality at all. To the extent that such 'descriptive explanations' do reflect historical developments, however, what seems to be involved is the restatement of the familiar (and psychologically *ir*rele-

[1] Nor is this an argument in favor of Jakobson's analysis; by the same token, Jakobson would have to demonstrate that those forms which he *cannot* unite lexically are *not* so related psychologically, etc.
[2] See 7.2.2 below for further discussion.

vant) 'diachronic' or 'historical' explanations of an earlier era, now formalized and recast under a new name.[1] Under this latter interpretation, most of the problems discussed in the previous chapter fall neatly into place. The extremely abstract base forms which appear in them are *counter-intuitive* because they represent not psychological reality, but long-lost and long-forgotten etymons of these forms. Many of the processes offered as being of 'general application' within the language are *not productive* in neologisms and new borrowings because they are no longer active processes, but accomplished historical changes which have restructured the lexicon in such a way that once-clear etymological relationships are now obscured (and a former lexical identity thereby lost). As a direct consequence, English orthography, being notoriously conservative, fails to reflect many of these lexical restructurings and is therefore *difficult to learn* by speakers of the modern language; Russian orthography, on the other hand, having undergone thorough modernization as recently as 1917–18, reflects more of these changes and is therefore easier to learn by contemporary speakers.

Much the same can be said of the second main argument in favor of Lightner's analysis, that only he was able to 'deal with a number...of hitherto completely baffling anomalies of Russian phonology' (p. 97 above). But on the reasonable assumption that these anomalies have been introduced into the language as the result of historical change, it is not surprising that a more-or-less accurate recapitulation of the history of the development of Russian phonology (such as Lightner's) *should* explain them. The correct *historical* explanations of these phenomena are not at issue, but rather the question whether or not Lightner's proposed analysis has any *synchronic* or *psychological* significance.[2] It is circular to argue that, because the correct historical explanations can be formalized, they must be psychologically valid as well, on the ground that they 'explain' anomalies which are themselves among the products of historical change. As in the previous case, it must first be asked whether the anomalies in question *require* explanation in any synchronic sense, and to know this we must know how the native speaker actually interprets such things as the strange behavior of the Russian /v/, for

[1] Chomsky has said himself that his notion of 'descriptive explanation' was originally 'very self-consciously modeled on the kinds of explanations that people gave in historical linguistics' (in Sklar, 1968, p. 215).

[2] As Chomsky himself says, 'If you want to describe history, you describe history. If you want to describe what the native thinks, you describe what the native thinks. They are different subjects' (in Hill, 1962, p. 63).

instance. Does he interpret this as an anomaly or as an 'explainable' phenomenon? Traditionally, Russian *linguists* have thought the phenomenon anomalous, and we have good reason for thinking that the child learning Russian might be as baffled by it as linguists have been. If so, we would expect him to make the same *ad hoc* adjustments in his internalized schema for language in order to accommodate such forms as the taxonomically-oriented linguist would. If the child is in *fact* unsophisticated in his approach to language acquisition, why attribute sophistication to him? Does the linguist describe what is true, or what he would like to think is true? Empirical truths are established by *getting the facts*.[1]

5.2 On 'simplicity' and 'naturalness' in generative phonology

The third argument in favor of generative phonological analysis was that only within its framework did it seem possible to formulate phonological rules which seemed phonetically plausible or 'natural'. Jakobson, for example, in restricting himself to the set of base forms permitted by his proposed discovery procedure, was forced to describe the ov-uj and resonant-null alternations (see pp. 93 and 99 above, respectively) and the phenomenon of transitive softening (see Jakobson, 1948, pp. 160–1) in an *ad hoc* and essentially taxonomic way (i.e. in terms of highly restricted rules which operated either in very artificial phonological environments or in terms of specific morpheme sub-classes). Lightner, however, was able to devise alternative analyses within the general framework of TGG which abrogated the imposition of such 'artificial' constraints on the abstractness of underlying lexical representations and in which the phenomena in question could be described as the result of an ordered sequence of highly general and 'natural' rules (i.e. in terms of rules which applied only to very 'natural' classes of segments within a highly constrained set of 'natural' phonological environments; see pp. 95–9 above). So Lightner's approach alone seemed compatible

---

[1] The arguments above illustrate a more general difficulty which underlies virtually all problems in TGG: although Chomsky has committed himself (and linguistics) to a psychological (or 'mentalistic') domain in principle – a salutary step – he has (apart from a commitment to the marginal sub-domain of 'linguistic intuitions') failed to consider evidence from that domain in evaluating his proposals. He relies instead on purely abstract principles of evaluation – such as 'generality' (= 'regularity') and 'simplicity'. Hence his claims about 'psychological reality' and 'empirical significance' are unsupported and will remain so until these notional criteria are either substantiated or supplanted by independent psychological investigation (see 7.2.3 below).

with any 'demonstrable scheme of natural universal constraints' which might unify linguistics.

And, indeed, it is in phonological theory that the close connection between linguistic descriptions in transformational-generative terms and Chomsky's hypothesis concerning innate linguistic universals can probably best be seen. It is Chomsky's main belief, we recall, that among the inborn apparatus which the child brings to language-learning is a detailed specification of 'what is common to all languages', hence, for Chomsky,

a certain schematism, a set of abstract formal conditions of a highly restrictive sort that *sets strict limits* on the choice of deep structures, surface structures, the transformational rules that interrelate them, the phonetic and semantic rules that interpret them (in Sklar, 1968, p. 214; italics added).

More specifically, this innate specification is assumed to be manifested in two supplementary ways: first, in a set of *universal formal constraints* which define the notion of 'possible' entity in a grammar and, secondly, by a set of *evaluation measures* which allow the child (as well as the linguist) to choose among these permissible entities (structures, forms, rules) those most appropriate to a given body of primary data. In generative phonology, these two broad assumptions have hardened into a fairly elaborate sub-theory of 'naturalness' or 'simplicity' in phonological description.

The association of these two notions within the framework of phonological theory was given its first detailed expression in Halle (1962). Here the proposal was made that the evaluation metric for phonological descriptions ought to be expressed in much the same terms as the set of formal constraints (thus to some extent obliterating the distinction), that is, in terms of 'the form of the statements admitted in such grammars' (p. 334), which is to say in terms of the specific symbols and abbreviatory or other notational devices employed in the formalization of grammars. In particular, it was proposed that these notational devices might be developed and employed in such a way that in all clear cases the most general statement would always be expressible in the smallest number of symbols, such that in doubtful cases, where the choice between descriptions in terms of generality was not clear, the simple technique of the symbol count would automatically make the choice. It was then argued that all phonological segments (as well as the rules which apply to them) would have to be expressed in terms of their composite phonetic properties (or features) rather than as unanalyzable (or global) entities. Though Halle's original argument is well known, it will be useful to repeat it here:

Halle argues, in part, that given a language possessing the three front vowels /i/, /e/, /æ/, the hypothetical rule /a/→/æ/ in the environment ___/i/, /e/, /æ/ (i.e. before a front vowel) is obviously a more general (hence 'simpler') statement than the second hypothetical rule /a/→/æ/ in the environment ___/i/ (i.e. before the high front vowel alone). Yet if these rules are expressed in this form (i.e. in terms of unanalyzable symbols), the latter, *less* general statement uses fewer symbols (3) than the former, *more* general statement (5 symbols). Halle concludes that the use of separate, indivisible symbols for each phoneme will not lead to a notation-based simplicity metric of the sort he desires. If the phonemes which participate in these two hypothetical rules are expressed as complexes of features, however, it is clear that the environment of the second rule (before a *high front* vowel) will require more feature specifications than will the environment of the first (before a *front* vowel). Thus if the two rules are expressed in these terms, the more general statement will need fewer symbols – the desired result. So, if one wishes to use a notation-based simplicity criterion of the sort proposed, Halle concludes that phonological segments must be regarded as complexes of properties, rather than as indivisible entities, and that all phonological rules should be expressed in feature notation (1962, pp. 336–7).

Halle then extends this newly established convention to define a notion of 'natural class' (p. 337), noting that a class such as /i/, /e/ and /æ/ – the class of front vowels – requires far fewer features for its specification than would some *ad hoc*, unsystematic collection of three random phonemes, such as the class /i/, /p/ and /z/ – the high front vowel, the voiceless bilabial stop, and the voiced dental fricative. At this point there emerges a rudimentary, yet intuitively satisfying, concept of 'naturalness' which receives its direct expression in the formal terms of a linguistic description: 'a set of speech sounds forms a *natural class* if fewer features are required to designate the class [as a whole] than to designate any individual sound in the class' (Halle, 1961, p. 90).[1]

This all seems well and good, perhaps, until one considers how a notational convention of this sort is to be actually used in linguistic

---

[1] Or, in relative terms, a *more* 'natural' (or homogeneous) class of phonological segments (and, similarly, a *more* 'natural' phonological rule) may be defined as one which requires fewer primitive symbols (in this case, phonetic features) for its specification than some *other* arbitrary class or rule which might be compared with it (cf. Chomsky & Halle, 1965, p. 122).

description. For it is, as advertised, to be employed as an *evaluation device* by which to determine the relative *adequacy* of one proposed solution (description) of a linguistic phenomenon as compared with some other; that is, if a description D_1 can be devised which accurately describes a given body of data by means of a set of rules expressible in terms of more natural or homogeneous classes than the rules of some alternative (and otherwise equally acceptable) description D_2, then D_1 is automatically to be preferred as the better (more accurate) model of the competence of the speaker. This surely means that Chomsky, Halle and their fellow transformationalists have incorporated into the formal devices of TGG an *a priori* assumption about the kinds of rules which the minds of children prefer when learning a language: they prefer rules expressible in terms of natural (homogeneous) classes (and which involve phonological environments) and reject rules which are expressible in terms of non-homogeneous classes (or which involve non-phonological environments). We have here one more in the rapidly growing list of transformationalist 'axiomatizations'.

Chomsky and Halle themselves interpret their proposals differently. Chomsky himself insists that 'it must first of all be kept clearly in mind that [an evaluation measure for grammars] is not given *a priori*, in some manner.[1] Rather, *any proposal concerning such a measure is an empirical hypothesis about the nature of language*' (1965a, p. 37; italics added). In fact, this theme is repeated over and over again in the literature:

(1) When we select a set of formal devices for the construction of grammars, we are, in fact, taking an important step toward a definition of the notion 'linguistically significant generalization'. Since *this notion has real empirical content*, our particular characterization of it may or may not be accurate as a proposed explication (Chomsky & Halle, 1968, p. 330; italics added; see also p. 335).

(2) Notice than an evaluation procedure (simplicity measure, as it is often called in technical discussion) is itself an *empirical hypothesis* concerning universal properties of language; it is, in other words, a hypothesis, true or false, about the prerequisites for language-acquisition (Chomsky, 1966b, p. 11; italics added).

(3) We stress once more that choice of an evaluation measure is *an empirical matter*. The problem of discovering an evaluation measure is much like that of evaluating a physical constant. We are given a certain pairing of empirical facts: primary linguistic data D_1 leads to descriptively adequate grammar G_1,

[1] So Chomsky and Halle chide Householder ('along with many others') for muddled thinking along these lines, i.e. for having 'fallen into the unfortunate habit of using the terms "simplicity", "economy", "generality", etc., as if they are somehow clear in advance and require no analysis' (1965, p. 109).

D₂ leads to G₂, etc. One can no more give an A PRIORI argument for a particular evaluation measure than one can for a particular value of the gravitational constant (Chomsky & Halle, 1965, p. 108; italics added; see also p. 114).

So the essential principle which is involved in this issue has been well stated, and I agree with it fully: 'There is no sense of "simplicity" in which [any particular] design for language can be intelligibly described as "most simple" ' (Chomsky, 1967c, p. 7) and hence 'the notion "simplicity of grammar"...[must be established] on empirical grounds, and there is no *a priori* insight on which we can rely' (Chomsky, 1969, p. 85). The question remains, however, whether or not work in generative grammar (and generative phonology in particular) has developed consistently with these principles. In particular, I am especially concerned here with the nature of that empirical evidence which supposedly stands behind the notions of 'simplicity' and 'naturalness' as generally understood in generative grammar.

To begin with, we are told, 'The major problem in constructing an evaluation measure for grammars is that of determining which generalizations about a language are significant ones' (Chomsky, 1965a, p. 42). This is no trivial matter, to be sure. Chomsky goes on to add that 'an evaluation measure must be selected in such a way as to favor these', that is, 'it is necessary to devise notations and to restrict the form of rules in such a way that significant considerations of complexity and generality are converted into considerations of length, so that real generalizations shorten the grammar and spurious ones do not' (p. 42). Fair enough – but no help in solving the first problem, of 'determining which generalizations about language are significant ones', which is the kind of information which would first have to be fed into such a proposed notational system. So how do we *get* such information? Chomsky says only this: we simply choose an evaluation measure which 'constitutes a *decision* as to what are "similar processes" and "natural classes" – in short, what are significant generalizations' (p. 42), that is, we devise a set of notational conventions to be used in presenting a grammar 'that *define* "significant generalization", if the evaluation measure is taken as length' (same page; italics added in both instances). We ask again: how can one resolve an *empirical issue* by making a 'decision' or by defining the problem away. For as Benjamin has indicated, 'Definition is an arbitrary act, and we cannot give the world the properties we want it to have merely by so defining it' (1965, p. 216). This, in fact, is the whole essence of the 'axiomatization' issue. Two theoretical statements can be meaningfully compared as to their relative formal 'simplicity' only if they make the *same empirical claims*; the rules which Halle (1962) compares, however, imply *different* empirical claims (assuming such 'rules' can be empirically interpreted at all; cf. 8.3 and 9.2.1).

I can anticipate two possible counter-arguments. The first might be that while Chomsky and Halle may have, in the choice of their notation-based simplicity metric for phonological description, incorporated into their theory a set of *decisions* or *definitions* about matters which are, in principle, empirical, they have not done so arbitrarily. Their choice of a particular simplicity metric is based on solid empirical evidence. If so, what is the *nature* of this evidence? One searches in vain for any experimental investigations into the notion of 'natural phonological rule' – or even of 'natural class' (but see 9.2.2 below). Nor do we have clear evidence from the study of language acquisition which would either support or deny Halle's implied hypothesis that the child must *necessarily* prefer a rule which operated in the environment before front vowels to one which operated (to take his most extreme example) before /i/, /p/ and /z/.[1] All we find, in fact, is a statement to the effect that the notational conventions which have been devised for phonological description 'were selected in such a way that what *seemed to be* linguistically significant generalizations gave rise to shorter, hence higher valued

---

[1] The 'naturalness' or phonetic 'plausibility' argument loses force once it is recognized that one consequence of the adoption of a general convention of *rule ordering* (and the major 'justification' of its adoption) is that it permits the stating of a rule in its most general form (e.g. 'all velars switch to palatals before *all* vocalic segments articulated in the palatal region'; cf. Lightner's rule (k:č) for Russian discussed on p. 146 below), despite the existence of numerous counter-examples at the phonetic level (cf. the Russian Dative or Locative case forms of 'river' *r'ek'e*, 'leg' *nog'e*, 'flea' *blox'e*, in which the velars are preserved before the front vowel *e*; see Lightner, 1965, pp. 161–3, for a discussion of the convention of rule ordering – together with facts about the history of Russian – which ostensibly remove these difficulties). I do not find it unreasonable to imagine that a child might extract some seemingly bizarre (but phonotactically *true*) generalization from any discernible set of morphological and/or phonetic environments (including even Halle's /a/→/æ/ if followed by /i/, /p/, or /z/) in preference to some other more 'natural' (but phonotactically *false*) generalization which could only be made to work in conjunction with extremely abstract lexical representations, a complex set of ordering relationships among rules, etc. If anything, it is the latter notion which is dubious – particularly since it is scarcely tenable except on the assumption that the child is endowed with an innate set of specifications which tells him what sort of rule is 'natural' and what sort is not, what the general conventions on rule ordering are, etc.; to learn a generalization of the former 'unnatural' sort, however, one need only think in terms of a general capacity for perceiving regularity in a wide range of forms and manifestations (see 6.2 below for further discussion).

grammars' (Chomsky & Halle, 1965, p. 109; italics added).[1] In other words, in the choice of one evaluation procedure, simplicity metric, or scheme of notational conventions over another, the deciding factor, in the last analysis, is *the professional intuitions or opinions of the analyst himself* – and at this level of discussion one might ask seriously why the opinions of one linguist (or group of linguists) on the matter of which rules are 'natural' or which express genuine 'linguistically significant generalizations' ought to be preferred over those of any other.[2] This is particularly true, it should be noted, if we also agree, with Chomsky, that 'there is no *a priori* insight on which [any of us] can rely' in answering such questions.

Alternatively, it might also be argued in rebuttal that the basis for the original selection of some particular set of notational conventions is a matter of theory *construction*, rather than theory *justification*, and:

Questions of this sort are not relevant to [linguistic research]...One may arrive at a grammar [and presumably also a theory of grammar – BLD] by intuition, guess-work, all sorts of partial methodological hints, reliance on past experience, etc....Our ultimate aim is to provide an objective, non-intuitive way to evaluate a grammar [or theory] once presented, and to compare it with other proposed grammars [or theories]' (Chomsky, 1957b, p. 56).

In other words, it doesn't matter much where your grammar or theory of grammar *comes from*; what matters is how one's hypotheses are *tested*.

How, then, *do* Chomsky and Halle go about testing these 'empirical hypotheses' related to the choice of some particular set of notional conventions for phonological description (and hence to the question of which generalizations are 'linguistically significant' and which are not). They state their position directly (if ambiguously) as follows: 'The notations that have been selected constitute an empirical hypothesis as to what is a significant generalization, a hypotheses which can be falsified *on grounds of descriptive inadequacy*, if it is incorrect' (1965, p. 109; italics added). Now this is an inadequate answer. We need only recall what the notion 'descriptive adequacy' refers to. According to Chomsky, the level of descriptive adequacy is achieved by a grammar if and only if it (1) 'give[s] a correct account of the linguistic intuition of the native

---

[1] Cf. also Halle's original 1962 paper, in which it is also obvious that it is merely 'the intuitively correct result' which is reflected in his proposed simplicity criterion (p. 337).

[2] Or why one linguist's professional opinions about 'possible rules' should be more significant than some other's about 'possible base forms', since native speakers are supposedly equally lacking in reliable intuitions on *both* accounts (see pp. 109–10 above).

speaker' and (2) 'specifies the observed data (in particular) in terms of significant generalizations that express underlying regularities in the language' (Chomsky, 1964, p. 63). We obviously cannot test our notational conventions (nor the rule-claims associated with them) by the first criterion, for we know that naive native speakers have no conscious awareness of the rules (much less the set of universal *constraints* on these rules) which they have internalized (furthermore, if they did, there would be little need for linguistic theoreticians). As for non-naive native speakers (i.e. linguists *qua* native speakers), we can hardly expect an independent judgment from them either, as it was their intuitions (or, more accurately, their *professional opinions*) upon which the hypotheses in question were initially formulated. So we move to criterion (2), and here we find that we are being asked to judge whether our original hypotheses as to 'what are significant generalizations' (Chomsky, 1965a, p. 42), which have since been converted into a set of formal notational conventions purposely 'designed in such a way that the greater the degree of linguistically significant generalization achieved in a grammar, the higher the value' (Chomsky & Halle, 1965, p. 108) can now be corroborated by inquiring whether the grammars we have written in terms of these notational conventions 'specify the observed data in terms of significant generalizations' in the sense in which we have defined them. Could we possibly find anything else? Obviously, the only grammars which can achieve descriptive adequacy in terms of the definition are those which conform to our *a priori* concept of what a 'linguistically significant generalization' *is* and, therefore, it is blatantly circular to inquire whether such descriptively adequate grammars are or are not descriptively adequate. I can conceive of only one way in which any proposed set of notational conventions could *possibly* fail 'on grounds of descriptive inadequacy', namely that grammars of the prescribed type *could not actually be written*, i.e. grammars which conformed both to the proposed notational scheme and were consistent with the known primary data. Chomsky admits as much:

To support or refute [some proposed evaluation procedure – i.e. 'an empirical hypothesis concerning prerequisites for language-acquisition'] we must consider evidence as to the factual relation between primary linguistic data and descriptively adequate grammars. We must ask whether the proposed evaluation procedure in fact *can* mediate this empirically given relation (1966b, p. 11; italics added).

Let us now consider that one.

First, the mere fact that a description *can* be formulated which is consistent both with the known data and with some specific set of formal preconditions or constraints by no means guarantees (or necessarily even attests persuasively to) the 'empirical validity' of the particular theoretical principles in question, even under the best of circumstances. It is always possible that equally satisfactory alternative descriptions could be formulated, based on different (or even similar) presuppositions.[1] Thus, to paraphrase Matthews, the only evidence which might be drawn from such a criterion of adequacy would be *against* Chomsky's position: his position will be refuted if such descriptions *cannot even be formulated*, but will not be strengthened even if such descriptions *can* be formulated (cf. Matthews, 1967, pp. 122–3).[2]

If that is the *most* to be gained from this approach, let us now inquire whether there is substance in this criterion of adequacy as it has been applied to generative phonology. The implication of the last few paragraphs is that given a rigid set of restrictions on the notion of 'possible phonological description', 'possible phonological rule', etc., it would be surprising (and therefore interesting in terms of the empirical adequacy of the set of proposed constraints) if all languages (or even a representative portion of a small set of languages) *could* be described in such restrictive terms, especially since efforts are continually being made to tighten these 'universal constraints' more and more.[3] That is, in Chomsky's words:

> To establish general principles of organization for grammar, we must show that these principles are consistent with the facts in a variety of languages and that, on the basis of these principles, one *can* explain phenomena that must otherwise be regarded as accidental (1967d, p. 126; italics added).

As far as the theory of generative phonology is concerned, however, there is one great difficulty, and this is in the lexicon. In particular, the phonological theory upon which the work of Chomsky, Halle, Lightner, Schane and company is based involves a significant departure from virtually all pre-transformational work in phonological analysis by introducing a level of lexical (morphophonemic) representation which is unique in the degree of abstraction or autonomy which it is permitted

---

[1] See Prideaux (1970a) for an excellent illustration of this point.
[2] This is a corollary of the more general falsifiability criterion, which is discussed at greater length in 7.2.1 below.
[3] Cf. Popper's dictum that the degree of falsifiability of a hypothesis or theory – and hence its intrinsic 'empirical content' – increases in proportion to its degree of restrictiveness (1965, pp. 112ff).

with respect to the level of phonetic representation. Chomsky and Halle scarcely mention this.[1] On the contrary, Chomsky in particular has insisted that his 'systematic phonemics' is essentially equivalent to the 'phonological orthography of Sapir' and, for all practical purposes, to the 'phonemics of Bloomfield's practice' as well (1964, p. 87). Thus in arguing convincingly against the legitimacy of invariantbiunique phonemics as a significant level of representation intermediate between the morphophonemic ('systematic phonemic') and the phonetic (cf. 6.1 below), Chomsky gives the (false) impression that he is simply returning to the good old 'two-level' days[2] which preceded the post-Bloomfieldian era (see especially Chomsky, 1964, pp. 85–112). Yet while Chomsky's proposed level of 'systematic phonemics' may with some justification be referred to as *a* type of 'morphophonemics', it is improper to equate it with the 'morphophonemics' of Sapir, Bloomfield, Jakobson, Harris, or any other of the structuralists. This point is made clearly (though more sympathetically) by McCawley, whose remarks on Sapir's phonologic practice are equally applicable to the other analysts mentioned, all of whom subjected their level of lexical representation to certain *specific constraints* which had 'the effect of making the set of possible analyses for [them] radically different from the set of possible analyses in generative phonology' (1967b, p. 107). And surely the 'most important of these constraints', as McCawley points out, was that their morphophonemic segment inventory was 'always a subset of [their] phonetic inventory' (p. 107).[3] That is, the practice of most pre-trans-

---

[1] I have been able to find only one brief reference in Chomsky's writings which suggests that generative phonologists might be departing from past standard approaches in this matter. This remark appears in Chomsky and Halle (1968, p. 76, n. 23).

[2] Cf. Bloomfield (1933, p. 85): 'Only *two kinds* of linguistic records are scientifically relevant. One is a mechanical record of the *gross acoustic features*, such as is produced in the phonetics laboratory. The other is a record in terms of *phonemes*, ignoring all features that are not distinctive in the language' (italics added). If 'not distinctive' here is interpreted to mean roughly the same thing as 'predictable', then Bloomfield's 'phonemes' would indeed be called 'morphophonemes' today (see 6.1 below) and even a cursory inspection of Bloomfield's practice (at least as outlined in his *Language*) shows this to be so. Cf. Joos, 1963, p. 92: 'When we look back at Bloomfield's work, we are disturbed at this and that, but more than anything else Bloomfield's confusion between phonemes and morphophonemes disturbs us.'

[3] There are rare exceptions to this generalization in the literature, typically in instances where the author has some specific extraneous problem in mind and merely exploits the convenient device of the morphophoneme to handle it. Cf., for example, the three nasal morphophonemes posited by Bloomfield (1939, p. 106) to account for the two nasal phones, *m* and *n*; the 'extra' morphophoneme °/N°/ is proposed merely to serve as a diacritic or 'exception' feature, specifically, to identify those *n*'s

formational phonologists was to limit the class of *candidates* for each segment of an underlying representation of a morpheme to those phones which *actually occurred* in that position in the various alternant shapes of that morpheme.[1] This is in striking contrast to the practice of generative grammarians in which the following principle obtains instead:

> It is often the case that the correct [*sic*] underlying form for a morpheme not only does not correspond to one of its alternants but indeed involves feature specifications which are not manifested phonetically in *any* of the alternants (McCawley, 1968c, p. 24).

The transformationalist innovation was to permit free utilization of the device by 'absolute neutralization', namely, to allow 'phonological distinctions which are never realized on the phonetic surface to appear in the lexical representations of morphemes' (Kiparsky, 1968a).

So the 'systematic phonemics' of Chomsky not only constitutes a radical departure from the morphophonemics of previous practice,[2] but also amounts to a serious *loosening of constraints* on the notion of 'possible lexical representation', and thus on the notion of 'possible phonological description' as a whole. For with lexical representations no longer confined within the range of their ultimate phonetic realizations, the analyst is in a position to posit virtually any underlying forms he wishes in his attempt to describe and 'explain' a given set of primary data in terms of whatever predetermined set of rule constraints or evaluation measures he finds to be fashionable at the moment.

In Lightner's work on Russian phonology, consider, for example, the problem of predicting the 'bare' palatalization of consonants within the verbal paradigm, which arose as an adjunct of the more complicated problem of 'transitive' softening. Jakobson's rule for 'bare' palatalization, was that it occurred with *all* consonants before the Imperative

---

which *failed* to undergo the common n∼s alternation (which Bloomfield obviously regarded as the typical case, despite its decidedly 'unnatural' character; p. 109).

[1] Thus, if a morpheme like 'wife' could end in either a phonetic *f* (as in 'wife') or in a phonetic *v* (as in 'wives'), then the underlying (lexical) representation of that morpheme must end with one or the other of these two segments. The only popularly endorsed exception to this with which I am familiar was in the use of *ad hoc* cover symbols which were understood to stand somehow for each of the variants 'simultaneously' (thus morphophonemic wayF = way [ʅ]). Harris says precisely the same thing in terms of the 'phonemic' alternants (the most common approach of the era), but this is simply a matter of abstracting away a certain amount of the variation at a lower level and has only the effect of restricting the range of possible lexical candidates somewhat (see Harris, 1951, pp. 224–5 and 6.1 below).

[2] Despite Chomsky and Halle's claim to the contrary: 'Postulation of phonetically unrealized segments is no great departure from established practice' (1968, p. 75).

desinence and with all consonants except the velars 'before any vocalic desinence which does not begin with -u' (1948, p. 161). This was very strange. Halle's formulation seemed more reasonable, since he predicted both palatalization and the shift from velars to palatals in two specific phonological environments, namely, before +o+C and before all front vowels (1963, p. 124). Lightner observed, however, that a far 'better', i.e. 'simpler' or more 'natural' rule (in terms of Halle's proposed simplicity metric) would clearly be one which had these same two palatalizing effects in the second of Halle's two environments *only* (i.e. only before front vowels). This rule not only makes good articulatory sense, but is (perhaps *because* it makes such sense) the sort of rule one finds evidence for in a variety of languages, not just in East Slavic. It was impossible for Lightner, however, to incorporate such a neat, general rule into his grammar of Russian and still get the correct phonetic output in many cases without also modifying Jakobson's highly constrained base forms. For example, given Jakobson's lexical representation °/p'ok+o+ t°/, Lightner would be unable to account for the correct phonetic[1] form *p'ečot* 'bakes' without patching up his highly valued rule. The solution to this problem, however, stated in these terms, is obvious. For if, as our putative rule states, palatalization and the velar-palatal shift may occur only before front vowels, we must posit front vowels in our underlying representations of all forms in which the palatals appear. So Lightner posits the lexical representation °/pek+e+t°/. His revised, more 'natural' rule now applies to both consonants of the root, yielding *p'eč'et*. To get phonetic *o* in the final syllable, all that it is necessary is to re-interpret Jakobson's old rule that '*o* changes to *e* between two soft consonants'[2] as a different rule which does just the opposite, namely, which changes *e* to *o* in all *other* environments (Lightner's (e:o) rule; see Lightner, 1965, pp. 22 and 214). Thus, by juggling his base forms, Lightner is able to construct a grammar which conforms to the prescribed criteria of rule naturalness and simplicity in this difficult case and which still accounts for (almost) all the phonetic facts.[3]

---

[1] Phonetic vowel-reduction has been ignored here, as elsewhere, as it would be accounted for in essentially the same way by both Jakobson and Lightner and is therefore not germane to any of the issues under discussion (see p. 92, n. 1, above).

[2] Though Jakobson does not state this rule explicitly, it is nevertheless implicit in his observation that '*o* is not admitted between two soft consonants of the stem, whereas both *o* and *e* occur between a soft and a hard consonant' (1948, p. 156). Furthermore, without this rule, Jakobson can only account for a number of verb forms by resorting to *ad hoc* devices (cf. his Section 2.5 on 'inserted vowels', for example).

[3] A few disturbing problems remain even in Lightner's analysis. The first of these he

One potentially serious difficulty arises in Lightner's proposed reformulation along these lines. One quickly discovers that, contrary to the presupposition implicit in Lightner's revised (e:o) rule, there are numerous Russian forms which preserve a phonetic *e* in environments other than between two soft consonants, as in the words *v'ek* 'century', *gr'ex* 'sin', *b'el* 'white', etc. Lightner deals with this problem as he does with the main one now under discussion, simply *by adjusting his base forms*. Specifically, Lightner postulates an *underlying* distinction between two *types* of *e* which is expressed in terms of the (abstract, i.e., 'absolutely neutralized') feature ± T(ense). He can then say that his proposed *e* to *o* rule applies *only* to those underlying *e*'s which are − T, and *not* to those which are + T. Thus the base form he finally postulates for the root 'bake' is °/pek°/, while the one for 'century' is °/vēk°/, etc. Once again, the freedom to manipulate lexical representations provides the loophole required. 'Absolute neutralization' as Kiparsky (1968a) puts it, is thus 'a consequence of setting up underlying distinctions for the *sole purpose* of classifying segments into those that do and those that do not meet the structural analysis of a rule' (italics added).

It is also obvious by this time that Lightner's 'insightful' analysis of the ov→uj (pp. 94–5) vowel–null (pp. 102–3) and resonant–null (p. 99) alternations, as well as his greatly 'simplified' treatment of transitive softening, rely directly on this same descriptive device. Lightner admits as much himself:

To explain [i.e. derive in terms of rules which conform to the proposed set of universal constraints on phonological rules] the different phonetic shapes in which morphemes may appear, we were *obliged* to posit underlying representa-

---

mentions (Lightner, 1965, pp. 137 and 164), namely, that the imperative forms of velar stems fail to undergo the predicted velar-palatal shift before the morpheme °/i°/ (cf. *p'ik'i* 'Bake!', *b'er'eg'i* 'Guard!', etc.) The second, and to my mind equally damaging, difficulty he appears to ignore. This is that the (2 P Pl) forms of *all* verbs (the velar stems included) which take the thematic suffix °/e°/ (according to Lightner's analysis) realize this vowel (under stress) as *o* – and thus must presumably undergo Lightner's proposed (e:o) rule. Yet the (e:o) rule should *not* apply in any such case, due to the appearance of a following *soft* consonant at a point prior in the deviation to the application of this rule (cf. *p'ečot'e* 'you bake', *id'ot'e* 'you run', *n'es'ot'e* 'you carry', etc.). Historically this phenomenon is usually explained in terms of analogical extension: since the old *e* has been replaced with *o* (by a process of regular phonological change) in *id'oš*, *id'om*, etc., why not replace it in *id'ot'e*, as well? (see e.g. W. K. Matthews, 1960, p. 165). Borkovskij and Kuznecov (1965) support this view, and also cite dialects (pp. 133ff) in which the analogy worked back again in the opposite direction (from *id'et'e* to *id'em*, etc.) But Lightner has no place in his work for anything so straightforward as this.

tions which bore no obvious relation to actual phonetic representations (1966b, p. 21; italics added).

But how does this provide empirical support for Halle's original evaluation scheme of 'naturalness' or the abstract lexical representations which come as its necessary complement? Clearly, we cannot speak of 'universal constraints' on phonological rules while leaving the analyst with freedom to posit whatever base forms he wishes; it is the *whole system* which must be constrained, not just half of it.

This can best be illustrated by describing one tactic which is permitted within the framework of any system which does not significantly constrain the notion of 'possible lexical representation' and, in particular, which allows the free use of absolute neutralization as a methodological device. Within such a metatheoretical framework nothing prevents the analyst from positing as his base forms for certain morphemes in some language those proto-forms which are provided in the standard handbooks on historical phonology. The analyst then finds that a certain set of generalizations has *immediately become statable,* namely, those generalizations which the historical linguists have found to be true of the historical development of the language. But what is to be concluded from this? Nothing at all. It would be patently absurd to argue that because of looseness in the metatheory of grammar which makes it a foregone conclusion that these purely diachronic generalizations will become statable within a supposedly 'synchronic grammar', these generalizations must now be 'psychologically real' as well. Yet this is what many generative phonologists (notably Chomsky, Halle, Lightner and Schane) have been doing. They have even gone so far as to applaud and defend one another in the process. Chomsky and Halle remark, for example, that:

It has been *shown* by Lightner...that *in the underlying representations of Russian* there are two parallel sets of vowels, tense and nontense. The nontense high vowels never appear in the output [absolute neutralization – BLD]; they are either deleted..., or they are lowered...and thus appear phonetically as [e] or [o] (1968, p. 379).

But Lightner has done no such thing – assuming that the phrase 'in the underlying representation of Russian' implies something of essential synchronic or psychological significance about present-day Russian. All Lightner has 'shown' is that, given a theory which is constrained only in part, almost anything is possible in 'synchronic' linguistic description – even the recapitulation of aspects of the history of a language. Consequently, given that there is no known external (non-linguistic) means to confirm or deny the rules or the base forms which such analysts have entertained in their descriptions, the abandonment of effective constraint on the abstractness of lexical representations has robbed the theory of generative phonology of empirical significance.[1]

A word is needed here on the use of the term 'effective' constraints. My general conclusion does not imply that generative grammarians have never proposed restraints on the notion of lexical representation. For instance, there was some discussion to the effect that lexical (or, at least, 'systematic phonemic') representations should consist only of fully specified (or 'pronounceable') phonological segments (cf. Stanley, 1967) though, more recently, this has given way to the proposal that the +, −, and O ('unspecified') markings of earlier descriptions be replaced with the values m(arked) or u(nmarked), which would be converted into (potentially) pronounceable phonetic sequences only upon application of a set of 'universal rules of interpretation' (see chapter 8 of Postal, 1968, and chapter 9 of Chomsky & Halle, 1968, for details).[2] And, clearly, the adoption of either formulation would constrain (or limit) the abstractness of lexical representations in the sense that it would eliminate at least two logically possible types of lexical representation, specifically (1) the view that the lexicon should constitute a 'perfectly arbitrary code' in which no intrinsic relation should obtain between it and the level of phonetics (see especially Fudge, 1967, and the critiques by Postal, 1968, pp. 56–7, and Kiparsky, 1968a), and perhaps (2) the earlier generative view (adapted from the Prague School) that incompletely specified 'archisegments' of various sorts might appear in the lexicon (i.e. that some segments in lexical representations might be left completely unspecified for certain of their phonetic properties). But while adoption of some such proposal would certainly tighten up the notion of lexical representation to a degree, it would still have no

---

[1] In an article which came to my attention shortly before this book went to press, I find that Crothers adopts this same position. Speaking of those generalizations which can be captured in an 'abstract description' (such as Lightner's) but are missed in a corresponding 'concrete' one (such as Jakobson's), Crothers argues that 'the basic issue is just whether it is proper to make such generalizations in synchronic phonology. Simply to indicate that such generalizations *can* be made solves nothing at all' (1971, p. 19).

[2] Technically speaking, according to Chomsky and Halle's scheme, these segments are not really 'pronounceable' until after the application of a set of phonetic 'detail' rules which convert the binary (classificatory) lexical matrix into a multinary (scalar) phonetic one. See Postal (1968, pp. 65ff) and Chomsky & Halle (1968, pp. 297–8).

bearing on the issue at hand, since under neither formulation is the constraint in question sufficient to proscribe absolute neutralization, the device responsible for the difficulties I have been discussing. I agree with Kiparsky's assessment that while contextual neutralization (where 'an underlying distinction is lost only in a specific environment') appears to be 'a linguistic fact which is beyond dispute', a serious dispute does begin 'where generative phonology parts company with more traditional approaches by also permitting absolute neutralization' (1968a).

We may now return briefly to an article already mentioned (Hyman, 1970, cf. p. 129, n. 1 above) in which abstract phonology (i.e. a phonology that permits absolute neutralization) is defended, in spite of Kiparsky's perceptive attack. Hyman's main point is that the rules he formulates for Nupe as part of his abstract analysis do appear to be fully productive to new forms borrowed into the language, as well; on these grounds he argues that his rules (and the abstract base forms which accompany them) must be 'psychologically real'. The conclusion does not necessarily follow. The argument from borrowings, like any other, can only be employed decisively for purposes of falsification, not confirmation (cf. 7.2.1 below). In particular, while the psychological validity of Lightner's analysis of Russian can be questioned because his proposed 'general rules' *fail* to be productive of new words borrowed into the language, the most we can conclude from Hyman's data is that his similarly abstract analysis of Nupe cannot be criticized on these same grounds. This is not to say that the explanation Hyman proposes for the Nupe borrowings is correct (namely, that unfamiliar incoming phonetic sequences are identified with Nupe *base forms* and treated accordingly). The arguments I have offered against the use of absolute neutralization in phonological analysis suggest, in fact, that some other mechanism must be at work. One is therefore inclined to believe that Hyman is simply wrong in asserting that 'the Nupe does not merely replace foreign sounds with those closest to them in his own language' (p.67). It seems reasonable to assume that in a language which lacks phonetic [ε] and [ɔ], both vowels might be interpreted as near-equivalents to the native vowel [a], with the frontness of the first (perhaps associated with a perceptible palatal on-glide) interpreted as palatalization of the preceding consonant, and the rounding of the second as labialization. Thus Yoruba [Cε] would be perceived as an approximation of Nupe [C^{y}a] and Yoruba [Cɔ] as Nupe [C^{w}a], as Hyman's data suggest. I find this interpretation generally more feasible than the one which Hyman proposes.[1] This view becomes more compelling when one considers that Hyman's original *linguistic* arguments in favor of his abstract analysis of Nupe phonology are the same as Lightner's for Russian, namely, maximum *generality* and *naturalness* (see Hyman, 1970, pp. 59–65).[2] The question immediately arises that if (1) these linguistic criteria provide valid guides to the construction of a synchronically legitimate and psychologically valid analysis of the phonology of a language and (2) the interpretation of new forms borrowed into a language is to be explained as Hyman suggests, then (3) why do the criteria proposed lead Lightner to formulate an analysis for Russian which is inconsistent with the facts of borrowings into that language, but lead Hyman to one which is not inconsistent with such facts? In the absence of any satisfactory answer to this question, I am disposed to suspect that it is Hyman who is mistaken.

To return to our main theme: apart from Kiparsky's (1968a) suggestions (which have not as yet been generally accepted by other transformationalists and which I shall therefore defer until 6.2 below), I know of only one other serious attempt within TGG to deal with the question of constraints on the abstractness of lexical representations. This is the one provided by Postal (1968, pp. 53–77). Here we read that the theory of generative phonology ('systematic phonemic theory') denies that there is 'any [significant] level of linguistic structure which is mechanically determinable *in full* from phonetic structure', i.e. from phonetics *alone*,[3] but insists instead 'that the level of systematic phonemic structure [lexical representation] is related to phonetics by the Naturalness Condition' (p. 73). This condition claims, as Postal puts it, that phonological [morphophonemic, lexical] and phonetic structure are

---

[1] So does Crothers, who offers the same alternative hypotheses which I suggest here (1971, pp. 20–1). Notice also that if Hyman's hypothesis were correct, some absurdities would follow from Lightner's analysis of Russian. E.g. the English word 'widow' would presumably be identified with the Russian base form °/uidou°/ and hence 'perceived' – by application of Lightner's rules – as [vdof]!

[2] Evidence from borrowings, while potentially useful in *evaluating* proposed analyses (and the general underlying metatheoretical principles) is surely no more legitimate for purposes of grammar *construction* than information related to the history of a language, since neither source of information is available to the typical child or language learner.

[3] The level of which Postal is speaking is that of 'autonomous' (or 'taxonomic') phonemics, whose status is not at issue here. Postal neglects to mention the more interesting alternative candidate for *lexical representation*, namely, the level of morphophonemics of Sapir *et al.*, i.e. a level which is mechanically determinable *in part* from phonetic structure and in part from *morphological* structure (see 6.1 below).

essentially similar and require special language-limited rules to relate them only with respect to a very limited number and kind of properties. Much of the work of generating phonetic representations from input systematic phonological structures is a function of universal rules and conditions... Hence, except in the irreducible cases of completely special language-limited facts ['true suppletion'], systematic structures automatically pass into phonetic structures without the need of setting up *ad hoc* rules (p. 77).

In other words:

If one considers those classes of systematic segments (morphophonemes) which must be referred to in the rules of natural languages, one will find that in general [that is, in all non-suppletive cases] these have phonetic realizations which form natural classes in terms of phonetic features, and that the variant phonetic mappings of a single systematic segment will form a natural class (pp. 73–4).

Clearly, Postal's proposed 'constraint' on lexical representations is not an independent hypothesis or constraint at all, but merely restates Chomsky and Halle's original assumption that the rules of a grammar and the classes upon which they operate are highly constrained from the standpoint of 'naturalness', and that an evaluation metric is needed to give formal expression to this 'fact' (see Chomsky & Halle, 1968, pp. 400 and 419, and the other references already cited). Postal's proposed 'constraint' can be accurately paraphrased as follows: 'Lexical representations consist of phonological strings which may be made more abstract than phonetic strings only to the extent that the mapping relation between this phonological level and the phonetic level can be described in terms of rules of the prescribed natural type.' This 'naturalness condition' imposes constraints on the abstractness of lexical representations only if the 'universal principles' which connect this level with phonetics are *known*; but since these proposed universals are not 'facts' but 'empirical hypotheses', the condition imposes no (independent) restrictions on the rules. That is, if one determines that some rule or proposed rule-constraint is 'universal' or 'natural' (i.e. if one decides that such a rule can indeed express a 'natural' *relation* between the lexical and phonetic levels of representation), then there is nothing in Postal's proposed 'constraint' to prevent you from incorporating that rule or universal feature into your grammars; so you are free to juggle with your underlying representations in order to fit the rule in.[1] It is therefore strange

---

[1] As a practical expedient generative grammarians have characteristically looked to language history for their ideas as to what base forms and rules to posit and thus have not yet managed to eliminate all *ad hoc* or 'non-natural' rules (see, for example,

to read that Postal thinks his proposed 'naturalness' condition involves 'a tremendously strong and nontrivial claim'[1] and even that *'the fact that it is true* is a fundamental characteristic of human languages' (1968, p. 75; italics added).[2]

I can only conclude that the transformationalists are simply convinced that their opinions about rule 'naturalness' or rule 'plausibility' (see Chomsky, 1967d, p. 126) are essentially correct, though there is no empirical evidence in support of these convictions. Such views are not unprecedented. We find a classic and strikingly parallel case in the early history of astronomy, for instancē, which also involves a set of *a priori* opinions about 'naturalness' (cf. Holton & Roller, 1958, pp. 105–17). Only the invention of the telescope finally brought these ideas to the ground: what had seemed obvious was simply not true (any more than were many other of the speculations of the early Greek philosophers, such as that most intuitively compelling common-sense notion that a force is needed to 'keep things moving' (see Holton & Roller, 1958, p. 62)). 'Science' can be said to have begun when man (or, more specifically, Galileo) broke with the Scholastic tradition which built on *a priori* common-sense hypotheses and a credulous deference to authority ('sterile introspection and blind subservience to dogma') and substituted in its place an all-embracing skepticism which insisted on the rigors of experiment and test (see Holton & Roller, 1958, p. 165). The lesson

p. 110, n. 1 and p. 146, n. 3. Surely in principle, however, a full set of rules of the desired type can eventually be worked in by taking full advantage of the freedom to shuffle base forms which the theory provides. Some of this has already been done, and so, as Chomsky points out (though for a different reason), the typical generative phonological description no longer recapitulates the history 'without qualification' (1967d, p. 127).

1 While the *claims* associated with the theory of 'naturalness' are certainly strong, they are, within the present framework of discussion, unsupported and hence *empty*. They cannot be falsified, given the escape-clause of abstract lexical representation. This is not to say that valid empirical hypotheses could not be made *of* them if they could be reformulated so that experimental evidence could be brought to bear. Those few observers who have attempted to bring even marginally new kinds of evidence (particularly evidence related to language change) to bear on such problems do not seem optimistic about the prospects that any 'theory of rule plausibility' of the sort which Chomsky and Halle propose (1968, p. 427) will hold out. See especially Kiparsky (1968a), Bach and Harms (1972) and my remarks in chapter 3 (p. 66, n. 2).

2 Postal says elsewhere that 'the question is to what extent are the differences between the phonetic representatives of phonological units predictable in general phonetic terms. This can ONLY be a question about universal phonetic and/or phonological rules and their relations' (1966, p. 167). Why so? Surely 'this assumption needs justification', for it, as much as any of the earlier structuralist assumptions, is also 'not a logical truth' (p. 163).

(supposedly) learned was that 'it is the duty of science to illuminate what *is*, not merely what is convenient, or what is traditional' (Allport, 1961, p. 11).

Chomsky and Halle themselves remark (in their rebuttal of Householder, 1965) that 'there is not the slightest reason to expect natural languages to be "maximally simple", assuming that some content can be given to this curious notion' (1965, p. 111, n. 8). By the same argument, what reason is there to expect that languages should be 'maximally natural', 'maximally general' (i.e. 'maximally *regular*' – see pp. 131–2 above), or, for that matter, maximally *anything*? Yet it is no exaggeration to say that many linguists subscribe to the view that 'the grammar of a language is precisely the simplest set of rules for accounting for the utterances in the language' and believe that 'such a position involves the strongest possible claim about the psychological validity of the formulation' (Saporta, 1965, p. 99).[1] But I assume that it is by now abundantly clear that it is not maximization of 'the simplicity and generality of the grammar as a whole' which is crucial in determining the best linguistic description (as J. Fodor suggests (in Lyons, 1970, p. 214)), but rather such empirical questions as are related to 'the way linguistic information is [actually] "stored" in the brain and "indexed" for "retrieval" in the perception (or production) of speech' (Lyons, 1970, p. 29).[2]

[1] Cf. McNeill, who argues that 'Relative economy is *always* an argument in support of one theoretical interpretation over another' (1970b, p. 1150; italics added). And why? Presumably because 'the argument of economy has special significance in the context of language acquisition. *We prefer to think of children doing the simpler thing, whatever that might be*' (same page; italics added).

[2] The information storage and retrieval analogy usefully illustrates this point (cf. Scriven, 1969a). If we interpret language processing in such terms, it is clear that Chomsky's (implicit) principles of maximum generality (or minimum lexicon) and maximum simplicity (or naturalness) both relate to the *storage* side of the ledger, so implying that the best linguistic description imposes the least burden from this standpoint alone (hence one which has as small a lexicon and as many rules as possible, and where each rule is maximally general and maximally natural). So Stanley argues that 'the best set of MS conditions is...essentially, the shortest set...that allows us to leave the greatest number of blanks in dictionary matrices' (1967, p. 434). What is ignored in this approach is the problem of *retrieval*: how difficult is it to learn, recall and use these very skeletal and abstract lexical representations and such a highly organized system of abstract rules in order to produce or comprehend speech? (See chapter 8 for further discussion.) Obviously, the most efficient storage–retrieval system is not the one which minimizes storage, but the one which adopts the optimal trade-off between economy of description (storage), on the one hand, and degree of abstractness (or ease of retrieval), on the other. Yet even striking the ideal balance in this respect is no solution to the *empirical* questions, since there is no reason to think that the language learner must necessarily be maximally efficient, either (cf. p. 244, n. 1 below). Without independent supporting evidence, no arbitrary criterion

To conclude, I readily concede that Chomsky, Halle and others have gone far towards giving explicit and formal 'content' to their *a priori* notions of 'naturalness', 'simplicity', 'generality', etc., yet there is still no reason to assume that languages must conform to the specifications which they provide. The issue is an 'empirical matter'. Nor is there the slightest doubt that 'it is an extremely difficult problem to construct an evaluation procedure that gives the *desired results*...[i.e. to justify] correct descriptions' (Chomsky & Halle, 1965, p. 107, n. 4; italics added). Most difficult of all is the part which Chomsky and Halle apparently take for granted, namely, determining what the 'desired results' and 'correct descriptions' are.

5.3   A brief syntactic interlude

Chomsky holds that only the phonological component of TGG is beyond a rudimentary stage of development at present (cf. p. 100, n. 1 above). It might nevertheless be useful to interject a few illustrations into our discussion to demonstrate that the same fundamental defects inherent in current work in generative phonological theory are characteristic of the entire transformational-generative approach, syntax included. Two illustrations will suffice. I have argued above that underlying current work in generative phonology are two arbitrary (though superficially reasonable) assumptions which have gradually hardened (been 'axiomatized') into the metatheory as implicit *principles of evaluation* – a first principle of maximum 'generality' or 'regularity' and a second of maximum 'simplicity' or 'naturalness'. We have also seen that underlying the generative grammarians' notion of 'explanation' is a set of equally indefensible assumptions about some particular domain of 'fact', e.g. assumptions concerning alleged morphological relationships among words, and the supposed synchronic significance of 'anomalies' involving the phonetic shapes of these words. Both developments have unmistakable analogues in transformational-generative syntactic analysis.

Consider the adoption of arbitrary principles of evaluation (i.e. apart from compelling extrinsic or empirical considerations; cf. 9.2 below for an alternative approach). Since we found phonological manifestations of this while exploring Chomsky's notion of 'linguistically significant generalization' as applied to phonology, we might expect to find syntac-

of 'simplicity' can ever 'validate' a grammar, and Lees is as mistaken as Chomsky in suggesting that one ever could (see Lees, 1957, p. 382).

tic parallels where this notion is applied and extended to syntactic analysis. And so we do. Moreover, this notion of 'linguistically significant generalization' as it applies to syntax has already been analyzed by Prideaux (1971a), who finds that there are three specific methodological criteria involved in its use. These are:

(1) 'Observational adequacy' must be met, i.e. the analyses must be consistent with the observed primary data (cf. Chomsky, 1964, p. 62, etc.),

(2) The rules must be conflatable in terms of some set of generally accepted notational convention(s), and

(3) At least some of the rules (and the more the better) must be 'independently motivated'.

Note that only the last two criteria are peculiar to TGG; moreover, these latter two principles are, as Prideaux points out, purely 'formal' (i.e. non-empirical). Each has its analogue in transformational-generative phonological theory: principle (2) can be identified with the Chomsky–Halle notion of 'naturalness' in phonology (cf. pp. 136–9 above), while principle (3) is the analogue of Chomsky's implicit principle of maximum 'regularity' (pp. 131–2). Since no definitive set of arbitrary principles of 'naturalness' has been devised for syntax (and perhaps this is why Chomsky considers this part of his theory relatively underdeveloped *vis-à-vis* phonology), we have to fall back on the analogy between 'independent motivation' and 'maximum regularity' here. This analogy holds up; just as one phonological analysis is preferred to another by the transformationalist if it 'predicts in' more phonetic information by general phonological rule (and hence 'explains' more about the phonetic structure of forms), the generative syntactician prefers that syntactic analysis which manages to interrelate the greater number of syntactic (surface) structures by general syntactic rule (so increasing the 'explanatory power' of the theory; cf. Chomsky, 1957b, pp. 85–91). The primary goal of the transformational-generative syntactician is therefore to minimize the number of independent syntactic structures which have to be posited (in the base) by maximizing the number which can be analyzed away as surface variants of a smaller set of underlying or 'deep' structures; this aim corresponds to the generative phonologist's concern to minimize the lexicon by 'predicting in' as much phonetic information as possible. So, just as the generative phonologist is led to prefer Lightner's analysis of the palatals in Russian, with its single, general and 'natural' (i.e. phonologically conditioned) phonological rule whereby all occurrences of morpheme alternants containing the segment-types in question are treated as predictable variants of underlying (lexical) representations containing a velar or a dental, so likewise the generative syntactician prefers Ross' (1967) analysis of the *that-* and relative clauses in English, where – with the help of a single, general rule of 'extraposition' – all occurrences of the clause-type in question are treated as predictable variants of underlying (base) representations in which they appear as embedded sentences immediately to the right of a noun or noun phrase (for details, see Prideaux, 1971a). What is entirely lost sight of is the empirical question about the kinds of structures and rules actually learned by native speakers: are they simple or complex, natural or unnatural (from the linguist's point of view), abstract or concrete, and so on? One can play any game he likes by setting up rules that appeal to him – and 'maximum regularity' is as good an arbitrary rule as any other – but one does not do empirical *science* that way.[1]

Of all on-going research in transformational-generative syntax, it is the current work of 'generative semanticists' like Lakoff, McCawley and Ross which best typifies this approach and which represents a straightforward extension of 'maximum regularity' (= Zwicky's 'Free-Ride Principle' (1970)) to its logical limits.[2] Consider, for example, McCawley's analysis of the 'causative' verb KILL (1968b, pp. 72ff), which develops ideas first presented in Lakoff (1970) (= Lakoff, 1965). The grounds of McCawley's analysis are clear enough: (1) he seeks to capture or 'explain' the supposed relation of paraphrase (synonymy) which is said to exist between such sentences as JOHN KILLED HARRY, JOHN CAUSED HARRY TO DIE and JOHN CAUSED HARRY TO BECOME NOT ALIVE by means of

---

[1] As I shall emphasize in the next chapter, the chief distinction to be made here is between imposing an arbitrary descriptive system on an artificially circumscribed body of data as opposed to genuinely seeking to establish knowledge about (underlying) empirical states of affairs.

[2] Though Chomsky himself introduced the principle and has used it a good deal in his work in syntax, as well as in phonology, I have to argue from the work of some of his students here in order to continue the demonstration. For Chomsky himself has resisted the unrestrained extension of syntactic theory in the direction of maximum regularity (and hence maximum abstractness), although the extension parallels his own incursion into these same realms of abstractness in phonology. This apparent inconsistency on Chomsky's part may be due to his having committed himself early (Chomsky, 1957b) to a notion of grammar in which syntax (and not semantics) was central (cf. the last sentence of Householder (1965, p. 16, n. 3), which sums up the situation).

the one device provided by the metatheory for doing so: to derive them all from the same (abstract) 'deep structure'.[1] He therefore (1) devises an extremely abstract structure of the sort required (a matrix sentence containing four 'lower' sentences embedded in it) from which each of the sentences in question can be derived by a succession of ordered transformational rules. In order to demonstrate that his proposed analysis is not *ad hoc*, but is 'independently motivated' he then (2) invokes the criterion of maximum regularity, arguing that the new 'predicate-raising' transformation which is novel to his analysis is justified because it 'includes as special cases the inchoative transformation and causative transformations of Lakoff (1970)' (p. 75).

We now turn to Lakoff's original work (1970) to fill out the remaining features of the analogy. Here we find (pp. 32–40) that in pursuing a parallel course to 'explain' another set of paraphrase relations among sentences involving either derived verb forms (e.g. THE METAL HARDENED; cf. THE METAL IS HARD) or some 'inchoative' verb such as BECOME or GET (e.g. THE METAL BECAME HARD or THE METAL GOT HARD), Lakoff is led to suppose that each set of sentences is derived from a single underlying syntactic structure containing an inchoative verb $[+V, -ADJ, +IN-CHOATIVE]$. To distinguish the two cases, the neutralized feature distinction $[\pm PRO]$ is then proposed: if the underlying verb is marked $[-PRO]$ it will be realized on the surface as the full verb BECOME (or GET); if it is marked $[+PRO]$ it will be realized as the suffix -EN. And as Lakoff sums up, 'The advantages of this analysis are that *we can postulate a single deep structure* for the *become, get*, and inchoative sentences *at the cost of only one new rule* – INCHOATIVE' (p. 38, italics added).

We see how closely related transformational-generative phonological and syntactic practices are. Compare Lightner's analysis of the $V \sim \emptyset$ alternation in Russian, for example (see pp. 101–3 above). Just as Lightner posits a single underlying phonological representation (combined highness and laxness in vowels) in order to characterize a given unitary phonological phenomenon (the vowel-null alternation itself), we

---

[1] McCawley would dispute my use of this term, since the main purpose of his article was to argue 'that there is no linguistically significant level [of "deep structure"] between semantic representation and surface structure' (p. 79). This issue does not concern me, since I find the entire notion of 'transformational-generative grammar' (constructed as a model of so-called 'linguistic competence' in any of the transformationalist senses) untenable (see chapter 8 for discussion). I therefore adopt here the terms 'deep' versus 'surface' representation in syntax merely as a set of convenient labels for distinguishing what is (overly) 'abstract' (or absolutely neutralized) from what is (reasonably) 'concrete' (or constrained).

find Lakoff positing a single underlying syntactic representation in order to characterize a given unitary semantic one (a specific example of synonymy or paraphrase). And as Lightner includes in his representation of all abstract 'base' forms which participate in the alternation in question an underlying phonological distinction (viz. $\pm T$ for high vowels) which is not realized as such on the phonetic surface, Lakoff includes in all abstract 'base' representations of sentences which are included in his paraphrastic set a corresponding absolutely neutralized syntactic distinction (marked $\pm PRO$ for inchoative verbs). To be sure, this is no accident, but a direct (and necessary) consequence of the fact that both are operating according to (essentially) the same metatheory and relying on much the same sort of argument. As clearly, however, a line of argument which is vacuous for phonology is also vacuous for syntax.[1] Yet Chomsky himself insists that 'the abstract character of underlying (deep) structure in both syntax and phonology is hardly open to question' (1966b, p. 57). I argue that it is very much open to question, both in syntax and phonology, because ingenuity or imagination alone cannot answer empirical questions, such as the kind of rules (if any) and structures which the speaker of a language actually learns in language acquisition and employs in speech production and perception.

I conclude that generative grammarians, syntacticians and phonologists alike, have the same set of fundamental difficulties: paradoxically, they are prone to excessive metatheoretical constraint and excessive metatheoretical looseness at the same time. On the one hand, they have made their theories (and hence all associated lines of inquiry) too specific in the sense that they have incorporated directly into their metatheory specific but arbitrary principles of evaluation which define or axiomatize away fundamentally important empirical issues; in order to permit descriptions of this arbitrary type which satisfy a minimum of external (empirical) conditions, we also find that they have been nonspecific in other areas of their metatheoretical framework – particularly on matters related to the degree of abstractness to be permitted to underlying representations (phonology) or 'deep structures' (syntax). They also have allowed themselves to lay their own ground rules in the sense of

[1] For further discussion of difficulties inherent in the principle of 'linguistically significant generalization' as employed by transformational-generative grammarians, see especially Prideaux (1971a, 1971b). I have benefited greatly from discussions with Dr Prideaux in developing the arguments in this section, and most of my illustrations are adaptations of his.

choosing which particular domain of 'fact' they will be primarily responsible for.

In phonology, we saw this second type of axiomatization manifested in morphological relationships and phonetic 'anomalies': whatever forms could be related, were related, and whatever phonetic anomalies could be 'explained' (even if one had to recapitulate history) were 'explained' – and so the descriptions were assumed to have synchronic or psychological significance. But the question now before us is whether we can also find manifestations of this second principle in transformational-generative syntactic practice, as well.

What facts does a synchronic syntactic description seek to account for? The four main ones are: (1) *grammatically* (Does the sentence belong to the language? Cf. Chomsky, 1957b, pp. 13ff), (2) *ambiguity* or 'constructional homonymity' (Can the sentence be analyzed in more than one way? Cf. Chomsky, 1957b, pp. 85ff), (3) *synonymy* or 'paraphrase' (Can two different sentences be analyzed in the same way? Cf. Katz and Postal, 1964, pp. 157ff), (4) *anomaly* (Is the sentence 'odd', 'peculiar', 'paradoxical' or 'bizarre'? Cf. Katz and Fodor, 1963, pp. 175ff). But of all the 'many facts about language and linguistic behavior' (Chomsky 1957b, p. 85), what is central or especially significant about the particular range of phenomena described?

First, all the phenomena in question belong to the single category of 'linguistic intuitions'. Why should an entire 'science of language' be built up around them? Of all the things which the speakers of a language *do*, it seems odd that it should be their ability to introspect on aspects of their own linguistic performance which should be regarded as the most fundamental, the most interesting, or (ironically) the most susceptible to serious empirical investigation (see 7.4 below for a discussion of one important factor in the dynamics of this development in TGG). To begin with, reliance on such a source immediately imposes on the discipline a number of methodological difficulties which might otherwise have been avoided (see 7.3 below for details). It is also difficult to imagine how the study of such 'intuitions' alone could lead to significant advances in our understanding of speech production and perception, which Chomsky himself has often implied is the 'central' consideration (1964, p. 50, and elsewhere).

Other difficulties also arise. Items (1) and (4), for instance, suggest an immediate and obvious possibility of conflict, which has not gone unrealized. Furthermore, as Householder has pointed out, it is by no means clear that making judgments about 'grammaticality' or 'anomaly' as such is a significant part of normal linguistic behavior.[1] Much more characteristic, surely, is the continuous attempt made by the listener to impose some meaningful interpretation on those frequent deviant utterances which he hears – and by the speaker to rephrase his remarks in a way that will further clarify his intended meaning (see Householder, 1971, p. 455). Yet this obviously central problem has been left virtually unexplored by generative grammarians, who are preoccupied instead with such considerations as (1) through (4).

Item (2) commands a good deal more interest as a demonstrable phenomenon, though even here it is difficult to understand why it must be regarded as a central or *key* notion. Notice that in generative syntax, for example, a grammar is evaluated in terms of its ability to capture ambiguities (among the other key notions on the list): a good grammar does and a bad one does not. This is surely a very crude criterion, however, since many grammars can be devised even within the 'standard' metatheory which capture those relatively few ambiguities which occur in a language. Yet it is not so much the relative rarity of ambiguity and homonymy which is significant, but rather the apparent fact that when these phenomena do occur, it is ordinarily under circumstances which are, as Chafe puts it;

accidental and unsystematic. That is, situations of this kind arise as a fortuitous result of unique processes which apply somewhere in the conversion of semantic structures into phonetic structures. It is simply the case that various processes of this kind frequently lead by chance to identical outcomes (1971, p. 9).

In short, while ambiguity may be central to the methodology of TGG, there is little reason to think that it is anything but a marginal phenomenon in normal language use. Its study can therefore hardly be expected to give substantial, much less definitive, results.[2]

[1] This is attested to by the many serious difficulties encountered by those few investigators who have tried to elicit such things as judgments of 'grammaticality' from naive speakers (cf. Maclay & Sleator, 1960; Hill, 1961; Sledd, 1962; etc.). Nor should it be lost sight of that even linguists resort to the question mark now and again.

By the same token, one can also seriously question the more general assumption that 'generating the sentences of his language' constitutes a normal function of the language user, as implied by Lees (1957, pp. 406–7).

[2] Furthermore, there is also good reason to believe that the *surface* syntactic structures (P-markers) associated with such classic examples of 'constructional homonymity' as FLYING PLANES CAN BE DANGEROUS (Chomsky, 1962b, p. 237) and THE POLICE STOPPED

Much the same can also be said of synonymy. The structuralists had little use for this notion at all. Bloomfield (1933, p. 145) and Nida (1949, p. 151), for example, even went so far as to deny its existence, in part on the ground that one of the more obvious forces of language change was an unmistakable pressure to *eliminate* synonyms from a language (cf. Bolinger, 1968, pp. 113–14).[1] The transformationalists have gone to the opposite extreme and now consider the notion of central importance in connection with what might be called *the principle of systematic paraphrase*:[2]

> Given a sentence for which a syntactic derivation is needed; look for simple paraphrases of the sentence which are not paraphrases by virtue of synonymous expressions; on finding them, construct grammatical rules that relate the original sentence and its paraphrases in such a way that each of these sentences has the same sequence of underlying P-markers (Katz & Postal, 1964, p. 157).

Transformational rules are here conceived primarily as devices which the linguist employs to derive diverse syntactic structures from the same underlying semantic (or semantically interpretable) 'deep' representation and (ever since Katz and Postal's book) without changing their meanings. A criterion of evaluation is clearly implied here, as well. That is, paraphrase-capturing (like ambiguity-capturing before it) provides the linguist with some basis for preferring one linguistic description over another (and even one *theory* over another, the best theory presumably being one which makes explicit provision for capturing synonymy).

But do speakers actually internalize rules specifically to capture the phenomenon in question, or might paraphrase (like ambiguity) be better regarded as a secondary or fortuitous consequence of the operation of a system established on some entirely different basis? There is a lot to say for the latter view. In speaking, for example, one's intention is rarely ever either to dredge up ambiguous expressions or to say something in a new or different way, but is directed instead to a communication which

DRINKING (Chomsky, 1966b, p. 7) are not identical at all, but actually differ in important ways (as to labeled bracketing, etc.); that is to say, such sentences are 'ambiguously analyzed *on the level of phrase structure*' (Chomsky, 1957b, p. 87; italics added). Hence there is no need to posit different 'deep' *syntactic* structures in order to distinguish these sentence types. See Prideaux (forthcoming) for discussion.

[1] Alyeshmerni and Taubr put it this way: 'When there is a distinction in form [available in a language], [the] language makes use of it with a distinction in meaning' (1970, p. 79).

[2] This term was suggested to my by G. D. Prideaux.

is adequate to the situation.[1] Moreover, what reason have we to think that a language should be so organized as to make explicit provision of complex syntactic devices *specifically* to permit the speaker to say precisely the same thing in many different ways? Is it not more reasonable to assume that structures are preserved in order to permit fine and subtle distinctions of meaning, emphasis, emotive content, etc. and that synonymy (or paraphrase) is the fortuitous consequence of the freedom to use a variety of devices interchangeably in situations when the distinctions in question are not really important? If so, the rationale for constructing grammars in such a way that synonymy is 'captured' seems tenuous, and the status of rules written primarily for this purpose is dubious[2] (see 9.2.1 below for an alternative scheme for the evaluation of proposed grammatical rules).

Yet Katz and Postal's original heuristic suggestion has become canonized as an implicit operational principle of considerable importance for TGG. This new principle might be stated in the following way: two sentences are synonymous if and only if both can be derived from the same underlying 'deep' structure (or putting it in a slightly different way, derivability from an identical deep structure is the only device provided by the metatheory for capturing or 'explaining' synonymy). And once again it is the work of Lakoff, McCawley and the other 'generative semanticists' which can be seen to represent the extension of this principle to its logical limits: from the domain of syntax proper (to which Katz and Postal restricted it – note the exclusion of 'synonymous expressions' in their original statement of the principle) into the domain of the lexicon. This extension is accomplished by introducing what McCawley has called 'lexical insertion' transformations, i.e. rules which

---

[1] Except, of course, when a pun is intended (ambiguity), or when one is specifically required to produce a sentence which means approximately the same as some other (paraphrase). I do not argue that these phenomena do not exist, but only that they are marginal to normal language use and thus need not necessarily have special metatheoretical provision made for them.

[2] If paraphrase seems the *closest* of the four phenomena in question to a normal language task, this may be due solely to the apparent fact that the language user retains in storage only his assessment of the *meaning* of an utterance, and not the syntactic frame, the phonological units, etc. (cf. Deese, 1970, p. 46). Thus if a speaker or listener is asked to repeat what he has just said or heard, he is forced to search out anew some lexical and syntactic frame which will suffice to convey the same general idea, and only rarely will these new structures be precisely identical – or even systematically related – to the original set. (This, incidentally, has important implications regarding the utility of rote memorization as a response measure in experimental psycholinguistics.)

'insert lexical items in place of portions of labeled trees' (1968e, p. 168). Presumably the paramount consideration behind McCawley's suggestion that this 'new' function be added to those traditionally performed by transformational rules[1] was the desire to make it possible to capture a whole class of relations of synonymy which were thought to exist between such syntactically disparate structures as simple verbs (such as KILL) and entire phrases or clauses (such as CAUSE TO DIE and, ultimately, CAUSE TO BECOME NOT ALIVE). The function of the lexical insertion transformation(s) in this instance would be to derive the simplest form in the set (the simplex verb KILL) from the partial P-marker represented by the most complex (the structure underlying CAUSE TO BECOME NOT ALIVE). Moreover, the choice of this alternative (rather than the reverse, for instance) is predicated upon the further desire to avoid introducing a fundamentally new and more powerful type of transformational rule capable of creating or 'building' new syntactic structure, rather than simply deleting or destroying structure already present in the base.

But the forms in question are *not* synonymous. Chomsky notes that 'as has often been remarked, "causative" verbs such as "kill"...etc., differ in meaning from the associated phrases "cause to die"..., etc., in that they imply a directness of connection between the agent and the resulting event that is lacking in the latter case' (1970a, p. 58, n. 7). Thus, to cite a classic case, while King David certainly 'caused' the death of his rival Uriah, he did not actually 'kill' him.[2]

Few of the classic purely 'syntactic' cases fare any better on this score, either. Take the old favorite, the active–passive distinction, for example. Katz and Postal insist that they 'can find no difference in meaning between actives and their corresponding passives' (1964, p. 73). This does not mean that there are no such differences to be found. An alternative interpretation is suggested by Chafe: 'a remarkable insensitivity to meaning differences exhibiting any degree of subtlety' (1971, p. 11). And a certain metatheoretical bias might have dampened somewhat the diligence with which Katz and Postal set to the task of searching such differences out (not to mention the fact that such differences become most apparent only at the discourse level, with which TGG has so far failed to concern itself seriously). In any event, Chambers had no such

---

[1] Namely, adjunction (or addition), deletion, permutation and substitution, all of which – including McCawley's 'new' function – are special cases of *substitution* (see Prideaux, 1970b, p. 46).

[2] We can assume that Nathan was making a moral, rather than a linguistic judgment in II Samuel 12:9 – or else that he was simply speaking loosely.

difficulty: he presents a host of examples exhibiting differences of this sort (1970; see especially pp. 1–21), as does Chafe (1970, pp. 219ff). As Chambers suggests: 'Active and passive sentence types do not [in general] occur in free variation but are conditioned by the "focus of attention" in the encoding situation' (p. v) and 'Since focus is semantically significant, the standard theory requires that it be accounted for at the level of deep structure' (p. vi).

In general, then, I tend to agree with Chafe that genuine synonymy is 'relatively rare in language', if it exists at all (1971, pp. 9ff). And in such relatively rare instances where apparently genuine 'free' or 'stylistic' variation does seem to be involved (as between Chafe's STEVE PUT ON HIS CLOTHES and STEVE PUT HIS CLOTHES ON (p. 10)), a straightforward surface generalization of the Harris type (1957) is all that seems to be required to relate the forms. In any event, numerous examples can easily be found (both for *avant-garde* 'generative semantic' models, as well as from the more classical 'centrality of syntax' view-point) in which syntactic structures which have been (and presumably still are) said to be derived from the same underlying structures prove upon close inspection *not* to be synonymous, at least not in general. That is, as many linguists have emphasized, many such structures are, at most, synonymous *only on one reading*. But how, in such cases, are the meaning differences on any remaining reading(s) to be characterized? Merely to say that the additional meaning(s) are 'latent', as Chomsky suggests (1965a, p. 224, n. 9), is to say nothing at all. The only course of action which seems relevant (apart from changing the metatheory in the direction of still greater power by introducing some new supplementary principles of 'surface structure interpretation' of the sort which Chomsky now seems to favor[1]) would be to provide some meaning-bearing marker in the base to distinguish between the two (as Chambers does). But can we then account for instances or readings in which the structures *are* used synonymously? This is a circular discussion, leading me to suspect that the whole frame of reference, according to which the speaker's 'paraphrasing skill' (Katz and Fodor, 1963, p. 175) is given so much analytical importance, may be misdirected.

At the other extreme we find forms and structures which seem synonymous enough, yet which *cannot in principle* be derived from the same

---

[1] See especially Chomsky, 1970a. For a discussion of some difficulties inherent in Chomsky's implicit notion of 'surface focus', see Chambers (1970, especially pp. vi–vii).

deep structures (at least not without giving the theory further power, once again, which hardly seems advisable).[1] Kinship systems, for example, manifest particularly acute difficulties in this connection. Chomsky (1970a, p. 59) mentions (but rejects) the possibility of deriving 'uncle' from the structure of the synonymous expression 'brother of (father-or-mother)'. By the same token, one might derive 'father' from its synonym (on one reading) 'son of (father-or-mother) of (father-or-mother)'; or from 'grandson of (father-or-mother) of (father-or-mother) of (father-or-mother)'; or from 'great grandson of. . .,' etc. Finding the syntactically most complex 'deep' representation from which all members of this paraphrastic set might be derived is likely to be difficult. Similarly, how is one to account for the obvious relation of paraphrase between such forms as 'tomorrow' and 'two days after yesterday' in terms of this criterion? For just as 'tomorrow' is synonymous with 'two days after yesterday', it is also synonymous with 'three days after the day before yesterday'; and with 'four days after the day before the day before yesterday'; and so on.

The argument that two structures are synonymous if and only if they can be derived from the same 'deep' structure fails in both directions:[2] we find both non-synonymous expressions which (traditionally) *are* derived in this way (and we are thus unable to account for the semantic distinctiveness of those readings which distinguish them) and we also find seemingly synonymous expressions which *cannot* be derived in this way (so proving that the 'common deep structure' approach cannot be the *general* solution to the problem of synonymy). I conclude, then, that synonymy is by no means so significant a phenomenon as generative grammarians have suggested, but is one that Chomsky himself might have 'abstracted' or 'idealized' away, had it not become so quickly and firmly canonized as part of his basic metatheory. In sum, there is reason to think that generative syntacticians may have picked the wrong phenomena to concern themselves with here – I would even argue that they have chosen the wrong *class* of phenomena (see 7.3). They might better have joined the structuralists in focusing attention more on the question of how speakers use the resources of their language in order to differentiate meanings as required, rather than on such contextually determined by-products as ambiguity (where two potential messages may fail to be

[1] See especially Peters and Ritchie (1969), Peters (1970) and Bach (1971a and 1971b).
[2] Cf. Chomsky's parallel argument against the notion that 'two utterances are phonemically distinct if and only if they differ in meaning' (1957, pp. 94–5).

distinguished formally when the situation does not require it, i.e. where the situation itself dictates which meaning it intended) and paraphrase (where formal distinctions which could be employed to distinguish potential messages may be used indiscriminately in situations where the distinctions are not crucial).

In any event, the question whether synonymy even exists – and if so, when we have genuine instances and when we do not – is not one which can be as easily answered as the transformationalists have suggested. The problem is of the same order of difficulty as that of establishing whether two forms are morphologically linked and, if so, how close the connection is in particular cases. The problem in both situations is the same: how do we determine what the semantic relationships 'in a language' really are? In more general terms, Sigurd asks:

Which units should be grouped as variants of one invariant? How great a formal and semantic variation should we allow? Should passive be grouped with active in spite of formal and semantic (or stylistic?) differences? Should the *green book* be grouped with *the book that is green*? Should *That he came was nice* be grouped with *It was nice that he came*? Should *Eliot refused the offer* be grouped with *Eliot's refusal of the offer*? (1970, p. 17).

These questions are fundamental, and we need answers to them *before* such issues as the evaluation of alternative linguistic descriptions can be taken seriously. Yet to find such answers we need both a basic conceptual reorientation and methods and techniques of research hitherto unknown to the linguistic community (see chapter 9 for suggestions).

5.4   A recapitulation

In the previous two chapters I have been concerned mainly with the kinds of linguistic descriptions which have flowed from the 'content' or 'innate universals' view of the language-acquisition device. In particular, I have directed attention chiefly to a specific set of representative problems of Russian phonology and Lightner's treatment of them. This work derives from Chomsky's criterion that:

To establish general principles of organization for grammar [i.e. the essential linguistic universals, etc.], we must show that these principles are consistent with the facts in a variety of languages and that, on the basis of these principles, one can explain phenomena that must otherwise be regarded as accidental (1967d, p. 126).

I assume that it is now obvious that there is no empirical content in the word 'can' so far as it relates to the theory of TGG. This is because there are no effective constraints on the notion of 'possible lexical representation' in generative phonology and on the notion 'possible deep structure' in generative syntax. Constraints on rules are meaningless so long as corresponding constraints are not also imposed on underlying representations; the whole linguistic *system* must be constrained, not just that part that one happens to be particularly interested in. I have shown that without effective constraints on the abstractness of lexical representations and rule ordering, it is a foregone conclusion that any (non-contradictory) system of proposed 'universal' constraints on phonological rules is in principle viable in terms of Chomsky's proposed criterion, the only limiting factors being the resourcefulness (say in taking advantage of known historical facts) and the ingenuity of the analyst.

Fortunately, there is an alternative. The one which I have in mind is admittedly old-fashioned and currently out of favor. But faced with the possibility that Chomsky's 'rationalist' speculation may have failed us, there is reason to think that the quick dismissal of an earlier 'empiricist' orientation may have been premature. The alternative is simply to give serious reconsideration to the old 'empiricist' idea that languages *can be learned*, after all. In the following chapter, therefore, I shall direct my attention to a number of alternative descriptive schemes which are in accord with this traditional view.

6 Some process-oriented counterproposals

6.1 Aspects of Chomsky's crusade against the phoneme

Two factors have been mainly responsible for the current state of disrepute in which the old 'data-analysis' orientation in linguistics rests today. The first was Chomsky's initially persuasive but ultimately self-contradictory argument against formulating a 'discovery procedure' for grammars. I have discussed this argument in sufficient detail in a previous chapter and no more need be said about it here. Chomsky's second approach was more complex and has had correspondingly more impact. This was his crusade against 'autonomous' or 'taxonomic' phonemics (see especially Chomsky, 1964). Although the status of the phoneme is of no essential relevance here – the possibilities inherent in the entire 'data-analysis' strategy being hardly exhausted by the attempts which the structuralists actually made within this frame of reference – the phonemic principle still represents a particularly outstanding product of the 'learning algorithm' approach and so has some bearing on the main problem at hand.

We must establish first which specific version of 'phonemic theory' Chomsky actually attacked. Though he admits that 'modern phonologists have not achieved anything like unanimity', he insists that 'a body of doctrine has emerged to all or part of which a great many [structural] linguists would subscribe' (1964, p. 91). To refer to this body of doctrine ('abstracting away from much variation'), Chomsky coins the term 'taxonomic phonemics' (p. 91), which he defines as that version of classical phonemic theory which subscribes to the following five conditions: (1) 'phonetic specifiability', (2) 'linearity', (3) 'invariance', (4) 'bi-uniqueness', and (5) 'local determinancy'. These are familiar enough by this time that I need not pause here to recapitulate Chomsky's definitions.[1]

---

[1] The first criterion ('phonetic specifiability') is perhaps exceptional in this regard. It states that 'each utterance of any language can be uniquely represented as a sequence of

But it must have struck the classical phonemicist of 1962 as strange to hear his work so described, since the terms (biuniqueness excluded) appear to have been coined (like the pejorative label 'taxonomic phonemics' itself) by Chomsky. Asked to state the major principles of phonemic analysis, the typical phonemicist of the period would surely have listed a different set. Hockett (1958, pp. 107–10), for example, argues that the 'four fundamental principles [of phonemic analysis] on which almost all specialists are in agreement' are as follows: (I) *The Principle of Contrast and Complementation* (= 'complementary' or 'mutually exclusive' distribution; cf. Pike, 1947b, pp. 73–104, and Gleason, 1961, p. 263); (II) *The Principle of Phonetic Similarity* (cf. Pike, 1947b, pp. 67–72, and Gleason, 1961, p. 261); (III) *The Principle of Neatness of Pattern* (= 'pattern congruity' or 'structural pressure'; cf. Swadesh, 1934, p. 35; Pike, 1947b, pp. 116–21 and 128–58; and Gleason, 1961, pp. 283–4); and, marginally, (IV) *The Principle of Economy* (usually construed as 'economy of inventory'). Is there any connection between these widely accepted principles (especially I–III in Hockett's list) and the ones which Chomsky presents? Lamb, for one, thinks not, but rather that 'C[lassical]-phonemics should not be confused with the fictitious framework which Chomsky calls taxonomic phonemics (T-phonemics), a system apparently created by him to serve as the helpless victim of a dramatic onslaught' (1966b, p. 540). But Lamb overstates his case. Chomsky's first criterion, for instance, is closely related to Hockett's second, and for our purposes we may regard the difference as terminological (but see p. 169, n. 1, above). As for the others, while we may agree that these do not necessarily describe a set of principles to which all classical phonemicists would necessarily have subscribed (Chomsky concedes this himself), I would argue that there is little question that the principles *were* employed (at least implicitly) by many if not most North American structuralists of the post-Bloomfieldian era. Moreover, the main reason for this seems clear: without

phones', presumably as defined by some theory of universal phonetics (Chomsky, 1964, p. 93). Though obviously fundamental, this assumption is rarely discussed, no doubt because it is regarded as non-controversial by most analysts (transformationalists included). Yet this is not so. There is much evidence that the *syllable* might serve as a better phonological prime (for many purposes) than either the *segment* or the *segment-feature*, even though most attention in recent years has been focused on matching only the latter two notions. (What is the status of a stop consonant, for example, apart from any associated vowel?) Although an important set of empirical issues is at stake in this discussion, I shall continue to take Chomsky's criterion of 'phonetic specifiability' for granted here.

supplementary criteria of linearity, etc. to accompany the more basic notion of contrast (cf. Hockett's Principle I), the specific *locus* of a contrast could not be determined unambiguously in any particular case.

Chomsky's terminological innovations are no doubt responsible for part of the confusion engendered on this point. For although Chomsky appears to be criticizing four *distinct* criteria, the four he mentions are not independent, but all reduce to one. Chomsky admits as much himself. On the one hand, he notes that 'the invariance condition has no clear meaning unless the linearity condition is also met' (1964, p. 94), and this is obvious from his examples (pp. 96ff). As for the criteria of 'biuniqueness' and 'local determinacy', Chomsky invokes the latter only in order to qualify what he means by the former, so far as 'taxonomic phonemics' is concerned. That is, the brand of phonemics which he is criticizing adopts that particularly 'strong' form of biuniqueness in which only 'purely phonetic' considerations (or 'considerations involving only "neighboring sounds" ') might be utilized in interpreting a particular sequence of phones or phonemes ('rather than literal biuniqueness in the technical sense', in which any considerations, morphological, syntactic or semantic, might be brought to bear in interpreting particular strings; see Chomsky, 1964, pp. 94–5). Finally, as Chomsky then goes on to say, this 'particularly strong form of the biuniqueness and local determinacy conditions' is precisely the one which can be deduced 'from the linearity and absolute invariance condition' (p. 95; note the singular form here). In the final analysis, therefore, there is only *one* condition at issue in this discussion (besides the 'phonetic specifiability' criterion, which I ignore here), namely the particular 'strong' form of *biuniqueness* described, the only purpose of the linearity-invariance subcondition being to insure that this criterion is satisfied. In order to distinguish this form of biuniqueness from other forms, let us refer to the criterion at issue as the SIB criterion (with S for 'strong' or 'strict', I for 'invariant' and B for 'biunique').

We can now readily identify the real-life historical analogue to the criterion in question. To Chomsky, the SIB criterion specifies that 'the unique phonemic representation corresponding to a given phonetic form can be determined [only] by "purely phonetic" considerations, or perhaps, considerations involving only "neighboring sounds" ' (1964, p. 95). Compare this with Joos' remarks that

phonemics must be kept unmixed from all that lies on the opposite side of it from phonetics: kept uninfluenced by the identities of the items of higher rank (morphemes and so on) which the phonemes 'spell', and hence free from all that their identities entail, such as their meaning and their grammar (1963, p. 96).

Clearly, the SIB criterion is nothing other than the old 'separation of levels' (or SOL) criterion of Bloch, Joos and many others now cast in a new guise. The (only) school of linguistic thought at which Chomsky directs his attack, therefore, is that school which held that a strict 'separation of levels' must be maintained in grammar construction, the chief implication for phonology being that the so-called 'phonemic' level of a linguistic description must be fully definable in terms of the phonetic evidence *alone*. In short, when Chomsky speaks of 'taxonomic' phonemics, he is speaking *only* of SOL-phonemics (equivalent to SIB-phonemics).

Though many linguists today tend to think of 'separation of levels' as a quaint and rather droll survival from pre-enlightenment times (something like alchemy or the idea that the world is flat), the SOL (or SIB) constraint was not really so ill-conceived as all that. Indeed, it is difficult to imagine how analysis could proceed if something like it were not invoked. All linguists might agree to the principle of contrast, i.e. that 'if X contrasts with Y, then the phonemic representation of X differs from the phonemic representation of Y, where X and Y are utterances (let us assume, phonetically transcribed)' (Chomsky & Halle, 1965, p. 128). But how does one determine the specific *locus* of a contrast when more than one segment is involved? For instance, тот (= [tat]), DOT (= [dat]) and NOT (= [nat]) contrast, and so must be represented differently on the phonemic level. But how should this phonemic difference be represented? SIB (together with 'phonetic specifiability', which is assumed throughout) provides the answer: the underlying phonemic distinction is the same as the overt phonetic one, namely, a distinction involving differences in voicing and/or nasalization in the first segment.[1] This makes perfectly good sense.

Next consider words like CAT (= [kæt]), CAD (= [kæ:d]) and CAN (= [kæ̃:n]), where the situation is a bit more complicated. What is distinctive here? Is it the voicing (and/or nasalization) of the final consonant, the length (and/or nasalization) of the vowel, or perhaps both together? Once again, SIB provides a determinate answer: since voicing (and/or nasalization) of a consonant has already been established as a *potentially* distinctive characteristic in one environment (word-initially

---

[1] Certain phonetic details are ignored here and elsewhere.

or pre-vocalically), it is reasonable to think that this might represent our best choice in word-final (or post-vocalic) position, as well.[1] So we phonemicize the last three words as follows: /kæt/, /kæd/ and /kæn/, thereby implying that vowel length (and/or nasalization) are non-distinctive or redundant phonetic properties which are predictable in terms of the distinctive properties of voicing (and/or nasalization) in the following consonant. All well and good: we were faced with indeterminacy and our criterion solved the problem for us, and in a way which did no violence to our intuitions as native speakers.

But what are we to do with CAN'T (assuming, with Chomsky, that this is correctly rendered phonetically as [kæ̃:t], at least in some dialects)? This is the first dilemma which Chomsky presents us with (1964, p. 96). We have already decided on the basis of the forms just discussed (and other analogous cases) that vowel length (and/or nasalization) is, in general, *redundant* for English; yet when we compare [kæt] with [kæ̃:t] we find a case where the features in question appear to function in the same way as consonantal voicing (and/or nasalization) did in our first set of examples. No matter. Unless we abandon SIB, the choice is automatically made for us: length and nasalization (whenever they appear together) are distinctive, after all. So CAN'T is phonemicized as /kæ̃:t/ and CAN is *re*-phonemicized as /kæ̃:n/, thus implying that *both* vowel length *and* nasalization of the final consonant function together in distinguishing this latter word from another like CAD (= /kæd/). This is counter-intuitive.

Further investigation (Chomsky's second dilemma) shows that this is not an isolated case. Vowel length alone can *also* distinguish words in English, as in WRITER (phonetically [rayDɨr] in some dialects) vs. RIDER (= [ra:yDɨr]). This forces us to re-phonemicize CAD as /kæ:d/. So our final analysis looks like this:

[tat] = /tat/	[kæt] = /kæt/	[kæ̃:n] = /kæ̃:n/
[dat] = /dat/	[kæ:d] = /kæ:d/	[kæ̃:t] = /kæ̃:t/
[nat] = /nat/		

---

[1] Why a 'choice' is necessary in this situation has never been made clear. If the *two* phonetic features of vowel length and consonantal voicing always co-occur in a word like CAD to differentiate it from CAT, how can we be certain that only *one* of these serves a truly 'distinctive' function, while the other is essentially 'redundant' (cf. 9.2.1 below). Furthermore, many phonetic details thought to be initially introduced into the speech event 'automatically' as the result of the articulatory habit patterns of the *speaker* may play an important role in maintaining or reinforcing a perceptual distinction which the *hearer* might otherwise miss (see, for example, Denes, 1955.) As

No indeterminacies remain, and all problems of phonemic assignment are taken care of. But, as Chomsky (and Bloch himself (1941, p. 96)) point out, the analysis is distorted (or, in Bloch's terms, 'lopsided'): while we were able to find *many* environments in which voicing (and/or nasalization) of consonants could be contrastive in English, we were able to find *few* in which either vowel length and nasalization (before voiceless stops as in CAT vs. CAN'T) or vowel length alone (before the flap [D] as in WRITER vs. RIDER) could be; and yet our SIB criterion forced us to regard *all* the features in question as (co-equally) distinctive in *all* environments. What is more, this asymmetry seemed to be paralleled by a persistent intuition that, in the problematical cases, at least, it did not 'seem' that the native speaker was ever 'conscious' of vowel length or nasalization in the same way as he 'seemed' to be conscious of differences in the consonants. All a bit vague, perhaps, but sufficient for Chomsky's purposes: it serves to show for him that the attempt to develop a theory of phonology (or anything else) along data-analysis lines was 'ill-conceived from the start' (1964, p. 99).[1] And, indeed, though the casual observer can hardly be expected to believe it, on this evidence (and very little else) the entire data-analysis approach to the study of language has been virtually abandoned by a generation of linguists in favor of an alternative approach which requires the positing of a complex set of innate linguistic universals.

So much for Chomsky's more extreme extrapolations. Less extreme (and correspondingly more manageable) is his best-known conclusion on this matter namely, that a level of SIB-phonemics is simply 'not incorporable into a descriptively adequate grammar' (1964, p. 111). In order to support this point, Chomsky must demonstrate that SIB-phonemics is neither appropriate as the level of lexical representation (which is the

implied by the model on p. 303 below, (the physiology of) speech articulation (State 2) and (that of) speech perception (State 4) are different things, and we should not be surprised to find each operating according to its own set of basic principles.

[1] Yet there are other possible answers to the question 'What is the significance of all this?' One alternative answer was adopted by the structuralists, as discussed on pp. 180–1 below: it might simply mean that one's analysis is *not yet complete*. Relatively few linguists regarded the SIB-phoneme as the absolute end-all of phonological description; the structuralists, it should not be forgotten, had their *morphophonemes*, too.

Few linguists, however, have managed to keep their heads on this issue. Matthews is one exception, noting as he does that 'the onus is as much on [Chomsky] to prove that there is no conceivable "empiricist" solution as it is on an "empiricist" to devise such a solution; it is not sufficient merely to belittle the proposals which have so far appeared' (1967, p. 123).

one in which we are most interested), nor as the level on which the 'terminal alphabet' of the grammar is defined (cf. Householder, 1965, p. 29), nor, finally, as an independent level intermediate between the two. Chomsky and Halle themselves have focused their main attack on the third interpretation, as though it were clear that the other two possibilities were not worth mentioning. I shall attempt to reconstruct some of the arguments against the first two interpretations, as well.

First of all, let us consider SIB-phonemic representation as a candidate for the *lexicon*. Postal states (correctly, I think) that this was the approach adopted by many American analysts of the post-Bloomfieldian era (from the mid-forties through the late fifties) 'which eliminated morphophonemic representation and stated all morphophonemic facts by means of lists of alternates' (1968, p. 99).[1] The major difficulty with this position, as Postal points out, is that it does not consistently distinguish between irregularities (which presumably should be expressed in the *lexicon*) and predictable alternations (which presumably should be expressed in the form of *rules*); in short, all alternations are 'assimilated...to wholly irregular suppletions' (Postal, 1968, p. 99).

Consider the following illustration from Russian. If the various alternants of the roots which appear in the respective paradigms of the words for 'table', 'village' and 'river' are transcribed (SIB-)phonemically and these transcriptions deemed appropriate for the lexicon, a complex context-restricted lexical statement results in each case.

$$(1) \quad \text{(table)} \rightarrow \begin{cases} \text{stal'} \ / \ \text{\_\_\_é} \\ \text{stól} \ / \ \text{\_\_\_\#} \\ \text{stal} \ / \ \text{Elsewhere} \end{cases}$$

$$(2) \quad \text{(village)} \rightarrow \begin{cases} \text{s'il'} \ / \ \text{\_\_\_é} \\ \text{s'ól} \ / \ \text{in Plural} \\ \text{s'il} \ / \ \text{Elsewhere} \end{cases}$$

$$(3) \quad \text{(river)} \rightarrow \begin{cases} \text{r'ik'} \ / \ \text{\_\_\_\{é, í\} in Sg.} \\ \text{r'ék'} \ / \ \text{\_\_\_i in Plural } (= \text{Nom. Pl. and Acc. Pl.}) \\ \text{r'ék} \ / \ \text{in Acc. Sg. and Gen. Pl.} \\ \text{r'ik} \ / \ \text{Elsewhere} \end{cases}$$

[1] Cf. Hockett, as late as 1968: 'The words of a language OCCUR. Morphemes – in the Bloomfieldian sense – also occur, though not in general alone. But morphophonemes do not occur at all, except in the linguist's description. They are not things in a language; they are a descriptive device, symbols invented by the analyst for the economical statements of certain kinds of alternations among actual forms' (1968a, p. 151). Compare Twaddell, thirty-three years earlier, where at least the distinction between what is real (or observable) and what is hypothetical (or abstract) is recog-

The difficulty with these representations is that all fail to capture the following generalizations, apparent even in the small sample of forms indicated:[1]

(a) All consonants are palatalized before *e*.

(b) Velars are palatalized before *i*, as well.

(c) Unstressed *o* is not differentiated phonetically from *a* after a hard (non-palatalized) consonant, nor from *i* after a soft (palatalized) one.

(d) Unstressed *e* is also not differentiated phonetically from *i*.

(e) Many nouns (which we may call class I nouns, such as STOL 'table'; cf. POLK 'regiment', KOT 'cat', SNOP 'sheaf', etc.) are always stressed on their desinence or ending (unless no ending appears, in which case the stem receives the stress).

(f) Many other nouns (class II nouns, such as SELO 'village'; cf. OKNO 'window', VESLO 'oar', PJATNO 'spot', etc.) are always stressed on their ending in the singular, but on their stem in the plural.

(g) Other nouns (class III nouns, such as REKA 'river'; cf. ŠČEKA 'cheek', RUKA 'hand', NOGA 'leg', etc.) manifest the more complex pattern in which stress appears on the stem in the Acc. Sg., Nom. Pl., Acc. Pl., and Gen. Pl., but on the ending elsewhere.

At this point it is clear that if we remove all the information from our earlier 'phonemic' lexicon which is predictable in terms of generalizations (a)–(g) above, and account for it instead within the 'rule' component of the grammar, our lexicon can be simplified to the point where we need only posit a single 'underlying' phonological representation for each root morpheme (provided we also associate with each a diacritic feature which relates it to a particular stress pattern), i.e.:

(1′) (table)→ °/stol°/ˌ I

(2′) (village)→°/s'ol°/ˌ II

(3′) (river)→ °/rek°/ˌ III

nized: 'It cannot be too strongly emphasized that a form is not a part of any specific utterance. An utterance is an event; a form is an abstraction from a large number of utterances' (1935, p. 70). Clearly, *all types* (as opposed to tokens) are abstractions and 'inventions of the analyst' – including words, morphemes, phonemes and everything else the linguist talks about (except, of course, the individual utterances themselves).

[1] Further analysis along the lines indicated would yield a large number of lexical entries involving alternate shapes which differed from one another *in the same ways*, thus indicating that these generalizations are highly productive. (There are a few (pat-

In doing this, we have re-established a consistent attitude towards our fundamental notions of *lexicon* (where irregularities and non-predictable entities are to be expressed) and *rule* (for the expression of generalizations which subsume large numbers of forms). Thus a (SIB-)phonemic lexicon may be criticized on the same grounds on which Bloch and Trager criticized any analysis presented in purely *phonetic* terms: 'Instead of giving us a clear picture of the language, it complicates the vocabulary and obscures the grammar with a profusion of incidental and irrelevant particulars' (1942, p. 39). We therefore conclude (with most structuralists – Hockett apparently excepted; cf. p. 175, n. 1) that the level of SIB-phonemic representation is, in general, inappropriate for the lexicon.

Let us now consider the possibility that SIB-phonemes might constitute an appropriate 'terminal vocabulary' for the grammar. This is apparently the position held by the stratificationalists (see especially Gleason, 1964, pp. 77–80) and defended by Householder (1965, p. 29). Postal (1968, p. 99) also attributes it to Bloomfield and to Z. Harris. The position has a number of pragmatic advantages over the alternative approach (supposedly adopted by the theory of generative phonology; but see Householder, 1965, pp. 28ff, and E. Pike, 1970, pp. 31–2, 44) which regards the final output of the grammar as *phonetic*. For one thing, as Householder points out, the terminal-phoneme approach permits the analyst to side-step the perplexing (and so far unsolved) problem of having to establish 'some solid basis for phonetic identity' (1965, p. 28), i.e. of having to formulate an empirically justified universal theory of phonetics; and so it enables him to avoid that 'morass of phonetic hair-splitting that the phonemic principle was intended to extricate us from long ago' (p. 29). The SIB-phoneme, in brief, is an ever-available, convenient and (thanks to the tightness of the SIB constraint itself, which insures that no phonetic detail will be lost or misplaced in the phonemic suffle) *safe* shorthand for representing utterances in a way which is not burdensome in terms of excessive detail.[1] And to consider the language learner, the SIB-phoneme concept seems plausible in the sense that it does not appear to be necessary to ascribe to the child any innate theory of phonetic identity in order to make it possible for him to acquire SIB-phonemes, since the two broad capaci-

terned) exceptions to some of the generalizations stated above, but these need not concern us here.)

[1] The notion is so useful for this purpose that I shall continue to use it throughout the remainder of this chapter, despite its apparent defects in other contexts.

ties to discriminate and generalize in terms of one's experiences appear sufficient (cf. 3.5 above).

But one powerful argument makes the notion of a phonemic-terminal alphabet unacceptable (despite its convenience as a useful shorthand device) on other than pragmatic grounds. This is the well-known fact that speakers do not articulate phonemes, but rather phone-types (or syllable-types; see p. 169, n. 1) which are highly specific (and which differentiate one foreign accent from another, for instance). Moreover, the same phoneme is by no means always realized in the same way in different phonetic contexts or environments; nor can all the 'allophonic variants' of a phoneme so produced be attributed to mere 'sloppiness' in speech. This implies that somewhere in the speaker's internal language-processing mechanism a large number of these various manifestations of a given phoneme must somehow be differentiated. In short, I cannot conceive of such things as ' "commands" to the articulatory apparatus', for example, as *not* constituting 'linguistic' information, as Gleason, for one, seems able to do (1964, p. 79). I make no claim of knowing how information of this sort ought best to be characterized in a linguistic description, or what form it might take in the central nervous system, yet it does seem fairly obvious that a certain amount of information about phonetic detail (namely, that part over which the speaker has actual control), which must inescapably be associated with some kind of 'neuro-physiological process' (Gleason, 1964, p. 78), must also be regarded as an essential part of language or linguistic processing.[1]

This brings us to the last and most disputed question of the three: whether SIB-phonemics might constitute a significant level of representation somewhere between the lexical (or morphophonemic) and the terminal (or phonetic). Chomsky and Halle say no, chiefly on the strength of an argument which first appeared in Halle (1959) and was repeated in Chomsky (1964) and elsewhere. This argument focuses on the fact that there is no voiced–voiceless contrast in native Russian vocabulary involving either the affricates (c, $\check{c}$) or the velar fricative (x). That is, whenever any of these three phone-types is articulated with voicing in Russian, this can always be predicted (for native vocabulary, once again) by means of a general rule which is statable in terms of the phonological (in fact, phonetic) environments in which these segment-types appear. For all the other obstruents in the language there are some

---

[1] For further clarification of this point, see my discussion of the communication event or language process in 9.1.1 below.

environments in which *either* the voiced or voiceless member may appear (i.e. they contrast). The difficulty arises when we consider what happens to these two obstruent sub-classes in those particular environments where the voiced–voiceless opposition is neutralized, such as immediately before another voiced obstruent. In this environment, for instance, *both* underlying (lexical) $°/t°/$ and $°/d°/$ are articulated with voicing, as well as underlying $°/c°/$, $°/č°/$, or $°/x°/$. It is reasonable to suppose, therefore, that a single generalization or rule of the following sort might be operative in all such cases: voice all obstruents immediately before a voiced obstruent.[1] If this rule is applied to an underlying $°/t°/$ or $°/d°/$ (or any other obstruent except $°/c°/$, $°/č°/$ or $°/x°/$), the result gives formal expression to the fact that an underlying voiceless–voiced distinction is (contextually) neutralized in such an environment into a single SIB-phoneme (in this case /d/). But this cannot be the case with $°/c°/$, $°/č°/$ or $°/x°/$. The output of the rule in question as applied to these morphophonemes cannot be the SIB-*phonemes* /c/, /č/ and /x/, because *there are no such phonemes*; the output in this case can only be construed as a *phonetic* representation. In order to insure that there will be some particular level or stage in a derivational sequence which is identical to the SIB-phonemic, therefore, the apparent generalization in question (which involves voicing *all* obstruents in the language) must, as Halle points out, be broken up into two parts, ordered as indicated:

(a) Voice all obstruents except $°/c°/$, $°/č°/$ and $°/x°/$ in the context before a voiced obstruent. (This is a 'morphophonemic' rule, since it relates the level of morphophonemics to the level of SIB-phonemics.)

(b) Now voice /c/, /č/ and /x/ (which are non-distinct from the underlying $°/c°/$, $°/č°/$ and $°/x°/$, respectively) in this same context. (This is an 'allophonic' or purely 'phonetic' rule, since it relates the level of SIB-phonemics to the phonetic output.)

By insisting, therefore, on the incorporation into the grammar of a distinct level of SIB-phonemics, we have rendered it impossible to state in its most general form *a generalization which is* (*phonotactically*) *true in this form.*[2] This argument is a very forceful one, since it involves (con-

---

[1] This generalization can be extended to incorporate all obstruents in an entire cluster and applies to devoicing, as well (see, e.g., Halle, 1959, p. 64).

[2] This situation is to be contrasted with one involving a 'generalization' of the sort 'Switch all velars to palatals in the context before front vowels' (cf. Lightner's (k:č) rule introduced on p. 146 above), a statement having certain implications which

trary to the situations discussed in 5.2 above) a legitimate use of the notion of simplicity, namely, that we don't posit more hypothetical constructs than are necessary to account for the facts.[1] For in this case our *a priori* insistence upon an independent level of SIB-phonemics breaks a legitimate (and learnable) generalization about Russian phonotactics into two fully complementary parts.[2] The artificiality is obvious. So on this ground I conclude (with Chomsky and Halle) that a level of SIB-phonemics has no obvious place within a generative grammar.

But this conclusion does not affect the over-all 'process' or 'dataanalysis' approach to language as a whole (even assuming that the notion of generative grammar itself is viable). It merely indicates that the 'taxonomic phoneme' – defined in the restricted sense of the SIB-phoneme and no other – may have problems associated with it. Furthermore, SIB-phonemics (the only brand which Chomsky brings any specific arguments against) was not universally accepted, even in North America, during the structuralist period. Householder makes this clear in an article which first appeared in 1959:

In phonological grammar the two chief nuisances are biuniqueness and 'once a phoneme always a phoneme' [strict or absolute invariance – BLD]. The former of these terms means that to any given phone-type in a given environment there must correspond only one possible phoneme, and to any phoneme in a given string there must correspond only one phone-type; the latter that if a given phone-type enters into oppositions sufficient to establish phonemic status in one environment, it carries phonemic status also in all environments. We have now enough experience with describing phonologies to know that a more useful prime is often capable of corresponding to more than one phonetype in a given environment, and need not always be uniquely determinable from the sequences of phones, i.e. several different phoneme sequences may have the same phonetic shape. We also know that it is frequently simpler and more elegant to have units so chosen that a given phone-type in one environment may be an allophone of one such phoneme, but in another an allophone (or the only allophone) of a different one (Householder, 1961, pp. 19–20).

In other words, the problems did not go unnoticed by the structuralists.

---

are demonstrably *not* true of Russian phonotactics in general (see chapter 5, p. 140, n. 1).

[1] This is to be sharply contrasted with the notion of 'simplicity' discussed in 5.2 which involved the incorporation into linguistic theory of a set of arbitrary assumptions regarding the *kinds or rules* which the language learner is said to prefer (see especially pp. 136–41).

[2] Notice also that the rule in question is fully productive of recent borrowings into Russian, as well (cf. *bejzbol*, 'baseball', *fudbol*, 'football', *žugboks*, 'juke box', etc.).

There were differences of opinion, however (and fortunately so; cf. 1.3.4), about their resolution.

One solution (proposed by Householder) was the one which Chomsky and Halle later chose to adopt: we might, as Householder put it, simply 'drop the useless term [SIB-]"phoneme" and treat morphophonemes as our phonological primes' (i.e. the SOL constraint might most usefully be abandoned and 'grammatical prerequisites' (cf. Pike, 1947a and 1952) re-introduced directly into phonological analysis). The SIB-advocates, too, recognized the problems and most accepted the notion of the morphophoneme as an appropriate solution, but they did not wish to equate the morphophonemes so devised with the notion of the 'phoneme' itself (as Bloomfield and Sapir seem to have been willing to do). Hence, attempts of the sort which Householder documents to relax the SIB restrictions on phonological analysis were not opposed in principle (i.e. as they related to a phonological descriptive as a whole), but only in relation to the SIB-phoneme, which some wished to preserve.[1] Grammatical information, in short, was not dismissed as irrelevant to *linguistic description*, but only as irrelevant to *phonemic analysis*. These points are clearly expressed by Hill in his 1955 summary report on 'Linguistics since Bloomfield':

In phonemic theory, perhaps the chief advance has been the elimination of an error [*sic*] on Bloomfield's part. Bloomfield, in his discussion of the unstressed central vowel of English, the schwa, said that the schwa was the unstressed representative of most of the vowel phonemes which appear in stressed syllables. This introduced a theory of phonemic overlapping, which had the unfortunate result of *making the boundaries between phonemes arbitrary*, and the whole analysis confusing. Bloch is primarily responsible for recognizing this danger, and countering it with the postulate that *identical sounds must always belong to the same phoneme* [= the SIB constraint in a nutshell –BLD]. It is this axiom which denies such statements as this about Icelandic: 'though /n/ and /ŋ/ contrast, when /n/ becomes /ŋ/ in a proper name like Jon Grimsson, the /ŋ/ is serving as an allophone of /n/.' All such statements are now shown to be *a result of mixing of levels*. THE VARIATION IS NON-SIGNIFICANT, OF COURSE, but belongs on the *morphemic* rather than the *phonemic* level (p. 254, italics and capitals added).

Today Hill's concern at 'mixing of levels' seems rather strange – not to mention the idea that 'non-significant' phonetic information should remain in any representation which is consistent with the phonemic principle. But at the time the chief preoccupation of phonemicists seems

[1] As Householder put it, 'Attempts at relaxing these restrictions... are usually countered by the charge "Those are morphophonemes".' (1961, p. 20).

to have been to avoid problems of indeterminacy in analysis, and this concern got them into some of the difficulties which Householder, Chomsky and others have noticed. This comes out clearly in Bloch's now-classic paper on 'Phonemic overlapping' (1941), to which Hill is obviously referring.

The basic problem, as Bloch saw it, was this: Suppose we encounter two occurrences of the same phone 'x' and want to consider the possibility of assigning them to different phonemes. If we consider the phonetic facts alone, we can never make a non-arbitrary choice, for 'there is never any clue in the utterance itself to tell us which kind of x we are dealing with' (p. 96). On the other hand, there are serious difficulties in bringing morphological evidence to bear in such decisions (cf. 4.5.3 above). In the case of the unstressed vowels of English, for example, we would be forced to

defer the phonemic analysis until we [should] chance to hear a stressed form of the same word, which may not occur at all in the dialect we are studying, or which, if it does occur, *we may fail to recognize as 'the same word'* (p. 95, italics added).

Even more serious are problems like how to analyze the dental stop segment in an English word like STOP; for in such cases there is no relevant morphological evidence available even if such evidence were allowed. That is to say, while some analysts might interpret the flap in WRITER as a phonemic /t/ because of the voiceless dental stop in the form WRITE (and the flap in RIDER as a /d/ because of RIDE), we find in the case of STOP that there are 'no alternate forms of the same word' which give additional information relevant to the analysis of the segment in question. Some other criterion, it was thought, must be appealed to in such instances, and Bloch proposed the very tight SIB constraint, so setting up a level of description for which (1) no morphological information is permitted (since such evidence is ambiguous or irrelevant) and (2) no overlapping is permitted ('once a phoneme, always a phoneme', as the old slogan put it). Now even the problem of STOP could be 'solved': the second segment must be analyzed as /t/ rather than /d/ on the ground of invariance with respect to the feature of *voicing*. Thus an English /t/ might be aspirated and released (initially), unaspirated and released (as in STOP) or even unreleased (as in word-final position), but at least it could always be recognized as a /t/ because it remained *voiceless* in *all* positions.

The SIB-phonemicist would object to the idea that WRITER contains the 'phoneme' /t/, for two reasons. First, the flap in WRITER (in the dialect in question) is *voiced*; to assign this segment to /t/ would eliminate all possibility of retaining voicelessness as a defining feature of the class. Second, the decision to distinguish the flap in WRITER from that in RIDER was grounded, at least in part, on morphological evidence, which has been disallowed for the reasons indicated. Therefore, the SIB-phonemicist would argue, the flap must in both cases be analyzed as a /d/ on the *phonemic* level, though the words may, of course, continue to be distinguished lexically (or *morpho*phonemically) in terms of a °/t°/ versus a °/d°/.

To Bloch this approach had advantages and disadvantages, though it is the disadvantages which stand out today. Bloch recognized that strict adherence to the SIB constraint in phonemic analysis led to a number of unsatisfactory results (such as calling the vowels in BIT and BID 'totally different phonemes', although vowel length can ordinarily be predicted in terms of voicing in a following consonant). Chomsky and Halle have since demonstrated the potentially more significant result that incorporation of a SIB-phonemic level of representation into a grammar makes it impossible in some cases to state true and valid generalizations in their most general form. For Bloch, this corresponding advantage was, however, decisive: by incorporating the SIB constraint he was

able to account for all the facts of pronunciation, which is surely *the more important requirement*. The resulting system is lopsided; but the classes it sets up are such that if we start from the actual utterances of the dialect *we can never be in doubt* of the class to which any particular fraction of utterance must be assigned (1941, p. 96; italics added).

I submit that it was at this point – and not in his basic concern to formulate a 'discovery procedure for grammars' along data-analysis lines, as Chomsky has suggested – that Bloch and his contemporaries went astray.

Consider first the decision to eliminate all but phonetic information from phonemic analysis. This was predicated on the relative inaccessibility of information about morphological relationships among words. To be sure, this information is not as easy to find as many latter-day linguists have suggested (see especially pp. 122–6 above). On the other hand, the decision to set up a particular level of analysis (the 'SIB-phonemic') at which such evidence may conveniently be ignored does not *solve* the problem, but merely *defers* it: it passes the problem up to the morphemic or lexical level. To the extent that the SIB constraint has been founded on pragmatic considerations of this sort, I see little value in it.

But this was not the *only* reason for the separation of levels. In particular, one goal of phonemic theory for most of this century (at least since Sapir) has been to attempt to account for the phenomenon of the foreign accent as manifested in the speech of adult speakers. That is to say, it has long been recognized that native speakers of one language show a strong and persistent tendency to mispronounce unfamiliar sequences of phones (whether presented as nonsense forms, as forms from another language, or whatever) in specific ways – a kind of faulty repetition which, as Householder points out, is to be clearly differentiated both from phonetic *mimicry* and from any possible reference to *morphophonemic potential*, and hence a phenomenon which would appear to be determined by the nature of 'the sound system' of a language *alone* (Householder, 1966, p. 99). The concept of the phoneme thus arose initially not as a notion to be associated with generative grammar (or with a theory which supposed that 'all the structural information there is about a given language' must be incorporated into a single set of ordered rules (Householder, 1965, p. 18)), but as an independent linguistic notion designed to account for a wide range of observed facts about the ways in which adult speakers of different languages interpret and repeat speech sounds differently, and, so far as I know, this concept is still useful in this connection.[1] Therefore, until some other concept can account for facts of this sort more satisfactorily (or until it can be argued why attempts to explain such perceptual facts should be abandoned in favor of some supposedly more productive activity, such as grammar writing), the SIB-phoneme (or something like it, to be defined below) may be allowed to live on for the time being.[2]

This does not imply, however, that the SIB-phonemicists are above criticism. For in their exaggerated concern over 'indeterminacy' in analysis, the SIB-phonemicists were led, in the end, to compromise the very principle which they sought to formalize. The ultimate short-

---

[1] See Derwing (1965) for an illustrative study of some problems of cross-linguistic interpretation between Russian and English and the role which the SIB-phoneme may play in their explication.

[2] I refer to the basic problem of deciding what should (or can) be explained in linguistics in 5.3 and chapter 9 below. By this point it should be clear that the transformationalist desire to explain 'forms' via a generative grammar has not produced the same interesting and predictive results as the phoneme theory can be credited with in elucidating the different ways in which a particular phone is interpreted by speakers of different languages.

coming of the SIB constraint is that it forces the analyst to make arbitrary choices with respect to the phonemic status of some phonetic feature even in those environments where the feature does not differentiate utterances. For example, though variants of /t/ and /d/ may contrast in most environments in English, they do *not* do so (in many dialects) either in the environment #s___ or V̇___V̆; nevertheless, the SIB-phonemicist is forced, by virtue of the first fact, to ignore the second, and to analyze the second segment in STOP as a /t/ (as though a contrast with /d/ *were* possible in this environment, after all) and to analyze the flap in WRITER or RIDER as a /d/ (though no voiced–voiceless contrast is possible for a dental stop in this environment, either, for the dialects in question). In other words, SIB-phonemics fails to recognize that 'features of a sound which are distinctive in one position may not be distinctive when that same sound is in another position' (Fudge, 1970, p. 85).

European linguists recognized this some time ago and gave formal expression to it in terms of a notion of the 'archiphoneme' (see especially Trubetzkoy, 1969, pp. 228–41). The question they asked might be paraphrased as follows: 'What is the point of assigning a particular phone in some particular environment to phoneme A (as opposed to phoneme B) when there is no possibility for A and B ever to contrast in the environment in question?' As far as I can see, there is no point at all, and to force a choice under such circumstances is arbitrary – and furthermore, does violence to the phonemic principle itself. The best 'phonemic' representation, therefore (one which is otherwise consistent with the SIB constraint and is arrived at via 'purely phonetic' considerations), would represent the dental stop in STOP and the flap in WRITER and RIDER as segments which are *unspecified* for voicing, rather than as *either* a full-fledged phonemic /t/ or /d/.[1]

Thus Bloch's overriding concern about indeterminacy in analysis seems misplaced, for here we find one of those areas where indeterminacy is apparently inherent in the data (cf. Hockett, 1949, p. 46) and can be eliminated only by arbitrary choice. In the absence of criteria by which a principled choice can be made, the language learner, like the linguist himself, must also leave the matter open. This is the conclusion

---

[1] Though native speakers' intuitions are vague about matters of detail like this, my experience with naive speakers has generally been that most seem able to decide only from the way a word is *spelled* whether a 't-sound' or a 'd-sound' is actually present in words such as these.

to which the evidence points in my example, and this fact enjoins the linguist to avoid imposing a more specific solution of his own design. As Malone has said, 'The linguist must not attribute to a language more than its speakers can do; if the model chosen forces the analyst into such a position, there's something wrong with the model' (1970, p. 333).[1]

I conclude that the SIB constraint must be relaxed in the direction of what Chomsky has called 'relative invariance' (1964, p. 94) by incorporating the proviso that no phonetic feature may be specified on the phonemic level under any conditions where an opposition is not possible; this limitation recognizes the phenomenon of (contextual) neutralization at the phonemic level. By incorporating this minor, but well-grounded principle into phonemic theory, we find that the analyses which result are no longer subject to the criticism which Chomsky and Halle have made of 'data-analysis' methods in general. To return to Halle's Russian illustration, for example, we find that the segment-types c and z, $č$ and $ž$, and x and y never contrast in native Russian vocabulary; hence, according to our revised theory, their proper representation on the phonemic level is /C/ (a class of dental affricates), /Č/ (a class of palatal affricates) and /X/ (a class of velar fricatives), respectively, all unspecified for voicing. By the same token, since t and d never contrast in the environment before a voiced obstruent, the proper phonemicization for them (*in this environment* only – or in other environments where the same distinction is neutralized, as in utterance-final position) is /T/ (a class of dental stops). The proper *morphophonemic* rule involved in such a neutralization is therefore as follows: 'all obstruents are *unspecified* for voicing before other obstruents' and the proper *phonetic* rule is precisely the generalization which Chomsky and Halle suggest: 'all obstruents are voiced before voiced obstruents' (or, more generally, 'all obstruents assimilate in voicing to the final obstruent of an obstruent cluster'). The first rule expresses the morphophonemic generalization that whereas voicing may be distinctive in Russian for most obstruents *lexically* (that is, at a level where *more* than purely phonetic considerations must be taken into consideration), voiced and voiceless obstruents never contrast *phonemically* before other obstruents; the second rule expresses the general phonotactic generalization which Halle advocates.[2] (Significantly, this latter rule is a purely 'phonetic'

---

[1] For further discussion on the matter of indeterminacy in grammar, see Teeter (1966) and Lyons (1968, especially pp. 152–4).
[2] This entire analysis is adapted from Householder (1967, pp. 942–3).

generalization; cf. pp. 201–2 below). Technically speaking, therefore, while I agree with Chomsky and Halle that a level of SIB-phonemics is not incorporable within a descriptively adequate generative grammar, I find nevertheless that a closely analogous level of RIB-phonemics (R for 'relaxed' or 'relative') – preferable to the SIB-phoneme on independent conceptual and empirical grounds – *is* so incorporable, and I therefore fail to see the significance of Chomsky's implied argument that the entire 'data-analysis' approach to the study of language is at stake in his critique.

The compatibility of the SIB- or RIB- or any other variety of the phonemes with Chomsky's notion of a generative grammar is, in any event, peripheral to our main theme. (See especially chapter 8 below, where I consider the entire notion of generative grammar, as conceived by Chomsky and his followers.) The main reason for reviewing so much old ground here was to establish a different and more important point. This is that none of the arguments offered by Chomsky (or by anyone else, to my knowledge) against the viability of the 'taxonomic' phoneme have any bearing whatever on the viability of the structuralist's notion of the *morphophoneme*, i.e. against the notion of a level of (lexical) representation which can be mechanically derived (or learned) from *both* phonetic *and* grammatical information. In fact, the only entities which Chomsky seems to pair off, in his 1964 paper and elsewhere, are 'taxonomic' phonemics (= SIB, but not RIB) against what he calls 'systematic' phonemics, arguing that the former represents the phonemics developed by such people as Jones, Troubetzkoy, Harris and Bloch (1964, p. 102), while the latter 'seems to be, in essence, the phonemics of Bloomfield's practice', as well as that of Sapir (p. 87). Assuming that Chomsky's analogies are fair (and I think they are) all he is therefore contrasting in his critique is one version of the structuralist notion of the 'phoneme' (the SIB-phoneme) against the familiar structuralist notion of the 'morphophoneme' ('in one of the several senses of this term', as Chomsky puts it (1964, p. 87)). Yet the first concept, as I have shown, is not an appropriate type of representation for the lexicon on any account, while the second concept has been considered all along to be a type of representation which *was* seriously proposed as a candidate for lexical representation (and specifically as not having the disadvantages of SIB-phonemics for this purpose). This is then an odd comparison to make: between an avowed candidate for lexical representation (the morphophoneme) and an avowed non-candidate for such a representation (the

SIB-phoneme), on the other.[1] Nor is it surprising that the SIB-phoneme suffers in such a comparison. The only comparison of any continuing interest here is the one which Chomsky fails to make, so forcing me to supply the omission: how does the structuralist notion of the morphophoneme (or lexical representation) – as an exemplar of the more general 'data-analytical' approach to the study of language – compare with the transformationalist notion of the abstract 'underlying representation' – the corresponding candidate for lexical representation involved in the more general 'innate universals' approach? If we want to compare these two opposed approaches to linguistic investigation we can only do so in areas which are actually comparable. At the level of lexical representation one fundamental characteristic which differentiates the two approaches is that the latter permits absolute neutralization, whereas the former does not, and so it is in this area that the 'innate universals' approach is so open to criticism.

6.2 A tentative set of 'learnability' constraints on phonological systems

Let us now retrace our ground a bit. In 4.5.3 I showed that the problem of establishing psychologically valid morphological relationships was complex and difficult. I have also noted in chapter 5 that the fundamental metatheoretical difficulty associated with the theory of generative phonology (as a typical representative – if not the ultimate epitomization – of the theory of TGG, and hence of the 'innate universals' approach to the study of language) was that all attempts to impose strict and testable constraints on the notion 'possible phonological rule' within the theory (giving the rules both maximum generality and 'naturalness') were frustrated by a lack of correspondingly effective constraints on the notion 'possible lexical representation' (i.e. absolute neutralization and extrinsic rule ordering were allowed, so making it possible in principle for virtually any rule or rule-type to be worked into a grammar). In the section above I also showed that it has long been recognized that *some* morphological evidence is often (if not typically) relevant to the establishment of an appropriate level of lexical representation, even in pre-transformational practice.[2] The problem now is one of developing, at

---

[1] Clearly, the only analysts who would have seriously considered the SIB-phoneme as a candidate for lexical representation would be those few who rejected the notion of the morphophoneme altogether (cf. pp. 175–7 above).

[2] That is to say, most structuralists recognized that phonetic overlapping could be

least in general outline, a substantially new version or interpretation of phonological theory which incorporates a set of appropriate constraints on both rules and lexical representations sufficient to yield a set of potentially viable phonological descriptions which can then be subjected to experimental testing. In attempting to do this we quickly find that, in order to illustrate the essential nature of the constraints which I have in mind, we have to make a few tentative first decisions related to some of the morphological evidence which may reasonably be brought to bear.

The most broadly acceptable such suggestion is the assumption which Trager adopted in his original analysis of 'The phonemes of Russian' (*not* SIB-phonemes, but morphophonemes in the sense of 6.1). His assumption was simply this: we may be reasonably certain that at least 'the paradigm exists in the mind of the speaker as a psychological reality'. This may be a reasonable starting point, for it seems obvious that if something of this sort were *not* the case (i.e. if each member of an inflectional paradigm were not identified by the mature native speaker as another form of the same basic 'word'), certain highly redundant (and seemingly quite productive) characteristics of the inflectional paradigm would have to be regarded as accidental. There is much evidence that the native speaker of a language like Russian has a productive ability to cast any noun in his language (including new or unfamiliar ones) in any of a number of case forms, depending on the role which that noun is to play in a given sentence. This could not be done if the case forms of each Russian noun were learned, stored and used by native speakers as though each were a distinct and unanalyzable lexical item (cf. Paul, 1891, pp. 100ff).[1] In any case, even if aspects of the apparent productivity of

allowed at the *lexical* level, provided that morphological evidence were available by which to distinguish the neutralized segments. As Trager put it, 'The same sound may belong to different [morpho]phonemes if the conditions covering its use can be so described as to make clear the distinction' (1934, p. 340).

[1] It is in the area of *derivation* that the most serious questions of productivity (and hence of morphemic relatedness) arise. It is not accidental that all the examples cited in the chart on p. 124 above involve potential or putative derivational, not inflectional, relationships. Note too that, besides the examples already cited from Chomsky and Halle (1968) for English and from Lightner (1965) for Russian, where dubious morphological connections are proposed and utilized, virtually without comment, Schane (1968) also appeals to far-fetched derivational morphology in his search for alternations in French. On p. 20, for example, we find that he unites both LÉVRIER 'greyhound' with LIÈVRE 'hare', as well as CROIRE 'to believe' and CRÉDIBILITÉ (though the noun in question, I am informed by B. Rochet, came into French only *after* those historical changes which Schane recapitulates in his 'synchronic grammar' had already been effected, i.e. e⟩...⟩wa). For an excellent critique of Schane's analysis of French phonology, see Creore (forthcoming).

this process are still in doubt, I shall assume for our purposes here that the inflectional paradigm constitutes one domain in which our search for productive morphological alternations is justified.

I now return to my earlier claim (p. 145) that most of the major American structuralists refused to countenance the 'setting up [of] underlying distinctions for the sole purpose of classifying segments into those that do and those that do not meet the structural analysis of a rule' (Kiparsky, 1968a). We have already noted several times that the trans-formationalists have allowed this device in phonology and that, primarily as the result of this metatheoretical looseness, they have made it possible for grammars to be constructed incorporating rules conforming to a specific set of *a priori* constraints, and which are capable of ordering even the most bizarre set of phonetic alternations.[1] Kiparsky seems to have been the first transformationalist to have recognized the problem, and he proposed that a constraint which he calls the 'alternation condition' ought to be imposed upon phonological analysis. The most notable effect of Kiparsky's proposed constraint on the abstractness of lexical representations (which effectively limits the number of candidates to those phonetic alternations which actually occur) would be to outlaw absolute neutralization (or 'the diacritic use of phonological features' in the way described above). So except for certain marginal details, Kiparsky's proposed constraint is not new, but is a recapitulation of a set of assumptions taken virtually for granted by the major pretrans-formational structuralists, including Whitney (who might even be con-sidered 'pre-structural'), Boas, Sapir, Bloomfield, Harris and many others. Yet none of these early investigators was as explicit in this matter as Jakobson. Furthermore, Jakobson's ever-so-concise discussion of this issue in his 'Russian conjugation' paper (1948) communicates the nature of his proposed constraint in such a way that his decidedly 'process' or 'data-analysis' orientation is not left in doubt, either. He says:

In presenting and analysing full-stems, we use *morphophonemic* transcription. If certain phonemic constituents of the given full-stem as compared with cognate [paradigmatically related] forms appear in different alternants, we take as basic the alternant which appears in a position where the other alter-nant too would be admissible (p. 156).

[1] Despite Swadesh and Voegelin's earlier conviction that this could not be accom-plished in the case of 'truly irregular' alternations (1939, p. 92). But Swadesh and Voegelin were operating always under the assumption that extremely abstract lexical representations of the sort which the generative grammarians now advocate were not permitted – and that no 'rules' could be formulated which were not in general true of the primary data.

On the first reading it might seem that Jakobson's procedure is simply to list the full set of alternate (phonemic) shapes (or allomorphs) which a given morpheme may adopt within the verbal paradigm, and to choose one of these full alternants as basic.[1] Jakobson's examples quickly dispel that impression, for in some instances the 'basic alternant' which he posits as a stem never appears *in toto* as a genuine alternate (allomorph) at all. Typical examples are his proposed basic alternants °/v'od°/ 'conduct' and °/gr'ob°/ 'row' (p. 160). In the first case the only allomorphs which appear in the paradigm are these (given, for convenience, in SIB-phonemic representation):

(1) /v'is'-/ as in the Infinitive form, /v'is't'í/
(2) /v'id-/ as in the 1P Sg Pres form, /v'idú/
(3) /v'id'-/ as in the 2P Sg Pres form, /v'id'óš/
(4) /v'ó-/ as in the Past Masc form, /v'ól/
(5) /v'i-/ as in the Past Fem form, /v'ilá/

The basic alternant °/v'od°/ is not, therefore, simply selected from this set *per se*, but is an artificial 'hybrid' form constructed from all the information provided by the entire set of alternants. This information might conveniently be presented segment-by-segment, perhaps as follows:

Segment 1: Only one candidate for the underlying form appears in this position throughout the paradigm, namely, /v'/.
Segment 2: There are two candidates for this underlying segment, /i/ and /o/.
Segment 3: There are four candidates for this underlying segment, /s'/, /d/, /d'/ and ø.[2]

This information can be more compactly represented by an abbreviatory schema of the following sort, which may be regarded as expressing the full range of (SIB-phonemic) variability manifested by this particular morpheme within the verbal paradigm:

[1] Which seems to have been Bloomfield's practice, at least as described in *Language* (1933; see especially pp. 164 and 209ff). This is not entirely true of his 1939 paper and other of his Amerindian work, where he sometimes resorted to the use of special cover symbols (cf. n. 3 on p. 144).

[2] Because of the possible operation of deletion or insertion rules (and the resulting appearance of ø in a position held by a full segment in some other alternant), it will not always be obvious what the appropriate segment assignments should be (cf. the problem of interpreting the final segment of /žeč/ 'to burn'), but this difficulty need not seriously concern us for the moment.

$$\text{'conduct'} = \text{v'} \begin{bmatrix} i \\ o \end{bmatrix} \begin{bmatrix} s' \\ d \\ d' \\ ø \end{bmatrix}$$

Jakobson's constraint implies, first of all, that the basic form of this morpheme must be selected from within this range of variation and the form he ultimately chooses ($°/$v'od$°/$) is one of eight possibilities.

Having unambiguously delimited the number and type of possible candidates for a basic (or lexical) representation, Jakobson then turns to the problem of selection (and so goes one step farther than most of his structuralist contemporaries). To do this, more must be known about the language in general. In particular, one must know what phonetic (or, equivalently, but with much detail omitted, SIB-phonemic) sequences are permitted in the language. This information can be brought to bear on the problem of selection. To take the second segment of this particular morpheme, for instance, we have two possible candidates for a basic representation, the /i/ and the /o/. If we consider all available information about Russian phonotactics as a whole, we discover that whereas both vowels may occur under stress in the language, only the first normally occurs in unstressed position. This environment is therefore useless for our purposes. Instead, following Jakobson's suggestion, we look at that complementary environment (viz., *under stress*) in which either /i/ or /o/ might possibly occur in the *language* in order to ascertain which does occur in connection with the *particular morpheme* in question. In this instance it is /o/ which appears (as in the past tense form /v'ól/), rather than /i/ (*/v'íl/). We therefore tentatively decide that the basic element (morphophoneme) which is to stand as segment 2 in our lexical representation for the morpheme 'conduct' is $°/$o$°/$ (see Jakobson, 1948, for further details).[1]

It is clear, I think, that one important effect of Jakobson's proposed discovery procedure for basic forms is to impose a strict constraint on the degree of abstractness which lexical representations may attain, so

---

[1] The general restriction on the occurrence of /o/ in unstressed environments may now be incorporated into the grammar as a general rule: $°/$o$°/$ must always be realized as /i/ in unstressed position (after a soft consonant only, as it turns out; cf. p. 176). So Jakobson's procedures do impose an implicit constraint of sorts on the notion of phonological rule, as well as on his base forms (contrary to what I now admit was a somewhat unfair characterization of his implied 'model of language acquisition' on p. 106 above), though considerable flexibility still remains in his system as to how these rules should be expressed.

limiting the range of possible phonological analyses allowed. In particular, it is no longer so easy to squeeze in rules of some predetermined type or form. Consequently we find that few of Lightner's rules – except for some which had their origin in Jakobson's work – can now be used to derive correct phonetic outputs from the kinds of base forms which Jakobson's procedures define. So we have an extremely effective constraint here. Moreover, the constraint is such that it can easily and naturally be associated with a plausible 'process' approach to language acquisition which assumes nothing more on the part of the language learner than a general capacity to induce or extract regularities from the data to which he is exposed.[1]

Stated in its present form, however, there are potentially serious difficulties with the constraint in question. One was noted by Kiparsky himself (1968a):

One of the effects of restricting phonology like this is to enter non-alternating forms in the lexicon in roughly their autonomous [= SIB] phonemic representation. That is, *if a form appears in a constant shape, its underlying representation is that shape* (italics added).

In Russian the root morpheme of the verb SLEDOVAT' 'to follow' contains the non-varying sequence *s'l'ed* throughout the paradigm, and so according to Jakobson's proposed procedure for deriving base forms would have to be entered in the lexicon in that shape. Yet we know that *l* (like every other consonant in the language which is ever palatalized) is predictably palatalized before the vowel *e* (cf. p. 176 above). Furthermore, the dental fricatives in Russian are also predictably palatalized immediately before another soft consonant (cf. Halle, 1959, p. 67). Thus Jakobson's procedures force us into a seemingly contradictory statement about these first two segments of this morpheme: on the one hand we specify both of them as (distinctively) palatalized in the *lexicon*; on the other we include *rules* in our grammar to the effect that both segments are predictably palatalized in precisely those phonetic environments in which they occur.

The reason for this difficulty is that no appropriate diagnostic environment appears in any of the variant forms of this particular morpheme

[1] Cf. Saussure's important observation, previously cited only in part, that 'we never know exactly whether or not the awareness of speakers goes as far as the analyses of the grammarian. But the important thing is that *abstract entities are always based, in the last analysis, on concrete entities*. No grammatical abstraction is possible without a series of material elements as a basis, and in the end we must always come back to these elements' (1959, p. 138).

which would allow us to apply Jakobson's *selection* technique to these segments; that is, the form and distribution of the morpheme SLED- are such that no environments are introduced within the verbal paradigm in which any possibilities other than the initial sequence *s'l'* are permitted by the phonotactics of the language, and in all such circumstances, clearly, Jakobson's selection technique is of no use. Moreover, the problem is not marginal, but is one which crops up again and again throughout the language (as one might expect, considering the large element of chance involved). In all these cases, one is forced either to follow the prescribed procedure rigorously and obtain seemingly contradictory results, or else arbitrarily to choose some other hypothetical 'potential' variant as basic.[1]

Trager adopted the second course. Consider his discussion of this same problem as it relates to the neutralization of voiced and voiceless segments in word-final position and elsewhere in Russian:

For words like sele*d*ka, no*g*ti, and the like, let us use the voiced symbols [for the italicized segments – BLD], since there exists at least one inflectional form of the word itself which retains the voiced sound; in this, then, we have the same rule in principle as for the etymologically voiced finals. For derivatives, however, in which the original sound does not reappear in any inflectional form of the *derivative*, I propose the use of the symbols for the *unvoiced* sounds.

---

[1] Or compromise and do both, as Jakobson did. Cf. his proposed basic form for the morpheme BEREG- 'spare', which he gives as °/b'er'og°/ (1948, p. 161). On the one hand, Jakobson includes the palatalization on the °/b'°/, although this is predictable before *e*; on the other, he posits the vowel °/e°/ in the first syllable, though there is no (non-comparative) morphological evidence in support: the only vowel which appears in this position phonetically within the paradigm is the unstressed vowel *i* (which could, theoretically, correspond to any one of at least *three* underlying vowels in this environment, namely, °/e°/, °/o°/ or °/i°/.) Similarly, the base form which Jakobson gives for the stem TRESTIROVA- (1948, p. 162) is °/tr'*est*'irova°/, although no form of this verb contains either an *e* or a hard *s*. Jakobson would no doubt want to posit the base form °/sl'ed°/ for the morpheme under discussion above (cf. Townsend, 1968, p. 103). Jakobson has apparently attempted to push this sort of detail back to the sub-phonemic level, where overlapping is still allowed. This is no solution to the problem, for as Bloch demonstrated, there is no non-arbitrary way to make decisions involving overlapping if the phonetic facts alone are taken into consideration.

Another possible solution which Jakobson fails to consider (surprisingly, considering his Prague School orientation) is to represent the *s'* in question lexically as °/S°/, i.e. as a voiceless dental fricative which is simply *unspecified* for palatalization (a kind of 'archi*morpho*phoneme'), on the ground that there is no evidence available to the linguist (nor, presumably, to the child) to enable him to decide non-arbitrarily one way or the other (cf. pp. 185–6 above).

The rule for voiced stops and spirants is this, then: the etymological voiced sounds... retain their psychological identity and distinction from the corresponding voiceless sounds in final position or before a voiceless sound in all words in which at least one inflectional form retains the original sound, even though they are, objectively, completely voiceless in the positions indicated; but in derivatives under the same conditions, where the original voiced sound does *not* reappear in any inflected form, we have complete psychological identification of the original voiced sound with the new, voiceless sound, and their merging into the voiceless [morpho]phoneme, despite the presence of the voiced sound in the original of the derivative, or in some other derivative (1934, pp. 341–2; italics added).

Despite the widespread appeal of this approach (especially to contemporary linguists of 'markedness' persuasion), the fact is that in the absence of experimental evidence which might give empirical content to the notion of 'psychological identity' as it is used here, the analysis must remain inescapably arbitrary. The crucial problem here, as elsewhere, is that while we have been toying with hypothetical procedures and hypothetical universals and with results which 'seem' this way or that, the essential empirical question is overlooked: What does the language learner *do*? For from the standpoint of the language learner, given a word or morpheme (or even a segment of a morpheme) which is always encountered in the same phonetic shape (with allowances for the presumably infinite but non-detectable range of 'sub-phonetic' variation), I see no *a priori* reason to suppose that he must necessarily invent abstract lexical entities which differ in any way from the forms he actually encounters. It is conceivable, in other words, that the lexical representation °/s'l'ed°/ might be the most appropriate one, despite the apparent 'contradictions' which the analysis implies for the linguist.

Certain other considerations lead me to suspect, however, that such an analysis (where a segment like *s'* is lexically marked for a feature which is seemingly redundant in the environment in which it always occurs) is most probably wrong and hence that Jakobson's (and Kiparsky's) proposed constraint – which restricts the segmental composition of a lexical entry to the range of variation defined by those particular (phonetic) segments which *actually occur* in one variant or another of the morpheme in question – is probably deficient in some important way. Consider, for example, cases which involve not the presence or absence of some particular (secondary) phonetic feature, but rather the presence or absence of an entire *segment*. A familiar example of this phenomenon involves the epenthetic *e* in Spanish. No Spanish word begins with the sequence sC (i.e. initial *s* followed by another consonant).[1] Many Spanish words, however, begin instead with the sequence esC (e.g. ESCUELA 'school', ESPAÑA 'Spain', ESTUDIANTE 'student', etc.). One possible explanation for both facts which has suggested itself is that a general 'Initial Epenthesis' rule of the following sort might operate in the language (which is to say that such a rule might be induced[2] by Spanish speakers from the primary data to which they are exposed and thereafter be part of their linguistic performance): ø → e /#___sC (i.e. all initial sC clusters are eliminated by the addition of a preceding *e*-segment; see, e.g. J. Harris, 1970, p. 928). What gives this hypothesis its credibility is not that it 'simplifies' or 'systematizes' the description of Spanish, but rather that the behavior of Spanish *speakers* gives every appearance of conforming to the rule even in the way in which they erroneously repeat foreign words (such that an English word like SCAR is characteristically rendered as *eskar* by the naive monolingual Spanish speaker, SPOON as *espun*, STOP as *estap*, etc.). So this rule (unlike Lightner's proposed (k:č) rule for Russian) is fully productive of new forms. If we, as linguists, believe in any phonological 'rules' for language, we can certainly believe in this one, and we shall be more than reluctant to accept some alternative analysis for Spanish which requires the abandonment or modification of this rule (unless it can be shown to be merely a special case of some more general rule *which has equally incontestable empirical support*).

But Jakobson's proposed constraint on the abstractness of lexical representations runs into the same difficulty here as in the previous (and more ambiguous) Russian example. If all forms of the Spanish word ESCUELA, for example, begin with the sequence *esk-* (as they do), Jakobson would be forced to posit an initial °/e°/ as part of the lexical representation for the root morpheme in question, although we find that this entire segment is fully predictable in terms of the well-founded rule for 'Initial Epenthesis'. We are much more reluctant, therefore, to accept the implied contradiction in this particular case.

[1] According to J. Harris (1970, p. 929), there are 'absolutely no exceptions'. 'Initial Epenthesis' is therefore an excellent candidate for a legitimate 'rule' of Spanish phonology in the sense of p. 202 below.

[2] Note that the term 'induce' is appropriate here, since the particular rule can be restated without difficulty as a generalization which is true of Spanish phonotactics in general and which might therefore be noted and learned by a child having no innate specific linguistic capacities – whether of the 'content' *or* of the 'process' variety – but merely a general capacity to extract regularity from his environment (cf. pp. 200–2 below for discussion).

At one level of discussion the argument may seem to be much the same here as with the Russian °/s'°/. But there are two important differences between the two. First, an *entire segment* is involved in the present case, not just a single feature. This makes any sort of 'neutralization' solution (cf. the last paragraph of n. 1 on p. 194) no longer tenable. (What is the 'neutralized' equivalent of a fully specified segment such as *e* and nothing at all?) Furthermore, the argument (not very convincing in the first place) that a speaker might go on retaining some highly specified lexical representation although part of it could be redundantly supplied by some independently operative phonological rule makes no sense at all in this context. The reason is that the *only* apparent advantage to be gained from learning and utilizing a rule like 'Initial Epenthesis' in Spanish would be precisely in order to permit the child to simplify the particular lexical representations in question in the way indicated.[1] Thus while it is conceivable that a child might learn a rule to account for one class of phenomena (such as morphophonemic alternations) and somehow fail to 'notice' that this rule was also relevant to certain morpheme-internal situations, it is a blatant contradiction to speak both of 'Initial Epenthesis' as a *rule* and of morpheme-initial °/e°/ as a *lexical* representation.

I conclude that while Jakobson's original suggestions have enabled us to focus attention on the general nature of the constraint we seek, we shall have to find some more liberal constraint in the long run (just as Jakobson's own constraint was more liberal than the one implied by Bloomfield and others). Before I can develop my proposals along this line any further, however, I must first make more explicit the kind of constraint which ought to be applied to the notion of possible phonological *rule*.[2]

One further small point ought to be mentioned here. This is that Jakobson's procedures, though apparently too strict to be fully satisfactory, do hold inherent practical advantages when it comes to the problem of deciding what morphological evidence is to be considered in resolving a question of phonological analysis. I have been making the

---

[1] This was not true of our previous example, where the rule was not suggested originally in order to simplify the lexical representations of such morphemes as SLED-, but rather to account for a set of regular *morphophonemic alternations* (across morpheme boundaries).

[2] As already indicated, both rules and base forms must be effectively constrained if either set of constraints is to be meaningful. The entire phonological system must be determined, not just one part of it (see especially pp. 145–8 above).

assumption that only morphological evidence related to the inflectional paradigm is relevant for such purposes (Jakobson made the same assumption, by implication, in writing exclusively on 'Russian conjugation'). We could further constrain or loosen these requirements and still apply his procedures by making appropriate, yet relatively minor, modifications in our over-all description. In considering inflectional evidence alone, for example, we are led by Jakobson's procedures to posit the basic stem °/v'id' + e°/ for the verb 'see' in Russian, i.e. with the final consonant of the root lexically marked for palatalization (since the only other segment-type which appears in the position within the paradigm is the predictable variant /ž/).[1] If we extend our search for morpheme variants by making the implicit claim that the noun form VID 'view, look, air' is 'psychologically identified' with this verb, we then would have grounds for introducing an additional candidate for the final basic segment of the root, specifically, the hard (non-palatalized) /d/, and we would surely then choose this segment-type as basic rather than the original /d/ posited on the basis of the verb paradigm alone.[2] Thus various analyses are possible, depending on the assumptions we make (or empirical evidence we have) regarding the essential relatedness of various forms (cf. Teeter, 1966, p. 478). Yet all these alternative analyses can be given in the form of *conditional statements* with no danger of contradiction. For example, in the case just cited, we have these alternative analyses:

Analysis I: *If* only the various inflected forms of a word are psychologically linked, *then* the basic form of the verb root which is given by application of Jakobson's procedures is °/v'id'°/ and that of the noun root is °/v'id°/ (two distinct lexical entries).

Analysis II: *If*, on the other hand, all the forms of the verb 'see' and

[1] Though I agree with Jakobson's general conclusion on this point, I strongly suspect that the *basis* for prediction actually involved in such cases is very different from the one Jakobson suggests (namely, phonological conditioning expressed in terms of a set of rather outlandish phonological environments). A more obvious generalization (and thus one more likely to be learned by the child) would involve the appearance of the palatals in a set of *specific paradigmatic forms* for a given sub-class of verbs (cf. p. 203, n. 3, below).

[2] Because /d/ is predictable palatalized before /e/. If our 'phonetic' transcription were more detailed, we should really introduce at least *two* new variants from the noun paradigm, both the /d/ (as in the G. Sg. form /v'ida/) and a /t/ (since the final segment of the N. Sg. form /v'it/ is voiceless and would remain so in the traditional SIB-phonemic representation). This /t/ would not be chosen as basic, however, since obstruents are predictably voiceless in Russian in word-final position.

of the noun 'view' are also psychologically linked, *then* we may replace these distinct lexical representations by their common single basic form °/v'id°/.[1]

In this way, although we must still make arbitrary decisions on matters of relevant fact, we are still able to keep our descriptions in line with the assumptions we *do* make, so making it possible for purely linguistic research to proceed in the absence of definitive psychological evidence in support of any particular analysis.[2]

I now return to the tentative constraint I should wish to see imposed upon the notion 'possible phonological rule'. Because I consider the 'innate universals' approach to language vacuous and self-defeating, I have been looking for an alternative approach along more traditional 'data-analytical' lines. One important qualification must now be made with respect to the treatment of this question in 3.3. There I outlined an 'alternative model of the AD' which involved not the positing of a full set of innate 'linguistic universals plus evaluation procedures', but rather a presumably innate 'algorithm or special technique for performing linguistic analysis' (p. 54). As first introduced, this formulation seemed to provide a useful alternative view of language acquisition which could be associated with the familiar frame of reference originally proposed by Chomsky and widely accepted since. Moreover, this view seemed consistent with pre-Chomskyan attempts to develop a set of 'discovery procedures' for linguistic analysis and description (as if one were trying to recreate in linguistic textbooks and field manuals the techniques which the child actually adopted in learning a language). But *neither* approach is completely satisfactory (though it is my conviction that the structuralists were much closer to the mark than the transformationalists are). The reason is by now obvious: so far as *any* acquisition model invokes the notion of 'innateness', it must be rejected (so far

---

1 Numerous additional alternatives are also possible. If we assume that not even the paradigmatic forms are linked, each form of the verb (or noun) will receive its own lexical representation (which would be identical with its SIB-phonemic representation). While this analysis seems untenable with respect to the language of a mature speaker, it may be the description most appropriate for a child in the earliest stages of language acquisition, that is, before he has learned anything about morphological relationships.

2 This is important, since we can be fairly certain that the questions posed by purely linguistic research will continue to affect the research questions which the experimental psychologist (hopefully accompanied by a 'new brand' of linguist as described in chapter 9) will ask in his study of language. I therefore think it one of the linguist's functions to supply the psychologist with plausible alternative hypotheses for experimental evaluation (see 9.2.1).

as current knowledge is concerned) as speculative, since there is no experimental technique at present available for testing claims about 'innate knowledge' – whether about *what* the learner is to look for or about *how* he might best look for it.[1] The closest analogue to 'innate knowledge' which experimental psychologists have so far elicited is in the area of 'species-specific' or 'unlearned' behaviors: by setting up control conditions so that a given organism has *no opportunity to learn* a given behavior or behavior pattern, it can be demonstrated empirically that such traits develop nonetheless (nest-building techniques in birds, for example). But this is not the same as demonstrating that the traits in question are 'innate' or 'genetically determined' (cf. pp. 64–5). In any event, even the weaker designation 'unlearned' behavior cannot legitimately be applied to human language, since no such experiments (for obvious reasons) have ever been performed on human beings.

We cannot hope, therefore, to build a science of linguistics on the basis of any particular set of presumed 'innate predispositions' for language, whether of the 'content' (or 'linguistic universals') variety or of the 'process' (or 'learning algorithm') sort. Instead of speculating about the unknown (even the unknowable), we should build our science on the foundation of the *known*. And one such known is the fact that a human being can extract regularity from his experience in the form of general 'principles' or 'rules'. Specifically (to cite an illustration provided by W. J. Baker), it has been demonstrated that a child, faced with a series of situations in which the response is called for to 'repeat behavior *x* one more time than on the previous occasion', can quickly (that is, on relatively few trials) abstract the principle desired and apply it unhesitatingly to novel situations of the same type. A chimpanzee does not seem capable of this; for him, each new situation in the sequence is a 'novel experience'.

An alternative model of language acquisition ought to be developed on the assumption that the human organism is initially completely *un*-informed both as to the essential nature of language and as to the best way to learn a language. My initial assumption is that no other 'special mechanisms' or 'secret abilities' are required for learning *language* than for learning anything else. In short, I shall assume that language acquisition can be fully accounted for in terms of such known (i.e.

---

[1] I am indebted to W. J. Baker for bringing this incontestable but embarrassing fact to my attention. Dr Baker also suggested to me the notion of 'extracting regularity from one's environment', which plays so important a role in the discussion to follow.

empirically established) capacities as the ability of the human organism to discriminate among and generalize from the sense-data to which he is exposed and, most importantly (since this capacity seems to be species-specific), to extract regularity – or induce a 'latent structure' (Brown & Bellugi, 1964, p. 151) – from his experience. This, I find, is the only rational starting point, given our present state of knowledge (cf. Schwarcz, 1967, pp. 43, 50). We want to know, first of all, whether human language can be explained in terms of *already established* general learning principles. To do so, we need make no assumptions at all about 'innateness'; it is an established fact that human beings have the capacities in question, and this is all that matters. If these are sufficient to explain language acquisition, there will be no need to look further for any 'purely linguistic' capacities. There will be sufficient scope for speculation once we have explored the few *testable* alternatives which face us at present. Furthermore, having explored these, we shall have some facts to base further speculations upon.

What sort of 'rule', then, might be 'learnable' by an organism so little endowed? For a definitive answer, the linguist must defer to the psychologist, who knows what there is to know about such things. The discussion immediately above suggests, however, that even the linguist can make some tentative judgments in this area, especially in certain more extreme cases. At one extreme, the 'learnability' constraint sketched above would eliminate from consideration most of the rules in a transformational-generative grammar (together with virtually all the 'essential linguistic universals' which underlie them, like the general convention of the 'transformational cycle', etc.) on the ground that the rules (and associated general conventions for 'grammar construction') are too far removed from the sense-data to which the language-learner is exposed to be directly extractable from them. Chomsky has advanced this argument himself (see especially pp. 67–8, above). At the opposite extreme, we find another class of descriptive statements about language which *could* be learned by an organism of the sort described. These would be statements which are in general true, as stated, of the primary linguistic data to which the language learner has been (or can be presumed to have been) exposed. One such statement would express what may be regarded as an exceptionless generalization about the phonotactic possibilities of a language.[1]

---

[1] Using the terms, 'exceptionless' and 'possibilities' not in any absolute or 'prescriptive' sense, but in the familiar 'descriptive' sense of what sequences generally occur under

I have already introduced a few such generalizations about English (see pp. 172–4 above). For example, (1) all vowels before voiced non-flap consonants in English are (relatively) long; thus we find no sequences of the sort $*V_1C_1$ (where V_1 is to be interpreted as a short or non-long vowel and C_1 as a voiced non-flap consonant). Similarly, (2) all vowels before nasals in English are nasalized; so we find no sequences of the sort $*V_2N$ (where V_2 is a non-nasalized vowel and N is a nasal). These statements express *true phonotactic generalizations* about any representative corpus of utterances in English, and each has associated with it a set of 'impossible' phonotactic sequences which it 'outlaws' (but see p. 201, n. 1). It is more than simply conceivable, therefore, that such generalizations might be learned (or, less acceptably, 'internalized') by a speaker of English in the process of acquisition. One might even suggest that the 'rules' in question express a pair of specific *articulatory habits* which the native speaker has acquired, over time, from endless repetition of forms which invariably involve these specific juxtapositions of phonetic characteristics. This is my proposed explanation for the absence of $*V_1C_1$ and $*V_2N$ sequences in English: because mature native speakers of that language (by the time they have reached that stage) have formed specific well-ingrained articulatory habits which strongly militate against such sequences; the regularities have simply been 'abstracted as rules from [the speaker's] unwitting practice' (Berko & Brown, 1960, p. 520; cf. Brown & Fraser, 1964, p. 44, and Shipley *et al.*, 1969, pp. 323–4). This makes sense to me, and I cannot see why Chomsky and his fellow transformationalists find the idea unreasonable or preposterous.[1]

We may now consider how far an essential 'learnability' constraint of the sort outlined (certain details have yet to be specified) is consistent with specific analyses which linguistics (and, in particular, generative grammarians) have found reasonable on independent grounds. For strategic reasons only, I shall limit the discussion to three analyses

conditions of normal language use by the naive, monolingual native speaker. This distinction, though fundamental, is sometimes lost sight of in a context of talk about what is 'impossible' or 'ungrammatical' in a language, as if the 'grammar' had some power or 'hold' on the language user which went beyond the familiar notion of *habit* or *skill* (that is, the ability to perform well-practiced activities on an unconscious or automated level).

[1] Cf. Chomsky (1965a) where he speaks disparagingly about 'speech habits' or 'habit structures' (p. 15) and insists, without empirical justification, that 'the child who acquires a language...knows a great deal more than he has "learned". His knowledge of the language...goes far beyond the presented primary linguistic data and is *in no sense* an "inductive generalization" from these data' (pp. 32–3, italics added). See also Chomsky (1966b, p. 4).

which Chomsky presented in his 1964 paper as evidence *against* the essentially 'taxonomic' or 'inductive' approach which I advocate here.

First, consider again the problem of CAT (transcribed as [kæt]), CAN (or [kæ:n]) and CAN'T (or [kæ:t]).[1] Chomsky argues that the following rules are responsible for these forms:[2]

(1) $V \rightarrow V: / \underline{\quad} C_1$ (where V: = long vowel, C_1 = voiced non-flap C)

(2) $V \rightarrow \tilde{V} / \underline{\quad} N$ (where $\tilde{V}$ = nasalized V, N = nasal C)

(3) $N \rightarrow \emptyset / \tilde{V} \underline{\quad} C_2$ (where $\tilde{V}$ = lax V, C_2 = voiceless stop)

It is clear that rules (1) and (2) represent the two articulatory habits which I have just discussed. It is also clear that rule (3) can easily be interpreted in the same way: no nasal consonants are articulated in English before voiceless stops if a lax vowel precedes. (For my dialect, this latter qualification seems to be unnecessary: I lack nasals in words like PAINT, WON'T, etc., as well). Under this interpretation, clearly, each of these rules may be taken to define a set of conditions which all phonological strings in English must meet before they can be regarded as acceptable (or 'normal') utterances phonetically; in more popular jargon each such rule represents a specific 'output condition' of 'surface structure constraint' (cf. Perlmutter, 1970) which must be satisfied in order for any phonological sequence in English to be 'correctly pronounced'. As such, all 'rules' of this sort are inherently unordered (see p. 208 below).[3]

[1] As on pp. 102–3 above, the phonetic transcriptions here are identical to Chomsky's except that I have added vowel length, where appropriate, in order to make the problem more interesting for illustrative purposes.

[2] Rules (2) and (3) here are schematic equivalents to Chomsky's rules (34i) and (34ii) respectively (p. 96), while rule (1) is a slightly modified substitute for Chomsky's rule (28) (p. 90). If we assume (with Chomsky) that short vowels do systematically appear in some English dialects before the (voiced) flap [D], one wonders how Chomsky's 'simpler' or more general rule – lengthen all vowel nuclei before *all* voiced consonants – could possibly be learned (except as a tentative first approximation which is later rejected, as indicated by the emergence of a [rayDir] vs. [ra:yDir] contrast in the learner's speech).

[3] The reader should not assume that broad phonotactic generalizations of this kind are the only kinds of generalizations which a language learner might induce from the primary data, given a 'learnability' constraint of the sort described. Presumably any generalization which is true of the data is a possible candidate, including those which are restricted to certain morphological categories or sub-categories, etc. It is an empirical matter to determine which of these possible generalizations the child hits upon, and to determine how these preferences are exercised. Presumably the broadest generalizations (of the set which the data allow in terms of our proposed constraint) will be preferred, since such generalizations have greater support in the data and are more likely to come to the language learner's attention. I restrict attention here to these broader types of generalizations only for purposes of this exposition.

But to continue; we have discovered (mainly by looking for instances of 'complementary distribution', in effect) that certain phonetic sequences are 'inadmissible' in English, and we have proposed plausible rules (or articulatory habits) to account for this. The problem is now to determine what base forms (or lexical representations) an adult speaker might reasonably associate with these rules. I have already argued that something like the classical SIB-phonemic level of representation, while possibly appropriate for a (child) speaker uninformed about morphological relationships,[1] is not appropriate to the normal adult speaker. For him there would seem to be no risk in assuming that he *does* know that CAN (SIB-phonemicized as $/kæ̃:n/$) and CAN'T (= $/kæ̃:t/$), are different forms of the same word (which is to say that he has recognized that both words contain the same *morpheme*). We may therefore broach the question of what lexical representation this common morpheme might be given.

According to Jakobson's suggested procedures (pp. 190–2 above), the appropriate representation would have to be culled from possibilities established by *pooling* the SIB-phonemic (or 'phonetic shorthand') representations of those variants of the morpheme which *actually occur*. In our example this would yield the following candidates:

$$\text{'can'} = \text{k æ̃:} \begin{bmatrix} n \\ \varnothing \end{bmatrix}$$

Neither of these representations (the two 'basic allomorphs' of Bloomfield, Nida, Hockett, etc.) is entirely satisfactory. We have already noted, on independent grounds, that Jakobson's proposed procedures are, in general, too restrictive. We are now in a position to consider an amended and more liberalized constraint.

The two-segment candidate, $°/kæ̃:°/$, is eliminated as an acceptable lexical representation for this morpheme on the ground that it will not even 'work'; i.e. there is no way of accounting for the form $[kæ̃:n]$ from this representation by means of any of the output conditions which have been proposed (since none of these ever insert an *n* in the position required). The three-segment candidate, $°/kæ̃:n°/$, is not defective in this respect, since the form $[kæ̃:t]$ (without the nasal) is automatically 'derived' from the sequence of lexical representations $°/kæ̃:n°/ + °/t°/$ by application of rule (3), which deletes the segment in question. (The form $[kæ̃:n]$ is supplied directly under this interpretation, since it

[1] For some interesting but unorthodox evidence for this, see Read, 1971, pp. 18ff, especially p. 20.

already satisfies the output conditions and is therefore unaffected by any of them.) But much the same difficulty faces us here as with the Russian °/s'°/ and the Spanish °/e°/, namely, that some of the phonetic information associated with the lexical representation proposed is redundant (and hence inappropriate for the lexicon), since it could be predicted by one or more of the rules which we have been led to postulate. In particular, with the hypothetical lexical representation °/kæ̃:n°/, both the length and nasalization of the vowel could be specified by application of rules (1) and (2) respectively, rather than included in the lexical representation itself.

But while only one of the two candidates for the lexical representation of the morpheme 'can' allowed by Jakobson's procedures is suitable or workable (given the set of reasonable rules which Chomsky suggests), there are other candidates which would also be compatible with these rules (although none of these others is actually realized phonetically in the data). There are three such possibilities, in fact. The first is °/kæ:n°/ (where the vowel is lengthened, but not nasalized). Notice that [kæ̃:n] can be derived from this representation by application of rule (2) alone, while the form [kæ̃:t] can be derived from °/kæ:n°/+°/t°/ by application of rules (2) and (3). By the same token, the sequence °/kæ̃n°/ is also a workable candidate, since both [kæ̃:n] and [kæ̃:t] are derivable from it as well (by application of rule (1) in the first case, and rules (1) and (3) in the second). The last candidate is °/kæn°/ itself,[1] from which each of the two words can be derived in the following way:

CAN	CAN'T
°/kæn°/	°/kæn°/ + °/t°/
⇓	⇓
[kæ̃:n]	[kæ̃:t]
by satisfying	by satisfying
conditions (1) and (2)	conditions (1), (2) and (3)

[1] No other candidates are consistent with the system as it now stands (i.e. without modifying the set of rules postulated). A base form like °/tæ̃:n°/ is unacceptable, for instance, because we have no rule to account for the replacement of the initial °/t°/ by [k]; similarly, a form like °/kon°/ is also excluded, since we have no principled way of accounting for any change in the basic vowel. Forms such as °/tæ:n°/ or °/tæn°/, °/ko:n°/ or °/kõn°/, etc. are excluded for the same reasons. In short, once a tentative set of rules (or output conditions) is established which satisfies the 'learnability' constraint on rules already discussed, there is only a highly circumscribed set of potential lexical representations which may accompany these rules and yield a workable total system; and it is this set (and *only* this set) with which we need to be concerned in any particular case. (If a new or revised alternative set of rules is proposed,

In this last case it is clear that we make maximum use of the rules available, i.e. we 'predict-in' as much redundant phonetic information as the system is capable of managing.[1] On these grounds I tentatively choose $°/kæn°/$ as the appropriate lexical representation for the morpheme 'can', in preference of the other seven possibilities which the system will allow.[2]

To recapitulate, I propose the following set of 'learnability' constraints on phonological systems:

(1) All tentative rules must be true, as stated, of the primary linguistic data, i.e. they must express valid (and easily falsifiable) generalizations realized in the data which is accessible to the child.

(2) Once a tentative set of rules is so formulated, a complementary set of possible base forms (lexical representations) for each proposed morpheme in the sample may be established. Each set is restricted to:

(a) the set of alternants (stated, for convenience, in SIB-phonemic representation) which actually occurs, given specific assumptions about morphological relations among words (= Jakobson's constraint);

(b) those additional representations which are also consistent with the

then the whole job has to be done over again.) My proposed constraint on lexical representations thus amounts to a condition of recoverability in terms of a set of *surface* generalizations (cf. Schane, 1971, p. 515).

[1] Notice the important distinction between something like 'predicting-in as much redundant phonetic information as is feasible' (given any metatheory – which implies that we choose that metatheory which will allow us to predict in all but a skeleton of distinctive features) and the phrase 'predicting-in as much redundant phonetic information as the system is capable of managing'. The chief difference between these approaches is the basic assumption in each case. Chomsky's basic assumption is that the child is pre-programmed to acquire a grammar in which as much information as might possibly be supplied by general rule is so supplied (the assumption of 'maximum regularity'). My basic assumption is that rules and lexical representations must be learnable, given an organism equipped to perform only in ways which can be supported by empirical evidence. I must therefore settle for maximum 'simplicity' or 'economy' in a system which is already very highly constrained from the standpoint of abstractness in rules and lexical representations. It is a purely empirical matter whether the language learner even opts for *this* kind of economy; my only claims, therefore, are in the direction of 'reasonableness' or 'viability', not 'correctness' or 'truth'. Independent experimental evidence is still required.

[2] Schematically, the eight candidates for the status of 'possible lexical representation for the morpheme "can"', given the system of rules already discussed, can be compactly indicated as follows:

$$\text{'can'} = k \begin{bmatrix} æ \\ \tilde{æ} \\ æ: \\ \tilde{æ}: \end{bmatrix} \begin{bmatrix} n \\ \\ ø \end{bmatrix}$$

system as developed so far (= my proposed 'liberalization' of the Jakobsonian scheme).

(3) We choose as basic that one of the available candidates for each morpheme which is least specific, i.e. from which the greatest amount of specific phonetic or other information can be extracted, given the particular rules proposed in step (1). This form is taken to be the lexical representation most appropriate to the phonological system.

These three rules present, in general outline, a tentative discovery procedure (or learning strategy) for possible phonological systems.

Two additional comments are now in order. First, the procedures outlined are not fully deterministic (nor should they be expected to be, at this early stage). Obviously, many 'possible phonological systems' will be admitted for a given body of data which are consistent with the procedures outlined here.[1] In particular, the results obtained from following steps (2) and (3) are highly (if not fully) determined by the results achieved under step (1): everything hinges, in the last analysis, on the set of rules or output conditions which the analyst tentatively regards as most likely to be extracted from the data by the language learner. (Nor is it at all unlikely that different learners might extract different generalizations, even if exposed to the same data.) In short, these procedures do not define 'the' phonological system for a language, but delimit a range of 'possible', 'feasible' or 'learnable' systems of this sort, around which a program of psycholinguistic investigation might be designed. No more grandiose goals can reasonably be expected of 'purely linguistic' research. There is no way (short of luck) in which the specific linguistic system which any individual employs in speech production and perception can be ascertained from primary linguistic data alone; the best the linguist can do at present is to outline those systems which the child would be *most likely* to hit upon (given some reasonable set of initial assumptions, such as the general 'learnability' constraint outlined here).

[1] One possible re-analysis of Chomsky's data, for example, would be to consider the nasal elision rule (Chomsky's rule (34ii) (1964, p. 96) and my condition (3) on p. 203 above) to be formulated not simply in terms of an 'unvoiced stop', but rather in terms of an 'unvoiced *homorganic* stop' (cf. Schane, 1971, p. 515). This formulation is also consistent with my proposed 'learnability' constraint and has the further advantage of allowing us to say (by step (2b) in the proposed discovery algorithm) that the *particular* nasal consonant in the base form of PUMP (presumably, the phonetic [pʌ̃:p]) is the labial °/m°/ (and not simply the indeterminate nasal °/N°/), of PUNT (= [pʌ̃:t]) is the dental °/n°/, etc. In these cases (unlike CAN or CAN'T) we have no morphological evidence (or alternation) to provide us with information regarding the *particular* nasal present (i.e. there are no morphemes 'pum' or 'pun' involved).

Whether any of these systems are true (i.e. whether any of them conform to the system which the child actually learns) can only be answered
by asking the child (or the adult, who once was a child), i.e. by performing experiments (see chapter 9 for discussion).

It is also important that in my proposed reconceptualization of
classical morphophonemic theory, I have effectively abandoned the
notion of rule ordering as far as phonological systems are concerned.
My analysis of the CAN–CAN'T problem differs in this one (important)
respect from Chomsky's. Chomsky suggests, for example, that his
nasalization and nasal elision rules must be ordered (1964, p. 96) and has
argued that, in general, a number of specific (and sometimes complex)
'universal principles' of rule-ordering are required for phonological
description (1967d). The first of these suggestions is incorrect (as indicated above, where the correct results are obtained by the 'simultaneous'
application of the rules to the base forms which Chomsky advocates),
while the second has no empirical support. (True enough, phonological
systems can be developed by linguists which incorporate the conventions in question, but this is not 'support'.) I therefore adopt (since my
metatheory and its associated conceptualization or interpretation *forces*
me to do so) the absolute limiting condition of Chafe's two proposals
(1968a): (1) to 'maximize simultaneous ordering' (p. 127) – I have *no
ordering at all* – and (2) to 'minimize the DEPTH of ordering' (or the
number of intermediate or pseudo-levels of representation between
the lexical and the phonetic; p. 127) and hence to 'apply each rule at the
latest possible point' (p. 128) – I 'apply' each phonological rule at the
same point in all 'derivations' (or, in terms more appropriate to
the interpretation of the notion 'phonological rule' suggested here, all
lexical representations must conform to a particular set of articulatory
habits, or 'output conditions', before they may be considered 'correctly
pronounced').[1]

Interestingly, all the other 'preferred' analyses which Chomsky presents in the 'taxonomic phonemics' section of his 1964 paper are also
compatible with the constraints I have outlined. Chomsky's WRITER–
RIDER example (p. 96), for instance, introduces no serious new complica-
tions. All that is required is to add to our system the additional output

---

[1] In some cases a phenomenon which gives the 'effect' or 'appearance' of rule ordering
is implicit in my theory (see pp. 215–18 below). This phenomenon (or something like
it) may have misled many linguists into thinking that phonological rules must be
ordered, and has thus led to the further loosening of constraints on phonological
systems which a general convention of extrinsic rule ordering necessarily implies.

condition (4) that $(t, d) \rightarrow D$ / $\acute{V}$___$\check{R}$, where $\acute{V}$ is a stressed vowel and $\check{R}$ an 'unstressed vocalic' (cf. Chomsky's rule (29) on p. 90), which correlates perfectly well with the absence of t and d in these environments (in the dialect in question), plus the appropriate adjustment of condition (1) to allow for the possibility of an intervening glide (cf. Chomsky's rule (28), also on p. 90).[1] The choice of an underlying $^\circ/t^\circ/$, in the first instance, and $^\circ/d^\circ/$, in the second, follows automatically from step (2a) of my procedure (if we may assume that WRITE and WRITER contain the same morpheme, and the same for RIDE and RIDER), or from step (2b), in any case. And, as before, no rule ordering is required (despite Chomsky's suggestion to the contrary (1964, p. 96)).[2]

By the same token, Chomsky's example using the ostensive /o/ – /o̜/ phonemic 'contrast' in Russian can also be analyzed in essentially the manner he suggests, given added data in the form of words like [mo̜l]

[1] W. J. Baker has pointed out to me (personal communication) that if there is, as Chomsky suggests, no acoustic basis for distinguishing the flap in WRITER (which Chomsky gives as [rayDɨr]) from the flap in RIDER (= [ra:yDɨr]) – or for identifying a nasal (consonant) in a word like CAN'T (= [kæ̃:t]) – and if it is the case that the mature native speaker of English in some sense 'perceives' a 't' in the first word, a 'd' in the second, and a segmental 'n' in the third, then the native speaker is, by definition, experiencing an *illusion* (cf. also Sapir's famous Sarcee illustration of this same phenomenon (1933, pp. 52ff)). In situations where a subject is presented with insufficient sensory input to provide a comprehensible pattern, what he typically does is to *fill in* the missing information by analogy with his previous experience in similar situations (cf. the familiar rotating trapezoid illusion, for example; see Ames, 1951, and Baker, 1963). The theory outlined above suggests one basis for the alleged 'phonological illusions' described here, namely, that *knowledge of other forms of the same word* constitutes one important source of the extra-sensory information required (cf. Sapir, who argues that 'it is possible for perfectly homonymous words to give the speaker the *illusion* of phonetic difference because of the different contexts in which they appear *or because of the different positions they occupy in their respective form systems*' (1933, p. 52; italics added)). This is not unreasonable.

On the other hand, this whole approach assumes that the 'phonetic facts' which Chomsky cites are correct, and my hypothesis concerning the possible role of morphological information in accounting for such 'facts' is grounded solely in the assumption that the problems which Chomsky outlines are genuine. Obviously, if there is a functionally constant acoustic cue in all tokens of the utterance-types transcribed here as [kæ̃:t] which the hearer might interpret as one manifestation of the segment-type [n], and another such cue which distinguishes the flap in WRITER from the one in RIDER, then Chomsky's argument collapses and the 'phonological illusion' with it. The point to make here, however, is that the more straightforward explanation of the native speaker's apparent interpretation of these forms ought to be explored before we conclude that illusion is the normal mode of perception in phonology, and before we search for some more esoteric explanation of a 'phenomenon' which might not even exist. See also Householder (1965, pp. 28–9).

[2] Procedure (2b) also supplies $^\circ/t^\circ/$ as part of the base form of LATTER, but $^\circ/d^\circ/$ for LADDER, etc., though no morphophonemic alternations involve these segments (cf. p. 206, n. 7 above).

'pier', [pọl] 'floor', [tọlk] 'sense', [dọlk] 'debt', [vólni] 'waves', [čọln] 'canoe' and [sóln'ičn'ij] 'sunny', which attest that while the phonetic sequences ọl and ọlC appear in Russian, the sequences *ol and *lNC never do (in non-deliberate speech, that is; cf. Chomsky's example [sóncal] 'sun' on p. 97 of his 1964 article). The following two output conditions (or articulatory habits) might therefore be included among the full set for Russian:

(1) o→ọ / ——l
(2) l→ø / ——NC

These statements correspond to Chomsky's proposed rules (36i) and (36ii), respectively (p. 97).[1] Similarly, my procedure (2a) – if we can agree that the noun 'sun' and the adjective form 'sunny' contain the same morpheme – or (2b) otherwise – will lead us to posit an °/l°/ as part of the preferred lexical representation for the Russian morpheme 'sun'. And, once again, no rule ordering is required.

The critique which Chomsky made in his 1964 article (and there-after) against the structuralists' notion of 'taxonomic' or strict in-variant-biunique phonemics has no bearing on the 'discovery algorithm' phonological analysis which I propose (which is little more than a re-conceptualized version of structuralist morphophonemic theory – which is what Chomsky should have focused his critique upon if it were really to have any force; cf. pp. 187–8 above). But Chomsky contrasted structuralist morphophonemics with SIB-phonemics, a peculiar thing to do; he then relabeled the traditional morphophonemics 'systematic phonemics' (1964, p. 92) and called it his own creation (but with rule ordering added). This was also peculiar. But nothing in all this is nearly as peculiar as his later attempt to equate the 'systematic phone-mics' of this 1964 article with the 'systematic phonemics' of his (and Halle's) later practice (as in Chomsky & Halle, 1968, for instance), which is an entirely different system.[2] I say this because by 1968, at least, it had become clear that anything approaching my learnability constraint

---

[1] I have incorporated a minor correction in the latter rule by adding a final C. Chom-sky's rule (36ii) deletes *l* in the environment V——N (where N = his 'Nasal Consonant', as in his rule (34i) on p. 96), a statement which is countermanded by such forms as [vólni], [čọln] (see above for glosses) and many others.

[2] Cf. especially chapter 1 of this latter work, where the authors' intended use of the terms 'lexical representation' (p. 10) or 'phonological representation' (p. 11) is pre-sented as a mere terminological preference over 'other terms that might have been used in place of [them, namely] ... "morphophonemic representation" or "systematic phonemic representation" ' (p. 11). And cf. the authors' own (unjustifiably qualified) admission on p. 76n.

(implicit in virtually all pre-transformational work) had been thrown to the winds.[1] Now anything was 'learnable', thanks to 'innate linguistic universals'.

Even generalizations which are objectively *false* with respect to the primary data are 'learnable' for the transformationalists. Kohler spotted a number of such 'generalizations' in his recent review:

A generative grammar should...state generalizations...independently from the idio-syncratic lexicon in language specific rules because in a foreign language learning situation, for example, the degree of phonic interference will be determined by patterns which govern *the articulatory behaviour* of a speech community in general...The adequacy of such an independent system of general rules...can be measured by the percentage of *correct predictions of learners' errors*. In a phonology that is principally interested in stating morphophonological processes and language universals in connection with a specific lexicon such predictability is greatly restricted and certainly not derivable in a straightforward explicit way from the phonological description itself. And in as much as a phonology fails to characterize the principles underlying this kind of performance [among others] it is not an adequate phonology of a language.

Thus phonological rewrite rules in English which only operate over the domain of the English vocabulary must not generate [ʌ] between a nonnasal labial segment and final [l], [ʃ], [tʃ] (p. 204), nor formative initial [ʃt-](p. 171), nor [ɔ:] in the context ____[+nasal]C, which, conversely, [au] is restricted to in polysyllabic formatives (p. 20), and these rules also pre-suppose identical feature specifications for [ɔ:] and [au] in the lexical matrices of polysyllables ([u:] is suggested) to state the complementary distribution of these segments. But *no native speaker of English shows the slightest difficulty* in producing and in auditorily identifying [pʌl]; [ʃtoun]; [au'deiʃəs], ['kɔ:nsil], whereas formative initial [ts-], [ps-], [ks-] or [pt-] prove far more troublesome, and in no way can he be said to possess, in his competence, an underlying identical feature column for the vowels in *au*dacious and council. *These are facts of a corpus of lexical items, not of articulatory and auditory potentialities in a given language*, and they are established by the *linguist* in the comparison of lexicon entries, they have no real status for the *speaker* (1970, p. 90; italics added in some instances).

All such rules would be excluded under my approach, and with them the kind of highly abstract 'absolutely neutralized' lexical representations which the authors repeatedly posit. The same is true of Lightner's work. A rule such as (k:č) as formulated on p. 146 above is automatically

---

[1] This was already presaged in the 1964 paper itself, where Chomsky's language acquisition model and its associated 'innate linguistic universals' received their first public airing.

excluded (in the very general form in which Lightner states it, at least),[1] as is virtually every other rule in his grammar which is crucial to any of the specific 'synchronic explanations' which he suggests (cf. 4.2 and 4.3). It is encouraging to find, therefore, that there is no real evidence of the productivity of any of these rules and hence that any of them might be 'psychologically real'. My approach, in short, prevents the analyst from engaging in either of two powerful descriptive tricks, and forces him to keep the number of possible analyses for a given language or corpus within reasonable bounds. I have already spoken at length on the first of these 'tricks': absolute neutralization or lack of constraint on the abstractness of lexical (and deep syntactical) representation. A few brief comments on the second are now in order. I am speaking now of that constraint-loosening stratagem called 'rule ordering'.

Suspicions about the possible counter-utility of this convention may arise after reading Chafe (1968a), in which two general proposals are suggested for determining a definitive or unique ordering among the rules of the phonological component of a generative grammar (pp. 126ff). The problem arose from Chafe's observation that some – presumably a small proportion – of these rules did not 'interfere' with many of the others and therefore could be placed almost anywhere in the ordered set with no effect on the output. Under the assumption that phonological rules must be linearly ordered (Chomsky's Principle 2 (1967d, p. 103)), the placing of such rules in the sequence would presumably have to be done in an arbitrary way every time the situation arose. On the other hand, if phonological rules needed only to be partially ordered (Chomsky's Principle 2′ (1967d, p. 105)), what was to be done with the remaining rules? Chafe's two proposals were designed to provide a principled basis for answering this question, by establishing a specific ordering without being forced to claim that certain rules are to be ordered before others in cases where there is no evidence to support such a decision (cf. Chomsky, 1967d, p. 105, who takes a different

---

[1] A (morpho)phonotactically true form of Lightner's rule might be one which changed *k* to *č* for certain sub-classes of verbs in certain specific paradigmatic forms (= *morphological* conditioning, rather than the kind of very general *phonological* conditioning implied by Lightner's own statement of the rule). There is no reason to assume that the child prefers phonological conditioning to morphological: I assume only that he is limited in his rule-inducing capacities to generalizations which are objectively true, in general, of the data to which he is exposed, and say nothing about the form these generalizations must take. The generalizations must follow from the data, not the reverse.

For some evidence in favor of morphologically conditioned rules, see especially Hale (1971), Prideaux (1971b) and Holden (1972). See also p. 198, n. 1 above.

tack). Chafe's specific proposals were to 'maximize simultaneous ordering' (that is, to group as many rules as possible into 'blocks' of 'simultaneous' rules, i.e. rules which all apply directly to the same level of representation) and to 'apply each rule at the latest possible point' (that is, to put as many rules as possible into the lowest block, then the next lowest, etc.). The result is to establish a specific ordering among all the rules of the phonological component (since each rule must now be in one block or another), as well as to establish a specific 'depth' of ordering in which as few intermediate levels of representation as possible are defined between the lexical and the phonetic.

The pedagogical advantages of adopting these conventions are obvious: it is easier to correct papers in which all rules are ordered in the same way then ones in which each student gives his rules (and his sample derivations) in any of a number of possible orderings which 'work'. For this reason I adopted these conventions in my beginning course in generative phonology. What happened was totally unexpected: I discovered that for almost all of my illustrative problems a large number of rules which I had previously assumed had to be ordered (if they were to be statable in their most general and most 'natural' transformational-generative form) did not have to be ordered at all; in fact, it was the rare rule indeed which really needed to be so ordered from this point of view. Even for the most complex problems in my corpus, I found that three to five 'depths' or 'levels' of 'rule-blocks' were all that were required, though sometimes three to four times as many individual rules were needed. My curiosity aroused, I next tried applying Chafe's conventions to the larger corpus of rules which Lightner presented in his thesis (1965) and found some equally surprising results of the same sort.[1] As a result, I came to suspect that the notion of rule ordering might not be as important as I had been led to believe.

[1] For example, of the 39 specific rule-ordering arguments which Lightner gives on pp. 218–19, I have found at least 12 which fail to stand up to the test of simultaneous ordering. So in a third of the examples which Lightner selects specifically to illustrate the need for some strict linear ordering in his grammar, the simultaneous application of each pair of rules yields the same results as does ordering the rules in the way he suggests; it is only the reverse ordering which fails, a situation which Lightner apparently considered a sufficient test. This is all the more striking when one considers that the system of rules which Lightner presents is only partially ordered to begin with (see his pp. 216–17), i.e. the examples under discussion represent a residual set of supposedly clear cases in which it was felt that ordering was required. It is also significant that the rules which apparently do have to be ordered in Lightner's grammar are, almost without exception, those rules which act upon absolutely neutralized lexical segments. (As for the exceptions, see p. 217, n. 1.)

An independent observation reinforced this suspicion and led me back to the version of traditional phonological theory sketched above, in which ordering among phonological rules is virtually eliminated. This was the realization (brought to my attention by R. T. Harms in 1970) that the lexicon was very definitely the wrong place to be dealing with such phenomena as sequential constraints (cf. the notion of 'morpheme structure rule' first introduced by Halle, 1959). For one thing, the constraints in question are not restricted to individual morphemes, but normally extend across morpheme boundaries as well,[1] so necessitating the addition of P-rules to the grammar which merely restate the information already given in the MS-rules (see Stanley, 1967). Moreover, as lexical representations became more and more abstract (and the associated phonological systems more and more unlearnable without some rich system of *a priori* linguistic universals), it also became more and more difficult to state the constraints in terms of the kinds of representations which were now appearing on the lexical level (which often contained segments not phonetically realized in the language at all). So where should such constraints properly be stated? If these were true phonotactic constraints, it seemed that the phonetic level was the obvious place.

A third consideration was then decisive: the full realization that the effect of ordering two phonological rules is merely to eliminate (albeit covertly) environments in which the rule does not really apply at all. The function of a general convention of rule ordering, in short, is to make a rule 'look' more general (and more 'natural') than it is (cf. p. 140, n. 1, above). In cases where *true* phonotactic generalizations are being expressed, we find that no rule ordering is required to make the rule 'look' good, for in such cases the rule *is* just as general and 'natural' as implied by the form in which it is stated.

A good example is the one provided by Chomsky and Halle (1965, pp. 111ff) and intended, ironically, as an argument against Lamb's claim (very much parallel to mine here) that the economy achieved in 'mutation' grammars of the generative sort is only apparent, since it is 'achieved at the cost of making rules ordered' (1964, p. 119). In this case Chomsky and Halle argue that their ordered 'mutation' grammar (3) is to be preferred over Lamb's (locally) unordered 'realization' grammar (4) on the ground that 'there is a significant relationship between the

---

[1] This is so commonly true that it has hardened into a notational convention regarding the 'formative boundary' (Chomsky & Halle, 1968, p. 364).

realization of /w/ and /k^w/ as [q^w]' which is implicit in their grammar but totally missing in Lamb's, which would imply that the phenomenon is purely accidental (see Chomsky & Halle, 1965, p. 112, for details). I do not opt here for 'realization' grammars (since these adopt unmotivated 'stages' of ordering of their own); what I do opt for is no extrinsic ordering among the phonological rules (since I am concerned with capturing those particular phonotactic or phonetic sequential constraints which may be interpreted as representing a set of articulatory habits which the speakers of a language have acquired, over time, as the result of constant practice).

Let us at this point adopt a tentative set of notational conventions for expressing generalizations of this sort. I assume that each such 'rule' has two essential parts: (1) a statement of the particular 'impossible' or 'outlawed' sequences of elements which the habit has produced and (2) a statement of the particular 'instruction' to be followed whenever an asterisked sequence of this sort is 'submitted' by the lexicon for articulation.[1] In these terms, the output conditions most appropriate for the data which Lamb and Chomsky–Halle describe would be as follows (with each statement rewritten in more conventional 'mutation rule' form immediately to the right):

(1) *hw; w→k^w w→k^w / h___

(2) *V$_1$hk^{w}V$_2$; k^w→q^w k^w→q^w / V$_1$h___V$_2$

Notice that stated in 'rule' form, my proposed conditions are precisely those rules proposed by Chomsky and Halle (p. 112), with one important difference: in order to insure the 'learnability' of rules, I have decided that all rules of this sort must express true phonotactic generalizations and hence be statements true on (and hence extractable directly from) the phonetic level. As such they must be *unordered*.[2] Also notice that this system of (extrinsically) unordered rules 'works' for the data which Lamb and Chomsky–Halle describe, i.e. it yields the correct results.

Assume that some lexical representation containing the sequence °/...hw...°/ were to be produced, for instance (cf. n. 1 below). In

[1] Notice that the implied ordering 'first choose your lexical elements' and 'then submit these for articulation' involves a specific empirical claim about linguistic performance (on the encoding side).

[2] I use the term 'unordered' to mean 'not *extrinsically* ordered' (cf. Ringen, 1971, and p. 217, n. 1 below). Koutsoudas (1972) argues on purely formal grounds that unordered rules are viable, but gives no independent reasons for preferring such a system of rules to any other.

order to be 'correctly pronounced' in this language, this representation, by definition (i.e. by convention), must satisfy all the output conditions stated. Obviously, condition (2) presents no problem in this instance (assuming that there are no sequences of the type $V_1hk^wV_2$ involved anywhere else in the lexical representation of the utterance). Condition (1) is another matter, and the sequence must be altered in order to satisfy it. According to the instruction provided, the sequence $°/\ldots hw\ldots°/$ is re-represented as the sequence...hk^w.... This sequence, we find fully acceptable (or 'pronounceable') – since there are no further conditions which it fails to satisfy – so we may supply the square brackets at this point: $[\ldots hk^w\ldots]$. The treatment of a lexical sequence $°/\ldots V_1hk^w$ $V_2\ldots°/$ is analogous.

But what about the lexical sequence $°/\ldots V_1hwV_2\ldots°/$? This is an interesting example, in that it illustrates a phenomenon associated with my theory which may have led to confusion and misconceptualization in the past. Let us consider the 'act of articulating' this sequence in terms of a sequence of steps, each consisting of a specific question (or instruction) and a specific answer (or adjustment), as implied by the conceptual framework I have proposed:

Step 1: Is the sequence $°/\ldots V_1hwV_2\ldots°/$ pronounceable as it stands? (I.e. does it satisfy all the output conditions established for this language?)
NO

Step 2: Which output condition(s) does it fail to satisfy?
CONDITION (1) – *only*.

Step 3: Follow the instruction associated with condition (1). This yields the representation ...$V_1hk^wV_2$...

Step 4: Is the sequence ...$V_1hk^wV_2$... pronounceable? (Notice again that, by general convention, no phonological representation is 'pronounceable' unless and until it satisfies all the output conditions provided.)
NO

Step 5: Which output condition(s) does it fail to satisfy?
CONDITION (2) – *only*.

Step 6: Follow the instruction associated with condition (2). This yields the representation ...$V_1hq^wV_2$....

Step 7: Is the sequence ...$V_1hq^wV_2$... pronounceable?
YES (It now satisfies all the stated output conditions.)

Step 8: Supply phonetic brackets to indicate this.
This yields [...$V_1hq^wV_2$...].

END

There are three important observations to be made from this example. First, we get the correct results. This is the paramount consideration against which any 'possible' phonological system must be measured. Second, we have managed to achieve this without imposing order among our rules (or, as I prefer to call them for conceptual and mnemonic reasons, 'output conditions'). Nevertheless, the sequence of 'steps' which a hypothetical language user might go through in articulating a lexical representation of the sort indicated does suggest an 'appearance' of rule ordering. That is to say, if we eliminated everything from the step-by-step procedure above except the phonological representations which appear as the 'output' of certain of these steps, we would have a sequence of representations indistinguishable from the 'derivation' associated with Chomsky and Halle's own 'mutation' grammar, in which the rules are ordered. But this 'appearance' of ordering which results from our model is a necessary consequence of that model and not an independent part of it.[1] That is to say, the sequence of stages or 'mutations' through which a phonological representation must go within my proposed framework does not follow from some special metatheoretical convention of rule ordering, but is a consequence of the single general metatheoretical requirement that 'all output conditions must be satisfied before phonetic brackets may be supplied'.[2] My rules (or conditions)

---

[1] For a parallel case in Russian, consider Lightner's claim (1965, p. 226) that his (l:ø) rule must precede his final devoicing rule (voice # #). Both rules represent true generalizations (though the former is apparently restricted to the class of true verbs; cf. Lightner, 1965b, pp. 81-2) and no extrinsic ordering with respect to these rules is required, given the single general convention described above. The ordering, in short, is purely *intrinsic*, since no sequence in Cl# # can ever be *eligible* for final devoicing unless or until the final resonant is deleted.

[2] This principle fails, however, in situations where the structural descriptions (SD's) of two rules overlap or conflict. Cf. the Russian /sASborAm/ 'with a collection' (from an underlying °/s + Sbor + om°/), where vowel epenthesis (to break up the non-permissible initial cluster s + fricative + stop) must apply *before* the rule for voicing assimilation (see p. 97 above). But notice that this ordering is also 'intrinsic' in the sense of n. 1 above: no sequence is 'eligible' for phonetic voicing assimilation until after its segmental (or canonical) structure has been definitively established. Hence, epenthesis rules are, in general, 'logically prior' to other rules which require information about the *segmental* composition of an utterance for their proper operation.

Sanders (see Koutsoudas, Sanders & Noll, 1971) has proposed a general convention of (intrinsic) rule ordering which seems sufficient to resolve all clear cases of this are unordered: they represent learnable phonotactic generalizations which may be extracted from the primary data directly. Extrinsic rule ordering (like absolute neutralization) is an analytical device which the generative grammarian has adopted to give his *a priori* notions of generality and 'naturalness' in grammar an appearance of credibility – and the general notion of 'innate linguistic universals' along with them. I reject such devices in favor of an alternative set of metatheoretical assumptions based on the overriding premise that every human language must be learnable, which is to say that the structure of each language must be such that it not only can but must be learned 'by an organism initially uninformed as to its general character' (cf. Chomsky, 1965a, p. 58).

6.3   Summary and conclusions

A general conclusion which emerges from the discussion of the past three chapters is that the whole framework of TGG is built on *a priori* assumptions about the nature of 'what is learned' in language acquisition. Finding this 'output' and the underlying principles upon which it is organized to be far removed from the 'primary data' to which the language learner is exposed, Chomsky develops the thesis that 'it can hardly be seriously proposed that abstract principles...of the nature of those discussed [in the transformationalist literature] are learned by any inductive process' (1967d, p. 127) and hence that 'knowledge of language cannot arise by application of step-by-step inductive operations...of any sort that have been developed or discussed within linguistics, psychology, or philosophy' (1967c, p. 11). He therefore concludes that

the child approaches the data with the presumption that they are drawn from a language of a certain antecedently well-defined type, his problem being to determine which of the (humanly) possible languages is that of the community in which he is placed. *Language learning would be impossible unless this were the case* (1965a, p. 27; italics added).

This argument hinges directly on the assumption that what is learned is roughly analogous to the system of rules which appear in a TGG. I find

sort: the rule whose SD incorporates the more extensive domain must always apply *first*. Sanders ignores, however, the further consideration which is ultimately crucial for the application of his principle, namely the question of determining what the proper formulation of a given rule *is*. (For a discussion of the distinction between *extrinsic* and *intrinsic* rule ordering, see Chomsky, 1965a, p. 223, n. 6, and Ringen, 1971.)

no good reason to believe that this is so. Indeed, my analysis of transformational-generative grammatical descriptions shows that combined
with the imposition of rigid constraints on the notion 'rule of grammar'
(intended to characterize, in part, that 'antecedently well-defined type'
of entity of which Chomsky speaks), there has been a corresponding
loosening of constraints in other areas of the descriptions, in particular,
on the notions of 'lexical representation' (in phonology) and 'deep' or
'base' structures (in syntax). This, combined with a general convention
of extrinsic 'rule ordering' (which permits the analyst to posit as many
rules and levels of rules – or 'intervening steps' – between his abstract
underlying representations and the surface as desired), has the inevitable
effect of making it possible in principle for the analyst to construct
grammars of the prescribed type for any body of data, so removing all
empirical significance from the specific set of 'universal constraints'
proposed for grammatical rules. Chomsky's system creates its own
evidence and then uses it to justify his more general philosophical
beliefs. I conclude from this that there is nothing in the transformational-
generative approach to linguistic description which supports the contention that language acquisition is predicated upon a highly structured
and specific set of innate 'content' linguistic universals. What Chomsky
and his fellow transformationalists have accomplished is merely to lend
an aura of 'plausibility to an otherwise preposterous thesis' (Goodman,
1969, p. 141).[1] Chomsky's claim that there is 'nothing known in psychology or physiology that suggests that the empiricist approach is well-
motivated, or that gives any grounds for skepticism concerning the
rationalist alternative' which he advocates (1967c, p. 11) is unsupported
assertion. Sufficient 'grounds for skepticism' concerning his proposed
'rationalist' alternative is this: 'innate knowledge' is beyond the bounds
of scientific inquiry as we know it. This is why we must look elsewhere
for understanding about the language acquisition process. Our only
present hope of *explaining* language acquisition is by assimilating it to

---

[1] Yet this 'aura' alone has been sufficient to convince most linguists and even some
psychologists that Chomsky is on the right track. McNeill, for example, observes in
his recent survey of 'The development of language' (1970b, p. 1067) that 'we operate
on the general assumption that the child's terminal state of knowledge is of the sort
represented by current transformational grammars', and Brown, too, insists that
Chomsky and his MIT associates 'put sharply in focus the remarkable terminal
state that is the regular outcome of language development' (1970, p. 2). Deese adds:
'A child has as part of his native equipment a device embodying a linguistic theory of
a high degree of complexity...[which] is best described as a universal grammar'
(1970, p. 11).

other kinds of learning. Moreover, as Chase observed, 'the very best way *not* to discover the essential substrate in experience for acquiring a capability [such as language] is to assume that it does not *have* a substrate in experience' (in Darley, 1967, p. 87; italics added). Chomsky proposes a model of linguistic description which puts unreasonable demands upon the language learner. To him, 'the normal assumption, unprejudiced by doctrine' which follows is that the learner must approach language with an essential foreknowledge of the system to be learned. To me the conclusion follows instead that the descriptive system itself must be at fault and so must be altered to eliminate the discrepancy. In this chapter, therefore, I have outlined tentative proposals of an 'empiricist' kind, a step which seems to call for no further justification.

One question remains: how did Chomsky so divert linguistics in the first place? Two possible explanations for the 'Chomsky phenomenon' come to mind. The first is related to Chomsky's undeniable skill as a polemicist: he succeeds in debate despite key arguments which include the fully specious (e.g. his attack on the notion of a 'discovery procedure' for grammars as discussed in 3.4), the mainly irrelevant (e.g. his campaign against the 'taxonomic' phoneme as discussed in 6.1), the grossly misleading (such as the argument that 'invoking an innate representation of universal grammar does solve the problem of learning...if in fact it is true that this is the basis...for it' (1969, p. 80))[1] and even the out-and-out false (e.g. 'It is a *widely confirmed empirical fact* that underlying representations are fairly resistant to historical change, which tends, by and large, to involve late phonetic rules' (Chomsky & Halle, 1968, p. 49; italics added)). Possibly the linguists' tractability can be excused, given the isolation of their study from other scientific disciplines (and most especially from psychology) and the poor training which the typical linguist receives in the aims and methods of empirical science. Furthermore, the history of linguistics has really been little more than a succession of dominant approaches, theories or 'fads' (each

---

[1] This statement is misleading, we recall, because it contains a hidden conditional which renders it meaningless. Consider this more complete formulation: 'If it *could* be established empirically that universal grammar were innate, then the principles of universal grammar *would* solve the problem of learning.' But it is impossible (so far as we know) to establish such a 'fact' empirically (which is why psychologists have largely abandoned the 'innateness' controversy altogether; cf. Carmichael, 1925, and Howells, 1945); so the statement is an assertion about a contrary-to-fact state of affairs which cannot be evaluated (cf. Chomsky & Halle, 1968, p. 332, for another statement of this same genre).

with its own set of pet dogmas and minor branch-offs or 'schools' based upon them) with almost no effort expended in any period to develop full-fledged competing alternatives to the dominant point of view. This, too, may have made linguists rather insensitive to theoretical foundations: our perspectives are so limited that we have no solid basis for comparison.[1]

Equally important, however, Chomsky introduced not simply a new 'model' or technique of linguistic analysis, but brought with it an entire linguistic philosophy, radically different in many respects from all past approaches (wherever comparisons are possible) and filling what was almost a methodological void until that time. He proposed to turn linguistics into an important, even central, discipline, with touchstones in both philosophy and psychology, and transform it from a simple 'taxonomic' or 'descriptive' enterprise into a full-fledged 'explanatory' science (cf. chapter 2). We cannot therefore complete either our critique of Chomsky's position or our evaluation of his influence on linguistics until we have looked at some of these deeper philosophical questions. This will be the task of the next two chapters.

---

[1] Compare the situation in psychology, where theoretical plurality is legend. Oddly enough, many linguists look down on this as something to be eschewed; psychologists take a different view (cf. Cattell, 1966, p. 17).

Part III

METHODOLOGICAL
AND
CONCEPTUAL
FOUNDATIONS

7 Chomsky's 'revolution' reconsidered

7.1 On the nature of scientific discovery

In his review of the first decade following the publication of Chomsky's *Syntactic Structures*, a period of turmoil in which 'almost every article of faith or working assumption held by American linguists prior to 1957 [was] called into question', Bach attempted to characterize two views of science which seemed to be in conflict in the dispute (1965b, p. 112). One, which he called the 'Baconian', he described as follows:

The purpose of science is to obtain secure knowledge about the world. The only sure basis for such knowledge is observation and experiment. The scientist collects a large body of statements about particular happenings in the world or the laboratory. Starting from these true statements about real events he proceeds by a method of induction to limited generalizations about classes of events. After verifying these cautious generalizations he proceeds to more general statements. A general statement is reliable to the extent that it is based on such inductive methods. Hence, it is of the utmost importance to give the evidence for any general statement. The theory – if we admit this term at all – which is based on the widest body of evidence and is thus most probably true is the one most worthy of acceptance. Any speculations, metaphysical or *a priori* statements about the world, are excluded from science (pp. 112–13).

At the opposite extreme Bach presented a second (and presumably competing) view of science, which he called the 'Keplerian'; it contrasted sharply with the first in that:

Whereas the Baconian stresses caution and 'sticking to facts' with a distrust of theory and hypotheses..., the Keplerian emphasizes the creative nature of scientific discovery, the *leap to general hypotheses* – often mathematical in form – whose value is judged in terms of fruitfulness, simplicity and elegance. This attitude is well illustrated in an article by the physicist P. A. M. Dirac who tells how Erwin Schrödinger succeeded in discovering by pure cogitation his wave equation but abandoned it when it did not give results that agreed with experiment (because the phenomenon of electron spin was not known at the time). He published only a weaker and more approximate form which agreed with experimental results. Later when the spin was discovered a complete agreement with the earlier equation was obtained. Dirac concludes:

225

'I think there is a moral to this story, namely, that it is more important to have beauty in one's equations than to have them fit experiment' (pp. 113-14, italics added).

Finally, Bach argues that 'the prevailing assumptions of American linguistics prior to 1957 were essentially Baconian in character' (p. 114) in that strict inductivist methods were employed, whereas Chomsky's main contribution was to replace these methods by a 'deductively formulated theory' of the Keplerian type. Furthermore, recent 'advances' in linguistics have tended to 'show the correctness' of such a methodological reorientation (p. 125). Lyons reports:

Although the inductive approach is still advocated in many standard text-books of linguistics, the deductive approach has been gaining ground in the last few years, especially in connexion with the development of generative grammar (1970, p. 8).

7.1.1   Is there a logic of discovery? It is not difficult to find support for this interpretation of scientific activity in contemporary writings on the philosophy of science. In particular, the idea that there can be any kind of a 'logic of discovery' at all has come under repeated attack (see, e.g. Hempel, 1966, p. 17; Popper, 1965, p. 31; Braithwaite, 1960, p. 21; and Holton & Roller, 1958, p. 255). There are, however, some dissenting voices (as in Cajori, 1934, p. 547, and Hanson, 1961, p. 31). Interestingly enough, the dissenters cited here are Isaac Newton and Johannes Kepler himself. Newton argues that

the best and safest method of philosophising [doing scientific work]...seems to be, first to inquire diligently into. the properties of things, and of establishing these properties by experiment, and then to proceed more slowly to hypotheses [theories] for the explanation of them (in Andrade, 1954, p. 64).

It is worth noting, then, that while many philosophers ascribe the devising of hypotheses to 'genius, intuition, imagination, chance, or other extralogical processes' (Caws, 1969, p. 1375), it is the 'common consent of reputable scientists' that certain forms of inductive inference are justified (Braithwaite, 1960, p. 264). Braithwaite asks: 'Why is there so much common consent? It has surely not arisen merely from scientists imitating one another. There must be some reason behind it' (p. 264). The distinct possibility exists that the philosophers may be wrong. After all, the philosophy of science is a young and developing discipline, not a repository of established fact (see Popper, 1965, pp. 13, 55). It would therefore be surprising if it did not contain difficulties, inconsistencies or even contradictions. And more recently some philosophers have begun to suggest that the 'approved answer' to the 'logic of discovery' question is one of these difficult areas (e.g. Hanson, 1961, p. 20). Caws expresses it this way:

If there were *no* rules of plausible inference, nobody could learn techniques of research, nor could the agencies responsible for funding it have any confidence whatever that the task undertaken by researchers would bear fruit. Yet people do learn, and suitably financed campaigns of research (like the Manhattan project) do regularly produce results. The task is then to find out what is going on, not dismiss it all as ineffable or mysterious (1969, p. 1376).

The first point to be made here is that there is nothing to be gained by setting up induction (generalization) and deduction (hypothesis-testing) as antagonistic methodologies which compete for the loyalties of the scientific community; they should rather be viewed as two *complementary* heuristic techniques, neither of which is much good without the other (for reasons which should become clearer below). We need no more opt for the essential 'correctness' of the 'Keplerian view' over the 'Baconian' (Bach, 1965b, p. 125) than argue, conversely, that the former has been 'irreversibly abandoned' in favor of the latter (cf. the Preface to Joos, 1963). *Both* are available for our use, and it is foolhardy to fail to take full advantage of this (cf. Braithwaite, 1960, p. 261, and Benjamin, 1965, p. 95). Outside linguistics, this is commonplace knowledge (see Hildebrand, 1957, pp. 25–6; Cattell, 1966, p. 15; and Fromkin, 1968, p. 53). Only in linguistics, it would seem, are we required to 'choose one' to the exclusion of the other.

A second important point is that if any priority must be assigned to one of these approaches, it is surely the inductive phase of scientific activity which must take precedence over the deductive phase, rather than the reverse. As Cattell puts it, 'If there is any part of the spiral which can be called the scientific beginning, it is in the induction rather than the deduction' (1966, p. 15). For, once again, it is a truism that scientists 'do not start from hypotheses; they start from data' (Hanson, 1958, p. 70). And they end in it (see Einstein, 1934, pp. 14–15). Yet, unaccountably, the transformational-generative grammarians have opted for the opposite course. The first main point which Lees attempts to make in his influential review of Chomsky's *Syntactic Structures*, in fact, is that:

Once it has developed beyond the *pre*scientific stage of collection and classification of interesting facts, a scientific discipline is characterized *essentially* by the introduction of abstract constructs in theories and the validation of those theories by testing their predictive power (1957, p. 376; italics added).

That is to say, after a relatively brief (and 'dull') data-cataloguing phase, scientific inquiry henceforth concentrates on 'inventing hypotheses as tentative answers to a problem. . . and then subjecting these to empirical test' (Hempel, 1966, p. 17). This philosophy seems close to the 'classic' hypothetico-deductive view which many philosophers of science have certainly espoused; it is the most simplistic interpretation of Popper's dictum that 'the work of the scientist consists [wholly?] in putting forward and testing theories' (1965, p. 31). Theories, according to this view, are freely invented and then tested against the available data (cf. Harris, 1970, p. 31). Moreover, this seems to be the view which Chomsky himself has adopted:

I suggest that we concentrate on the problem of specifying [investing hypotheses about] the form of grammars and on ways of selecting among [testing] proposed grammars of the appropriate form (in Hill, 1962, p. 161; see also p. 11 of Chomsky, 1957b).

But although the transformationalists can appeal to the writings of some philosophers of science on this issue, one suspects nonetheless that it is not entirely 'irrelevant' whether a hypothesis is arrived at by 'sifting [through] vast amounts of material' or whether its imply 'pops into one's head while shaving' (Bach, 1964, p. 186; cf. Popper, 1969, p. 49). Once a useful and testable hypothesis or theory is *already available*, it is, of course, of no consequence where it actually came from; in this sense one might well argue that it is the *testability* of a theory which must be regarded as the prime consideration. On the other hand, we may doubt the further suggestion implicit in these accounts that such hypotheses are *characteristically generated* on the basis of so haphazard a set of events as accident, intuition or even 'genius', and more recent discussions in the philosophy of science suggest that the importance of this question is at last beginning to be realized (see, e.g. Caws, 1969).

But if logic of discovery exists, what is it? Is it deductive logic? Inductive logic? Or what? Hanson has shed some important light on the matter in his own 'uphill argument' against the authorized view. He begins by distinguishing between (1) 'reasons for accepting a hypothesis H' and (2) 'reasons for suggesting H in the first place' (1961, p. 22). Most philosophers have repeatedly and emphatically denied that there was any *logical* distinction to be drawn between the two; Hanson argues, however, that there *is* a question of logic involved, and that the logic of

(2) is basically a type of *analogical reasoning* (1961, pp. 22–5). He sums up his main points with the following remarks:

So the inductive view rightly suggests that laws are somehow related to inferences *from* data. It wrongly suggests that the resultant law is but a summary of these data...

Yet the original suggestion of hypothesis type is often a reasonable affair. It is not as dependent on intuition, hunches, and other imponderables as historians and philosophers suppose when they make it the province of genius but not of logic...

H-D accounts begin with the hypothesis as given, as cooking recipes begin with the trout. Recipes, however, sometimes suggest 'First catch your trout'. The H-D account is a recipe physicists often use after catching hypotheses. However, the conceptual boldness which marks the history of physics shows more in the ways in which scientists *caught* their hypotheses than in the ways in which they elaborated these once caught.

To study only the verification of hypotheses leaves a vital part of the story untold (pp. 30–1).

From this perspective it becomes clearer why the philosophers ('who do not really know what it is like to be a scientist' (Caws, 1969, p. 1375)) and the scientists themselves have often seemed to be at odds on this issue. It is simply because the former, until recently, have started 'from what are regarded as completed scientific theories as data' (Introduction to Nidditch, 1968), thereby developing an account which merely 'analyzes *the argument of a completed research report*' (Hanson, 1961, p. 29). But in science 'the reasoning is from data to hypotheses ...', not the reverse' (Hanson, 1958, p. 88). Thus, 'by the time a law has been fixed into an H-D system, really original physical thinking is over' (p. 70). The scientist disagrees with the H-D theorist, in short, chiefly because his theories have almost nothing to say about the most interesting aspect of the scientist's work: the process of *discovery*. For it can hardly be seriously doubted that scientific discovery *does* have a systematic and rational basis, perhaps a logic of its own (if Hanson is correct), distinct from Baconian induction on the one hand (since it involves analogical 'leaps' to hypotheses) and from deduction on the other (since it is 'non-demonstrative' (Carnap, 1966, p. 22)), yet a logic nonetheless. But whatever its true form, one thing seems sure: it is a far cry from the 'free invention' of the classic H-D variety. The idea that scientific hypotheses arise by a random, uncontrolled mechanism like this is a caricature of the process of scientific discovery. Moreover, useful scientific theories do not ordinarily arise spontaneously *ex nihilo* (cf. Caws, 1969, p. 1380). Theories *may*, but useful (i.e. testable) ones seldom, if ever do – and the ones which arise in this way are normally referred to as 'idle speculations', at least until proven otherwise. Yet, as we shall see below, it is out of just such clay that much (let us even say *most*) of the model of TGG has been molded.

7.1.2   The steps to theory. I have suggested that fruitful theories tend not to blossom spontaneously. Instead, they arise slowly, hesitatingly and even modestly as the culmination of a sequence of well-ordered steps (cf. Caws, 1965, p. 280). And the first step towards theory is gathering, classifying, associating, ordering, measuring and idealizing facts (Nagel, 1961, p. 31, n. 2; Benjamin, 1965, p. 98). It is therefore odd that transformational grammarians should be so contemptuous of Bloomfield's 'pre-occupation with observable data' (Rosenbaum, 1966, p. 179), 'taxonomic' methods of 'segmentation and classification' (Chomsky, 1964, p. 113) and 'data-collection' in general (Postal in Woodworth & DiPietro, 1963, p. 10). If workers in a young, developing science like linguistics often seem to be overly preoccupied with the work of collecting and classifying facts, it may not be because they 'would not *like* to do other things but because they are still laying an observational foundation' (Caws, 1965, p. 91; italics added). Thus many practicing scientists have seen the major practical problem often to be 'not so much of finding hypotheses, as of holding them in check' until a sufficient observational basis has been laid (Caws, 1969, p. 1377; see also p. 1376, and Holton & Roller, 1958, pp. 27 and 238–9).

It is often said that 'data is cheap'. If so, hypotheses or 'bright ideas' (Chomsky in Hill, 1962, p. 174) are surely even cheaper. At least the data must be collected; the ideas are absolutely free for the thinking. Hypotheses are, to begin with, nothing more than guesses or conjecture. But science, says Caws, 'has something to do with knowledge – acceptable explanations cannot be based on mere conjecture' (1965, p. 14). Hence constraints have been established in science on the kinds of pre-conditions which must be met before any particular set of 'bright ideas' are taken seriously. And Schrödinger (cf. Bach's remarks on p. 225 above), as a scientist, was playing by these rules, and rightly so; there was no guarantee, in advance, that his ideas would turn out any better than anyone else's, there being no *empirical* evidence available at the time to cause him to think so.

How, then, does science attempt to differentiate between those hypotheses which are mere conjecture or speculation and those which represent established knowledge or fact? For one thing, it insists that the constructs of the theoretician contain what Hempel and Oppenheim call 'empirical content' (1948, p. 56). This is because the potential testability of a given theoretical system can only be measured in terms of the extent to which the hypothetical constructs which appear in the theory have associated with them suitable 'reduction sentences' which relate them to a set of 'observation terms', such that 'a question about a theoretical construct can be *reduced* to a question about observables' (Caws, 1965, p. 57). In other words, scientists recognize that the theoretical concepts with which they deal 'should *in principle* have meaning in terms of possible operations' (Holton & Roller, 1958, p. 221; italics added) since 'only that part of the theoretical structure, questions about which can be reduced to questions about observables, can be known to be empirically meaningful' (Caws, 1965, p. 58).

We may now inquire what empirical interpretations have been assigned to the proliferation of theoretical constructs which characterize contemporary (transformation-generative) linguistic theory? We are told that a major innovation of TGG was to reinterpret 'Saussure's conception of *langue*' as an 'inventory of elements' as rather a 'system of rules' (Chomsky, 1964, p. 60), and, to be sure, the notion of rule is fundamental to the transformational-generative framework. But in reading Chomsky's most detailed treatments of this topic (Chomsky, 1961 and 1963, and Chomsky & Miller, 1963), we note that while he has much to say about how a rule is to be defined within the formal domain of the *grammar*, he has virtually nothing to say about how this notion is to be related to the domain of *observables*. We look in vain for any kind of 'reduction' statement which connects Chomsky's notion of 'rule of grammar' to any experimental idea.

This alone should make us wonder about the empirical status of the theory; but there is more. Transformational-generative grammars not only have *rules*, but many *kinds* of rules (cf. Chomsky, 1965a, and Chomsky & Halle, 1968). None of them is interpreted in terms of any observational or experimental parameters, either. We could then return to the artificially curtailed list of organizational, formal and substantive universals presented in 3.1 and show that the same is true for almost all of these, as well (with the exception of such notions as 'sentence', 'constituent', 'word', etc. which Chomsky has taken over from structural and traditional linguistics). We have in TGG a vast, complex, and detailed hypothetical system of concepts, almost none of which has any interpretation in the world of observables. As Stuart puts it:

The linguistic statement describes orderings which are combinatorial possibilities admitted by the primary data, but the orderings *do not exist within an empirical space* so that we are not entitled to say that they 'describe the way in which language is organized' (1969, p. 397; italics added).

The theory of TGG, in short, is almost exclusively restricted to the formal domain wherein its fundamental concepts are defined and, therefore, like any other logical construction of formal (as opposed to empirical) science, until interpretations of the hypothetical concepts associated with this theory are provided within an empirical domain, the whole apparatus must remain 'a mere exercise of intellectual ingenuity' (Caws, 1965, p. 331).

But no, the reader may protest, you are asking too much. What you opt for is a requirement of strict operationism, the doctrine that 'there is nothing in the world of science except operations, a kind of metaphysical purification' the price of which is recognized, in our enlightened age, to be 'very high indeed. It is in fact the almost complete sterilization of science' (Caws, 1965, pp. 322–3). True enough. Every theory has some 'surplus meaning' (Caws, 1965, p. 58). Theoretical concepts should, however, be definable in terms of experimental operations *in principle* (cf. p. 231 above) and the long-term goal of scientific research should be to provide such definitions for as many of the theoretical concepts which it employs as possible, since the status of each concept *remains in doubt* until such an interpretation *is* provided for it (cf. Agnew & Pyke, 1969, p. 11).

It is most misleading to argue, therefore, as Lees does (1957, p. 407) that 'in the construction of a theory *very abstract* concepts and models must be postulated and then verified against the data in question' (italics added; cf. Chomsky, 1957b, p. 49), the reason being that if the postulated concepts or models are so *very* abstract, such 'verification' may be well-nigh impossible. Lees' own supposed illustration, for instance, the election theory of chemical valence, was only conceived as a theoretical model within the context of a long history of careful experimental research which made it clear that a concept of 'valence' was necessary in the *first* place. Moreover, the concept of the electron *is* operationally defined within the framework of modern experimental physics (not only that, but even the notion of the electron *jump* – see Caws, 1965, p. 57, and Nagel, 1961, p. 101). In other words, the hypothetical concepts of modern physics are nowhere near as 'abstract' as Lees and his fellow transformationalists would have us believe, and the 'leap' to the electron theory of valence was not so great a conceptual hurdle as Lees suggests. For physics and chemistry have been built upon an empirical foundation, which is to say that physicists and chemists, at least, have sought to give empirical content to their primitive hypothetical concepts.

So we do not refuse to *consider* uninterpreted concepts, but we do *suspect* them (particularly if they appear suddenly in large bundles), and we must try to supply interpretations for them. Actually, in the normal case, these interpretations arise naturally as an integral part of the inductive-hypothetico-deductive spiral (Cattell, 1966, p. 16) which generates the hypotheses in the first place. The important implication of the notion of a 'spiral' effect here is that experiment is by no means employed exclusively to *test* antecedently conceived theories, as the classic H-D paradigm implies, but also plays a fundamental role in the process of theory *construction*; thus, in the typical case, 'interpretation is not something a [scientist] *works into* a ready-made deductive system. . . He rarely searches for a deductive system *per se*, one in which his data would appear as consequences *if only interpreted physically*' (Hanson, 1958, p. 72).[1] The cry of 'Operationism' (or 'Positivism!') is therefore inappropriate in this context, for there is a wide gap between not insisting that *all* the hypothetical terms associated with some theory be operationally defined at some given time, and insisting that practically *none* of them need to be. So I ask once again: what evidence attests to (or even suggests) the psychological existence of *any* of the fundamental hypothetical concepts of transformational-generative grammar? Before one can claim to have an 'empirical hypothesis' he must first have isolated an *empirical concept* or two. Furthermore, while many of the fundamental concepts of a science like physics, both primitive (e.g. mass, time, distance) and derived (e.g. velocity, acceleration, momentum), may seem self-evident today, they were 'gained through the centuries only at the cost of enormous effort and long struggle' (Holton & Roller, 1958, p. 18). There is no reason to think that the search for useful empirical concepts in linguistics will be shorter or less arduous. It will certainly not be speeded up by trying to take methodologically untenable short-cuts.

So empirical science as it is recognized by physicists, chemists and the

[1] See chapter 8 below for a view of the strikingly disparate picture which has emerged within contemporary linguistic theory.

like has arisen in an orderly progression, starting with the mundane, but essential, preliminary stage of collecting and arranging potentially important facts. There is a second stage, intermediate between this groundwork and formal theory construction. This is the stage at which 'empirical rules' (Holton & Roller, 1958, p. 257), otherwise referred to as 'natural' (Popper, 1965, p. 63) or 'experimental' (Nagel, 1961, p. 80) laws, or simply 'empirical generalizations' (Caws, 1965, p. 76), are formulated. These are statements which 'summarize in a simple and convenient manner a great amount of observational materials, although the person who formulated the rule may have no idea *why* the rule should hold in nature' (Holton & Roller, 1958, p. 257). This stage is significant because 'by far the greater proportion of scientific activity has in the past been concentrated at this stage' (Caws, 1965, p. 283). Caws also suggests two good reasons for this:

First, the practical benefits of science lie mainly in the possession of information about regularities in the world, even if those regularities cannot be explained...Second, it may be a very long time, even when many generalizations are established, before a hypothesis which accounts for more than a few of them occurs to anybody...The day-to-day work of the great majority of experimental scientists consists, then, of discovering new but minor regularities...and of checking and refining the accuracy of our knowledge of such regularities (1965, pp. 283–4).

But consider the following remarks by Fodor and Garrett, in this context:

There is no reason at all to suppose that...psychology is...primarily in the business of arriving at generalizations about behaviour. On the contrary, psychology is primarily concerned with understanding the nature and capacities of the mechanisms which underlie behaviour and which presumably cause it. The observation and experimental manipulation of behaviour is of interest in so far as (and almost solely in so far as) it sheds light upon these mechanisms and capacities (in Lyons & Wales, 1966, p. 136; cf. Sutherland's retort on p. 155).

There are also other important methodological considerations involved in the generation of fruitful hypotheses in science, and chief among them is that scientific advance flourishes when there is a broad range of inquiry along a number of diverse, even contradictory paths, than when effort is concentrated instead along a single line of inquiry. This is implicit in what Toulmin refers to as Popper's 'two fundamental maxims – freedom of conjecture, and severity of criticism' (1967, p. 471), neither of which is of much use without the other. For Chomsky, however, 'the real problem is almost always to restrict the range of possible hypotheses' (1965a, p. 35). That this approach is counterproductive should now be clear. For the chief effect is the simultaneous repudiation of *both* 'cardinal virtues of science' (Toulmin, 1967, p. 471). On the one hand, Chomsky's one-metatheory approach to linguistic description insures that almost all original thought will be limited to that which arises when attention is directed along a few sharply delineated channels (so insuring that the available 'pool of variants' will be as small as possible), and, as a direct consequence, that the scope of critical evaluation will be restricted to those problems of detail which arise *within* the accepted framework (so insuring that the degree of 'selective pressure' brought to bear against the fundamental postulates of the theory will also be minimal). But perhaps the most baffling aspect of this whole situation is that the transformationalists seem unable to understand why their predecessors should be so hesitant (in many cases) to follow along, except on grounds of irrational reaction. Thus when the issue of alternatives arises, their characteristic response is that this must be a sign of muddled thinking (see 2.3), as in this retort by Chomsky and Halle to one of Householder's suggestions:

In any serious field of investigation, the discovery of two mutually inconsistent descriptions, each somehow suggestive, would be taken as posing a *problem* for research, a challenge to the investigator to be resolved by showing how the two inconsistent...descriptions can be replaced by a single, consistent description...because in all serious intellectual pursuits...it is taken for granted that the goal of research is to discover the *truth* about the object under investigation (1965, pp. 105–6; italics added).

But most scientists recognize the distinction between *research in progress* and the attainment of one's *ultimate goals* and give a different view of the matter. Holton and Roller observe that:

History reveals many...instances in which two rival views contradict each other in certain respects and yet have other features that make both of them useful. This often means that both views will *later* turn out to be partly valid and partly invalid, and that we may therefore expect the *eventual* development of a new conceptual scheme that will be a synthesis of the earlier, rival views – a synthesis that serves not only to reconcile the contradictory features, but to deal with a wider range of phenomena than did either of the earlier views alone (1958, p. 490; italics added).

In the meantime research along both lines of inquiry serves to define the limitations of each and the development of a successful synthesis may have to await some 'startling new discovery' which neither approach could originally have envisioned.

7.2   On justifying theories

7.2.1   On confirming and falsifying theories. A (logical) argument form which is often used to justify scientific hypotheses is the argument $(q \wedge (p \supset q)) \supset p$, where p is a hypothesis and q is whatever empirical generalizations follow from it. Unfortunately, this argument is invalid in a crucial circumstance, namely, if p is false, and is therefore not very useful, since we never know in advance whether p (the hypothesis) is true or not. This argument-form, in short, commits the familiar fallacy of affirming the consequent (cf. Caws, 1965, p. 111). For this reason, therefore, philosophers such as Popper have concluded that scientific hypotheses may not be decisively *confirmed*, i.e. validated, but can only be decisively *falsified* (by demonstrating that some of their consequences are contrary to fact), since there does exist a valid argument form (*modus tollens*) according to which 'the falsification of a conclusion entails the falsification of the system from which it is derived' (Popper, 1965, p. 76).[1] Thus, Popper insists:

what characterizes the empirical method is its manner of exposing to falsification, in every conceivable way, the system to be tested. Its aim is not to save the lives of untenable systems but, on the contrary, to select the one which is by comparison the fittest, by exposing them all to the fiercest struggle for survival (p. 42).

Compare, however, the following remarks, which are typical of others scattered through the literature of TGG:

(1) [Linguistic universals] in effect constitute an empirical hypothesis as to the class of possible human languages. Such a hypothesis can be *confirmed* in two ways: by showing that it is compatible with the diversity of human language, and that it is sufficiently powerful to offer explanations for particular phenomena (Chomsky, 1965b, p. 15; italics added).

(2) To *establish* general principles of organization for grammar, we must show that..., on the basis of these principles, one *can* explain phenomena that must otherwise be regarded as accidental (Chomsky, 1967d, p. 126; italics added).

Chomsky's philosophy of linguistics is embued with the idea that

[1] It should be noted here, however, that even the notion of falsification can only be utilized in any decisive way provided certain important 'methodological rules' are also observed (see especially Popper, 1965, pp. 81–4, and pp. 237–8 below).

theories are tested by inquiring whether the data at hand are or are not *compatible* with a transformational-generative description; rarely does one find a transformationist exposing the basic tenets of TGG to falsification 'in every possible way', or exposing them to 'the fiercest struggle for survival' against equally well-conceived and well-developed alternative accounts.

Theories in empirical science are developed from their own *observational basis* (Caws, 1965, p. 182) and are only as sound as the observational base which supports them (cf. 7.1.2 above); such theories are characteristically arrived at slowly and incrementally (with occasional drastic 'reshufflings' of the Kuhn variety, perhaps, when serious difficulties arise), each hypothetical concept arising out of a broad base of data-collection, organization and reorganization, and controlled experiment. It is obvious that no such firm empirical base has *ever* been laid in linguistics: we know a bit about sentences, words, and phones, perhaps (thanks mostly to the structuralists and a handful of experimental phoneticians), but practically nothing about more abstract structures than these, not even about rules. We know a bit about the *output* of an 'internalized grammar', in short, but virtually nothing about whatever underlying psychological reality the grammar *itself* supposedly represents. As far as this psychological reality is concerned, the approach of TGG is essentially one of guesswork: try to guess at the nature of something which will provide the proper output. No experimentation, no attempt to develop a set of empirically interpreted psychological concepts – nothing but speculation about a 'possible state of affairs' called 'linguistic competence' (see chapter 8).

No conclusive falsification, either. But this, after all, is to be expected. In Braithwaite's words, given any complex theoretical system:

complete refutation is no more possible than is complete proof. What experience can tell us is that there is something wrong somewhere in the system; but *we can make our choice* as to which part of the system we consider to be at fault (1960, p. 19; italics added).

Given only 'ultimate' or 'remote' consequences of the theory to go by, it is *never* the case that one need abandon a theory in its entirety; there will always be 'some parts of [the] theory which, if we very badly want them, can be preserved in the face of all opposition' (Caws, 1965, p. 324) by resorting to what Popper has called a 'conventionalist stratagem' (1965, p. 82). Caws explains:

No hypothesis stands alone as the explanation of a given state of affairs – it must always be supplemented by other generalizations or hypotheses...Let us call the hypothesis in question *h* and the ancillary statements which accompany it collectively {*a*}, and let the state of affairs be described by a protocol sentence *p*. The traditional view regarded the explanation of *p* by *h* as resting on the simple inference

$$h \supset p$$

so that in the event of a contrary instance $\sim p$, *h* would be refuted by *modus tollens*. Duhem points out, however, that with the set {*a*} of supplementary assumptions the situation is really

$$h \cdot \{a\} \supset p$$

and in this case the occurrence of $\sim p$ leads, not to $\sim h$, but to $\sim (h \cdot \{a\})$, which by De Morgan is seen to be equivalent to $\sim h \lor \sim \{a\}$. We can always choose the second disjunct of this pair, and by abandoning {*a*} preserve the truth of *h*...Our convention is to retain *h*, and we have succeeded in doing so in the face of apparently contrary evidence (1965, p. 325).

The history of the theory of TGG since its inception in the mid-fifties may be summed up in these words: a set of unquestioned basic assumptions *h* has been proposed (following Chomsky, 1957b, p. 11) and a long series of different *a*'s have been tried and rejected in conjunction with these until a reasonably close fit has been achieved between the predictions of the theory and those limited clear (or unclear) data readily available about sentences and their interpretations. The theory has changed in many respects, but the fundamental assumptions related to the 'essential linguistic universals' remain as unsullied (and untestable) as ever. The theory is almost totally empty because it is almost totally uninterpreted, and ignores Popper's insistent and explicit advice:

The only way to avoid conventionalism is by taking a *decision*: the decision not to apply its methods. We decide that, in the case of a threat to our system, we will not save it by any kind of *conventionalist stratagem*. Thus we shall guard against exploiting the ever open possibility just mentioned of 'attaining for any chosen...system what is called its correspondence with reality'.

A clear appreciation of what may be gained (and lost) by conventionalist methods was expressed, a hundred years before Poincaré, by Black who wrote: 'A nice adaptation of conditions will make almost any hypothesis agree with the phenomena. This will please the imagination but does not advance our knowledge' (1965, p. 82).

Given the kinds of data presently used in formulating linguistic descriptions, the basic assumptions of TGG are unfalsifiable (see chapter 8). That is to say:

once the combinatorial possibilities admitted by our initial selection of descriptive features ha[ve] been established, all we can do is to improve the description rather than to falsify it. Correctness is thus *a matter of goodness-of-*

fit with respect to the primary data, and *not a matter of testing hypotheses about empirical states of affairs that underlie these data* (Stuart, 1969, p. 397; italics added).

7.2.2 On prediction and explanation in science and in TGG.

Another technique commonly employed in empirical science for the evaluation of theories is to judge them in terms of their ability to *predict* phenomena not considered in their original formulation. It is required of a good theory, in Benjamin's words, 'that it should have consequences in addition to those which suggested it in the first place' (1965, p. 129). Chomsky interprets this as follows:

It is no trick to predict the structure of sentences which have already been uttered. To do so would be like a physicist's limiting his predictions to the experiments he has already performed...What I have been trying to do is to have the native speaker give me a set of sentences, then to construct a device which will *extend* the set, without including sentences the native would not accept. There is nothing trivial about such a task – *it is exactly what any scientist tries to do*. If I were merely trying to list every new sentence that the native speaker says, then I would admit that the procedure was trivial (in Hill, 1962, pp. 159–60; italics added).

Thus, the 'great predictive power' of TGG (cf. Lees, 1957, p. 380) is predicated upon the ability of the theory to account for a wide range of grammatical and ungrammatical sentences and their interpretations which were not *specifically* utilized in constructing the grammar in the first place. It is claimed that even the 'simplest generalization [of a transformational description]...immediately commits one...to an IN-FINITE set of possible data, and it commits one in a way which can be evaluated against rival claims' (Lees, 1965b, p. 23).

Much of the force goes out of this argument, however, if we consider the predictions of a transformational grammar not in terms of individual sentences *per se*, but rather in terms of sentence *types*. That is, once we have already taken into consideration such sentences as 'Cows eat grass', 'Horses eat oats' and 'Pigs eat garbage', we should not be astounded to find that a grammar adequate for these should also predict the occurrence of 'Horses eat grass'. Or that 'Grass is eaten by horses' should stand in the same relation to the (novel) sentence 'Horses eat grass' as 'Grass is eaten by cows' stands with respect to 'Cows eat grass'. Even in less trivial cases, the argument still holds: how much of a 'trick' is it, really, to predict the structure of new sentences which are of precisely the same character or *type* as other sentences which *have* been considered in constructing the grammar? Even the poor structuralists could do this with their sentence-type classification schemes (though since they lacked the property of recursion in their grammars, they could not extend their results to a potentially 'infinite' number of cases).[1]

In Caws' words, to be scientific, explanations must take *predictive risks*, for 'it is only when scientific theories take risks and make predictions which are *antecedently improbable* that the confirmation of these predictions lends any strength to the theory' (1965, p. 311; italics added). Thus for any 'candidate for the title of scientific theory' to be taken seriously, it must be 'prepared to stake its reputation' on the predictions it makes and declare itself willing to withdraw from consideration should these predictions be falsified (Caws, 1965, p. 95). For if we follow Popper's ground rules and do *not* resort to the conventionalist stratagem, we are committed to the consequence that even if only *one* logical consequence of our theory fails to gibe with accepted observation statements, the *entire theory* (the 'whole system') has been falsified (see Popper, 1965, p. 76, and Hanson, 1958, p. 103). And under these circumstances one is as justified in devising a new theory as in modifying the old one (provided that, as in the case of TGG, no unique aspects of the old theory have been individually and independently verified). A more realistic strategy might be to *start small*, i.e. to begin with hypotheses of limited scope which lend themselves to attempts at *direct* experimental falsification, rather than to persist in dealing with such 'heroic', but untestable, schemes as those to which we have by now grown so accustomed in the field (cf. 'Introductory Remarks' to Stuart, 1964).

Compare how the theory of TGG has reacted over the first few years of its existence to new facts and the way in which Newton's theory of

---

[1] Admittedly, the structuralists failed almost totally to come to grips with the problem of recursion (but see Hockett, 1961, for an outline of an approach which does take the language user into consideration). The transformationalists seem to have failed in the opposite direction. That is, there often seems to be a singular disparity between the real linguistic processing capacities of human beings and the unlimited 'recursive' abilities implicitly attributed to them by transformational-generative grammars (cf. the case of self-embeddings, where there is an upper limit of one – or, at the very most, two – which any speaker or hearer seems able to process under circumstances of normal language use (see Reich, 1969, pp. 831-3). Memory limitations (unlike lapses, shifts of attention, etc.) seem to constitute inherent pyschological constraints on language processing, so it is not at all clear why the linguist should want to abstract away from them. The key question, then, is not whether Dixon is using the term 'infinite' in some 'special and rather obscure sense' (Chomsky, 1965a, p. 198), but whether Chomsky might not be using the term 'language' in such a way (cf. chapter 8 below).

universal gravitation reacted to the discovery that, after some years of predicting the precise orbit of the planet Uranus, certain minor discrepancies began to emerge. This was immediately cause for alarm in the scientific community, and suggestions were made that Newton's law of gravitation might not hold precisely over longer distances (Holton & Roller, 1958, p. 196). Rather than patching up the theory or abandoning it,[1] however, two young mathematicians independently demonstrated their confidence in it by risking the prediction that some hitherto *undiscovered planet* must be producing the observed perturbations, and undertook the 'immensely difficult mathematical task of calculating the positions of this suspected perturbing body from the observations of Uranus' motion and the assumption that Newton's law of gravitation applied to the interaction between the hypothetical planet and Uranus' (p. 197). The result was the discovery of Neptune, which astronomers found almost exactly in the position predicted by these two independent sets of calculations – and over a century after Newton's death. (A similar approach also led to the discovery of Pluto a century later.) It is predictions of *this* sort which inspire confidence in theories. But in current linguistics

prediction can only be said to appear *trivially*...once we have ensured a sufficiently large sampling [of primary data] to avoid new and major combinatorial possibilities within our initial selection of descriptive features. In this connection, we may [also] note that it follows immediately from the nature of the mapping relation between linguistic descriptions and primary linguistic data that *no new empirical phenomena, i.e. of a kind not already present in the primary data, will be implied by the description* (Stuart, 1969, p. 397; italics added).

Thus 'accuracy of prediction beyond one's corpus' provides no more assurance today than when Hockett originally proposed the criterion (1948, p. 280) that one's description may be regarded as equivalent or isomorphic to 'a state of affairs in [the] nervous system' of the speaker of a language.[2]

---

[1] It is often remarked in linguistic metadiscussion that TGG is the only theory we've got, so we're not to abandon it without 'good reason'. But, if Popper is correct, this condition only applies to a theory, like Newton's, which has 'proved its mettle'; furthermore, a sufficiently 'good reason' may be, for instance, 'replacement of the hypothesis by another which is *better testable*; or the falsification of *one* of the consequences of the hypothesis' (1965, pp. 53–4; italics added).

[2] Moreover, as Joos has correctly pointed out, predictions in linguistics are never carried out with the rigor and comprehensiveness applied in the well-established sciences (1963, p. 280).

Yet another criterion of evaluation is offered by transformational-generative grammarians in favor of their formulations: they are said not only to have predictive power, but also 'explanatory power' (see Chomsky, 1957b, chapter 8), and 'theories which explain the data have *ipso facto* some claim to be considered true' (Fodor, 1971, p. 121). But just as in the previous case, when a transformationalist speaks of 'explanation' he is talking about a different thing than what the natural scientist talks about under the same name. Consider the following characterization offered by Chomsky, for example:

As a long-range task for general linguistics, we might set the problem of developing an account of [the] innate linguistic [metatheory] that provides the basis for language learning...

To the extent that a linguistic theory succeeds in selecting a descriptively adequate grammar on the basis of primary linguistic data, we can say that it meets the condition of *explanatory adequacy*. That is, to this extent, it offers an explanation for the intuition of the native speaker on the basis of an empirical hypothesis concerning the innate predisposition of the child to develop a certain kind of theory to deal with the evidence presented to him (1965a, pp. 25–6).

Chomsky thus seeks to 'explain' various facts about utterances and native-speaker intuitions by means of a set of specific hypotheses about the general form of grammar (the so-called 'essential linguistic universals' and the associated evaluation measures), under the general assumption that 'it is sufficient in explaining a given phenomenon to show how it is deducible from a certain theoretical framework' (Lees 1965a, p. 37). But it is unacceptable to assert, as Fromkin does, that 'by explanation of a given thing, we mean [simply?] the demonstration that this thing follows necessarily from other things' (1968, p. 53). One vital ingredient is missing: there must be independent reason to believe that those 'other things' which are served as the *explicans* here are factually *true*.[1] As Scriven emphasizes, 'an explanation is essentially a linkage of what we do not understand to what we *do* understand, and there can be no such linkage if we understand *nothing*' (1969b, p. 98; italics added). Hypotheses, speculations or guesses are not explanations; otherwise, any theory not inconsistent with some body of data would have to be considered 'explanatory' (and hence 'true', by Fodor's dictum) solely by

---

[1] This is the 'empirical condition of adequacy' which Hempel and Oppenheim argue must be satisfied in order for any proposed explanation to be sound (1948, pp. 55–6). Thus the scientific explanation of a given phenomenon does not involve merely subsuming it under a more general *statement*, but rather 'under a more general *law*' (p. 55, italics added).

virtue of the fact that it was conceived by the mind of man. The fact that true empirical consequence can be derived from false theories is of little interest (cf. 7.2.1 above).[1] If, on the other hand, we know beyond reasonable doubt that something *is* true, at least under certain well-defined conditions (such as Newton's second law, F = ma), and we can deduce from this knowledge specific empirical consequences, then we can claim that the consequences have been explained, in the scientific sense. But no unknown (such as man's innate capacity for language) can ever be employed to 'explain' another (such as the equally mysterious process of language acquisition);[2] an event is explained only 'when it is traced to other events which require *less* explanation' (Hanson, 1958, p. 94; italics added).

Talk of 'explanation' in contemporary linguistics is therefore absurd, for not only are the 'generative explanations' of the transformationalists untested in their own right but they remain, for the most part, uninterpreted (if not uninterpretable) as hypotheses about some underlying empirical state of affairs. Moreover, we shall see that no other source of evidence apart from the form of utterances and certain auxiliary 'linguistic intuitions' is ordinarily considered in the formulation of such hypotheses, though this is precisely the body of data thought by the generative grammarians 'to be explained' by these theories, as well. The Chomskyan thus puts himself in the awkward position of claiming that there exists a unique body of data (the class of well-formed human utterances plus native speaker's judgments about certain features of these utterances) which can be employed to *explain itself* (see 7.3 below).

7.2.3 On simplicity. Having its basic presuppositions well insulated against falsification by any known means and being unable to make predictions of any but a trivial sort, the theory of TGG nonetheless has one further criterion of justification available: simplicity. As Postal puts it, 'The question of justification of grammars is handled in generative grammar as in other sciences. We justify a grammar by showing that it is the simplest theory, capable of explaining all the facts' (in Woodworth & DiPietro, 1963, p. 8). Katz elaborates:

---

[1] This truism becomes all the more obvious when conditions are set up, as in TGG, with such metatheoretical looseness as to insure that the *purely formal* requirement involved will necessarily be satisfied (see 4.5 and Chapter 5 for a long list of specific illustrations).

[2] Chomsky helped to found his own reputation by berating Skinner for this same mistake (Chomsky, 1959b, especially pp. 42ff).

The linguist, like the physicist and biologist, can only achieve scientific understanding by constructing a model of the system which contains a hypothesis about the structure of the components of the system that are not observable. If the logical consequences of the model match the observable behavior of the system and would not do so without the hypothesis, the scientist may say that this hypothesis accounts for the behavior of the system in terms of the behavior of the unobservable but causally efficient component. If the model is the simplest one which enables the scientist to derive all the known facts and predict previously unknown ones as effects of the hypothesized component, he can assert that his model *correctly* pictures the structure of the system and its unobservable components (1964, p. 128; italics added).

For the transformational-generative grammarian, then, simplicity represents, in Chomsky's words, 'the only ultimate criterion in evaluation' (1957b, pp. 55–6).

There is something odd about this. If we search through Holton & Roller (1958) – a major sourcebook on the way workers in the natural sciences view their own efforts – we find little mention of the notion of simplicity. The index, for example, refers the reader only to Dalton's proposed 'rule of greatest simplicity' for determining molecular formulae, a postulate which 'did not stand the test of time' (p. 385). Despite the popular cliché that 'Nature is simple', the search for simplicity in the history of science has been complicated by a great 'difference of opinion as to what constitutes simplicity' (p. 393).[1]

One reason is that simplicity can be meaningfully interpreted only *in retrospect*; as Popper puts it, the 'simplest system' ordinarily means, in practice, the ' "classical" system of the day' (1965, p. 81). Thus any well-confirmed physical theory gives the impression of great elegance and 'simplicity' relative to the seeming chaos before the major laws of the system were established. Nevertheless, it is often suggested that the Copernican (heliocentric) scheme was victorious over the Ptolemaic (geocentric) one primarily because of its advantages in mathematical simplicity or elegance. And no doubt such considerations had much to do with its original appeal. Yet it is also true that central to Copernicus' own disillusionment with the Ptolemaic system was not the cumber-

---

[1] Furthermore, if nature is so parsimonious, why does the human optic nerve have over a million fibers where 100,000 or so would be sufficient – or why does the salmon lay over a million eggs to produce an average yield of six? Considerable redundancy seems to be required in physiological systems in order to insure that the job gets done. Similarly, 'speech perception is geared more towards a high degree of *security of communication* than towards a maximum exploitation of channel capacity' (Hörmann, 1971, p. 68; italics added).

someness of the system *per se*, but rather the growing 'dissatisfaction he and many other astronomers felt with *the accuracy of prediction* attainable by contemporary astronomical methods of calculation' (Holton & Roller, 1958, pp. 118–19; italics added). In any event, it was not the maximally 'simple' mathematical formulation of Copernicus which eventually won out, but rather the mathematically more 'complex' one of Kepler which followed about half a century later.[1] That both Copernicus and Kepler seemed to have the same essential belief 'in the simplicity and uniformity of nature' (p. 148) was of no particular consequence in determining whose theory was correct.[2] As Popper says (citing Schlick), 'It is certain that one can only define the concept of simplicity by a convention which must always be arbitrary' (1965, p. 145), an observation which helps explain why the notion fails us in all critical cases (cf. Yngve, 1969, p. 456).[3]

But the devoted Chomskyite seems to remain undaunted by this kind of talk. One transformationalist takes the position that not only is a grammar 'validated' by considerations of simplicity (Lees, 1957, p. 382), but that in formulating such 'explicit criteria of excellence' for grammars linguistics may even 'be able to go one step further' than the other sciences. He argues: 'To reject the worse alternative of a pair of proposed theories; the best that the natural scientist can do is to propose a so-called "crucial experiment" ' (pp. 380–1). However, as P. Harris points out, there are certain difficulties with Lees' characterization of the nature of scientific inquiry, here as elsewhere:

The natural scientist actually applies *a wide range of criteria* in assessing theories. Bunge (1967 II: 352–4) lists twenty criteria of several different sorts. One of them is that of depth, the most important result of which is that *the set of relevant data becomes more varied*. Despite Lees' implication, the setting up of an evaluation procedure in linguistics can hardly be construed as going beyond the natural sciences in rigor, because linguistic theories have not survived attempts at disconfirmation of the psychological claims made for them. *In fact these attempts have not been made, and this is the reason for the indeterminacy which the evaluation procedure is supposed to resolve* (1970, pp. 39–40; italics added).

[1] One might even speculate whether the masterful Newtonian synthesis would have been possible had Kepler been unwilling, on *a priori* grounds, to sacrifice some of the simplicity of his descriptive system in the face of what seemed to others at the time to have been almost negligible observational discrepancies.

[2] See Holton & Roller (1958, p. 373) and Caws (1965, p. 166) for other interesting examples to illustrate this same point.

[3] Popper eliminates simplicity from his scheme by subsuming it under the notion *degree of falsifiability* (1965, pp. 140ff).

Consider the Aristotelian model of the universe as a case in point. We find a theory most elegant in its original conceptual simplicity: four terrestial elements, each having its own 'natural place' relative to the others in the terrestial region, plus a unique fifth element characteristic of the celestial region and having a 'natural motion' all its own. Furthermore, this scheme accounted for all physical facts known at the time, not to mention that it was also compatible with a larger conceptual scheme which incorporated poetry, ethics and theology, as well (see Holton & Roller, 1958, pp. 19–20). It was only when *new kinds of data* were introduced into the picture that serious difficulties began to emerge (cf. pp. 153–4 above). As a consequence, the so-called 'principle of simplicity' now always contains the qualification 'always choose the simplest function *compatible with the data at hand*', which indicates that 'whenever there is a conflict between simplicity and fidelity to observation, the latter takes precedence. *Science need not be easy, but it must be accurate*' (Caws, 1965, p. 165; italics added).

In short, simplicity is invoked in science (and normally then only as a holding operation) once a wide range of data from that domain regarded as crucial to the evaluation of a specific theory has already been taken into consideration; it is never invoked as a *substitute* for data. Again, we find that this is a rule of the science game which the transformational-generative grammarians, following Chomsky, do not obey. In particular, while Chomsky admits that 'choice of a grammar for a particular language L will always be much underdetermined by the data drawn from L alone', he nevertheless holds that this data-shortage problem can be overcome provided the linguist 'concern[s] himself with the problem of developing an explanatory theory of the form of grammar' (1965a, p. 41), that is to say, a theory which is 'sufficiently rich, detailed, and highly structured' that it will be capable of 'select[ing] from the store of potential grammars a specific one that is [most] appropriate to the data available' (p. 36). Thus, in the *absence* of data, an arbitrary 'evaluation measure' or 'simplicity metric' will suffice; for Chomsky, 'simplicity' constitutes the *ultimate axiomatization*, something the analyst is apparently free to invoke in order to resolve any problem of indeterminacy which may face him.

Chomsky himself insists that the choice of a particular evaluation measure is always 'an empirical matter' (1965a, p. 37), involving what he chooses to call 'an empirical hypothesis' or 'empirical *assumption*', yet, about the form of grammar and thus, 'ultimately, about the native intellectual capacity (*faculté de langage*) that makes language acquisition possible' (Chomsky & Halle, 1965, p. 109). Probably no word in the language suffers more in the hands of the transformationalists than 'empirical'. One illustration should suffice here:

We have argued that there is *strong empirical support* for the claim that declaratives have abstract underlying structures and that this support derives primarily from considerations of *the simplicity and generality of grammatical rules* (Bever *et al.*, 1965b, p. 289; italics added).

Bach correctly notes that 'simplicity' is employed by grammarians as 'a technical term...defined in general linguistic theory' (1964, p. 180; cf. Chomsky, 1965a, pp. 37ff); 'empirical', on the other hand, means 'based, acting, on observation..., not on theory' (*The Concise Oxford Dictionary*, 1964, p. 397). How considerations of 'simplicity and generality' constitute 'empirical support' for any position is a question only the transformationalists seem capable of answering.[1] However disguised beneath a rhetoric which speaks of 'empirical import' (Chomsky & Halle, 1965, p. 111), the fact remains that considerations of 'simplicity' in linguistics are purely formal. The notion of 'rule simplicity' is no less arbitrary and unmotivated as a principle of evaluation than many of the principles which the structuralists devised before them (cf. Lees, 1957, p. 389). In linguistics, as Pike observed a quarter of a century ago, 'we are not after simplicity first, but rather a representation of the structure of language as it functions, whether the result be simple or complex' (1947a, p. 172).

7.3. On the use of introspective evidence in TGG

This brings us to the linguist's data sources and data-gathering techniques. It has been suggested that one accomplishment of the transformationalist revolution in American linguistics was that it enlarged the empirical base (or domain) of linguistic investigation by taking into consideration both the primary data of speech forms (or utterances) and certain kinds of native-speaker judgments about them (see 2.4 and 5.3 above). This provided more data on which theories might be constructed,

---

[1] Moreover, a good deal of the 'generality' has been purchased at the expense of increased *abstractness* of description (aided by the general convention of extrinsic rule ordering; see 5.1 and 5.2 above for details); then, to complete the circle, a specific 'innate schematism' is invoked which '*makes possible* the acquisition of a rich and highly specific system on the basis of limited data' (Chomsky, 1969, p. 67).

and provided important new 'external, empirical requirements' (Lees, 1957, p. 382) by means of which they might be evaluated.

It is well known, nevertheless, that there are many problems associated with the use of introspective evidence. Popper says that 'the *objectivity* of scientific statements lies in the fact that they can be *intersubjectively tested*' (1965, p. 44) or, in Caws' words, '*intersubjectively corroborated*' (1965, p. 74). This objectivity is fundamental to science. In the first place, the subject matter of science is the class of public, not private, events (Caws, 1965, p. 96); furthermore, the scientist is not as interested in conclusions about individuals (or individual events) as in discovering general laws or principles characteristic of entire populations (or universes). Yet unless one can show that the crucial observations in question are (within reasonable limits imposed by considerations of statistical probability) essentially 'invariant between different observers' (p. 74), there is no empirical basis for extrapolating beyond the individual to the population in general. It has been a 'central concern of science' to increase the degree to which observations are tied to 'shareable objects and events' and to decrease that to which they are tied to 'personal objects and events, and therefore not readily open to test by other researchers' (Agnew & Pyke, 1969, p. 30; cf. Robins, 1966, p. 9). Yet transformationalists have a practice of constructing their own data-sets, for the most part; if anything, this tendency has increased in recent years (see especially the new journal *Linguistic Inquiry*, from MIT). Yet other observers find 'the "linguistic intuition of the native speaker"...too shifty and variable (both from speaker to speaker and from moment to moment) to be of any criterial value' (Householder, 1965, p. 15).

The apparent lack of concern of most transformationalists on this question may be because a good deal of inter-subjective agreement *can* be found in this area, at least by them; in short, they find themselves, as a rule, in general agreement on the acceptability of those data-sets which they construct (see Postal, 1966, pp. 156–9). But if all the linguists in the world *were* to agree on these data-sets (and such agreement does *not* exist, particularly as we cross from one linguistic school to another), there would remain the problem of justifying extrapolation from *these* results to the population as a whole. For the linguist is not seeking to characterize the linguistic capacities of *linguists*, but those of 'the typical native speaker' (see Schwarcz, 1967, pp. 40–1). So the standard practice of the linguist in supplying his own data *qua* native speaker can only be justified to the extent that the linguists involved can be regarded as 'typical'. But how is *this* question to be answered objectively without comparing the results obtained between the two groups, i.e. between the naive and non-naive native speakers of a language? In the absence of the demonstration of equivalence, we are free to doubt whether conclusions drawn from examination of the first group may legitimately be extrapolated to the second. For one thing, with professional linguists 'the problem of the self-fulfilling prediction comes in' (Householder, 1966, p. 99) – hence the disagreements across theoretical schools (and even sub-schools) already alluded to.[1] It is unrealistic to assume that any scholar with vested interests can remain immune from the influence of his own prejudices; in this respect linguists are human, too. It is because of these human tendencies that objective data-gathering methods are insisted upon in science in the first place.

The problem is compounded when we consider that few linguists have managed to limit their introspective activities to those judgments they might be capable of in their role as 'typical' native speakers (i.e. to judgments about the interpretation of utterances in their language), but have often extended them into the domain of the underlying mechanisms being described (i.e. to judgments about the form of grammar, the nature of 'linguistically significant generalizations' and the like).[2] In such cases, the danger of being unduly influenced by such factors as 'the investigator's own overtrained bias' (Olmsted, 1955, p. 47) clearly increases; moreover, it is obvious that if this is the sort of data relied upon in deciding between alternative formulations, there is going to be no objective way of assaying the correctness of the formulations, since independent data from naive native speakers is excluded in principle from such accounts (see Leech, 1968, and Peters, 1970). So Householder remarks that 'all arguments based on bare intuition whether the linguist's or the native speaker's constitute a hindrance to communication, since there is no way of evaluating conflicting claims' (1965, p. 15, n. 2).

My first serious disagreement with Chomsky on the use of intro-

---

[1] Householder cites the case of 'the beautiful 4-stress 4-pitch dialects spoken by some of the Foreign Service Institute personnel some years back' (p. 99). Cf. the vacillation at MIT over the proper interpretation of sentences involving quantifiers (Chomsky, 1957b, pp. 100–1; 1965a, p. 224; and Katz & Postal, 1964, pp. 72–3.)

[2] Thus we find one expressed central object of concern among contemporary grammarians to be that of 'justifying correct descriptions' or constructing an evaluation procedure 'that gives the desired results' (cf. 5.1 and 5.2 above).

spective evidence in TGG is thus with respect to his claim that, although the 'gathering of data is informal' in linguistics with 'very little use of experimental approaches, the arguments in favor of this informal procedure seem...quite compelling' (1969, p. 56). Such 'arguments' are not compelling at all. The choice here is between proven data-collection methods and the reliable (or 'hard') data to which they lead, or inferior 'informal' methods and the 'soft' data which inevitably result (cf. Agnew & Pyke, 1969, p. 155). This is hardly a choice. In linguistics there is reason to believe that the choice is *available*, but has been ignored or neglected in the rush to theory (cf. 7.1.2 above). All that is necessary is 'to replace intuition by some more rigorous criterion' (Chomsky in Hill, 1962, p. 24) and attempt to establish, under con-trolled experimental conditions, whether naive native speakers really can do all the things which Chomsky says that they can (such as make consistent judgments of grammaticality, paraphrase and anomaly, or judge such things as morpheme relatedness and phonetic similarity). There is very little to say positively about *anything* which Chomsky has done until this is accomplished (cf. Maclay & Sleator, 1960, p. 282).

The problem goes deeper. Consider the following assertion from Chomsky & Halle (1965):

All linguistic work is, obviously, guided by certain assumptions about the nature of linguistic structure and linguistic patterns; and such assumptions, which are the heart of linguistic theory, can be tested for adequacy in *only one way*, namely, by determining whether the descriptions to which they lead are in accord with tacit knowledge concerning the language (p. 103, italics added).

Yet as I have argued in 7.2.3, grammars are notoriously underdeter-mined by the data available, even when introspective judgments of dubious reliability are admitted. If such data represent the *only* way in which linguistic theories may be tested, they must remain untestable indefinitely. The basic problem with reliance upon intro-spective evidence is that linguistically naive native speakers have virtually *no* intuitions (as far as we know) about the mechanisms which underlie speech, any more than the biologically naive individual has any intuitions about how any of his other internal mechanisms operate. As Chomsky himself admits:

Any interesting generative grammar will be dealing, for the most part, with mental processes that are far beyond the level of actual or even potential consciousness; furthermore, it is quite apparent that a speaker's reports and viewpoints about his behavior and his competence may be in error (1965a, p. 8).

Thus the kinds of data which transformationalists currently rely upon are 'restricted in a crucial way – that is, in a way crucial to Chomsky's own goals' (P. Harris, 1970, p. 65).

7.4 On idealization in science and in TGG

There is one further consequence of heavy reliance upon introspective evidence in linguistics. It has led to a concept of linguistic 'competence' (which is said to 'underlie' language use) which does not represent an idealized model of language use at all (see 8.1 below for details), but is viewed instead as a model of 'the speaker-hearer's knowledge of his language' (Chomsky, 1965a, p. 4). At first blush, the logical basis for this interpretation seems unimpeachable: since the basic data against which theories of 'linguistic competence' are to be evaluated (i.e. introspective judgments about grammaticality, ambiguity, paraphrase, etc.) themselves represent aspects of what might be called the native speaker's knowledge of his language, it is reasonable to think of the hypothetical model which accounts for such knowledge as itself an idealized model of linguistic 'knowledge'. This seemingly straightforward interpretation is complicated, however, when we find that a grammar of a language purports to be both 'a description of the ideal speaker-hearer's intrinsic competence' (same reference), and (on the same page) 'the underlying *system of rules* that has been mastered by the speaker–hearer' (italics added). Paradoxically, we are next reminded (p. 8) that the speaker–hearer is, at the same time, 'not aware' of the rules of this grammar which he is supposed to have internalized. Putting these propositions together in an attempt to determine the meaning of 'linguistic competence', one finds that (1) competence is knowledge; (2) competence is also a system of rules; yet, at the same time, (3) there is no knowledge of the rules.

Chomsky attempts to reconcile the statements along the following lines: some of this 'knowledge' which a native speaker is said to have of his language is 'tacit' (1965a, pp. 19, 21, 27) or 'unconscious' (1968b, pp. 14–15, and in Hook, 1969, p. 153). Thus, Chomsky says, 'a generative grammar attempts to specify what the speaker [of a language] actually knows, not what he may report about his knowledge' (1965a, p. 8). Chomsky seems to want to place both linguistic intuitions (judgments of grammaticality and the like) and the presumably internalized 'knowledge' of a generative grammar together, but on a scale of 'consciousness' or 'awareness', such that the speaker–hearer is capable of bringing his 'knowledge' to awareness at one end, but where it becomes increasingly more 'tacit' or 'unconscious' at the other (cf. Postal 1966, p. 156).[1]

This is a difficult position to maintain. In the first place, is it useful (or even proper) to consider both 'linguistic intuitions' and this 'knowledge' of the grammar itself (i.e. of its basic components, its rules, the general constraints imposed upon it, etc.) as two forms of the same thing, i.e. 'knowledge'? There are important differences between these two notions. For one thing, the first, at least, can be brought to conscious awareness (and *must* be so realized if they are to be of any use to the linguist); but the second seems incapable in principle of being brought to conscious awareness. We also notice that 'linguistic intuitions' represent interpretations placed upon the *output* of a generative grammar (and hence part of the *data* of linguistics which the grammarian is concerned to account for), while the grammar itself represents a body of hypotheses (in the form of a set of rules) designed to 'explain' these data. So there is a potentially significant distinction to be made here, which is obscured by Chomsky's terminological equivocation and which is, in turn, responsible for the apparent contradiction that knowledge $\neq$ knowledge. Thus we have on the one hand the overt (or potentially overt) knowledge (let us call it knowledge$_1$) referred to in the literature as 'native speaker intuitions', while on the other we have the fully covert ('tacit' or 'unconscious') kind (call it knowledge$_2$) which appears in such phrases as 'knowledge of a grammar' or 'knowledge of the language' (as in Chomsky, 1965a, p. 9). These notions can be readily interpreted in terms of fig. 7.1 below, where C stands for a competence model (or generative grammar – in Chomsky's terms, 'a system of rules that in some explicit and well-defined way assigns structural descriptions to sentences' (1965a, p. 8)) – and LI refers to those linguistic intuitions which this model has been constructed to explain.

Now it seems appropriate to speak of LI (i.e. interpretations placed on the *output* of the grammar) as 'knowledge' which the native speaker has about his language, for we are speaking here of native-speaker judgments about sentences which can in principle be brought to con-

[1] Apparently the accessibility of this 'knowledge' to introspection diminishes rapidly in this latter direction, so allowing Chomsky to conclude that 'any interesting generative grammar will be dealing, *for the most part*, with mental processes that are far beyond the level of actual or even potential consciousness' (1965a, p. 8; italics added).

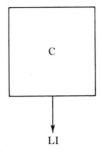

FIG. 7.1 Chomsky's model of linguistic competence

scious awareness (say by manipulating the data in various ways; see Chomsky, 1965a, pp. 18ff, for discussion). The fact that 'a speaker's reports and viewpoints about his behavior' in this respect 'may be in error' (p. 8) does not attest to the covert status of judgments of this sort, but merely to the *unreliability* of the methods used to bring these judgments to consciousness (and hence to the relative unreliability of the data themselves). As far as the native speaker's reports about his underlying 'competence' (i.e. reports about the grammar or the competence model itself) are concerned, however, these simply do not exist. It is only knowledge$_2$, therefore (i.e. 'knowledge' of the grammar), which can properly be described as going 'far beyond the level of actual or even potential consciousness', and one begins to wonder whether the term 'knowledge' is even appropriate here. In any event, Chomsky's failure to distinguish clearly between knowledge$_1$ and knowledge$_2$ leads to the difficulty in making sense out of his notion of 'linguistic competence'.[1]

One possible (and, to my mind, reasonable and useful) way of distinguishing between these two notions is the one suggested by Harman (1967). He argues that knowledge$_1$ is knowledge in the familiar propositional sense of 'knowledge that' (as in 'knowledge that such and such is the case'), whereas knowledge$_2$ is best regarded as knowledge only in the dynamic or procedural sense of 'knowing how' (i.e. in the sense that one may 'know how to ride a bicycle').[2] Under this interpretation know-

---

[1] In Harman's terms, Chomsky simply 'muddles together' here notions which philosophers (and others) have been at great pains to distinguish (p. 86). In this particular case, 'Chomsky's use of the phrase "tacit competence" betrays a confusion between the two sorts of knowledge of a language' (p. 81).

[2] Harman does not claim, as Chomsky suggests (in Hook, 1969, pp. 87 and 154–5), that the ability to use a language is a close analogue to the ability to ride a bicycle; the example is given merely as an illustration to clarify the important distinction between 'knowledge how' and 'knowledge that', and to demonstrate the inappropriateness of viewing a skill or ability in terms of the latter.

ledge₁ involves awareness or cognizance of *facts* or *information* (i.e. knowledge in the ordinary sense), while knowledge₂ involves a behavioral *skill* or *ability*. The value of this interpretation rests, in part, in that it makes it possible to replace Chomsky's terminological equivocation by a conceptual distinction of considerable utility. Furthermore, this distinction is consistent with the facts regarding accessibility to introspection: it is generally the case that no well-fixed habitual or automatic form of behavior acquired as the result of practice is normally under the individual's conscious control (as in Harman's bicycle-riding illustration). What other interpretation *can* be placed on the word 'know' in such remarks as the following?

> When a person has command of a language,...what kind of things does he *know*?...Command of [a] language involves...the *ability* to select, when one of the signals is presented, the correlated semantic content; also the *ability*, given some idea in mind, to find the appropriate signal to express it (Chomsky, 1967b, p. 75; italics added).

Chomsky, however, rejects Harman's proposed interpretation, asserting that 'knowledge of language cannot be discussed in any useful or informative way in this impoverished framework. In general, it does not seem... that the concepts "knowing how" and "knowing that" constitute exhaustive categories for the analysis of knowledge' (1969, p. 87). He argues that 'obviously knowledge of a language is not a matter of "knowing that"' (p. 86),[1] yet also sees 'no reason to suppose that knowledge of language can be characterized in terms of "knowing how"' (p. 87), either. Chomsky presumably has some third sense of 'knowledge' in mind when he speaks of knowledge₂ (or of knowledge₁ and knowledge₂ *together*), although he does not say what it is: adding the descriptive term 'tacit' is not in itself enlightening.

Chomsky complicates the picture even further. For he also tells us that his model of linguistic 'competence' which attempts to charac-

---

[1] Otherwise, of course, 'knowing' the rules of the grammar would necessarily imply the ability to exhibit what Wiest (1967) refers to as 'the verbal performance called "uttering the rules of [the] grammar"' (p. 220). On the other hand, any native speaker of English can probably be made aware of the fact *that* the sentence 'What disturbed John was being disregarded by everyone' (from Chomsky, 1967b, p. 77) is acceptable, but ambiguous. So at least *part* of the knowledge one has of his language is knowledge *that*, is it not? Then what about the other part? Furthermore, there is one sense of 'knowledge of rules' which *does* involve the ability, at least in principle, to state what the rules are (as in football or chess – see, e.g. Searle, 1970, pp. 33ff). In short, the notion 'knowledge of a language' needs a great deal of conceptual polishing up – not to mention the notions of 'grammar' and 'rule' themselves.

terize 'what the speaker of a language *knows* implicitly' (and not what he *does*), nevertheless 'describes and attempts to account for the *ability* of a speaker to understand an arbitrary sentence of his language and to produce an appropriate sentence on a given occasion' as well (Chomsky, 1966b, p. 3; italics added). That is to say, linguistic *competence* in Chomsky's scheme ('the speaker–hearer's knowledge of his language') is described as a kind of 'idealization' of linguistic performance ('the actual *use* of language in concrete situations'); thus competence represents 'a mental reality underlying actual behavior', abstracting away from a variety of (supposedly) irrelevant factors such as 'memory limitations, distractions, shifts of attention and interest, and errors' (Chomsky, 1965a, pp. 3–4). Since such idealizations are common in other sciences, Chomsky feels justified in claiming that 'in this respect, study of language is no different from empirical investigation of other complex phenomena' (p. 4).

What is so peculiar about the description is the difficulty of envisaging how competence (construed as a model of 'knowledge' and *not* of ability) can be regarded as 'underlying' or representing an 'idealization' of performance (which *is* construed as a description of linguistic ability or behavior). There seems to be a disparity between these two notions in *kind*, which we fail to find between the idealized concepts of the natural sciences and their paired counterparts in the real world. In physics, for example, we find 'ideal gases' and 'real gases', 'ideal (frictionless) surfaces' and 'real surfaces', 'ideal (perfectly elastic) bodies' paired with 'real bodies' and even 'ideal (point) masses' underlying 'real masses', but never any mention of 'ideal forces' paired with 'real fluids' or 'ideal charges' underlying 'real springs' or anything else so absurd.[1] For the hypothetical entities or models postulated in the natural sciences are always assumed to be identical to their observational counterparts in the real world in all their essential properties, with one qualification: a few of these properties are typically ignored (or disregarded) in the hypothetical model in order to eliminate the problem of confounding variables, and so to facilitate the mathematical manipulations involved in making

---

[1] Equally absurd consequences follow from the suggestion that it is 'ideal knowledge' which *directly* underlies 'real behavior' in linguistics. Under such a straightforward 'idealization' interpretation, for example, the aphasiac must presumably be said to suffer from some kind of a 'depletion' or 'shrinkage' in his 'knowledge', and not regarded as an individual whose *abilities* have been incapacitated (as in the case of stroke victims who lose the capacity to walk, rather than to speak). I fail to see how the former interpretation could possibly be useful.

quantitative predictions on the basis of the model.[1] This is the essence
of the notion of idealization or abstraction in science. Consequently,
hypothetical models are not construed to be 'empirically true' in every
particular, but are recognized to represent 'approximations' or 'over-
simplifications' of the true (underlying) state of affairs; hence any
predictions made on the basis of such models are not expected to correspond *exactly* with the observed facts, but only approximately – under
the assumption that the factors which have been left out of consideration are only marginally significant to the phenomena which are the
main focus of attention. As Cohen puts it, 'theories about ideal counterparts represent a simplified description of observable data' (Lyons and
Wales, 1966, p. 164), since when science abstracts from the world its
abstractions invariably involve nothing more than the simple 'omission
of something' (Caws, 1965, p. 303).

The rationale for constraining the notion of idealization (or abstraction) in science in this way is implicit in the discussion of 7.1 above: it
follows directly from the fact that the ultimate goal of any science is
generally understood to be the construction of *empirically true* models
of certain aspects or domains of the universe (see Caws, 1965, p. 68).[2]
Yet hypothetical models can only be regarded as empirically true to the
extent that they may be regarded as isomorphic with the state of affairs
which they purportedly represent (p. 184) and this goal can presumably
be achieved only if the scientist sets out with the intention of developing
a hypothetical model whose basic characteristics are *in principle* capable
of being interpreted in terms of some particular empirical space or
domain and vice versa.

The completion of such a task must be enormously complex and

---

[1] Thus Holton and Roller (1958) agree that 'a very powerful procedure in physical
science [is] *the isolation and individual study of a specific and small part of the total situation* when the remainder is either inaccessible or too complex for a successful study
as a whole' (pp. 79–80).

[2] Compare the highly idiosyncratic view propounded by Fodor and Garrett (see p. 34n
above), that science is concerned instead 'to understand the laws that determine the
behavior of *ideal objects*'. To borrow an analogy from Fodor himself (1968, p. 227),
'To explain how an internal combustion engine works is to account for its normal
performance; the account will not [necessarily] include an explanation of backfires,
misfires, and overheating.' Thus a theory of the ideal internal combustion engine is
an oversimplified account of the performance of a *real* engine (which is *not* backfire-
free under all conditions). A theory of 'ideal gases' is also an oversimplified account
of the behavior of *real* gases, etc. It follows that any theory about some aspect of
human behavior (such as linguistic performance) must also be an oversimplified
account of behavior, as well (in this case, an idealized model of linguistic performance).

difficult for any but the most circumscribed and trivial of empirical domains; thus it is to be expected that such models will be arrived at through successive approximations which must necessarily involve simplifying assumptions and idealizations along the way. But the point remains that, to be heuristically useful in empirical science, the idealizations must conform to the general constraint under discussion. Yet Chomsky's proposed idealization, in which 'competence' is said to represent some obscure form of 'knowledge', fails to conform to such a constraint. Rather, the sort of 'idealization' which distinguishes Chomsky's notion of competence from performance involves *far more* than the mere 'abstraction away' of vagaries of performance like false starts, hesitations, lapses and the like. Chomsky's notion of 'idealization' is extreme and unprecedented – certainly far from 'uncontroversial' (cf. Chomsky, 1966b, pp. 8–9) – with a consequent effect on the conceptual clarity of his entire linguistic theory.

Yet conceptual clarity is essential. Chomsky insists that a model of linguistic competence of the sort he proposes can be tested in only one way, namely, 'by measuring it against the standard provided by the tacit knowledge that it attempts to specify and describe' (1965a, p. 19). Obviously, then, we must have some idea what this 'tacit knowledge' is if we are to know what evidence is relevant in evaluating any hypothetical model which purports to represent such an entity. It is as clear (or as unclear, in this case) as that.

Given the essential incoherence of Chomsky's concept of 'knowledge', one might ask why he should have adopted it. Hiz (1967) suggests that the dictum that linguistics is about 'competence' rather than performance 'is to be understood as saying that introspection is a source of linguistic knowledge. Our introspection about performance is to be admitted as linguistic evidence' (p. 69). Chomsky rejects this interpretation: 'I do agree that introspection is an excellent source of data for the study of language,' he says, 'but this conclusion does not follow from the decision to study linguistic competence' (1969, p. 81).

But which came first – the decision to focus attention on introspective evidence or the decision to study 'competence' (in Chomsky's idiosyncratic and restricted sense of the term)? Clearly, it was the former. There is, for example, no mention of 'competence' in either *Syntactic Structures* or among Chomsky's remarks in Hill (1962), though both emphasize native-speaker intuitions:

(1) It is undeniable that 'intuition about linguistic form' is very useful to the

investigator of linguistic form (i.e. grammar) (Chomsky, 1957b, pp. 93–4).

(2) I claim...that study of the native speaker's reactions is what all linguists are studying (Chomsky in Hill, 1962, p. 167).

(3) I am interested in explaining intuition. If you cannot accept this as the purpose of linguistic study, I am lost. I would like to get a theory which will predict intuitions (Chomsky in Hill, 1962, p. 168).

As a direct result of this interest, generative grammars were developed to account for these intuitions. Only later did the empirical or psychological status of these grammars come into question. And when it did, the notion of 'linguistic competence' came with it – together with the interpretation of competence as a model of the native speaker's 'knowledge' of his language. (See especially Chomsky, 1965a, p. 27, where the phrase 'linguistic intuition' is used inter-changeably with 'tacit competence'.) It is quite feasible that this particular interpretation is a direct (historical) consequence of Chomsky's earlier decision to emphasize introspective data and we have to be skeptical of his assurances that that prior decision had 'nothing to do with the distinction between competence and performance' (1969, p. 81).

8   On 'competence' and 'performance'

8.1   Three interpretations of Chomsky's competence/ performance distinction[1]

Chomsky has asserted that 'the goal of the descriptive study of a language is the construction of a grammar' (Chomsky & Halle, 1968, p. 3), where 'a grammar of a language purports to be a description of the ideal speaker–hearer's intrinsic competence' (Chomsky, 1965a, p. 4). The notion of 'linguistic competence' is thus central to Chomsky's conception of linguistics as a discipline. Yet few notions in the transformationalists' repertoire are as poorly understood as the notion 'model of linguistic competence' (or C-model). One reason for this seems to be that Chomsky himself is uncertain of the proper interpretation. At one time or another he seems to have advocated as many as three distinct interpretations. I shall examine each in turn.

8.1.1   Competence as an idealized model of linguistic performance. Whenever the issue of the competence/performance distinction first comes up in one of Chomsky's writings, he is careful to give the initial impression that the sort of idealization he has in mind differs in no important way from anybody else's: a C-model is simply an idealized model of linguistic performance (or P-model), that is, a model of what the speaker–hearer actually does when he produces or comprehends utterances (abstracting away from such extraneous factors as distractions, shifts of attention, hesitations, and the like). Consider the following citations from his works, for example:

(1) By a 'generative grammar' I mean a description of the tacit *competence* of

[1] The development of the arguments presented in this section has benefited immeasurably from discussions with P. R. Harris. I have also benefited from the study of Mr Harris' (unpublished) University of Alberta M.Sc. thesis (1970), which contains what is probably the most complete and clear unraveling yet available of the competence/performance distinction as employed by Chomsky. The interested reader is referred to that work for the original, more concise statement of many of the issues developed below.

the speaker–hearer that *underlies his actual performance in production and perception* (*understanding*) *of speech.* A generative grammar, ideally, specifies a pairing of phonetic and semantic representations over an infinite range; it thus constitutes *a hypothesis as to how the speaker–hearer interprets utterances*, abstracting away from many factors that interweave with tacit competence to determine actual performance (1966a, p. 75, n. 2).

(2) A grammar, in the traditional view, is an account of *competence*. It describes and attempts to account for the *ability* of a speaker to *understand* an arbitrary sentence of his language and to *produce* an appropriate sentence on a given occasion. If it is a pedagogic grammar, it attempts to provide the student with this *ability*; if a linguistic grammar, it aims to discover and exhibit the *mechanisms* that make this *achievement* possible (1966b, p. 3).

(3) The most striking aspect of linguistic *competence* is what we may call the 'creativity of language', that is, the speaker's *ability to produce* new sentences, sentences that are immediately *understood* by other speakers although they bear no [*sic*] physical resemblance to sentences which are 'familiar'. The fundamental importance of this creative aspect of normal language *use* has been recognized since the seventeenth century at least (1966b, p. 4; italics added, as in the previous two examples).

Now in such accounts Chomsky seems to be arguing that linguists ought to become concerned with explaining linguistic performance or language use and I have no quarrel with that view, or with the implication that 'competence' refers (or *ought* to refer) to this underlying performance mechanism. It is, after all, the facts of *verbal behavior* (i.e. the facts of *language use* or *linguistic performance*[1]) which the linguist and/or psychologist are really concerned to account for, including such characteristics as its creative and apparent 'rule-governed' aspects which Chomsky himself emphasizes.

One analogy often made in this connection is between Chomsky's competence/performance distinction and Saussure's distinction be-

---

[1] Due to Chomsky's influence, there is a striking tendency among linguists today to equate 'linguistic performance' exclusively with those particular 'performance factors' which Chomsky specifically excludes from consideration (often with good reason) as irrelevant. This tendency is apparent in Katz's blanket assertion that 'linguistic description can be no more concerned *per se* with the *speech performance* of members of a language community than a physicist is concerned *per se* with meter readings or a biologist is concerned with individual specimens of various sorts. Like other scientists, the linguist idealizes away from the heterogeneous phenomena that directly face him in nature' (1966, pp. 116–17; italics added). However, as Fromkin points out (1968, p. 48), because *some* 'performance factors' are heterogeneous and uncontrollable, it does not follow that 'all aspects of [linguistic] performance are random and unpredictable' (cf. Chomsky, 1968a, pp. 85–6, n. 5).

tween *langue* and *parole* (as in Chomsky, 1964, p. 52). Now there are a number of objections to this analogy. For one thing, as Chomsky is always careful to point out, Saussure seems to have spoken only in terms of a system of inter-relationships among *elements*, whereas Chomsky is interested instead in an idealized system of *rules* (or, better, elements and rules).[1] For another, Saussure saw language as 'purely social and independent of the individual' (1959, p. 18) – as a sort of reified 'super-system' of elements and relations having a separate metaphysical existence in some undefined hyper-space and with only a 'potential existence in each brain' (p. 14). A more suitable interpretation for linguists today, surely, is to see language as existing in a specific empirical space (the individual mind) but to abstract away individual (idiolectal) and dialectal differences in order to concentrate on a certain 'common core' of psychological elements, relations or rules which may be regarded as representative of *all* the speakers of a language or dialect, hence of the 'typical' speaker (see, e.g. Hockett, 1958, pp. 332ff and chapter 9 below).

Despite these difficulties, I think there is still something important for today's linguist to learn from Saussure's *langue* vs. *parole* distinction. Saussure provides a useful analogy of his own which can be invoked here. This is his famous SYMPHONY analogy, which he introduces as follows:

Language is comparable to a symphony in that what the symphony actually is stands completely apart from how it is performed; the mistakes that musicians make in playing the symphony do not compromise this fact (1959, p. 18).

Katz and Postal (1964, p. ix) pick up this analogy and develop it in the following way:

In any linguistic study, it is necessary to distinguish sharply between *language* and *speech*... A language is a system of abstract objects analogous in significant respects to ... a symphony. Speech is the actual verbal behavior that manifests the linguistic competence of one who has learned the appropriate system of abstract objects. Thus speech is analogous to the performances of a symphony in just the sense in which the language is analogous to the sym-

---

[1] Chomsky (1964) nevertheless proceeds to speak next of a 'classical Saussurian assumption' related to '*generative grammars* that describe [langue]' (p. 52, italics added). Chomsky's students also reinterpret Saussure along lines currently in favor among generative grammarians. Bever (1968), for example, insists that Saussure 'drew a basic distinction between the *knowledge* of a language and the *performance of that knowledge* in actual speech behavior' (p. 4, italics added). This is distinctly Chomskyan, not Saussurian. What does the phrase 'performance of knowledge' mean?

phony itself. But just as symphonic performances are not invariant realizations of a symphony, so speech performances are not invariant realizations of the abstract objects that comprise the language. In both cases, besides the competence of performers who have learned the appropriate abstract objects, many other parameters partially determine the character of actual performances, among which are the skills and abilities of the performers, the context of the performance, and the character of the audience.

So the performance of a symphony will involve many factors which do not contribute significantly to an understanding of the symphony itself; these may be considered essentially irrelevant. But what *is* the 'symphony itself'? What is the nature of these 'abstract objects' which represent its idealized pristine state yet which may be 'realized differently' by different performers under different conditions – or by the same performers at different times? Stated in this way, the question may well seem to be a purely metaphysical one, since the notion of the true 'essence' of symphony, construed as a pure abstraction totally removed from human minds or actual performance, cannot be said to represent a discoverable empirical entity. But suppose we rephrase the question in this way: how might the idealized form of any symphony *most usefully be represented*? Now we can readily find an answer. For among musicians there seems to have been established virtual unanimity on this point: a symphony (or any other piece of music) is invariably represented as *a set of instructions for playing music* (including instructions as to the particular notes to be played, the meter, tempo, dynamics, instrumentation, etc.). And certain important consequences result from this decision. For one thing, viewed in this way (as a set of *instructions*, rather than as a pure abstraction), a symphony can only be said to have a fully *dynamic* interpretation or realization, when some particular orchestra actually attempts to play the music according to the instructions provided (cf. Lamb, 1966a, p. 10). Different orchestras (or the same orchestra) may play it well or badly on different occasions, and no two performances will be exactly alike. Furthermore, under this interpretation, there is also something feasible for the 'symphonic scientist' to do (assuming that he does not already have the score available; otherwise the analogy with language would be destroyed): he must feel his way through these variations in the realization of the work in question in order to arrive at the *idealized model* which has served to underlie them all (the original score itself). But what is perhaps the most important point of this illustration is that this idealized model is itself *a model of performance* (as it must be in order to preserve the notion of 'idealization' as employed in empirical science) and not something different in *kind* from the target aimed at in each actual performance (cf. 7.4 above).

Now the same is surely true of language, under any sensible interpretation of the notion 'model of linguistic competence'. Only if a competence model is to be understood as *an idealized model of linguistic performance* (or *language use* – I shall use the two terms interchangeably throughout) can any sense be made of Chomsky's claim that the model is intended to characterize 'the basis for actual *use* of language' or to 'determine how sentences are to be *formed, used,* and *understood*' – or of Katz and Postal's remark that speech is 'the actual verbal behavior that *manifests* the linguistic competence of one who has learned the appropriate system of abstract objects'. Just as a symphony can most usefully be regarded as a set of instructions for performing music, a language can perhaps most usefully be regarded as *a set of instructions for performing speech*.[1]

Chomsky starts out in *Syntactic Structures* as though he had adopted a very sensible approach of just this sort. He considers first the possibility of interpreting a finite state grammar as an 'elementary communication theoretic model of language' in which one might

---

[1] The analogy does break down in a number of places, some critical. First of all, with the symphony, the conductor and his musicians have the set of instructions symbolized before them in black and white, and are in a position to commit them to memory or otherwise come to *know* (in the ordinary sense of the term) just what these instructions are; the instructions for performing a symphony, in brief, are overt, whereas those for performing speech are covert. Secondly, as a consequence of this first fact, the symphony may be said to have an independent existence above and beyond its dynamic realization on any particular occasion; one may go into a music store and buy a *copy* of Beethoven's 'Fifth' or Schubert's 'Unfinished', fondle it, show it to a friend, etc., whereas one may not manipulate a 'language' in this way. As a further consequence, the musicians may also choose to change or distort the instructions symbolized before them in any particular place or manner they like, and even with respect to certain specific and minute details; this is a far more difficult proposition for the speaker of a language who has no real awareness (or knowledge) of just what the particular instructions are and can thus manipulate them only in rather gross and poorly understood ways. Thus mistakes in speech tend to be more 'mechanical' or 'accidental' (due to carelessness, inattention and the like) than directed or purposeful (although this need not necessarily imply that such mistakes must be random, unstructured or inexplicable). In addition, while each performance of a symphony normally includes the realization of the *full set* of instructions indicated in the score, few individual speech events will ever be required to take into account more than a small portion of the full range of instructions actually available to the speaker. And, finally, there is no provision within the symphony model for anything analogous to the notion of a set of interpretation (or comprehension) formulas for the *hearer*, so that the analogy is useful only insofar as it clarifies the *production* phase of a fully articulated model of linguistic performance.

view the speaker as being essentially a machine of the type considered. In *producing* a sentence, the *speaker* begins in the initial state, *produces* the first word of the sentence, thereby switching into a second state which limits the choice of the second word, etc. Each state through which he passes represents the grammatical restrictions that limit the choice of the next word at this point in the *utterance* (p. 20, italics added).

Clearly, Chomsky is concerned here with the problem of articulating a hypothetical *model of speech production*, ostensibly to be incorporated directly into a more general (idealized) model of linguistic performance or language use (i.e. a model of speech production *and* perception). An attitude of primary concern with the construction of such a model is also indicated in Chomsky and Miller (1963, p. 271):

The fundamental fact that must be faced in any investigation of language and linguistic *behavior* is the following: a native *speaker* of a language has the *ability* to *comprehend* an immense number of sentences that he has never previously heard and to *produce*, on the appropriate occasion, novel *utterances* that are similarly understandable to other native speakers. The basic questions that must be asked are the following:

1. What is the precise nature of this *ability*?
2. How is it put to use?
3. How does it arise in the individual?

There have been several attempts to formulate questions of this sort in a precise and explicit form and *to construct models that represent certain aspects of these achievements of a native speaker.*

Now, given comments such as these, it is hardly surprising that many people (including many linguists and certainly most psychologists) should have taken Chomsky at his word and assumed he was working towards a model of speech production and/or perception; for the psychologists, in particular, the prospect of a 'precise and explicit' model of linguistic behavior (or even of some limited domain of linguistic behaviors) must have seemed an appealing one indeed. What most early commentators failed to note was that, having dispensed with finite state models (of *speech production*), Chomsky then moved on to his discussion of phrase structure and transformational models in quite *different* terms. Just what these new ground rules were was never made clear in *Syntactic Structures* ('linguistic competence' not yet having been conceived), but that there was a drastic (though unannounced) shift in interpretation of some sort is no longer in doubt by p. 48:[1]

[1] Although transformational and finite state models are still being compared as late as p. 47, as though both were to be interpreted as models of the same kind of thing! Presumably Chomsky intended his readers to have reinterpreted the finite state model, too, in similar 'neutral' terms by this time, but who was to know this?

One further point about grammars of the form (35) [i.e. transformational grammars]. . . We have described these grammars as devices for *generating* sentences. This rather familiar formulation [borrowed from automata theory – BLD] has occasionally led to the idea that there is a certain asymmetry in grammatical theory in the sense that grammar is taking the point of view of the speaker rather than the hearer; that it is concerned with the process of producing utterances rather than the 'inverse' process of analyzing and reconstructing the structure of given utterances. Actually, grammars of the form that we have been discussing [since chapter 3? – BLD] are quite *neutral* as between speaker and hearer, between synthesis and analysis of utterances. A grammar does *not* tell us how to synthesize a specific utterance; it does *not* tell us how to analyze a particular given utterance. In fact, these two tasks which the speaker and hearer must perform are essentially the same [*sic*], and are *both outside the scope of grammars of the form* (35) (italics added).

So here we find that transformational-generative grammars are *not* intended to be interpreted as idealized production and/or perception models, after all, but as models of something else 'neutral' between the two; in other words, a model of 'linguistic competence' (as this 'something else' has since come to be known) is *not* to be regarded as an idealized model of linguistic performance. Clear enough, but (for reasons which Chomsky seems to find baffling) the illusion died hard, especially among psychologists.[1] So Chomsky is forced to restate his position in unambiguous terms in his *Aspects of the Theory of Syntax*, as well (p. 9, italics added):

To avoid what has been a continuing misunderstanding, it is perhaps worth while to reiterate that a generative grammar is *not* a model for a speaker or a hearer. It attempts to characterize *in the most neutral possible terms* the knowledge of the language that provides a basis for actual use of language by a speaker-hearer...When we say that a sentence has a certain derivation with respect to a particular generative grammar, we say *nothing* about how the speaker or hearer might proceed, in some practical or efficient way, to construct such a derivation. These questions belong to the [non-existent – BLD] theory of language use – the theory of performance.

Thus while Chomsky himself speaks of the *desirability* of constructing and testing models of linguistic performance (see especially the citation from Chomsky and Miller on p. 264 above), he has from the beginning

[1] Chomsky seems surprised at the frequency with which his remarks have been 'misinterpreted' on this point. But he has *repeatedly* used the term 'generate' in contexts where only the interpretation 'produce' makes sense (e.g. paired with the notion of 'interpretation' within a general context of discussion of 'language use'; see especially Chomsky, 1965a, p. 18, and 1968b, p. 9). Halle, too, has spoken of 'generative grammar' in the context of an implied 'process of synthesizing an utterance' (1961, p. 92).

refused to interpret his own work in *generative grammar* in such terms, whenever the question is put to him straight. Now why has he done this? Surely the answer is obvious: because generative grammars would *fail* under such an interpretation. True enough, generative grammars are somewhat suggestive in this connection. For one thing, they incorporate a feature of *recursiveness* which, as Chomsky himself has emphasized, allows in principle for the possibility of accounting for the well-publicized '"creative" aspect of language use' (Chomsky, 1965a, p. 205, n. 30), more often abbreviated (significantly, I think) to the 'creative aspect of *language*' (as in Chomsky, 1964, p. 51; 1966b, p. 4; 1966a, p. 4 and elsewhere), i.e. for the ability of the speaker of a language to produce (and the hearer to understand) sentences which he has not previously encountered. In addition, Chomsky's generative model possesses a certain apparent 'dynamic' quality which many observers have also found attractive in this connection (see, e.g. Hörmann, 1971, p. 45). Nor is there any denying that Chomsky's was the first explicit linguistic model which incorporated either of these highly suggestive properties. At the same time, however, there are other equally central and equally essential characteristics which any satisfactory model of linguistic performance must have and which Chomsky's model (of linguistic 'competence') does *not*. One of these, is the feature of *selectivity*. For as Chomsky and Miller themselves point out, the native speaker of a language not only has the ability simply to 'produce novel utterances' but also to produce them 'on the appropriate occasion'. (Furthermore, the context of an utterance obviously has much to do with the way a hearer interprets or understands it.) Lyons is right to say that 'the ability to use one's language correctly in a variety of socially determined situations is as much and as central a part of linguistic "competence" as the ability to produce grammatically well-formed sentences' (1970, p. 287). The normal use of language is not only 'innovative' (Chomsky, 1968a, p. 10), but also has the properties of 'coherence' and 'appropriateness to the situation' such that 'we can distinguish normal use of language from the ravings of a maniac or the output of a computer with a random element' (p. 11). Thus it seems clear that any model of linguistic performance capable in principle of capturing such central aspects of language use as these must have the property of selectivity. Yet no generative grammar of the 'standard' or 'classic' mold has this property. Katz and Postal (1964, pp. 166–7) describe the situation which actually does obtain:

The syntactic component, which is the generative source for the whole linguistic description, enumerates the infinite set of sentoids in an order and in a way that must be considered essentially *random* from the viewpoint of actual speech production and comprehension. The phonological and semantic components cannot change this fact, because they are merely interpretative devices which assign interpretations to sentoids in whatever order those sentoids are given to them by the syntactic component. Therefore, within the framework of a linguistic description, there is *no provision* for describing how speakers equipped with a linguistic description of their language can extract from it just the sentences they wish to produce and just the analyses required to understand the sentences produced by others. The systematic description of these abilities is the province of what can be called 'models of speech production' and 'models of speech recognition' (italics added).

So Campbell and Wales (1970) reasonably express the following misgivings about current linguistic models:

Although generative grammarians, in particular Chomsky, claim that their work is an attempt to characterize the nature of competence$_2$ (that is, the nature of those human abilities that are specific to language) their main effort has in fact been directed towards a more restricted sort of competence, which we will call *competence$_3$*, from which by far the most important linguistic ability has been omitted – the ability to produce or understand utterances which are not so much *grammatical* but, more important, *appropriate to the context in which they are made* (1970, p. 247).[1]

Yet, though Chomsky (1967b, p. 76) argues that 'the basic, most elementary fact that has to be accounted for by anyone who is interested in dealing with the phenomenon of human language in a serious way' is that in normal language use the speaker repeatedly encounters 'absolutely new signals or produces them *on the appropriate occasion* without any feeling of strangeness or feeling of novelty' (italics added), he concludes (p. 81) that 'a person who knows a language has represented in his brain some very abstract system of underlying structures along with an abstract system of rules that determine, *by free iteration*, an infinite range of sound–meaning correspondence' (italics added). The logic of this escapes me. Transformational-generative grammars may not be construed as performance (or even production) models *per se* because under such an interpretation they must have some property akin to recursiveness (which they do), and also the added feature of selectivity (or non-randomness of generation), something which all standard or Chomskyan generative grammars – the models of 'genera-

---

[1] See also Schwarcz (1967, p. 41) and Saporta (1965, pp. 99–100).

tive syntax' – demonstrably lack.[1] Hence generative grammars (of the Chomskyan variety) are excluded *in principle* from serving in the capacity in question.

There are other features which any acceptable model of linguistic performance must possess and which generative grammars also lack. To keep our discussion within bounds, let us consider only one. Let us assume, with Chomsky, that the ultimate integrated performance model will contain a single central linguistic component which is *common* to both language production (encoding) and perception (decoding); (see, e.g. Miller and Chomsky, 1963, p. 422).[2] Now under this interpretation the linguistic model (or component) must also possess the property of *bidirectionality* (or interchangeability); that is, it must be capable both of translating semantic representations into phonetic ones (on the production or encoding side) and interpreting phonetic representations in terms of semantic ones (on the perception or decoding side). Both of these active and dynamic processes are obviously required of any fully articulated overall model of linguistic performance.[3] Yet

[1] One way to meet this difficulty would be to change the model from one in which the syntactic component is central (as in Chomsky's 'standard' approach) to one in which the semantic component is the generative source. In such a case, the sentence generated in any particular instance would presumably be predetermined (up to free variation) by the initial choice of semantic representations. Such 'generative semantic' models have been proposed in recent years as off-shoots of the transformational-generative tradition, but still as models of 'competence' in Chomsky's highly restricted sense (i.e. they have not been proposed for the reasons indicated). Though such models remain insufficiently explicit to allow for much in the way of critical evaluation, they also appear to fail under the interpretation in question on other grounds. For one thing, like Chomsky's 'standard' models, they lack the further requisite feature of bidirectionality (not to mention a self-monitoring capacity and other characteristics; see the discussion below). Moreover, as alternative models of linguistic 'competence' in their own right, they also suffer from the same logical and conceptual defects of their Chomskyan predecessors (see 8.2 and 8.3 below).

[2] This suggested 'common' aspect of the otherwise *disparate* processes of language production and perception is presumably what is often referred to loosely in the literature as the 'linguistic code', i.e. that general *consensus* achieved between speaker and hearer which makes effective communication possible. (Chomsky, however, might disagree on this, holding that speech production and speech perception are 'essentially the same' (1957b, p. 48).)

[3] Chafe, who also proposes a model in which semantics is generative (cf. n. 1 above) and hence one which would appear capable in principle of satisfying the two fundamental requirements of creativity and selectivity, explicitly rejects the bidirectionality characteristic in favor of a 'directionality of well-formedness' (1970, pp. 57–9). All he apparently means by this is that the speaker initiates the communication act and it is meaning which is communicated (1971, p. 8). Chafe apparently overlooks the important point that no meaning actually resides in an utterance *per se*, but is imposed on the utterance by the hearer (correctly or incorrectly) as part of a process of inter-

this requirement, though also fundamental, cannot be met by any version of what may properly be called TGG.[1] In particular, no grammatical model which incorporates a phrase-structure (or constituent-structure 'rewrite') component, for example, is capable in principle of satisfying the requirement, because the relation represented by the symbol → in all such grammars is defined as being, among other things, *asymmetric* (Chomsky & Miller, 1963, p. 292). Thus, as F. W. Householder, Jr, has put it (personal communication), the one–many relation proceeding from left to right is represented directly in the PS-rules, but the one–many relation from right to left can be found only by searching through the rules. Moreover, it is clear that the *transformational* relation is also to be interpreted in this way, i.e. as specifying a *unidirectional* process or operation (see, e.g. Chomsky, 1961).[2] So Schwarcz observes that 'the second problem in parsing with transformational grammars is that the reverse transformations and their ordering are not explicitly specified, and in some cases it may be impossible to specify some of them' (1967, p. 42).[3]

In sum, then, a transformational-generative grammar is inherently incapable of serving as an idealized model of linguistic performance because it lacks certain properties which any model of this sort must possess. Of the three important properties under discussion, a generative grammar has only the property of *recursiveness* (or creativity), so

pretation which is as active, dynamic and even 'creative' as that by which the speaker attempted to impose his intention 'into' the original phonetic signal in the first place. It is as reasonable to talk about 'well-formed phonetic structures' (those having one or more semantic representations associated with them in the hearer model) as to talk about well-formed semantic ones (those having one or more phonetic realizations in the speaker model). In short, a fully specified model of linguistic performance will have to account for both state transformations of the communication act (from meaning to sound and from sound to meaning). And I see no ground for divorcing the notion of a 'linguistic description' from this performance model (see 9.1.1).

[1] The only reasonably explicit linguistic models which I know which do appear capable of satisfying this requirement in principle – or which even recognize that bidirectionality must be incorporated in the model – are the 'stratificational' model of Lamb (see Lamb, 1966a and Gleason, 1964, especially pp. 75 and 90–1) and the 'equational' grammar of Sanders (1970). See also Sigurd (1970, p. 18).

[2] This is to be contrasted with Harris' original notion of transformational rule which was bidirectional (see Z. Harris, 1957).

[3] Chomsky has argued that this sort of directionality is not meaningful (see especially Chomsky, 1970a, and pp. 288–90 below), presenting a model which is said, once again, to be absolutely 'neutral' with respect to either the speaker or the hearer. Thus, under Chomsky's own interpretation, a generative grammar makes no provision for the language production or the language perception processes, but merely generates (i.e. enumerates) sentences in the formal mathematical sense.

limiting its capabilities under a fully (and in Chomsky's view, un-warranted; see p. 269, n. 3) dynamic interpretation to serving at best as a model of *random sentence production*; such a grammar has no possible interpretation as a model of speech *perception* of *any* sort.[1] To the extent, therefore, that some researchers (notably psychologists) have been attracted to TGG in the hope of gaining insight into the processes of normal speech production and/or perception, they are bound to be disappointed, for, by his own admission, Chomsky's model of linguistic 'competence' has nothing to say about either of these processes.

8.1.2   Competence as a central component of an idealized performance model.

So far we have managed to establish one thing which a competence model is *not* – it is not (and cannot be) an idealized model of linguistic performance in and of itself. We have yet to see what such a model *does* represent. Fortunately, other interpretations are possible. One was suggested as early as 1963 by Miller and Chomsky, who proposed to construct a model for the language user that 'incorporates a generative grammar as a fundamental component' (p. 465). 'No doubt,' Chomsky asserts, 'a reasonable model of language use will incorporate, as a basic component, the generative grammar that expresses the speaker–hearer's knowledge of the language; but this generative grammar does not, in itself, prescribe the character or functioning of a perceptual model or a model of speech production' (1965a, p. 9).[2]

---

[1] None of these observations is original. Gleason, for example, as early as 1964 (p. 91) wrote that: 'A transformational-generative grammar is theoretically designed to do just one thing – to generate sentences.' Actually, few advocates have been able to maintain consistence in distinguishing 'generate' in the sense of 'enumerate' or 'define' from 'generate' in the sense of 'produce'. In fact, their grammars are readily adaptable to a second function, *the random production of sentences*. All that is necessary is to read the arrow as 'rewrite as' instead of 'consists of' or the like (italics added). Gleason also recognized the desirability of developing a model which formalized 'the processes of *both* transductions through language' (pp. 90–1), i.e. 'from experience to sound and from sound to experience' (p. 75) and saw that 'a transformational-generative grammar has insuperable difficulty with one of the two' (p. 91). (Gleason fails to distinguish between the constituent-structure and the transformational 'arrows' in the first citation above, but this has no effect on his conclusions.)

[2] This assertion has been stated in progressively stronger terms as time goes by:

(1) 'A perceptual model that does not incorporate a descriptively adequate generative grammar *cannot be taken very seriously*' (Chomsky, 1964, p. 114; italics added).

(2) 'The grammatical rules that generate phonetic representations of signals with their semantic interpretations do not constitute a model for the production of sentences, although any such model *must* incorporate the system of grammatical rules' (Chomsky, 1967a, p. 399; italics added).

(3) 'A theory of performance *will necessarily* incorporate the grammar, but will also

In the first major published paper to pursue this particular line of inquiry, Miller and Chomsky (1963) summed up the current state of development of 'finitary models of language users' which incorporate generative grammars:

We have suggested that a generative grammar can give a useful and informative characterization of the competence of the speaker–hearer... The question [now before us] is, therefore, *how does he put his knowledge to use in producing a desired sentence or in perceiving and interpreting the structure of presented utterances?* How can we construct a model for the language user that incorporates a generative grammar as a fundamental component? This topic has received almost no study, so we can do little more than introduce a few speculations (pp. 464–5, italics added).

They suggested a few, which all involved the postulation of

a component M that contains rules for generating a matching signal... components to analyze and (temporarily) to store the input,...a heuristic component that could make a good first guess, a component to make the comparison of the input and the internally generated signals, and perhaps others (p. 465).

Though rather schematic, the general nature of the proposed link between the competence model C (the generative grammar) and the remaining components of a more general performance model P is presumed to be the familiar one of *analysis by synthesis*: the P-model searches through the C-model for a suitable match for the desired output (production) or the available input (perception). In another programmatic paper, Halle and Stevens (1964) attempt to explicate these proposals in connection with the development of a model (specifically) for speech recognition (perception). They point out the necessity of including in their model a whole 'group of components performing the functions of storage, preliminary analysis, comparison, and control', which they lump together as 'strategy' (p. 610). The purpose of these components is to cut down the time required to pair a given input signal with that internally generated signal which provides the best match for it (p. 607), since it seems obvious that a model which involved a simple *random* search among *randomly* generated internal signals would be highly deficient; human speech recognition evidently does not involve the potentially infinite delays required by such a model (also see Katz & Postal, 1964, p. 167, and Fodor & Garrett, 1966, pp. 139–40). Hence

attempt to study the many other factors that determine the actual physical signal. Any investigation of grammar *is*, then, a contribution to the study of performance, but it does not exhaust this study' (Chomsky and Halle, 1968, p. 110; italics added).

the need for additional components to perform a preliminary analysis, store the input signal, and engage in a more systematic search for an appropriate match. Their general conclusion is, however, that:

While certain components in both major stages of analysis can be designed from present knowledge, further research is necessary before the remaining components can be realized and before the system can be designed to function as a whole (p. 611).

Now as a 'model and a program for research', few objections can be made to these proposals; such a 'program' need only satisfy plausibility and practicability requirements to be acceptable. It is what is *done* with such programs that counts. And this is the difficulty: though the proposals are by now nearly ten years old, almost *nothing* has been done with them, as far as one can judge from the published literature. Most linguists seem satisfied with a schematic suggestion as to how a generative grammar *might in principle* be incorporated into a workable model of linguistic performance, and do not seem concerned with the question whether or not such a program can actually be carried out.[1] Consequently, the research program outlined by such people as Halle and Stevens has not been realized, so that the development of models of linguistic performance hardly differs today from the one described by Miller and Chomsky in 1963:

there seems to be little that we can say about the speaker and the hearer beyond the obvious fact that they are limited finite devices that relate sentences and structural descriptions and that they are subject to the constraint that time is linear. From this, all that we can conclude is that self-embedding (and, more generally, nesting of dependencies) should cause difficulty, as indeed it does...Further speculations are, at the present time, quite unsupported (p. 475).

There has been no serious effort made by linguists to develop models of the language user, whether incorporating generative grammars or not. As Chomsky admits, 'the question of how a grammar is used in production or perception of speech is, of course, quite open' (1967d, p. 125).[2]

[1] There are a few notable exceptions. Fromkin (1968), for example, argues that 'the interrelationship between competence and performance is the concern of linguistics' (p. 47) and that linguists must be 'concerned with discovering and explaining how a speaker utilizes his knowledge, his competence, to perform' (p. 49). And such a program must necessarily involve specifying in detail those additional components which Miller and Chomsky (1963), Halle and Stevens (1964), Katz and Postal (1964), Katz (1964) and Chomsky (1965a and 1970a) discuss in only general terms.

[2] It is therefore difficult to understand what basis Chomsky has for the claims made in the sources cited on p. 270, n. 2, above. Presumably, if the issue is truly 'open', one logically possible resolution is that generative grammars play *no role at all* in linguistic performance or language use.

Chomsky's model of linguistic performance, therefore, is hardly more than the 'schema' Steinberg describes as follows:

Chomsky's competence-performance distinction is based on the notion that language knowledge (competence) is to be distinguished from language use (performance). Such accomplishments as the uttering of a sentence are conceived to be the result of an interaction between the *knowledge we have of our language* and various *application factors* such as (1) memory limitations, (2) distractions, (3) shifts of attention and interest, (4) errors, (5) beliefs, and (6) rules for competence use. It is performance which is concerned with the processes of production and understanding. Our language knowledge, competence, is thus considered [just] a part of such processes (1970a, pp. 180–1).[1]

To be sure, factors 1–5 in Steinberg's list might be irrelevant from the point of view of some particular idealized system of linguistic performance (though I have expressed misgivings about the exclusion of item (1) (see p. 240, n. 1) and Fromkin has raised doubts about item (4) (1968, 1971)). Abstracting away from these to an idealized model of language use which incorporates a competence model C, a set of 'heuristics' or 'use rules' H and various 'other components' suggested by Halle and Stevens and others, the overall picture shown by fig. 8.1 emerges.

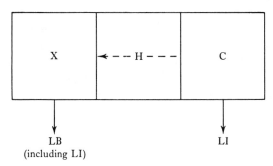

FIG. 8.1   Chomsky's model of linguistic performance

In this framework, the competence model C relates logically only to a highly circumscribed set of (unobservable) behavioral tokens[2] which I have labelled (after Chomsky) 'linguistic intuitions' (LI), i.e. judgments about grammaticality, constituent structure, ambiguity, paraphrase, etc. (cf. fig. 7.1 on p. 253 above). The relation between C and *all*

---

[1] See Chomsky (1969, p. 83) for an explicit acceptance of Steinberg's last sentence.
[2] Hiż (1967, p. 69) appropriately refers to judgments of this sort, as 'introspection about our linguistic performance' and Chomsky admits that such 'judgments about sentences' are to be included under the rubric 'performance' (1969, p. 82).

other aspects of linguistic behavior is mediated by at least two components of unknown character, dimension and scope. The first of these is component H in the diagram, which encompasses the various 'heuristics' referred to by Miller and Chomsky (1963, p. 465), Katz and Postal (1964, pp. 167ff) and Fodor and Garrett (1966, p. 139) and/or the 'use rules' implicit in Chomsky's 1970a paper (see especially p. 58). The second is a catch-all component (labelled X in the diagram) which stands for whatever other components or properties (over and above the ill-defined component H and the relatively well-defined component C) an empirically adequate performance model incorporating C might require. (So little work has been done on models of this sort that even the suggested division into 'components' is decidedly artificial; my purpose here is to suggest the extent to which such models remain unspecified.) Whatever the details, the important point is this: by no stretch of the imagination can there be said to exist any direct or well-specified logical link within the overall model between the chief object of linguistic investigation (the generative grammar or competence model C) and the data of linguistic behavior or language use (except for that sub-class of such behaviors called 'linguistic intuitions'). Only the component C of the performance model is specified in any explicit way, while the remaining components are merely assumed to exist and to be operative; thus the way in which the (presumably central) C-component even interrelates or 'interacts' (Chomsky, 1968a, p. 23) with the other components is not indicated. It is therefore impossible to make logical inferences about linguistic behavior in general (with the small class of exceptions already noted) from properties of the competence model C; equally, no particular conclusions are to be drawn from the observed facts of linguistic behavior about the appropriate form and structure of grammars.[1] There is a crippling *inferential gap*[2]

---

[1] Cf. Fodor (1971): '[W]hat is at issue is the problem of characterizing the relationship between the "performance" devices psychologists investigate and the "competence models" that grammarians study. In particular, *at present there exists no satisfactory account of the relationship between a grammar capable of recursively enumerating the sentences and their structural descriptions, and a device (a performance model) capable of simulating the speaker/hearer by recognizing and integrating utterances of sentences*' (p. 121, italics added). See also Schlesinger (1971, pp. 63ff).

[2] The term is from P. Harris (1970, p. 7): 'The difficulties I find in Chomsky's position are of two main sorts: (1) conceptual – notions like "competence", "performance", and "intuition" demand explication, and (2) logical – there is what might be called an *inferential gap* between linguistic formalisms and observable events; indeed, the logical apparatus necessary to bridge this gap is not part of the theoretical structure as such (italics added).

between the linguist's grammar and the bulk of the observable facts of linguistic behavior. Transformational-generative linguistic models, in other words, do not make predictions about linguistic behavior directly (i.e. by logical implication), but only in a way which Chomsky himself has recently called 'no more than intuitive' or 'suggestive' (1970a, p. 58). As a consequence, even abstracting away from such supposedly 'grammatically irrelevant factors' as those listed in Steinberg's characterization above, we find we are still in no position to adopt Chomsky and Halle's suggestion to 'think of the study of competence as the study of the *potential performance* of an idealized speaker–hearer who is unaffected by such...factors' (1968, p. 3; italics added).[1] Nor has Chomsky any basis for claiming that a generative grammar (or C-model) characterizes 'the knowledge of the language that *provides the basis for actual use of language* by a speaker–hearer' (1965a, p. 9, and many other places; italics added). Chomsky denies that a generative grammar does this directly. But to defend the assertion that a generative grammar does this even indirectly, Chomsky must surely be required to specify the details of the operation of the components H and X in fig. 8.1, i.e. in his (implicit) idealized performance model. Until he does so, i.e. until he can demonstrate at least that a generative grammar is capable in principle of functioning as an integral part of some workable performance model which overcomes the difficulties discussed in 8.1 and which does not involve the inferential gaps of which we are now speaking, we must again agree with Chomsky's assessment that grammars tell us literally 'nothing' about how sentences are either produced or understood (1965a, p. 9). Chomsky's competence/performance distinction, in sum, involves far more than mere abstraction away from such 'grammatically irrelevant factors' as those listed by Steinberg;[2] a great

---

[1] Chomsky is not consistent on this point. As part of his attempt in 1964 to 'clarify' the competence/performance distinction, he remarks (p. 52) that 'clearly the description of intrinsic competence provided by the grammar is not to be confused with an account of actual performance...*Nor is it to be confused with an account of potential performance*' (italics added). Chomsky wants his model to be interpreted as having something useful (even explanatory) to say about language use – and, in particular, about the ability of a mature speaker to 'produce a new sentence of his language on the appropriate occasion' and for other speakers to 'understand it immediately, although it is equally new to them' (p. 50), yet, when interrogated specifically on the point of whether his C-model is to be interpreted as a model of language use (albeit idealized), he consistently backs away (and lately he has been backpedaling at an accelerated rate; see Chomsky, 1970a, for example). Is it any wonder that Chomsky's commentators are confused on this point?

[2] Cf. Lyons (1966, p. 394): 'The distinction between linguistic "competence" and

deal of important *additional* structure is also hidden under item 6, in particular, *all that structure which is required to demonstrate whether generative grammars play any significant role in language use or not.* On the matter of developing explicit models of linguistic performance, therefore, it is difficult to see how Chomsky, too, 'attempts to go beyond traditional grammar in a fundamental way' (1966b, p. 4).

How, then, are we to evaluate such claims as the following: 'Obviously, every speaker of a language has mastered and internalized a generative grammar that expresses his knowledge of his language' (1965a, p. 8)? First, there is no way of assessing this 'knowledge' directly (since such 'knowledge' is 'tacit' or 'unconscious' and therefore inaccessible to introspection). Now we also find that generative grammars are insulated inferentially from nearly all aspects of actual language use. The *only* data which can be logically related to a generative grammar are that small and relatively uninteresting subclass of behaviors commonly called 'linguistic intuitions'– and these refer only to interpretations placed upon the output of a generative grammar, not to the inner workings of the model.[1] So how can one decide whether or not any particular characterization of this 'knowledge' is correct? He cannot, except on some set of arbitrary 'evaluation' criteria (as already noted in 7.2.3).

Yet Chomsky pushes his claims further. In *Aspects*, for example, he claims that 'a child who has learned a language has developed an internal representation of a system of rules that determine how sentences are to be formed, used, and understood' (1965a, p. 25) and that a generative grammar specifies 'the underlying system of rules that has been mastered by the speaker–hearer and that he puts to use in actual performance' (p. 4). What empirical basis is there for such claims? What 'system of rules' has been shown to 'underlie' linguistic performance in the sense of being demonstrably 'put to use' in determining 'how sentences are to be formed, used, and understood'? Obviously, it would require a fully articulated model of linguistic *performance* which incorporated some particular set of *performance* rules and which was consistent with those major aspects of language use

linguistic "performance" is overworked: too many aspects of language are lumped together as "performance" and dismissed as linguistically irrelevant.'

[1] It would not be proper to argue that a generative grammar is even concerned with accounting for the form of actual utterances, since it is generally assumed by transformationalists that only those utterances which are construed by them to be fully 'grammatical' are within the province of grammar (but see Lakoff, 1970). Thus even the notion 'the form of utterances' is highly contaminated in TGG by the notion 'linguistic intuition'.

outlined in 8.1 to make a case along these lines. Chomsky has only one argument in defense of these claims: he has devised a unidirectional recursive system of rules which randomly generates 'grammatical' sentences and their structural descriptions, etc. as output. Hence this system (or some system like it) *must* serve as part of the basis for language use, though no attempt has been made to demonstrate a connection between the two. The logic of this argument, too, escapes me.[1]

Now if generative grammars are as empirically uninteresting as this, why should linguists have devoted so much effort to their construction? Of what possible utility is a 'competence' model, after all, apart from an associated performance model? The argument Chomsky himself usually offers is that an issue of 'logical priority' is involved. Claims of this sort go back to the Chomsky and Miller collaborations of 1963:

The first of our three basic questions concerns the nature of language itself. In order to answer it, we must make explicit the underlying structure inherent in all natural languages. The principal attack on this problem has its origins in logic and linguistics; in recent years it has focused on the critically important concept of grammar. The justification for including this work in the present handbook is to make psychologists more realistically aware of what it is a person has accomplished when he has learned to speak and understand a natural language (pp. 271–2).

Thus, it is asserted, the linguist must first 'isolate and study the system of *linguistic competence* that underlies behavior but that is not realized in any direct or simple way in behavior' (Chomsky, 1968a, p. 4), since the 'investigation of performance will proceed only so far as understanding of underlying competence permits' (1965a, p. 10). But is this not difficult to accept, given that it is not clear in what sense linguistic

---

[1] Chomsky says elsewhere (in Hook, 1969, pp. 154–5): 'As to the question...why one should say "that a speaker of a language has an unconscious knowledge of the rules of his grammar" when we do not make an analogous statement about the "unconscious knowledge of the principles of mechanics" by the bicycle rider, I think the answer is simple...[W]e do not attribute knowledge of mechanics to the bicycle rider if in fact this assumption does not help explain his ability to ride a bicycle; we *do* attribute knowledge of the rules of grammar to the speaker–hearer *if* this assumption does contribute to an explanation of *his ability to use a language*. Or, to eliminate the irrelevant reference to the skill of the bicycle rider, the answer is, simply: we postulate that a speaker of a language has an unconscious knowledge of the rules of grammar *if* this postulate is empirically justified *by the role it plays in explaining the facts of use and understanding and acquisition of language*' (italics added). Yet it has never been shown that any grammar plays such a role. So we conclude (with Chomsky?) that there is no empirical basis for attributing 'knowledge of the rules of [a transformational-generative] grammar to the speaker–hearer' (cf. P. Harris, 1970, p. 26).

competence (in Chomsky's restricted sense) may be said to 'underlie behavior' in the first place (since it is not even proposed as a model of behavior)? Such arguments are necessarily question-begging: what justification can there be at the outset for asserting that the rules of any competence model represent 'the knowledge of the language that provides the basis for actual use of language' (Chomsky, 1965a, p. 9)? Or that, as a consequence, 'generative grammars...must be the "output" of an acquisition model for language' (p. 57)? Or that any reasonable performance model 'must' incorporate a competence model as a central (or even essential) component? There is none. The arguments are *mere* assertion, unsupported by evidence. In order to support such claims one must first *demonstrate* that such a P-model can at least be constructed, and to do so in such a way that the unified model can be tested against a set of essential facts related to normal language use. Therefore, any 'logical priorities' involved must surely work in just the opposite direction than Chomsky suggests: C-models can only be justified in terms of role they play in the construction of P-models, not the reverse.[1] Yet no explicit and testable P-model which incorporates a C-model even exists.

On occasion, Chomsky recognizes that this problem exists: 'Honesty forces us to admit,' he says (1968a, p. 11), 'that we are as far today as Descartes was three centuries ago from understanding just what enables a human to speak in a way that is innovative, free from stimulus control, and also appropriate and coherent.' The reason is explicit in his next sentence: 'This is a serious problem that *the psychologist and biologist must ultimately face* and that cannot be talked out of existence ...' (italics added). Why not the linguist? Presumably, he has already done his part in specifying (what is asserted to be) the central component of whatever P-model must ultimately be developed by these outsiders, following basic guidelines supplied to them by the linguist, and it is the task of these other investigators in other fields to show how the C-model will fit in. But it should by now be obvious that the task of specifying the internal structure of the components H and X in fig. 8.1 will not be a routine matter of 'polishing off of rough edges', and may well involve more difficulties than it would to scrap the unmotivated

---

[1] Consider the suggestion implicit in Chomsky (1970a, p. 58) that 'any number' of equivalent C-models might be envisioned which could be incorporated into a given P-model; the reverse is also true (cf. Chomsky, 1967a, p. 436). It is useless to attempt to consider the two notions separately if decisions are to be made on other than arbitrary grounds.

C-model concept and to begin work on an appropriate P-model un-hampered by the *a priori* constraint of having to work in a C-model which generates sentences randomly and unidirectionally. In any event, the view that the construction of P-models (presumably of a type which incorporates C-models, which is axiomatic to the generative gram-marian) is the province of the psychologist, and not of the linguist, is a popular one among linguists today, as can be seen from the following remarks of Fodor and Garrett (1966, p. 138):

The question of HOW linguistic information is put to use in the production or processing of sentences is left to the psychologist. *His* problem is to construct a 'performance model' where this means not a model of behavior but a model of how the speaker's linguistic information [the C-model] interacts with other psychological mechanisms in the production of behavior (italics added).

Schlesinger (1967, pp. 399–400) demolishes this view in his commentary on the exchange between Bever, Fodor and Weksel (1965a and 1965b) and Braine (1963 and 1965):

They [Bever *et al.*] see linguistics as providing a '...part of the total theory of language behavior' (p. 494). Thus, since linguists take account of behavioral data (other than those pertaining to language as a corpus of utterances), the boundary between linguistics and psychology can no longer be as clearly drawn as it can according to the [Bloomfieldian] view described above, and the relationship between psychological and linguistic models can become a problem.

What, then, is the task of the psychologist? Bever *et al.* do not give any explicit answer to this question, but the standpoint implicit in their paper seems to be somewhat as follows: The linguist constructs a model of language competence, and it remains for the psychologist to explain what makes the linguistic model work. Hence, Braine's theory and similar theories can be taken to task for being in principle unable to show how a child acquires the information about language contained in the linguistic model. An explicit statement of this view has been made by one of Bever's co-authors (Weksel, 1965). The theory of competence, according to him, 'has specified' *what* the child learns, and the psychologist who 'attempts to' account for language learning must show *how* it is learnt. Therefore, the theory of competence 'rules out what appear to be fruitless approaches'. Weksel does not seem to be aware that it would be just as reasonable...to argue that a theory specifying *how* language is learned can serve to evaluate theories describing *what* is learnt.[1]

He [Weksel] does not show on what his claim of the primacy of the linguistic model rests...[Presumably] linguistics 'has specified' already what linguistic

---

[1] Note that this is precisely the alternative approach which I have adopted in this book (see especially 3.5 and 6.2).

competence consists of, and the psychologist, who is a newcomer, and only 'attempts' to show how language learning proceeds, must accommodate himself to the rules which the linguist has laid down once and for all. This approach imputes to the linguistic model a finality no scientific theory can be said to have.

The 'logical priority' argument, then, is pure hand-waving: no one has ever demonstrated either that generative grammars 'are acquired by the learner and put to use by the speaker or hearer' or even that they 'provide the devices that are employed...in the production and understanding of speech' or 'underlie the observed use of language' in any way. And there is surely no way of demonstrating (i.e. empirically, or in *a posteriori* rather than in *a priori* fashion) 'what facts about a speaker's language underlie his ability to communicate with others in that language' without first developing a model which shows how this linguistic 'knowledge' is 'put into operation to achieve communication' (cf. Katz, 1964, p. 130).[1] And, by the same token (and this is Katz's own argument) the development of a well-specified P-model is also an essential prerequisite to the development of any testable theory of language acquisition, since such a theory seeks to explain 'how a non-verbal infant who is exposed in the normal way to a sample of sentences and non-sentences, and perhaps other data as well, comes to possess a linguistic description and procedures of sentence recognition and sentence production' (pp. 130–1), i.e. to explain how he comes to possess a performance model. The output of a language acquisition model is not, in short, 'a

[1] Yet many linguists and psychologists seem willing to grant Chomsky his main premise regarding the essential primacy (and inviolability) of C-models. Fromkin, for example, in formulating her plea that more work be done on P-models, writes in terms of the need to specify how the speaker of a language 'utilizes the rules he *has learned*' and argues that the construction of such P-models 'should be considered as falling *as fully* within the realm of linguistics as the construction of a competence model' (1968, pp. 47 and 48, respectively; italics added in both cases). Fromkin writes almost as though there were a need to justify or defend performance models, as if there were some doubt or question as to *their* status.

In turn, Sutherland, a psychologist, at the end of a largely critical commentary on Fodor and Garrett's (1966) paper and the principles which underlie it, still feels obliged to concede (while 'crossing himself') that 'thanks to the work of Chomsky..., Halle, and others, our knowledge of competence is at a much more advanced stage at present than our knowledge of the [performance] mechanism...Although *we know what [speakers] are competent to do*, we still have no very clear idea of the mechanism by which they do it. Although people do follow rules in carrying out other tasks, the rules followed in language behavior are much more complex than in any other kind of behavior; and it is Chomsky's great achievement *to have given us a systematic account of these rules*' (in Lyons and Wales, 1966 p. 162; italics added). But, how do we *know* that 'the rules which Chomsky has given us' correctly specify 'what speakers are competent to do' or are 'the rules followed in language behavior'? We don't.

generative grammar' (or a C-model alone), but rather a fully specified P-model, which (if it incorporates a C-model at all) must also specify how this C-model (in Schlesinger's terms) 'works'. It is the structure of the overall P-model which is crucial, and the ultimate viability (not to mention simplicity)[1] of C-models can only be determined in this larger context. Or, as Schwarcz puts it, 'the dictum that performance is to be considered a reflection of competence is to be supplemented by the converse dictum that *competence must be viewed as something that can effectively lead to performance*' (1967, p. 51; italics added).

8.1.3 Competence as an independent abstract entity remote from linguistic performance.
I conclude that the first order of business for linguistic theory is the construction of tentative models of linguistic performance. It is a matter of indifference, really, who does the work, though I suspect that the best approach would be for linguists and psychologists to collaborate on the problem (see 9.2). But at least it is clear that a great deal of work has to be done by somebody before *anybody* can defend any serious claims relating to 'the underlying system of rules that has been mastered by the speaker–hearer and that he puts to use in actual performance' or anything of that sort. Two general approaches to this problem are implicit in the previous discussion. The first is that one might be inclined, despite the difficulties, to accept Chomsky's notion of competence (the C-model) as potentially viable and to set out to develop a workable and testable P-model which incorporates a generative grammar in some specific way (i.e. to attempt to specify the internal structure of the components H and X in fig. 8.1 above). This is the position advocated by Fromkin (1968), who sees the problem of developing performance models within linguistics as equivalent to the task of specifying the 'interrelationship' between competence (the C-model) and performance (an overall P-model).

This course does have inherent advantages. It minimizes the 're-tooling' problem associated with any paradigmatic shift (cf. Kuhn, 1962, p. 76), since it would not require that linguists change drastically any of their major theoretical notions, but merely endeavor to add more structure to them. Thus this approach makes it possible to 'cut one's

---

[1] Cf. Schlesinger (1967, p. 401): 'Even if it is true that the assumption of underlying structures currently made by linguists provides the simplest explanation, some of this simplicity may have to be sacrificed for the sake of the simplicity of an overall theory of language behavior (cf. Braine, 1965, 490, n. 6, who makes essentially the same point).'

losses': it would not require the abandonment of all that work of the past decade and a half which has been concentrated upon the construction of competence models of the Chomskyan sort. Yet there are also risks associated with this course. In particular, if competence models (in the Chomskyan sense) should prove incapable of the ultimate task assigned to them, i.e. if they should prove to be incompatible with any workable model of linguistic performance (or, at best, compatible only under forced accommodation), then one can only foresee another decade or two washed down the drain along with a good deal of the first. For what is at issue in this discussion are such fundamental matters as the appropriate goals and methods for an entire discipline, and questions of such import ought not be dealt with perfunctorily. So let us suppose that before we embark on another great adventure along 'competence' lines, we stop long enough to ask ourselves a couple of questions: 'How difficult is it likely to be to develop P-models which incorporate C-models as an essential component?' and 'How reasonable a line of inquiry is this, given the facts already at our disposal?' I shall argue in this section that present evidence suggests that the answer to the second question must be 'not very reasonable', and hence that the answer to the first is likely to be 'very difficult indeed'.

Although it is true that Chomsky has insisted from almost the beginning that an important distinction had to be made between a model of language use and his own proposals about generative grammar, it is clear that (until recently) he also felt that there must be a close connection between the two. In 1963, for example, Miller and Chomsky suggest that:

The psychological plausibility of a transformational model of the language user would be strengthened..., if it could be shown that our performance on tasks requiring an appreciation of the structure of transformed sentences is some function of the nature, number, and complexity of the grammatical transformations involved (p. 481).

Even as late as 1967, while now admitting that 'the question of how a grammar is used in production or perception of speech is...open', Chomsky still persisted in the view that 'it is not unreasonable to assume, as a first approximation, that the process will increase in complexity as the number of applicable grammatical rules increases' (1967d, p. 125, n. 21). Others have restated this idea in the following way:

If...the grammar is involved in sentence processing in anything like the way that analysis-by-synthesis models suggest, then we have a right to expect a very general correspondence between such formal features of derivational histories as, for instance, length in rules, and such performance parameters as perceptual complexity, ease of recall, and so on (Fodor and Garrett, 1966, p. 141).

Psychologists were quick to seize on this suggestion, dubbing it (among other things) the 'Derivational Theory of Complexity',[1] and a series of experimental studies were carried out in order to assess its general feasibility. Interestingly, except for a few early and relatively unsophisticated and uncontrolled studies, almost all serious work along these lines has yielded spectacularly negative results. (For details, see the summaries provided by Fodor and Garrett, 1966; Bever, 1968; and Watt, 1970. An independent yet equally significant study not mentioned in any of these papers is Fagan, 1969.) Watt sums up this whole effort as a series of experiments 'designed to show, not whether performance mirrored competence' in all, most, or even many respects, but merely to show 'whether performative complexity mirrored competence complexity' (1970, p. 144). This question is a weaker version of a more general 'Correlation Hypothesis' which might state that the 'linguist's grammar' and a 'mental grammar' were similar in many important respects (p. 138); thus, even 'if it were upheld, the stronger version would remain still in doubt; but, (of more immediate importance) if it were disconfirmed then the stronger version would be seriously threatened' (p. 144). By 1970, clearly, this hypothetical threat had become real and troublesome (at least to psychologists). Stated in terms of the frame of reference provided in 8.2, Chomsky's original suggestion that the relationship (or 'interactions') between the C-model (or component) and the overall P-model must be close or straightforward amounted to a suggestion that the contribution of the added components H and X must be relatively insignificant. But now it is seen that this suggestion fails to hold even when so crude a measure as *general sentence complexity* is utilized for purposes of comparison between the two domains, i.e. between the C-model and the facts of linguistic behavior which this model is said to 'underlie'. We must therefore conclude that in any P-model which incorporates a C-model as a fundamental component, the contribution of the unspecified components H and X is going to be more substantial than originally assumed. In effect, these

---

[1] The 'transformational decoding hypothesis' (Gough, 1966) or simply the 'coding hypothesis' (Bever, 1968) have also been suggested for different versions of the same general idea, but the term used here (following Watt, 1970) appears the favorite.

added components must drastically change and/or reorder the rules of the generative grammar if anything approaching the proper predictions are to follow from the overall model as it relates to the facts of language use.

Hence the question raised by Steinberg (1970a), that if the effect of Chomsky's 'governing use rules' is anything like what it seems to be from the above account, what is the point of having the C-model in the first place? Take the matter of rule-ordering, discussed by Chomsky (1970a), as a case in point. Steinberg asks:

> If a person is presumed to have one order of competence rules for production and another for understanding, why would he still need another order, that of Chomsky's model of competence? The postulation of the existence of an organization of language knowledge such as Chomsky's is *theoretically super-fluous*. A competence model where language knowledge is *ordered [directly] for performance* is all that is required (p. 187, italics added).

In other words, given that a C-model may not serve as P-model directly, and also given that no known C-model may serve even as a component of a P-model without having to be substantially altered by the effects of the remaining components H and/or X, why need we think that a generative grammar must find some natural place in the P-model at all? I find no good answer to this question. As far as I can see, the linguist (and the occasional psychologist who has been led to believe that the linguists have evidence to support their extravagant claims)[1] is saddled with models of 'linguistic competence' for one reason: because early in his career Chomsky saw the usefulness of the analogy between the notion of a formal language (as known in mathematics within the theory of recursive functions or, more specifically, automata theory), and a natural language. On this analogy, a natural language could be construed as a set of sentences (an interpretation not far removed from a traditional one held by many linguists) and an explicit and recursive generative system devised for these, just as for their formal analogues in mathematics. From this point it was only a step to look for a useful *psychological* analogue to the new generative system.[2] For reasons already

---

[1] An influential example is Jenkins, one of whose 'reflections on the conference' as reported in Smith and Miller (1966) was that 'the paradigm of the [generative] grammarian will soon be seen to be the most fruitful way for both linguist and psychologist to approach language' (p. 349). Another is provided by Deese, whose most recent book (1970) is a classic (though often muddled) illustration of how many of Chomsky's unsupported assertions have been picked up by others and converted into facts.

[2] But, as P. Harris has observed, there is 'something very questionable about con-

noted, the most desirable candidate, 'model of linguistic performance', would not work directly, so something new had to be devised, and the idiosyncratic notion 'model of linguistic competence' associated with Chomsky thus came into being – all by way of analogy. There is no *a priori* probability that generative grammars have any useful empirical interpretation and it becomes increasingly obvious that such grammars may be mere historical artifacts which failed to pan out, i.e. arbitrary descriptive devices for a corpus of sentences and structural descriptions which are of no psychological significance.

This was the conclusion drawn by Fodor and Garrett in 1966 (though they construed the matter differently). For what Fodor and Garrett did was to present experimental evidence against Chomsky's early suggestion that 'a performance model ought to consist of a model of linguistic competence (a grammar) plus some further component or components at present unknown' (1966a, p. 138). From this they concluded that a generative grammar must represent only an axiomatization of sentences and their structural descriptions,[1] such that only the structural descriptions which the grammar assigns have empirical (or psychological) reality, but not the operations or rules 'whereby grammars generate structural descriptions' (p. 152).[2]

Bever, in a later paper (1968), reaches the same conclusion on the basis of more experimental evidence:

The result of these studies is that behavioral processes manipulate linguistically-defined structures but do not mirror or simulate grammatical processes. The import of this is to invalidate the perceptual interest of any speech recognition routine which attempts to incorporate directly grammatical pro-

---

structing an elegant formal algebraic theory and then searching for a psychological model (with appropriate quantifiable variables) to tack on as confirmation' (1970, p. 65). Cf. p. 233 above.

[1] Chomsky himself frequently adopts this position. In *Aspects*, for example, Chomsky states that 'by a generative grammar I mean *simply* a system of rules that in some explicit and well-defined way assigns structural descriptions to sentences' (1965a, p. 8; italics added), and on the next page he says that 'when we speak of a grammar as generating a sentence with a certain structural description, we mean *simply* that the grammar assigns this structural description to the sentence' (italics added).

[2] The extent and significance of the disparity between this view and that of Katz (1964) can hardly be exaggerated. Katz's position was that 'every aspect of the mentalistic theory involves psychological reality' (p. 133); now Fodor and Garrett opt instead for the view that *no* aspect of the theory is to be so interpreted (except for the sentences and their [surface] structural descriptions which serve as output). Chomsky's own position is ambiguous but one can detect a tendency in his recent work to align himself with the extreme abstractionist view of Fodor and Garrett, as shown below.

cesses as part of its recognition process...That is, linguistically isolated *structures* are reflected in behavior, but not linguistically postulated *processes* (p. 15).

In his most recent formulation of this idea, therefore, Fodor allows that 'the mental operations which underlie the behavior of the speaker/ hearer are not identical to, *and probably do not include*, the grammatical operations involved in generating sentences' (1971, p. 134; italics added).[1]

So much for the Derivational Theory of Complexity: obviously, there can *be* no such theory if the rules in generative grammars have no empirical status. Thus the theory of TGG does not have to confront the experimental results which Fodor, Garrett and Bever cite: the C-model can always be saved, if required, by adopting the view proposed by Fodor and Garrett that

an acceptable theory of the relation between competence and performance models will have to represent that relation as abstract, *the degree of abstractness being proportional to the failure of formal features of derivations to correspond to performance variables* (1966, p. 152; italics added).

But under such an extreme 'abstractionist' interpretation the theory of TGG is also relieved of all empirical significance, since the grammar (or C-model) is automatically relegated to a purely formal system which expresses nothing.[2] For current theories of generative grammar do not distinguish themselves noticeably in terms of the novel kinds of (surface constituent) structures which they provide; in fact, except for certain minor differences (which reflect such things as an immediate-constituent vs. a string-constituent bias among pre-generative syntacticians), the structural descriptions which generative grammars assign are virtually identical to those recognized by linguists of practically all

---

[1] Fodor's own proposed 'solution' to this problem is to axiomatize away even the relation between competence and performance, i.e. 'to assume that the child's innate linguistic endowment is *even richer* than most transformational grammarians have supposed. In particular, that the child must be construed as having not merely an innate ability to select a correct grammar of a given natural language on the basis of exposure to a sufficiently rich corpus of primary linguistic data drawn from that language, but also that he must have available procedures for constructing a recognizer/producer for sentences in a language given an appropriate grammar of the language' (p. 137, italics added).

[2] As Chomsky has put it, 'Without principles of interpretation, a formal system expresses nothing at all. What it expresses, what information it provides, is determined by these principles' (1970a, p. 61).

persuasions for a century or more (with some of them traceable even to antiquity).[1] Thus the fact that empirical content is assigned to these structures has no bearing on the empirical significance of one linguistic theory as opposed to any other. It is the unique systematization of (ordered) grammatical rules and operations (together with the set of underlying supposed universal constraints) which is the heart of the transformational-generative model, and the ultimate fate of the theory must rest upon these. (Of what significance is a 'generative explanation', for which no psychological reality is even claimed?) Yet these aspects of the model (the internal workings, as opposed to the data output) are not supported by the experiments in question.

What is more, given the proliferation of uninterpreted theoretical apparatus associated with any generative grammar, it is clear that a great deal of manipulation within the inner workings of the model need not affect the output appreciably – as has become obvious to many linguists (see especially Bach, 1971b, pp. 3–4).[2] When various alternative 'axiomatizations' of this sort are proposed in this way, what is to be done? One suggestion is made by Peters and Ritchie: to enlarge the range of data to be accounted for by the grammar (p. 152). But how is this possible, given 'competence' models of the Chomskyan sort? For as already indicated in 8.1 and 8.2, such models seem to be restricted in principle to the highly circumscribed domain of 'linguistic intuitions'; in particular, they can have no behavioral or performance interpretations or implications beyond this domain (and especially under the conception of grammar here under review). Thus the possible relation to generative grammars of 'the actual data of linguistic performance' (Chomsky, 1965a, p. 18), evidence from 'linguistic change' (Kiparsky, 1968b, pp. 174ff) or of 'borrowings' (Hyman, 1970) and other such potentially 'new sources of data' is at best obscure and is rendered dubious by the same 'inferential gap' I have already discussed (pp. 274–5 above). One can 'enlarge the range of data' which reflects on a compe-

---

[1] But cf. such observers as Hörmann, who associates even the notion of constituent structure specifically with Chomsky's name (1971, p. 244). Such misrepresentations give some idea of the extent to which Chomsky's influence has become dominant in linguistics, particularly to observers from other disciplines.

[2] Cf. Salmon (1967, pp. 115–16): 'The basic trouble with the hypothetico-deductive inference is that it always leaves us with *an embarrassing superabundance of hypotheses*. All of these hypotheses are equally adequate to the available data from the standpoint of the pure hypothetico-deductive framework. Each is confirmed in...the same manner by the same evidence... It is always possible to construct an unlimited supply of hypotheses to fill the bill' (italics added).

tence model only by changing the nature of the model itself so that it is forced to make predictive claims about such data.

This point can best be illustrated by reviewing Chomsky's 1970a paper, which, perhaps more than any other, exposes his own close affiliation with Fodor and Garrett in their movement into abstractness. In this paper Chomsky is primarily concerned with clarifying the status of the so-called 'generative semantic' competence models *vis-à-vis* his own 'standard' theory, in which it is the syntactic component which provides the generative source. One of his major points is the following:

It is easy to be misled into assuming that differently formulated theories actually do differ in empirical consequences, when in fact they are inter-translatable—in a sense, mere notational variants. Suppose, for example, that one were...to counterpose to the 'syntactically-based' standard theory a 'semantically-based' theory of the following sort. Whereas the standard theory supposes that a syntactic structure Σ is mapped onto the pair (P, S) (P a phonetic and S a semantic representation), the new theory supposes that S is mapped onto Σ, which is then mapped onto P as in the standard theory. Clearly, when the matter is formulated in this way, there is no empirical difference between [the two approaches]...The standard theory generates quadruples (P, s, d, S) (P a phonetic representation, s a surface structure, d a deep structure, S a semantic representation). It is meaningless to ask whether it does so by 'first' generating d, then mapping it onto S (on one side) and onto S and then P (on the other); or whether it 'first' generates S..., and then maps it onto d, then s, then P; or, for that matter, whether it 'first' selects the pair (P, d), which is then mapped onto the pair (s, S); etc. At this level of discussion, all of these alternatives are equivalent ways of talking about the same theory. *There is no general notion 'direction of a mapping' or 'order of steps of generation' to which one can appeal* in attempting to differentiate the 'syntactically-based' standard theory from the 'semantically-based' alternative, or either from the 'alternative view' which regards the pairing of surface structure and semantic interpretation as determined by the 'independently selected' pairing of phonetic representation and deep structure, etc. (pp. 56–7; italics added).

Now I disagree that the alternatives in question are only different ways of talking about the 'same theory'. The theories implied by the alternatives in question are very different. Yet Chomsky is correct, I think, in arguing that these different theories do not differ in any of their empirical consequences (since the domain of relevant data to which they are all restricted is so highly circumscribed and uninteresting); hence they would appear to be empirically 'equivalent' (in the sense that they are all equally uninteresting). And this is true for the reason which Chomsky suggests: because the formal differences which distinguish these theories as *theories* are nonetheless meaningless *empirically*, since they involve (theoretical) differences which relate to such things as 'direction of a mapping' and 'order of steps of generation' and the like which, in a 'competence' model, are incapable of having any empirical interpretation associated with them.[1] Hence these theories (and many others) are all empirically non-distinct and can well be called mere 'notational variants' of one another.

But what happened to such 'empirical hypotheses' as notationally based 'evaluation measures' or ordering relations among individual rules of the grammar and the like (cf. Chomsky & Halle, 1965, pp. 109–14)? Is 'the proper balance between various components of the grammar', an 'empirical' (Chomsky, 1970b, p. 185) or a purely 'notational' issue (1970a)? Surely if 'empirically equivalent' reformulations of competence models are possible which involve such drastic reshufflings of the theoretical apparatus as those which Chomsky considers in this paper, then the potential for this sort of juggling within the grammar at lower levels and involving matters of intricate detail is even greater, so increasing the number of such empirically non-distinct 'notational variants' almost indefinitely.[2] Peters and Ritchie (1969), suggest that there is *no limit* to the number of reformulations conceivable.

But what, after all, is the point of opting for a model (such as the so-called 'competence' model) in which such notions as 'direction of a mapping' or 'order of steps of generation' play a role (even a central one) in the formal domain of the theory but which can have no empirical

---

[1] The same is apparently true of such other fundamental notions as 'derivation' and the like. Just what does it mean (empirically) to say that two sentences are 'derived' from some particular underlying structure?

[2] To return to the rule-ordering example, it is clear that any sequence of ordered rules can be written as a list of unordered rules, provided one repeats some information as part of several rules, rather than as part of one. Thus any ordered set of (seemingly simple or general) rules can apparently be rewritten as an unordered list of (seemingly more complex) rules. Yet both would have the same empirical consequences in the final output. Reformulations along these lines would be additional full-fledged 'notational variants' in their own right. What generative grammarians ordinarily do in such cases is to opt for the least complex set of rules on the basis of some arbitrary 'simplicity' or 'evaluation' measure which says that ordering of rules is 'more highly valued' (i.e. inherently less 'expensive' or 'simpler') than relative complexity of (or redundancy in) rules – although this assumption apparently makes the rules in question inherently *unlearnable* by a human organism without positing the prior availability of the full set of 'essential linguistic universals' built into his genes from the start (see especially 5.1, 5.2 and 6.2 for discussion). Rule-ordering is another of those historical artifacts now embedded within the current tradition of descriptive linguistics, this time on loan from historical linguistics, as Chomsky admits (in Sklar, 1968, p. 215).

interpretation associated with them, i.e. which are inherently meaning-less, or, as Chomsky puts it, 'have no more than an intuitive, suggestive role' (1970a, p. 58)? Such questions are especially important in that opting for a competence model of this sort one is preferring it to a *performance* model in which it actually 'makes sense' (as Chomsky puts it) to speak of such things, i.e. where directionality and ordering of choices have a direct and natural interpretation in terms of a hypo-thesized successivity (in real time) of operations which a speaker or a hearer performs in the process of speech encoding or decoding. To borrow from Chomsky, once again: 'Before the standard theory can be compared with [some proposed] modification, it is necessary to formu-late both in such a way that there is an empirical distinction between them' (1970a, p. 57). Yet the only way to accomplish this is to propose such drastic reformulations of current linguistic theories that they can be interpreted directly as models of linguistic performance, so rendering the theoretical apparatus capable of empirical interpretation, and simul-taneously exposing the theory to falsification by the observed facts of language use, thereby enlarging the domain of data relevant to the theory.[1] Only in this case, surely, can progress be anticipated with respect to our current understanding of language and language acquisi-tion.

Now why should linguists have devoted so much time and effort to the articulation of models which are inherently meaningless (since the inner workings of such models seem incapable of empirical interpreta-tion in principle)? Part of the problem, I suspect, has been that few linguists have ever given the matter of 'competence models' and their interpretation much thought, despite the obviously central character of the notion: like Kuhn's trainees in 'normal science', perhaps, young linguists are trained to think in terms of specific kinds of conceptual boxes and can hardly be blamed for accepting them (cf. Agnew & Pyke, 1969, p. 31). Consider also the following remarks by Steinberg, in a paper devoted specifically to the 'notational variants' issue (1970b, pp. 258–9):

---

[1] At present we cannot falsify any particular part of or rule in the grammar, but only the grammar as a whole. Clearly, what is needed is a set of experimental analogues for each rule in the grammar, which might then be tested against the facts of linguistic performance. But since grammars are not models of linguistic performance, cor-respondence formulas of this sort are excluded in principle – hence the problem of 'notational variants'. This is a major difficulty (but see 9.2.1 below for some suggested possible escape routes).

The set of rules, this 'mental reality' called competence, is information which we have of our language and which we tap in order to produce and understand sentences. It is a specification of precisely what language knowledge is stored in the person. Competence is thus a psychological resource which is available for use.

From this account it follows that two grammars which differ in terms of the nature, number, or organization of rules *must necessarily* differ with respect to the knowledge they impute to the human organism, regardless of whether the linguistic functions of the grammars are assessed as equivalent or not. Hence, the child who must master the system of rules known as the Standard Theory must master a different set of rules and thus acquire different knowledge when compared to the child who must master the system of rules which any other grammar might posit. Since any two grammars *necessarily* make different claims with regard to what rules or what specific system of rules a person is said to acquire, a different developmental history of rule acquisition will be required in order to accommodate each of these grammars . . . [Furthermore, since] Chomsky holds that a theory of performance (production or perception) incorporates a theory of competence, i.e. a generative grammar . . ., it then follows that grammars *which differ in any way*, be it in terms of the nature, number, or organization [for the utilization] of its rules, *must require different performance specifications* for the utilization of such knowledge . . . Since different performance specifications represent different empirical claims, an evaluation of the empirical adequacy of such formulations may provide a basis for selection among grammars (italics added).

Implicit in this discussion is the naive assumption that alternative theories must have different empirical consequences associated with them which will eventually serve to distinguish them. If a truly 'important' issue is at stake, I have heard it said, there *must* be empirical consequences *somewhere* to settle the matter. This is extremely unrealistic, for such arguments are only tenable granting one further implicit assumption which may or may not be true of the particular theories or models at issue: this assumption is that such theories or models are fully interpreted. If they are not, the problem of 'notational variants' is automatically introduced in principle and may well arise in practice. On this point I agree with Chomsky: under conditions of less than full empirical interpretation, it is 'easy to be misled into assuming that differently formulated theories actually do differ in empirical consequences'. They may not. Clearly, empirical interpretation is the key both to rendering a hypothetical model experimentally testable and to eliminating non-uniqueness (cf. pp. 231–3 above). Without it (or with only limited doses of it), we shall be in serious difficulty on both counts. There are at least three important facts to be kept in mind here:

(1) It is easy to axiomatize away any number of potentially significant empirical issues as part of any particular 'idealization'. When this is done, these particular issues become untestable from the point of view of the theory or idealization involved, because no provision is made for them in the model. They are converted into assumptions. I have already noted several questionable assumptions or axiomatizations of this type in the theory of TGG (see especially 3.6, 5.1, 5.2, 5.3 and 7.2.3).

(2) Empirical data can be brought to bear in evaluating a given theory only to the extent that the hypothetical concepts associated with the theory are assigned appropriate empirical interpretations, allowing the theory to be related inferentially to potentially disconfirmatory evidence. We have already seen (in 8.2) how this presents problems from the standpoint of evaluating 'competence' models in terms of data from linguistic performance.

(3) Models can even be constructed in such a way that the hypothetical machinery involved in them is incapable in principle of having any interpretation assigned to it within any empirical (or experimentally manipulable) domain, thus making all attempts to resolve questions involving 'notational variants' on a non-arbitrary basis futile. In the final analysis, this particular feature is the major conceptual difficulty inherent in Chomsky's notion of a C-model.

Steinberg's remarks on p. 291 above, therefore, would make sense if it were the case that Chomsky was proposing a theory of linguistic performance in which all of his theoretical terms were empirically interpreted (surely far too much to ask, when put so boldly), for only in such a case would a differentiable set of empirical consequences necessarily be implied by any and all reformulations of the theory. Even a partially interpreted theory of this sort would be of some help, as some of the possible reformulations could be eliminated. Yet Chomsky makes it clear that (1) he is *not* offering a performance model and that, consequently, (2) it is only the *output* of his model which has any empirical content (cf. p. 288 above).[1] Sanders (1970) is therefore correct in his

---

[1] Saporta observes (1965, p. 98) that: 'It has not always been clear what kind of "psychological reality" could properly be ascribed to linguistic elements, since there have apparently been different kinds of claims made or implied for the abstract notions included in linguistic descriptions...[I]f one adopts the view that such notions constitute terms in an over-all theory of considerable abstraction, it is difficult to know how one would go about asking for behavioral correlates for a given part of such a theory, in any way that could be said to constitute a crucial test.' I find these remarks perceptive and apropos (especially for 1965) as an implied characterization of the empirical status of the theory of TGG. Saporta apparently did not recognize

observation that 'all properties traditionally called syntactic [plus many others – BLD] are entirely hypothetical, being postulated solely for the purpose of accounting for an infinite set of symbolic equivalences between semantic and phonological structures by means of a finite set of explanatory statements' (p. 71); what he fails to note is that this situation must change if alternative linguistic theories are to be evaluated on empirical grounds. For at present the hypothetical concepts in linguistic theories have associated with them, at most, only vague, implicit definitions,[1] with the result that questions related to the role these notions play in the derivation of sentences cannot be experimentally tested, but must simply be taken for granted. Thus other intervening concepts and processes might also be imagined to play a role in such derivations (see 9.2.2 below for further discussion). The 'notational variants' problem threatens contemporary linguistic theory for the reason which Peters and Ritchie (1969) suggest:

because the empirical checks on a grammar are actually rather limited. The only empirical restriction. . . on a grammar is that of descriptive adequacy. This means that the grammar of a given natural language must assign a number of properties of sentences in a way which agrees with the linguistic intuitions of native speakers of that language. These are properties such as being grammatical (vs. ungrammatical), being *n* ways ambiguous and being a paraphrase of such and such another sentence (on at least one reading) (pp. 151–2).

And that is all. Therefore, though Steinberg may be correct in asserting that 'different performance specifications represent different empirical claims' (1970b, p. 259), given some highly interpretable model of linguistic performance, he apparently fails to recognize that different 'competence' specifications of the Chomskyan sort do not. For Chomsky,

---

them as such; for rather than using them to expose a weakness in transformational-generative grammatical theory, he used them instead as an intended argument against Osgood's (presumably misguided) 'interest in "behavioral correlates of language units" ' (p. 98). See also Popper's discussion (pp. 112ff) on the intimate connection between the falsifiability of any theoretical system and that theory's empirical content, i.e. 'the amount of empirical information conveyed by a theory' (p. 113).

[1] Popper is as contemptuous of such 'implicit' definitions as he is of the 'conventionalist stratagem' and for the same reason: both render a theory unfalsifiable. He observes that 'undefined concepts can always be used in the non-empirical sense (1), i.e. as if they were implicitly defined concepts. Yet this use must inevitably destroy the empirical character of the system. This difficulty, I believe, can only be overcome by means of a methodological decision. I shall, accordingly, adopt a rule *not to use undefined concepts as if they were implicitly defined*' (1965, pp. 74–5; italics added).

at least, 'competence' and 'performance' are by no means the same kinds of thing!

Nowhere is this made more explicit than in Chomsky's 1970a paper. After arguing that such notions as 'order of selection of structures' and 'direction of a mapping', etc. could only make sense if 'we were to interpret this account as an intuitive instruction for *using* the rules of the grammar' (p. 58, italics added), i.e. as part of a performance model, he returns to his competence model (for the duration of the paper) in which such notions as these

> have no more than an intuitive, suggestive role; the informal instruction would be one of any number of equivalent instructions for using the rules of the grammar to form structural descriptions. To confuse the two kinds of account would be *a category mistake*. In short, it is necessary to observe *the difference in logical character* between performance and competence (p. 58, italics added).

At last we see clearly the nature of the kind of 'idealization' which Chomsky employs with respect to his competence/performance distinction: it is an 'idealization' in which a relation of *logical incompatibility* obtains between the real-world entity (performance) and its idealized counterpart (competence). How much structure must then be assigned to the missing components H and X in Chomsky's implicit model of linguistic performance? No amount will suffice, for these components are being asked to do the impossible: to bridge a logical gap between two logically incompatible entities – linguistic behavior and 'linguistic competence'. Indeed, if 'competence' and 'performance' differ in their essential make-up or logical character (as Chomsky suggests, rightly), how are the two to be found compatible within one theory (cf. P. Harris, 1970, p. 55); in particular, how is it possible to construct a P-model which 'incorporates a generative grammar [C-model] as an essential component'? The sort of 'heuristics' or 'use rules' required to accomplish such an amalgamation would presumably be of the same sort as might be required to transform grapefruit into spider monkeys. So, unless Chomsky changes his mind, it is clear that he has aligned himself with the Fodor–Garrett characterization of a generative grammar: it represents only a (non-empirical) axiomatization of sentences and their structural descriptions. And just as clearly, if this is *all* that a generative grammar is (and is capable in principle of being), then a generative grammar is a mere 'formal and frozen abstraction' (Toulmin, 1963,

p. 109). Chomsky's competence/performance distinction is immutably established, but at a price![1]

One remembers the remarks in Chomsky and Miller (1963), for example, about explaining the abilities of speakers of a language to construct novel and appropriate utterances, of hearers to comprehend them, and even of explaining language acquisition itself. It was *this* which interested people in generative grammar in the first place, in the hope that this new concept might shed light on the nature of linguistic performance and language acquisition. *These* are the important issues, and generative grammars justify their existence to the extent that they may help exploration into these areas. Yet linguists, on the whole, still appear indifferent to such matters; so enamoured are they with their formalisms that they cannot see the forest for the trees. Arbitrary descriptive systems are of no more inherent interest today (regardless of their formal intricacy and elegance) than they were in Bloomfield's time. If linguistics is to become a serious scientific discipline, determined to establish knowledge, we linguists must concern ourselves with performance models. If competence models (or generative grammars) are to play a role in the construction of such P-models, this must be demonstrated before any claims can be defended involving any 'mental reality underlying actual [linguistic] behavior' (Chomsky, 1965a, p. 4). But if generative grammars are the mere axiomatization systems for sentences and their structural descriptions which they now appear to be, they are useless for purposes of P-model construction and ought, therefore, to be abandoned.

A by-now fourth-hand quotation (from W. A. H. Rushton via Platt, 1964, via Fromkin, 1968, p. 51) sums up this issue: 'A theory which cannot be mortally endangered cannot be alive.' Competence models cannot even be wounded, much less mortally endangered. They belong, like all such 'hypotheses which cannot be tested but somehow are "true" in and of themselves for all time...to the field of metaphysics, not to science' (Fromkin, 1968, p. 52). When Warnock (1958, p. 9) speaks of 'metaphysical systems' below, therefore, he is, by direct implication, also presenting a valid commentary on the Chomskyan notion, 'model of linguistic competence':

[1] Cf. P. Harris (1971): 'To put it bluntly, perhaps grammars are *semantically abstract*, that is, *incapable of empirical interpretation*. If so they are invulnerable, but also irrelevant to Chomsky's own professed goals. And if linguists are not interested in these goals – in explaining language use and acquisition – then they might as well close up shop and declare bankruptcy.'

[M]etaphysical systems do not yield, as a rule, to frontal attack. Their odd property of being demonstrable only, so to speak, from within confers on them also a high resistance to attack from outside. The onslaughts of critics to whom, as likely as not, their strange tenets are very nearly unintelligible are apt to seem, to those entrenched inside, mis-directed or irrelevant. Such systems are more vulnerable to *ennui* than to disproof. They are citadels, much shot at perhaps but never taken by storm, which are quietly discovered one day to be no longer inhabited.

8.2 The transformational-generative paradigm: an overall assessment

In the last two chapters I have considered in detail the major suggestion implicit in the discussion of chapter 2, the popular view that chief among the accomplishments of the so-called 'Chomskyan revolution' in American linguistics has been the introduction of the rigorous methods of theory construction and validation characteristic of the natural sciences (cf. Lees, 1957, pp. 377–8, and such recent restatements as Micklesen, 1971, p. 30), together with a corresponding shift in attention and concern from problems of description to problems of prediction and explanation (cf. Chomsky, 1966a, p. 58). I have argued that there is little evidence that that has happened. We find instead an enterprise which might better be described in Steiner's (1967) terms as a 'fallacy of imitative form' in which the terminology of the natural sciences is invoked as a vehicle for stating the basic principles, methods and empirical claims of the discipline, but where little attention is paid to playing the game according to those well-established rules which the natural scientists have laid down. I have deplored the suggestion implicit in virtually all work in TGG that viable (i.e. testable) scientific theories arise out of thin air (7.1). This misconception has been responsible for the major dilemma which confronts the linguistic theorist today, the fact that his theories are overwhelmingly underdetermined by the data at his disposal (mostly data inherited from a previous generation of more empirically-oriented investigators). The increased 'external conditions of adequacy' imposed on linguistic theories through acceptance of 'linguistic intuitions' as data against which to evaluate these theories have not been sufficient to unscramble the proliferation of alternative proposals possible even within the framework of the standard meta-theory.

In the attempt to overcome this fundamental difficulty, the transformationalists have distorted the basic principles of theory validation in science, as well, by (1) placing heavy emphasis on the search for corroboratory rather than disconfirmatory evidence (7.2.1), (2) accepting a notion of prediction which is trivial and one of explanation according to which the statement of a possible generalization is regarded as insuring empirical significance (7.2.2), and, finally, (3) the detailed articulation of arbitrary criteria of simplicity and generality whose ultimate role is to take the place of the missing empirical evidence (7.2.3). Thus while arbitrariness has not disappeared from contemporary linguistics, the *awareness* of it has. We have further seen how that most venerable rule of all, objectivity, has also been abandoned by the transformational-generative grammarians, for the most part (7.3).[1]

Considering the *un*scientific methods typically employed in TGG, therefore, we should not be surprised to find that the theories or models which these methods have produced are also defective in fundamental ways. In particular, we have seen how Chomsky has done violence to the straightforward notion of 'idealization' in science in the effort to construe his originally purely formal notion of a generative grammar as part of a theory which has something to say about the actual behavior of real speakers or hearers, and about language acquisition (7.4). Further analysis showed that while this supposed connection between a generative grammar and a model of linguistic performance (via its 'creative' or 'dynamic' properties) has had a good deal to do with the 'sex appeal' of TGG (cf. Putnam, 1967, p. 14), there is no evidence that such a grammar (i.e. a system of rules which recursively defines the surface structures of well-formed utterances) has anything to do with language production or perception. Thus while speaking may very well be a process which *somehow* involves a set of rules whose function must ultimately be construed as relating semantic and phonetic representations, there is still no reason to think that the rules in question look anything like the set of rules which appears in the typical transformational-generative grammar (8.1).

In any event, Chomsky's failure to specify how the 'knowledge' of a language purportedly represented by the set of rules which appears in a generative grammar is actually brought to bear in actual speech production and/or perception turns his insistence upon the existence of

[1] The only reason which Chomsky has given for this radical departure from standard scientific practice is that 'objectivity can be pursued with little consequent gain in insight and understanding' (1965a, p. 20). This may be true under some circumstances, but non-objectivity is worse.

some necessary connection between the two into a mere article of faith. Non-believers may still doubt 'that the full apparatus of the generative grammar...is brought to bear immediately in carrying out [such a task as sentence comprehension]' (cf. Chomsky, 1964, pp. 113–14). Though Chomsky chides other investigators (psychologists) for providing 'only the most programmatic (and often implausible) kinds of answers' to the problem of providing 'a formal characterization of, or model for, the users of natural languages' (Chomsky & Miller, 1963, p. 272), it is obvious that after a decade of concerted attention to the problem, he has done no more himself (8.2). For what is more 'programmatic', after all, than to say that the connection between a generative grammar and an overall performance model is 'open' (Chomsky, 1967d, p. 125) – or more 'implausible' than the view that a model of the speaker–hearer's 'knowledge' of his language (and specifically *not* a model of behavior) represents 'a mental reality underlying actual behavior' (Chomsky, 1965a, p. 4)? It is difficult to see in what sense Chomsky's competence/performance distinction represents 'a major methodological clarification' (Fodor & Garrett, 1966, p. 137).

Chomsky is not only unable to justify this notion of linguistic 'competence' as the 'psychological' interpretation belatedly attached to his formal notion of a generative grammar; he is also unable to justify the choice of one *version* of such a model over any other (8.3). This problem has arisen, I have argued, primarily because competence models have been so constructed that only data related to the introspective reports of speakers have any direct bearing on them (despite unsupported claims to the contrary, as in Chomsky, 1965a, p. 18).[1] And this situation, in turn, has arisen from Chomsky's own basic unwillingness to break away from the Bloomfieldian tradition which dealt only in facts related to the speech *output* and refused to take into account evidence from the domain of psychology.[2] The linguists' tenacious attachment to 'competence'

---

[1] Cf. P. Harris' (1970) summary that 'psycholinguistic data concerning a performance model must be considered in order to solve the problem of justification,...[yet] this cannot succeed [at present] because grammars cannot be linked to psychological events' (p. iii).

Cf. P. Harris (1970): 'Chomsky has not really foregone the Bloomfieldian dichotomy, and is still playing it safe...He is making deep representational claims while at the same time refusing to develop any specific theory containing those claims and implying that linguistics is not properly concerned with the kinds of data necessary to justify those claims [cf. pp. 278–80 above – BLD]. Linguists are to describe competence and to account for its acquisition, psycholinguistics is to show how all this is realized in performance. My position is that if linguistics must study competence in order to be a serious discipline, then it must also investigate the ways of justifying models of the Chomskyan sort can therefore best be explained in terms of a long-standing (and still continuing) search for a useful descriptive system for the facts of speech and no more than this (cf. Fromkin, 1968, p. 47). But if the Chomskyan dream of *explaining* language use is ever to be realized, we linguists are eventually going to have to learn to play some new tunes (see 9.1 below). As Hill has said, Chomsky's task is indeed a 'dazzling' one, yet 'at present one can only say that its very recognition is the chief step so far taken towards achieving it' (1967, p. 106).

I have no quarrel with TGG as one of an unlimited number of descriptive systems for the well-formed utterances of a language, i.e. as one possible 'reordering of the primary data...according to an arbitrary set of descriptive labels which has become fossilized within linguistic tradition' (cf. Lees, 1957, p. 377). From this point of view generative grammars have distinct advantages in clarity and economy of statement over the other systems so far devised, and this must certainly be put to Chomsky's credit. But in the time since the publication of *Syntactic Structures*, Chomsky has been unwilling to let matters stand on this purely taxonomic plane; instead, he has extended the range of his claims into human psychology, far beyond the limits of any available empirical evidence (cf. Broadbent, 1972, p. 79). No longer is he offering a neat and compact way of organizing the primary data of a language, but is now dealing in genuine 'psychological explanations' of these data (cf. Chomsky, 1969, pp. 61–2).[1] Hence this long counter-statement.

I do not suggest that the entire Chomskyan period has been a total loss. It is very much to Chomsky's credit that he got linguists even interested in problems of theory construction and explanation, and ultimately in psychology. Unfortunately, Chomsky's original inspiration has now become bogged down in a new dead-end philosophical tradition, but eventually the original impetus will surely bear much healthy fruit, once the full extent of current foundational difficulties comes to be recognized by more linguists. Chomsky has also introduced into linguistic theory standards of explicitness hitherto unknown, though here, too, the overall effects of this innovation have been largely wasted

claims about competence as well if it is to be taken seriously. We can afford to play it safe only at the risk of becoming uninteresting despite our delusions about ourselves' (pp. 65–6).

[1] Halle now goes even further with the assertion that 'we have more detailed knowledge about language than about any other human activity involving man's mental capacities' (1971, p. 177).

on a domain of quite *in*explicit empirical reference. Yet in the long run this kind of care in formal model construction will also serve future linguists (and, hopefully, psychologists) in good stead, and may some day lead to theories of linguistic performance which *will* be testable. And, thirdly, of course, Chomsky has also done much to redress an imbalance in the proportion of linguistic attention devoted to problems of syntactic description, previously a neglected area. We shall also find that there are a number of especially useful elements of the Chomskyan model which, properly reconceptualized, may provide a basis for the radical reconstruction of linguistic research. In the final chapter I shall attempt to explore some of these possibilities.

9   *Towards a redefinition of linguistic research*

9.1   What is linguistics?

The common thread running through the modern linguistic era (the period from Saussure onwards) is the view that linguistics should be properly concerned with the facts of speech, i.e. with the form of utterances. This was put most explicitly by Bloomfield: 'In the division of scientific labor, the linguist deals only with the speech-signal' (1933, p. 32). We may refer to this as the language *product*.[1]

One consequence of this early decision was the establishment of a discipline of linguistics which was logically independent of psychology: the linguist deals with the overt speech-signal, the psychologist with the mental operations which underlie it. Bloomfield argued persuasively in favor of this division in terms which still make sense today: the linguist, he said, 'is not competent to deal with problems of physiology or psychology. The findings of the linguist, who studies the speech-signal, will be all the more valuable for the psychologist if they are not distorted by any [uninformed] prepossessions about psychology' (1933, p. 32).[2] On these terms a good case can be made for an *autonomous* discipline of linguistics. As a temporary exigency, the division of labor has already enabled the linguist to concentrate sufficient attention on the overt facts of speech to provide us with a good initial idea of what languages (i.e. language products) are like. But this view of linguistic inquiry has associated with it inherent limitations which can no longer be overlooked. In particular, it has the effect of restricting the discipline to the

---

[1] I extend the conventional psychological distinction between process and product to language at the suggestion of W. J. Baker, whose collaboration has been indispensable to the development of this chapter. See also Broadbent (1972, p. 79).

[2] Cf. Bloch & Trager (1942, p. 40): 'The linguist is concerned solely with the facts of speech. The psychological correlates of these facts are undoubtedly important; but the linguist has no means – as a linguist – of analyzing them.'

status of a taxonomic science which is, by its nature, beset by insoluble problems of arbitrariness (cf. pp. 30–7 above). All the taxonomist can ever do is (1) set up arbitrary schemes of classification for the data with which he is concerned (in this case the form of utterances) and (2) proceed to classify those data according to these schemes (cf. Hockett, 1942, p. 97). No other consequences necessarily follow.[1]

In recent years many linguists have found such a view of their discipline confining and stultifying. Repeated reference can be found in the literature to the desirability of escaping the endless cycle of classification and reclassification by isolating that one 'best' classificatory scheme which may finally be regarded as 'true'.[2] This is an admirable and natural development, but how is it ever to be accomplished? Obviously, non-arbitrary uniqueness in linguistic description can only be achieved from a set of criteria *external* to the original data; moreover, these criteria must *not* be arbitrary. To find such criteria is no simple matter. The task which the linguist has set himself under this new (non-arbitrary) conception of his discipline is inseparable from that of determining the *ultimate purpose* of linguistic description. Only when we have settled on a tentative answer to *this* question, can the question of what criteria are 'relevant' to linguistic description be broached. The question, what is the 'most useful' form of linguistic description, presupposes the further question, 'most useful for *what?*' This question does not involve an empirical issue, but is rather one of those fundamental 'general methodological questions' which can only be dealt with by rational argument (cf. Botha, 1968, p. 49). We need some starting point, some overall conceptual scheme or basic frame of reference, in order to proceed.

9.1.1   A schematic model of the language process. One such frame of reference widely discussed by linguists (e.g. from Lotz, 1950, p. 712, to Chafe, 1971, p. 8), psychologists (e.g. Miller, 1951, pp. 6–7, Carroll, 1955, pp. 88ff, and Hörmann, 1971, pp. 17, 30; see also Osgood & Sebeok, 1965, pp. 1–2) and communications engineers (e.g. Denes & Pinson, 1963, pp. 3ff) is the following scheme (fig. 9.1), which may be

---

[1] So Sledd properly remarks (speaking of English): 'I do not know of any way in which the language must be described. I think we have seen very clearly that the language may be described in more ways than one' (in Hill, 1962, p. 116).

[2] Even Bloch & Trager (cf. p. 301, n. 1) remark that 'the linguist's task...is to classify the facts of speech, and to reveal *the* system of the language' (1942, p. 39; italics added).

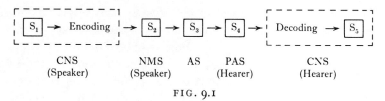

FIG. 9.1

referred to as a schematic model of the communication event (or language *process*).[1]

Here the speech-act is conceived (in oversimplified fashion) as a sequence of five successive discrete *states*, each of which represents the transformation or re-representation of an original 'message' into or within some specific *empirical space*:

(1) S_1 represents an original *message* (an 'idea' or 'meaning') conceived in the mind of the speaker. Whatever the nature of this message, its existence is presumably manifested in the central nervous system (CNS) of the *speaker*.

(2) This message is next 'encoded' (no doubt by means of a complex series of sub-transformations) into the form of a time-sequenced series of speech articulations (S_2). At this point the speech event may be said to have a purely *articulatory* existence within a neuro-muscular space (NMS), namely that of the *speaker*.

(3) The articulatory movements involved in S_2 produce in the external medium (air) surrounding the speaker a disturbance which may be referred to as an acoustic wave-form (S_3). At this stage the speech event consists (solely) of a set of *pressure changes* (or molecular movements) within an acoustic space (AS), that is, in the atmosphere.

(4) This acoustic wave-form next impinges upon the auditory apparatus of the hearer (as well as upon that of the speaker, providing a feedback loop which I ignore here, though it is important), where it goes through a series of preliminary physiological transformations. At this stage (S_4), the speech event may be said to have a purely *auditory* existence within the peripheral-auditory space (PAS) of the *hearer*.

(5) Finally, the speech event is 'decoded' (once again, via a further process of successive sub-transformations which no doubt provide for re-analysis on a number of different levels), ultimately providing some particular *interpretation* (that is, some *new* message or meaning) within the CNS of the *hearer*.

---

[1] The particular formulation of this familiar model which is presented here has been borrowed from C. I. J. M. Stuart.

Though schematic and obviously defective in many respects, a model of this sort is a useful starting point in our discussion, if only to clarify two important matters which might otherwise be obscure:

(1) The language *process*, as conceived here, is almost exclusively a psychological (and ultimately physiological) phenomenon, in the sense that almost everything of real interest which goes on in it takes place between States 1 and 2 and between States 4 and 5 in the model, that is, during the so-called 'encoding' and 'decoding' phases. The only directly observable phases of the process, however, are those represented here as States 2 (articulations), 3 (physical wave-form) and 4 (peripheral-auditory stimuli). This presents the linguist (or psychologist of language processing) with his major methodological dilemma: how is one to gain understanding of the remaining stages?

(2) As a corollary to (1), such things as the meaning or syntactic (constituent) structure of an utterance are not to be discovered in the utterances themselves (i.e. in the observable language *product*), whether represented in State 2, 3 or 4), but only in the mind of the speaker (on the encoding side) or the hearer (decoding side). That is to say, meaning and 'linguistic structure' are not entities which are somehow 'present' in actual utterances (i.e. they do *not* exist in an articulatory, acoustic or auditory space), but rather entities associated with or imposed upon utterances by speakers and hearers (i.e. they exist instead in the CNS's of language *users*).

9.1.2 Linguistics or 'psycholinguistics'? The implicit suggestion is that a scientific discipline might be conceived whose natural domain would be that of *normal language processing* and whose goal would be to specify in detail those operations of speech production and comprehension which language users actually perform (as represented in fig. 9.1 in only crude hypothetical outline). The goal would be to develop and test alternative models of *linguistic performance* (where a performance model would be indistinguishable from what Jakobovits has referred to alternatively as a 'psychological model of the language user' (1969, p. 157)). But what shall this discipline be called? The accepted name is 'psycholinguistics', defined by Osgood as 'the science of encoding and decoding processes in individual communicators' (in Koch, 1963, p. 248). In my view this is an unfortunate term, for it seems by implication to support the damaging misconception that the scientific investigation of language as a natural phenomenon can proceed independently of the study of the psychology of language users. The interpretation of autonomy at issue here is often stated this way: 'To find out what the structure [of a language] is like, is the task of linguistic science; to find out how the structure functions and how it is acquired, is the task of psycholinguistics' (Hörmann, 1971, p. 31; cf. also the remarks of Chomsky and others on pp. 278–80 above). This is the view that a branch of psychology (called 'psycholinguistics') can be seriously entertained which is forced to rely on an essentially independent science of linguistics 'for its "raw material"' (Hörmann, 1971, p. 233).

But what is the source of this 'raw material'? What is it that the linguist studies under this plan? As always, the linguist restricts his attention to *utterances*, the language *product*. Yet linguistic 'structures' do not exist in utterances, regardless of the particular state in which they are actually observed. Articulations are only articulations, acoustic waves are only acoustic waves. The domain of observable utterances (whether conceived in terms of minimal utterances or words, as sentences or even as entire discourses)[1] does not constitute a natural domain for anything except some arbitrary classification scheme (which, I have argued, is what a TGG represents, just like any other linguist's 'grammar'). Even phonetics (as distinct from physics, which would distinguish every speech token from every other) is essentially a psychological phenomenon, and the attempt to impose any additional 'higher' structure directly upon the domain of observable utterances is a conceptual absurdity. Does a linguistic form 'have' a meaning, for example? Surely not. A form or sign 'means' only what a speaker or hearer (i.e. a language user) thinks or has been taught it means. And, in general, a linguistic unit at any 'level' exists as a unit only because the language user treats it as a unit (cf. Hörmann, 1971, p. 31). Linguistic structure is not something which is either 'built up' out of utterances or 'overlaid' upon the language product, but is (according to the conceptual scheme which I have adopted) something which receives its only possible empirical realization as part of the language process of speech production and comprehension. The most that can be said about utterances is that they exhibit regularities which indicate that both speakers and hearers are

---

[1] I agree with Sanders (1970) that 'words, phrases, and sentences do not constitute natural domains for any empirical theory whatever', but dispute his further claim that 'the set of all discourses of [a] language' does (p. 52). Language is a psychological phenomenon; hence a science of language must concern itself primarily with the language *user*. Utterances alone represent only a small part of the total language process.

going about their tasks in a systematic fashion; to ascertain what that system *is*, however, is a problem for experimental psychology. The explanation of the form of utterances is not to be found in the utterances themselves (though these provide helpful cues), but within the language user, and facts, not speculation or decision-making, are needed before we can understand those language processes which the user actually goes through. In short, it is impossible to determine what the structure of a language is without broaching the question how that structure functions, since language has no structure independent of the process (cf. Yngve, 1969, pp. 459–60, and Jakobson, 1961a, p. 250).

This means that while psychology and physics may be extensively pursued independently of one another – and their possible inter-relations considered only later in some new 'hyphenated' discipline like *psychophysics* – linguistics and psychology may not develop independently in this same way. For language is inherently a psychological phenomenon. Hence, to be a viable scientific discipline, linguistics must be recognized as a branch of psychology (and in more than name only; cf. Chomsky, 1968a, p. 1). To invoke an analogy suggested by W. J. Baker, the serious study of language can no more progress independently of psychology than anatomy could independently of biology; without a knowledge of biological function, the anatomist would have no non-controversial basis for describing anatomical structure in the particular way in which he does. In much the same way, 'foundational considerations [also] preclude a completely autonomous science of language – an empirical base is necessary' (P. Harris, 1970, pp. 55–6). As a descriptive term, therefore, 'psycholinguistics' is no less redundant and misleading than 'bio-anatomy'.

Within the general frame of reference which I have suggested, only two views of linguistics make any sense. The first is to conceive of linguistics as a purely taxonomic discipline governed by considerations of convenience, simplicity and/or aesthetics, in which case linguists must remain mere 'hewers and drawers' of endless possibly (but never certainly) useful descriptive schemes for psychologists or others to evaluate experimentally (cf. p. 199, n. 1 above). In this way alone can linguistics and psychology continue to 'develop' independently, each employing its own set of 'logically independent' methods or procedures: speculation by the former, experiment by the latter (cf. Greenberg & Jenkins, 1964, p. 158). Alternatively, linguistics may be redefined as that particular branch of psychology which deals with problems of linguistic behavior or language processing, in which case linguists must become active in experimental research themselves. It is a matter of personal taste which route any particular linguist follows, though he should not have illusions about the implications of his choice. In the remainder of this chapter, I shall be concerned only with the problems which must be faced by linguists who are inclined to adopt the second alternative.

9.2 On the initial contributions of formal linguistics and experimental psychology

There has been a lot of confusion among linguists and psychologists as to the proper integration of their disciplines, as the unstructured hodgepodge of studies currently called 'psycholinguistics' shows. These difficulties stem from two main sources, each peculiar to one of the disciplines in question. I have been suggesting that linguists in recent years have been concerned primarily to develop conceptual schemes designed to account for the form of utterances. Since these linguists have characteristically refrained from any sort of experimental investigations, these schemes remain untested (and in many cases untestable) and can be dismissed at present as brilliant but unsupported exercises in creative imagination. The psychologists' general approach suffers under a different handicap: a characteristic lack of discrimination which results in a scattering of energies over too broad a range of research problems. To many psychologists the term 'verbal behavior' (and lately 'psycholinguistics', as well) seems to incorporate any phenomenon which has anything to do with language, so that few of the problems which these psychologists study have more than marginal relevance to the central problem of normal language processing (take the familiar case of word associations, for example). In some cases one wonders whether the studies have any bearing on linguistic behavior at all (as when verbal stimuli are employed in the study of long-term memory). The experimental techniques which psychologists employ in these studies are often sophisticated and effective, but they are often wasted on questions scarcely worth answering.

We can more constructively consider the situation which faces the prospective scientist of language behavior today in terms of what the disciplines of linguistics and psychology might possibly contribute to his initial efforts. From this standpoint I would argue that each has something substantial and valuable to offer, and the contributions are complementary. From the side of the linguist, who has devoted himself almost exclusively to speculation, the most important initial contributions will be mainly *conceptual*: a reservoir of potential research questions which, once framed as testable experimental hypotheses, might tell us a good deal about what normal language-processing is like. And what the linguist lacks, the psychologist has to offer in abundance: a reliable set of experimental vehicles for exploring empirical questions. The chief initial contributions of the psychologist will, I suspect, be mainly *methodological*. Let us consider a few specific examples.

9.2.1 Some fundamental linguistic concepts. Two fundamental linguistic concepts underlie virtually every important recent linguistic controversy.[1] These are the notions of *list* (or lexicon) and *rule*. The first is associated with those aspects of linguistic behavior which Saussure called 'lexicological' or 'unmotivated' and which modern linguists have referred to variously as distinctive, non-predictable, irregular or arbitrary. The second has been associated with those aspects of language use which Saussure thought of as 'grammatical' or 'motivated', and which are regarded in contemporary terms as non-distinctive, predictable, regular or redundant. Clearly this distinction is central to the continuing controversy in linguistics as to how regular the various features of linguistic structure really are (cf. chapter 5). The structuralists leaned towards the lexical side, as indicated by their general acceptance of Saussure's view of grammar as 'a system of elements' (or 'items and arrangements', as they commonly came to be called in North America), while the transformationalists have now reverted to the opposite extreme. To Chomsky, a grammar is 'a system of rules' which express the 'basic regularities' of a language (1965a, pp. 4–5) and the notion of list therefore plays a smaller role in his grammar than with any of his predecessors. The truth must lie between the extremes: the grammar of a language is a system of elements *and* rules.

It is to Chomsky's credit that he revived the notion of rule in the post-Bloomfield doldrums and re-emphasized its intimate connection with another traditional concept, that of productivity or 'creativity' (cf. pp. 34–5 above). I say re-emphasized, because the idea was not original. Paul, for example, wrote this before the turn of the century:

One of the fundamental errors of the *old* science of language was to deal with all human utterances...as with something merely reproduced by memory...

[1] Lyons traces these notions back to the ancient Greeks (1968, pp. 6–8).

True it is that W. v. Humboldt insisted on the fact that *speaking is a perpetual creation*...The fact is that the mere reproduction by memory of what it has once mastered is *only one factor* in the words and groups of words which we employ in our speech (1891, p. 97; italics added).

Bloomfield adds:

we may say that any form which a speaker can utter without having heard it, is regular in its immediate constitution and embodies regular functions of its constituents, and any form which a speaker can utter only after he has heard it from other speakers, is irregular. Strictly speaking, then, every morpheme of a language is an irregularity, since the speaker can use it only after hearing it used, and the reader of a linguistic description can know of its existence only if it is listed for him...

If we make this restriction, it is obvious that most speech-forms are regular, in the sense that the speaker who knows the constituents and the grammatical pattern, can utter them without ever having heard them; moreover, the observer cannot hope to list them, since the possibilities of combination are practically infinite (1933, pp. 274–5).

At one level of discussion, Chomsky's notion of a rule of grammar and the structuralists' notion of a regular language function or grammatical pattern may be regarded as much the same.

There are important differences, however. Both Paul and Bloomfield linked their notion of linguistic creativity to a general principle of analogical formation. The process of 'freely creating' novel forms, says Paul, 'we call formation by analogy' (1891, p. 97), while Bloomfield argues that 'a regular analogy permits a speaker to utter speech-forms which he has not heard; we say that he utters them on the analogy of similar forms which he has heard' (1933, p. 275). It is reasonably clear what is meant from the examples which Paul and Bloomfield provide: an analogical pattern represents a 'common element' (Paul) or 'regularity' (Bloomfield) manifested in the surface form of utterances, hence one which is extractable from them as a generalization which can be applied to all utterances of a given type or class. Paul expressed it this way:[1]

In the process of naturally mastering one's mother-tongue no rule, as such, is given, but only a number of examples. We hear gradually a number of sentences which are connected together in the same way, and which hence associate themselves together into one group. The recollection of the special contents of the single sentences may grow less and less distinct in the process; the common element is always strengthened anew by repetition, and it thus

[1] I am indebted to F. W. Householder, Jr, for bringing this reference to my attention. See also Sturtevant, 1947, pp. 96ff, and Hockett, 1968b, pp. 89ff.

comes about that *the rule is unconsciously abstracted from the examples* (1891, pp. 98–9; italics added).

We are talking about a notion of linguistic rule which can be directly 'elicited from surface structures' (Schlesinger, 1967, p. 399), hence one which does not put unreasonable demands upon the language learner: all that is required to learn rules of this sort are general capacities which human beings possess: power to discriminate, to generalize and, most important, to extract regularity from the environment. Consequently, this is the notion of linguistic rule which I have endeavored to resurrect for serious reconsideration (see especially chapter 6).

This plausible notion of rule is to be contrasted with the esoteric concept which Chomsky presents under the same label. For Chomsky rejects this notion of analogy (on the ground that it is 'mysterious'; see Chomsky, 1968a, p. 30) and opts for rules which 'involve mental operations of a very abstract nature, applying to representations that are quite remote from the physical signal' (p. 53). I have argued that this notion of rule is itself a mystery, since such rules are defined only within the formal domain of an empirically uninterpreted theory of linguistic 'competence' (see chapter 8), and seem unlearnable without attributing to the child a complex and specific repertory of innate linguistic knowledge, none of which is open to empirical examination (see chapters 3–4). It is improper, therefore, for transformationalists to argue that their rules are simply 'analogies made precise' – or that once the notion of analogy is made precise, it is 'indistinguishable from a transformation' (Lakoff, 1969, p. 126). For transformations (of the Chomskyan type, to which Lakoff is referring here),[1] as Lakoff himself has emphasized on many occasions, are formal devices which operate on abstract hypothetical structures and some of which yield surface structures only as output. Such rules suffer from the dual disadvantage of being incapable of a direct behavioral interpretation (8.1), as well as inherently unlearnable. There is ground for Jakobovits' suspicion that 'the conception of "rule" that is to be psychologically relevant as the basis of a psycholinguistic theory of language performance must be something quite different from the [currently popular] linguistic one' (1969, p. 157).

Suppose, therefore, that we replace Chomsky's abstract notion of rule with a reconceptualization specifically designed to represent part of

---

[1] It would appear that Z. Harris' original notion of transformation is exempt from this criticism and so represents a potentially acceptable interpretation of syntactic rule (cf. p. 165 and p. 269, n. 2).

a model of linguistic behavior (a performance model), that is, a model in which 'putting rules to use' means simply behaving according to the rules. This immediately places a behavioral interpretation on our notion of rule like the one originally suggested by Bloomfield: the rules express behavioral regularities directly.[1] This decision has the important immediate consequence of implying that one kind of evidence is necessary if we are to justify the formulation of any *particular* rule: we must demonstrate that the linguistic behavior of the speaker, at least, is creative or 'regular' in the manner stated by the rule. We must demonstrate, in short, that the speaker does behave according to the rule in a situation which is novel to his linguistic experience (for example, in Bloomfield's characterization, in using a form or utterance which we can be reasonably certain he has not previously heard). We may then postulate that the rule in question is a general surface-structure constraint (or 'output condition') on the form of utterances, and the language user has learned he must conform to it if he is to communicate effectively and creatively (cf. pp. 201–8 above).

It is one thing to have an idea of the kind of evidence *required* to justify postulating a particular rule, and another to know how to find it. There is little hope of obtaining the needed evidence from the simple naturalistic observation of adult speech (the data with which linguists have traditionally been most concerned).[2] The reason is obvious: we seldom know with certainty when (or in what particular respects) a mature native speaker is being creative. To be certain that an adult speaker has not heard a given utterance before, we would need an accurate record of all the utterances to which he had been exposed in his

---

[1] Note that previously Chomsky was able to speak of rules and still insist that 'there [are] no "*behavioral* regularities" associated with... the understanding and production of speech' (1968a, p. 86; italics added), while Ziff could counter with the position, 'I am concerned with regularities: I am not concerned with rules' (1960, p. 34). Under a direct behavioral interpretation of the sort I advocate, it will no longer be possible to hide behind a competence/performance distinction and speak of one without the other.

[2] King interprets this obvious fact as an indictment of the entire principle of analogy (1969, pp. 131–2). Granted, the phenomenon is poorly understood. Though we have some understanding of basic principles, the details are less clear. With few exceptions, we have little idea, for example, which particular generalizations are extracted by children from the primary data, or what factors motivate the induction of one set of generalizations rather than some other. This is a problem for research, not a case for dismissal. If the same attention and energy had been devoted to the study of such problems over the past fifteen years as was devoted instead to the study of formal grammars and the abstract uninterpreted rules which they contain, we might have had by now a much better understanding of normal language acquisition.

lifetime – and then we could not be certain which he had failed to comprehend or even attend to, which he might have forgotten in the meantime, and so on. Dunkel puts the problem in this way:

> The most important fact about the functioning of analogy (and one which is frequently overlooked) is that we become aware of it *only when it is unsuccessful*. If a child [or an adult] says *cows*, we do not know (and usually have no way of knowing) whether he formed this plural by analogy without ever having heard it or whether he is repeating a form he has heard. Similarly with all the other phenomena of accidence and syntax, the successful use of analogy (trial-and-success, so to speak) passes unnoticed as an acceptable speech form. Only in cases of trial-and-error, when mother has to say, 'The dog *ran*, not *runned*', do we become aware of the linguistic principle which the child has discovered and is using (1948, pp. 25–6; cf. Faust, 1970, pp. 45–6).

If the linguist wishes to continue to restrict his research to the technique of naturalistic observation, his most productive field of exploration would be the speech of children, rather than adults. For it is reasonably well established that after an initial stage of lexicalization or imitation, during which he apparently learns forms essentially as unanalyzed wholes,[1] the child quickly proceeds to a second stage of grammaticalization or analogy where he begins to identify and extract generalizations from his lexicon. Some of these apparently serve the definitional function of partitioning his vocabulary into a number of lexical classes, while others are separated out as rules which are applied indiscriminately to all members of a given class. So Ervin (1964) found that such forms as FEET and WENT appeared at the earlier stage in English-speaking children, but were soon supplanted by the forms FOOTS (or FEETS) and GOED (or WENTED). There is no adult model for such forms, leading us to believe that they represent novel creations of the child himself. Such 'systematic anomalies'[2] in the behavior of the developing child give us an excellent (though under-exploited) source of evidence of the kinds of rules which the child has tentatively extracted from his experience (cf.

---

[1] This lexical principle is apparently extended to whole utterances at an early 'holophrastic' sub-stage of this period (cf. Osgood & Jenkins, 1965, p. 132, and McNeill, 1966b, p. 63 and elsewhere). Notice also that it is only at this first stage that the paradigm of imitation or association learning can account for the observed facts; concurrently, this also seems to be the only stage at which close parallels can be drawn between human language and the communication systems employed by any of the lower species. See, e.g. Chao (1968, p. 9).

[2] Corder (1967) calls them 'systematic errors' and provides a discussion of some useful criteria for distinguishing these from simple lapses or 'mistakes'. See also Berko & Brown (1960, p. 520), Brown & Fraser (1964, p. 45), Kiparsky (1970, p. 311) and Bellugi (1970, p. 35).

Campbell & Wales, 1970, pp. 257–8). Presumably the systematic study of a wide range of such 'anomalies' – in phonology and syntax proper, as well as in morphology – would provide the analyst with information as to the kind of behavioral rules which children adopt, and hence provide evidence which might have some important bearing on the question whether the notion of simple analogy (the extraction of surface regularities) will have to be supplemented by more powerful or abstract principles.[1]

This strategy breaks down in those instances when the child gets his generalizations 'right' (that is, good enough to allow him to produce utterances acceptable to those with whom he seeks to communicate). This is a serious problem if it is the set of adult rules which the investigator is most interested in, for as the child's rules approach those of the adult, his systematic errors will decrease,[2] yielding fewer clues as to what new or revised rules he has adopted. Here the experimental linguist has to go beyond naturalistic observation and introduce artificial heuristic techniques specifically designed to answer questions of productivity or creativity. One promising technique was introduced by Berko in 1958: to insure novelty by requiring the subject to manipulate nonsense material. But this technique, too has inherent limitations, some of which can usefully be indicated here.

Let us assume that Berko's technique, if extended to naive adult speakers in connection with a fully representative set of nonsense noun-like words, would yield the following results for plurals:[3]

(1) The plurals of all name-words ending in the segments *p, t, k, ө,* and *f* are all formed by adding a final *-s*.

---

[1] See Slobin (1971a) for an excellent illustration of the kind of useful inductive generalizations which might be established from the cross-linguistic investigation of children's systematic errors.

[2] Though his lapses may not, thereby providing another data source of considerable potential which Fromkin, in particular, has endeavored to exploit (1968, 1971). Foreign 'accents', of course, should also continue to provide valuable data (cf. Kohler, 1970, p. 90).

[3] I know of no attempt to do this in full, but judging from Berko's partial set (which was presented to 12 adults, as well as to her child subjects) and one's own introspections, there is little doubt that the results would follow substantially as indicated. I ignore here the important matter of defining the term 'segments' in my statement of these hypothetical results. (Presumably these are to be regarded as either 'phones' or 'phonemes'. But since both terms define *psychological*, not physical, concepts, how do I justify referring to them as 'observations'? Rough impressionistic perceptual judgments are involved in such studies and some attempt should be made to induce objectivity by the use of several raters and some measure of inter-rater agreement.)

(2) Those in b, d, g, ∂, v, m, n, η, l, r, y, w and the vowels add $-z$.

(3) Those in s, z, $\check{c}$, $\check{z}$, $\check{s}$, and $\check{z}$ add $-\partial z$ (or $-iz$) (cf. Berko, 1958, p. 360, and Halle, 1964, p. 324).

Assuming further that the subject sample is representative, this experiment would justify the conclusion that the overt linguistic behavior of the typical mature native speaker of English conforms to the following rule: 'The plural form of a picture-name word is produced by articulating an $-s$ after the final segment of the word if that segment is a member of the class C_1, a $-z$ if it is a C_2 and an $-\partial z$ if C_3', where C_1, C_2 and C_3 refer to the classes of segments listed in (1), (2) and (3) above, respectively; or, schematically:

$$(\mathrm{PL})_N = \left\{ \begin{array}{l} s/ \ \ldots C_1]\underline{\quad}\# \\ z/ \ \ldots C_2]\underline{\quad}\# \\ \partial z/\ldots C_3]\underline{\quad}\# \end{array} \right\}$$

On the reasonable premise that this highly structured form of behavior is not accidental but is based on some learned schema for utterance-construction in the language, we may now postulate with confidence that the rule may also have some kind of 'psychological equivalent' (cf. Slobin, 1971c, p. 7).

It is important to note some conclusions which would *not* follow. One such would be that two separate rules of the following sort are involved in pluralization in English:

(1) Pluralization is realized *syntactically* as a process of suffixation, i.e.:

$$(\mathrm{N}), (\mathrm{PL}) = (\mathrm{N}) + (\mathrm{PL}).$$

(2) The particular *suffix* involved is $-s$, $-z$, or $-\partial z$, i.e.:

$$(\mathrm{PL}) = \left\{ \begin{array}{l} s/ \ \ldots C_1 +\underline{\quad} \\ \dot{z}/ \ \ldots C_2 +\underline{\quad} \\ \partial z/\ldots C_3 +\underline{\quad} \end{array} \right\}$$

Although not unreasonable as a speculative claim or as a hypothesis subject to further study, the conclusion that there are two distinct processes involved in pluralization (one purely syntactic, the other lexical) is not justified by the evidence outlined above, which shows only that the segments in question appear at the end of the forms indicated. The 'two' discrete events hypothesized above always co-occur in the data, which provide no empirical basis for differentiation. A *single* behavioral rule is all that can be justified: plurals are formed by suffixing the segments in question.

This singular statement is empirically non-distinct from the bifurcated restatement more typical of most linguistic analyses. Scientists resolve such problems of 'notational variants' (cf. pp. 288–94 above) by adopting a criterion of level parsimony (cf. Bunge, 1967, p. 354), which forces the investigator to adopt that solution involving the fewest intervening variables or unmotivated levels of representation (namely, *none*). Contrast Chomsky's technique of 'presupposing the legitimacy' of successive multi-level abstractions (1967a, p. 401), a strategy which opens the door to limitless empirically non-distinct alternative analyses (cf. 8.3). To avoid this, each new level of representation must be empirically validated before it can be accepted as a scientific statement.[1]

A second interpretation of these hypothetical data, corollary to the first, would be that one more abstract representation is actually suffixed and that a set of intervening 'phonological rules' changes this 'basic' representation in specific phonological environments. That is, in place of Rule (2) in the above example, we substitute Rule (2') and Rules (3) and (4) below:

(2') The lexical representation of the morpheme Plural is $/z/$, i.e.:
$$(\text{Pl}) = {}^{\circ}/z^{\circ}/$$

(3) This ${}^{\circ}/z^{\circ}/$ is devoiced at the end of a word if it is immediately preceded by a voiceless segment, i.e.:
$$z = s \ / \ C_{vl}\underline{\quad}\#$$

(4) If two successive sibilants (C_4) occur at the end of a word, a ∂ is inserted to break up the cluster, i.e.:
$$\emptyset = \partial \ / \ C_4\underline{\quad}C_4\#$$

As in the previous case, each of these new rules requires independent justification. Unlike the previous case, however, it seems clearer in this instance what kind of evidence would be required: the investigator would have to demonstrate that the naive speaker's morphophonemic behavior (as when sequences of learned nonsense forms are joined together in novel ways) conformed to the generalizations indicated. In

---

[1] Cf. the parallel problem of accounting for visual perceptions. Given only data involving the presentation of various visual stimuli and the responses RED, BLUE, etc., the investigator is justified in concluding only that $S_1 \rightarrow$ RED, $S_2 \rightarrow$ BLUE, etc. and can only speculate about intervening physiological or psychological steps. If the physiologist can talk about such intervening activities as photo-chemical changes in the retina, neurological transmission from the retinal ganglia through the optic nerve to the lateral geniculate body, synaptic transmission and projection upon the occipital lobe of the cortex, etc., he can do so with confidence only because experiments have justified each of these intervening steps independently. (I am indebted to W. J. Baker for this observation and example.)

the absence of such a demonstration, only our original statement of the rule can be supported by the evidence (cf. Bloomfield, 1933, p. 213).

A third unwarranted interpretation of the data would be to restate the original rule in terms of some alleged 'feature composition' of the segment-classes involved, such as to represent C_1 as non-vocalic, consonantal, grave or non-strident and voiceless, C_2 as non-vocalic, consonantal, grave or non-strident and voiced, and C_3 as non-vocalic, consonantal, non-grave and strident (as in Halle, 1964, p. 328).[1] There is no support in the data for any claim that the language user adverts to these phonetic properties or any others more abstract than the *full* representation of the segment-types in question. The facts show *only* that *s* appears after *p*, after *t*, after *k*, etc. One would hardly deny that the fact that these conditioning segments fall into classes which seem very 'natural' (i.e. definable by a small set of basic articulatory and acoustic properties) is a highly suggestive observation. It suggests that the language user may advert to some such subsegmental properties rather than (or in addition to) the fully specified segments; but the present data do not demonstrate this. This conclusion, too, must therefore remain entirely speculative until empirical evidence is available to justify the claim.[2]

This brings us to the general problem of establishing what kinds of units the language user actually deals with. In general, it seems to me that this problem is not amenable to empirical investigation in terms of the more simple techniques (naturalistic observation and the forced manipulation of nonsense material) so far discussed. To study such problems, the linguist must eventually look for more sophisticated and indirect research vehicles. The experimental psychologist may fill the bill, hence the linguist is well advised to begin to seek his cooperation.

9.2.2 An illustrative research paradigm from experimental psychology.

One experimental technique from the cognitive psychologist's repertoire well suited to the investigation of such problems is

---

[1] Unless these terms are used merely as mnemonic labels for the segment-classes in question (as I have used C_1, C_2 and C_3). This was clearly not Halle's intent.

[2] One way of exposing this particular claim to falsification might be to include among the nonsense forms some *new* final segments which also conform to the feature specifications indicated (e.g. ϕ, β and c). Unfortunately, none of these segment-types exists in standard English, and so the results of such an experiment might be confounded by a serious discrimination problem with naive speakers. (Should the naive speaker interpret ϕ as *f*, β as *v* and *c* as *ts*, for example, the purpose of the exercise would be defeated.)

the 'concept formation' (CF) paradigm (see, for example, chapter 12 of Deese & Hulse, 1967). At the suggestion of W. J. Baker, a group of us at the University of Alberta have adopted a variation of this general technique to the study of some of these problems:

(1) The experimenter chooses a class of homogeneous stimuli and divides it into two sub-classes on the basis of a particular set of characteristics which the first sub-class shares but the second lacks. One of these sub-classes (normally the first) is identified as the 'target' class, the other as the 'non-target'.

(2) The individual stimuli are presented to each subject in random order and the subject is required to indicate which items belong to the target set (YES) and which do not (NO). Each response is immediately reinforced as CORRECT or WRONG. Initially, the subject will have no idea which items qualify and which do not. In order to insure a common initial strategy, we instruct each subject to respond NO to all items until he is informed that his response is WRONG, indicating that the item in question *does* belong to the target set.

(3) This continues until it is obvious that the subject has correctly identified the target set, as indicated by a long string of consecutive correct responses.

(4) Experience with this technique has shown that more trials to criterion are ordinarily required to identify a class of items on the basis of a complex set of shared properties or attributes (e.g. a TRIANGLE which is both BIG and RED) than on the basis of a simple set (e.g. a TRIANGLE, a RED object, etc.).[1] Analysis of the errors which each subject makes in the course of his training also represents a useful method of interpreting the results of such studies.

As an example of the kinds of problems amenable to experimental investigation by a research strategy of this sort, consider the problem raised in chapter 4 of determining what particular *semantic* relationships exist (in the mind of the language user) between different words (pp. 122–6) or sentences (pp. 162–7). The CF paradigm seems ideally suited to this kind of problem. Presumably a class of words or other structures which the language user associates through a set of shared semantic attributes will be easier to identify than an arbitrary or less systematically organized class – and the ease with which the language

[1] To insure that the subject is identifying the items in the target class by their properties and not simply memorizing them individually, we must also see that the number of items in the target set is overwhelmingly large, or at least force the subject to deal with novel test items at frequent intervals. ·

user can identify a particular class of such items ought to serve as an empirical measure of the closeness or directness of the semantic connections in each case. One would expect an attempt to adopt the CF technique to verify the results obtained by Luria and Vinogradova (1959) – who adopted a more cumbersome research strategy based on elusive physiological response variables – would lead to this set of differential results (for native speakers of Russian):

(1) Easiest to identify (based on shared semantic features or 'sense-links'):

KOŠKA 'cat', SOBAKA 'dog', MYŠ 'mouse', etc.

(2) Next easiest to identify (based on a shared superficial phonetic resemblance):

KOŠKA 'cat', OKOŠKO 'window', KROŠKA 'crumb', etc.

(3) Most difficult to identify (the unsystematic class, having no significant semantic or phonetic attributes in common):

KOŠKA 'cat', MAŠINA 'automobile', LOPATA 'spade', etc.

This same technique might also be extended to the empirical investigation of a wide range of fundamental questions in *phonological* theory. The essential logic is unchanged: a class of forms which share common phonetic or phonological properties ought to be easier to identify than a class which does not – and the ease of identifying a particular class on this basis ought to serve as an empirical measure of the phonetic or phonological similarity of the forms (provided no overriding semantic connections interfere). This suggests a way of evaluating claims which linguists have made about the status of phonetic features as phonological primes, for example (see pp. 136–7), as well as providing a technique for assessing the advantages of one set of proposed phonetic features *vis-à-vis* another.

Consider first the question of the status of the phonetic feature. Many formal arguments have been offered by linguists in support of the idea that the phonetic feature, rather than the unanalyzed phonetic segment (or syllable), is the prime phonological unit of a language. For one thing, many phonological rules (such as the pluralization rule discussed in the preceding section) indicate a persistent tendency in natural language for classes of segments to be grouped on a 'natural' basis (that is, in terms of a relatively small number of shared phonetic attributes). For another, the segment-types which appear in a given language also tend to be restricted to a range defined by a relatively small number of such basic attributes, and do not seem to have been arbitrarily selected from a larger set of segment-types which reflects the range of variation from one language to another and across language families. None of these arguments provides empirical evidence that the language user *adverts* to these properties, nor indicates what set of properties, if any, is being adverted to; the evidence is entirely circumstantial. If the language user does advert to such properties in normal language use, we have reason to believe that he would also have subconscious access to them in performing other tasks.[1] So a pilot study of the following sort is now in progress at the University of Alberta:

(1) A set of CVC units (for consonants) and VCV units (for vowels) was made up (all the logical combinations of 12 consonant and 8 vowel phonemes in English, the initial and final segment being identical).

(2) The CVC units were grouped in the following three ways:
  (a) Experiment 1: Units containing voiced consonants versus units containing voiceless consonants
  (b) Experiment 2: Units containing fricatives versus units containing stops
  (c) Experiment 3: Two unsystematic classes containing an equal mixture of stops, fricatives, voiced and voiceless consonants

(3) The VCV units were grouped in the following ways:
  (a) Experiment 4: Units containing high vowels versus units containing non-high vowels
  (b) Experiment 5: Units containing front vowels versus units containing non-front vowels
  (c) Experiment 6: Two unsystematic classes containing an equal mixture of high, non-high, front and non-front vowels.

(4) Each naive subject is randomly assigned one task (experiment) from each group (consonants and vowels) during each of three successive sessions. Eventually each subject will participate in each of the six experiments.

(5) If naive native speakers of English advert to the (binary) features of voicing and continuance in consonants, it is to be expected that significantly fewer trials to criterion will be required in Experiments 1 and 2 than in Experiment 3.

---

[1] One outstanding advantage of the CF paradigm in investigating such problems is that subjects are known to be able to derive concepts from common properties even when they are unable to state explicitly what the common properties are (cf. Deese & Hulse, 1967, p. 416). Experience at Alberta with the CF paradigm in connection with syntactic properties (see below) bears this observation out.

(6) By the same token, if native speakers of English advert to the (scalar) features of height and frontness in vowels, it is to be expected that the tasks outlined in Experiments 4 and 5 will be significantly easier than the task outlined in Experiment 6. It may also prove interesting to compare the results obtained from Experiments 1 and 2 with those obtained from Experiments 4 and 5.

Preliminary results indicate that naive subjects can classify nonsense syllables on the basis of shared phonetic properties. The class of continuant consonants, for example, is markedly easier to learn than the unstructured class. Interestingly, this does not appear to be the case for the class of voiced consonants. The class of front (non-grave) vowels also seems to be somewhat easier to learn than the class of high (diffuse) vowels. The general applicability of the CF paradigm to the study of such questions thus seems established and this suggests the possibility of extending it to the investigation of more problematical features (such as 'compactness', 'tenseness', 'flatness' and the like), and to the evaluation of alternative systems of phonetic features. McCawley (1967a) has argued that the high vowels group more naturally with the palatal and velar consonants than with the labials and dentals (as in Jakobson's original scheme) and Chomsky and Halle have incorporated this suggestion in their revised system of 'universal phonetic features' (1968, pp. 304ff). This suggest that a class of high vowels, palatal and velar consonants ought to be easier to learn than a class of high vowels, labial and dental consonants, etc. Obviously, many specific problems of this sort might be answerable by means of the technique.

The CF paradigm does have some serious drawbacks. One is the inordinate amount of subject-time required to answer a small number of specific questions. In the pilot project described above, approximately three *hours* of experiment time was required of each subject to provide information about each of the four specific features. Given the number of questions which remain to be asked within the traditional articulatory and acoustic taxonomic schemes, not to mention the problem of comparing alternative schemes, alternative research programs will also have to be considered.[1] My only purpose here is to illustrate how one specific

---

[1] This pilot project has also shown defects in the original design which ought to be corrected in further attempts to adapt it to these problems. For example, the idea of repeating the crucial segments (cf. (1) above), originally conceived in order to provide the subject with some redundancy and thus minimize any potential discrimination problem, seems counterproductive. Due to environmental conditioning, the 'repetitions' in question often differ markedly in some phonetic properties and some

heuristic technique might be applied to each of the three fundamental linguistic areas.

We have already found the CF technique useful with syntax. In our initial pilot project, now completed, for example, we were curious to learn whether classes of sentences could be readily identified by naive speakers from shared *syntactic* properties like voice (active versus passive), mood (declarative versus interrogative) and modality (affirmative versus negative) and, if so, what the relative difficulty would be in identifying these features *vis-à-vis* one another and in various combinations. Our pilot project showed that the answer to the first question was a resounding affirmative, so this technique might be usefully extended to more complex and problematical areas of syntactic analysis. Due to overwhelming individual variation, no clear answer to the second question emerged from this study in terms of the trials to criterion measure; we have found, however, that various schemes of analysis of the *error patterns* exhibited by our subjects have yielded interesting and suggestive results along this line (for details, see Baker, Prideaux & Derwing, forthcoming).

The CF paradigm is not the only – or necessarily the best – experimental technique available for the study of the problems I have outlined. Other techniques have been tried, though none, to my knowledge, has been extensively followed up by linguists (cf. the various rating scales for phonetic similarity described in Greenberg & Jenkins, 1964, and the perceptual confusion strategy adopted by Miller & Nicely, 1955). It is to be hoped that serious efforts will soon be made to replicate and extend this work, as well.

9.3 A concluding summary and prognosis

The chief argument of this book has been that contemporary linguistics has gone fundamentally astray, both conceptually and methodologically. I have offered suggestions about how some of these aberrations might be rectified. In this final chapter, in particular, I have attempted to outline

of our early subjects attempted to form classes from these differences (e.g. a 'target' class where the two segments were 'identical', a 'non-target' where they were markedly 'different'). This is normal behavior, and it is hard to anticipate and eliminate all such 'alternative' or 'detracting' strategies in advance. Hence the pilot studies.

We have also learned that the total number of errors for a fixed number of trials is, in general, a more useful response measure than the more conventional trials to some arbitrary criterion.

a basic conceptual reorientation which seems to clarify the nature of the major phenomena of interest and hence the basic problems with which the student of language is confronted. These problems are such that they can be investigated only with the help of new research tools, unfamiliar to linguistic inquiry as commonly understood today. It also seems likely that most such tools will have to be borrowed from experimental psychology, at least for the foreseeable future. The linguist seriously interested in establishing knowledge about human language processing must become familiar with those techniques which the experimental psychologist has developed, and try to adapt them to the investigation of natural language phenomena.

We do not start in a complete vacuum. Some of our predecessors, particularly Bloomfield and his 'structuralist' followers, have provided valuable, even indispensable, groundwork; they have, in fact, provided the basic conceptual and empirical foundations upon which a science of language-processing might now be cautiously constructed. Moreover, Bloomfield, for one, seemed to have few illusions about what he was doing and the limitations upon the interpretation of his results. Our current generation of linguists, however, at least that portion of it which has been heavily influenced by Chomsky, wants to travel a good deal farther than their methodology will permit. They have taste for the fruits of scientific labor, but none for the labor itself. One of these tastes will have to be adjusted. One does not make an empirical science out of a discipline merely by wishing or proclaiming it to be so. We can hope to extend the range of our scientific interests beyond the traditional bounds of the overt speech-signal (the language product) only if we are prepared to deal with new problems which have no simple solutions, and especially not solutions which are accessible by 'thought experimentation' alone.

In sum, linguists have to face the question whether a science of language (the language process) is possible and, if so, whether or not we want to participate in its development. If we do, we shall require new methods and new modes of thinking but, above all, a new kind of cooperation and free exchange of ideas. The journey ahead should be exciting, and courtesy dictates that every interested party should be invited to join in the adventure. More pragmatically, we have every reason to believe that the road will also be long and arduous. If the trip is to be enjoyable for any of us, it will require all of us to help clear the way.

BIBLIOGRAPHY

Bibliography

Agnew, N. M. & Pyke, S. W. (1969). *The Science Game*. Englewood Cliffs, N.J.: Prentice-Hall.

Allport, G. W. (1961). *Pattern and Growth in Personality*. New York: Holt, Rinehart & Winston.

Alyeshmerni, M. & Taubr, P. (1970). *Working with Aspects of Language*. New York: Harcourt, Brace & World.

Ames, A., Jr (1951). 'Visual perception and the rotating trapezoidal window', *Psychological Monographs*, **65**, no. 324.

Anastasi, A. (1958). *Differential Psychology*. New York: Macmillan.

Andrade, E. N. da C. (1954). *Sir Isaac Newton: His Life and Work*. Garden City, N.Y.: Doubleday.

Bach, E. (1964). *An Introduction to Transformational Grammars*. New York: Holt, Rinehart & Winston.

  (1965a). 'On some recurrent types of transformations'. In Kreidler (1965), pp. 3–18.

  (1965b). 'Structural linguistics and the philosophy of science', *Diogenes*, no. 51 (Fall), pp. 111–28.

  (1968). 'Nouns and noun phrases'. In Bach & Harms (1968), pp. 90–122.

  (1971a). 'Questions', *Linguistic Inquiry*, **11**, 153–66.

  (1971b). 'Syntax since *Aspects*'. In O'Brien (1971), pp. 1–17.

Bach, E. & Harms, R. T. (eds.) (1968). *Universals in Linguistic Theory*. New York: Holt, Rinehart and Winston.

  (1972). 'How do languages get crazy rules?' In Stockwell & Macaulay (1972), pp. 1–21.

Baker, W. J. (1963). 'Subject Variables in the Perception of the Trapezoid Illusion'. Unpublished Ph.D. dissertation, Fordham University.

Baker, W. J., Prideaux, G. D. & Derwing, B. L. (forthcoming). 'Grammatical properties of sentences as a basis for concept formation.' (To appear in *Journal of Psycholinguistic Research*).

Bellugi, U. (1970). 'Learning the language', *Psychology Today*, vol. 4, no. 7 (December), pp. 32–5, 66.

Bellugi, U. & Brown, R. (eds.) (1964). 'The acquisition of language', *Monographs of the Society for Research in Child Development*, vol. 29, no. 1.

Benjamin, A. C. (1965). *Science, Technology, and Human Values*. Columbia, Mo.: University of Missouri Press.

Berko, J. (1958). 'The child's learning of English morphology', *Word*, **14**, 150–77. Reprinted in Saporta (1961), pp. 359–75. (Page references to the latter.)

Berko, J. & Brown, R. (1960). 'Psycholinguistic research methods'. In Mussen (1960), pp. 517-57.

Bever, T. G. (1968). 'A survey of some recent work in psycholinguistics'. In Plath (1968), pp. 1-66 (Section iv).

Bever, T. G., Fodor, J. A. & Weksel, W. (1965a). 'On the acquisition of syntax: a critique of "contextual generalization" ', *Psychological Review*, **72,** 467-82. Reprinted in Jakobovits & Miron (1967), pp. 257-73. (Page references to the latter.)

Bever, T. G., Fodor, J. A. & Weksel, W. (1965b). 'Is linguistics empirical?' *Psychological Review*, **72,** 493-500. Reprinted in Jakobovits & Miron (1967), pp. 285-93. (Page references to the latter.)

Binnick, R. I., Davison, A., Green, G. M. & Morgan, J. L. (eds.) (1969). *Papers from the Fifth Regional Meeting of the Chicago Linguistic Society*. Department of Linguistics, University of Chicago.

Bloch, B. (1941). 'Phonemic overlapping', *American Speech*, **16,** 278-84. Reprinted in Joos (1963), pp. 93-6. (Page references to the latter.)

Bloch, B. & Trager, G. L. (1942). *Outline of Linguistic Analysis*. Baltimore: Waverly Press.

Bloomfield, L. (1926). 'A set of postulates for the science of language', *Language*, **2,** 153-64. Reprinted in Joos (1963), pp. 26-31. (Page references to the latter.)

(1933). *Language*. New York: Holt, Rinehart & Winston.

(1939). 'Menomini morphophonemics'. In Trubetzkoy (1964), pp. 105-15.

Bolinger, D. L. (1948). 'On defining the morpheme', *Word*, **4,** 18-23.

(1950). 'Rime, assonance, and morpheme analysis', *Word*, **6,** 117-36.

(1968). *Aspects of Language*. New York: Harcourt, Brace & World.

Borkovskij, V. I. & Kuznecov, P. S. (1965). *Istoričeskaja Grammatika Russkogo Jazyka*. Moskva: Nauka.

Botha, R. P. (1968). *The Function of the Lexicon in Transformational Generative Grammar*. The Hague: Mouton.

Braine, M. D. S. (1963). 'On learning the grammatical order of words', *Psychological Review*, **70,** 323-48.

(1965). 'On the basis of phrase structure: a reply to Bever, Fodor and Weksel', *Psychological Review*, **72,** 483-92.

Braithwaite, R. B. (1960). *Scientific Explanation*. New York: Harper & Row.

Broadbent, D. (1972). 'On some issues in psycholinguistic theory', *American Psychologist*, **27,** 78-81.

Brodbeck, M. (ed.) (1968). *Readings in the Philosophy of the Social Sciences*. New York: Macmillan.

Brown, R. (1968). 'The development of wh questions in child speech', *Journal of Verbal Learning and Verbal Behavior*, **7,** 279-90.

(ed.) (1970). *Psycholinguistics: Selected Papers*. New York: The Free Press.

Brown, R. & Bellugi, U. (1964). 'Three processes in the child's acquisition of syntax'. In Lenneberg (1964), pp. 131-61.

Brown, R. & Fraser, C. (1964). 'The acquisition of syntax'. In Bellugi & Brown (1964), pp. 43-79.

Bunge, M. (1967). *Scientific Research*. vol. II. *The Search for Truth*. New York: Springer-Verlag.

Cajori, F. (ed.) (1934). *Sir Isaac Newton's Mathematical Principles of Natural Philosophy and His System of the World*. Translated by A. Motte. Cambridge: Cambridge University Press.

Campbell, R. & Wales, R. (1970). 'The study of language acquisition'. In Lyons (1970), pp. 242–60.

Carmichael, L. (1925). 'Heredity and environment: are they antithetical?' *Journal of Abnormal and Social Psychology*, **20**, 245–60.

(ed.) (1954). *Manual of Child Psychology*. Second edition. New York: Wiley.

Carnap, R. (1966). *Philosophical Foundations of Physics*. New York: Basic Books.

Carroll, J. B. (1955). *The Study of Language: A Survey of Linguistics and Related Disciplines in America*. Cambridge, Mass.: Harvard University Press.

Cattell, R. B. (ed.) (1966). *Handbook of Multivariate Experimental Psychology*. Chicago: Rand McNally.

Caws, P. (1965). *The Philosophy of Science: A Systematic Account*. Princeton: Van Nostrand.

(1969). 'The structure of discovery', *Science*, **166:3911**, 1375–80.

Chafe, W. L. (1965). Review of Longacre (1964). *Language*, **41**, 640–7.

(1968a). 'The ordering of phonological rules', *International Journal of American Linguistics*, **34**, 115–36.

(1968b). Review of Lamb (1966a). *Language*, **44**, 593–603.

(1970). *Meaning and the Structure of Language*. Chicago: University of Chicago Press.

(1971). 'Directionality and paraphrase', *Language*, **47**, 1–26.

Chambers, J. K. (1970). 'Focused Noun Phrases in English Syntax'. Unpublished Ph.D. dissertation, University of Alberta.

Chao, Y-R. (1934). 'The non-uniqueness of phonemic solutions of phonetic systems'. *Bulletin of the Institute of History and Philology, Academia Sinica*. vol. IV, part 4, pp. 363–97. Reprinted in Joos (1963), pp. 38–54. (Page references to the latter.)

(1968). *Language and Symbolic Systems*. Cambridge: Cambridge University Press.

Chomsky, C. (1969). *The Acquisition of Syntax in Children from 5 to 10*. Cambridge, Mass.: MIT Press.

Chomsky, N. (1957a). Review of Jakobson & Halle (1956). *International Journal of American Linguistics*, **23**, 234–41.

(1957b). *Syntactic Structures*. The Hague: Mouton.

(1959a). Review of Greenberg (1957). *Word*, **15**, 202–18.

(1959b). Review of Skinner (1957). *Language*, **35**, 26–58.

(1961). 'On the notion "rule of grammar" '. In Jakobson (1961b), pp. 6–24.

(1962a). 'Explanatory models in linguistics'. In Nagel *et al.* (1962), pp. 528–50.

(1962b). 'A transformational approach to syntax'. In Hill (1962), pp. 124–58. Reprinted in Fodor & Katz (1964) pp. 211-45. (Page references to the latter.)

(1963). 'Formal properties of grammars'. In Luce *et al.* (1963), pp. 323–418.

(1964). 'Current issues in linguistic theory'. In Fodor & Katz (1964), pp. 50–118. Also published separately under the same title by Mouton.

(1965a). *Aspects of the Theory of Syntax.* Cambridge, Mass.: MIT Press.

(1965b). 'Persistent topics in linguistic theory', *Diogenes*, no. 51 (Fall), pp. 13–20.

(1966a). *Cartesian Linguistics: A Chapter in the History of Rationalist Thought.* New York: Harper & Row.

(1966b). 'Topics in the theory of generative grammar'. In Sebeok (1966), pp. 1–60. Also published separately under the same title by Mouton.

(1967a). 'The formal nature of language'. In Lenneberg (1967), pp. 397–442.

(1967b). 'The general properties of language'. In Darley (1967), pp. 73–88.

(1967c). 'Recent contributions to the theory of innate ideas', *Synthese*, **17**, 2–11.

(1967d). 'Some general properties of phonological rules', *Language*, **43**, 102–28.

(1968a). *Language and Mind.* New York: Harcourt, Brace & World.

(1968b). 'Language and mind'. In Rothblatt (1968), pp. 3–31.

(1969). 'Linguistics and philosophy'. In Hook (1969), pp. 51–94.

(1970a). 'Deep structure, surface structure, and semantic interpretation'. In Jakobson & Kawamoto (1970), pp. 52–91.

(1970b). 'Remarks on nominalization'. In Jacobs & Rosenbaum (1970), pp. 184–221.

(1971). 'Conditions on transformations'. Unpublished MS. Reproduced by the Indiana University Linguistics Club.

Chomsky, N. & Halle, M. (1965). 'Some controversial questions in phonological theory', *Journal of Linguistics*, **1**, 97–138.

(1968). *The Sound Pattern of English.* New York: Harper & Row.

Chomsky, N. & Miller, G. A. (1963). 'Introduction to the formal analysis of natural languages'. In Luce *et al.* (1963), pp. 269–321.

Church, J. (1961). *Language and the Discovery of Reality.* New York: Random House.

Corder, S. P. (1967). 'The significance of learner's errors', *International Review of Applied Linguistics*, **5**, 161–70.

Creore, J. A. (forthcoming). 'Schane vs. the French language'. Paper read at the Banff meeting of the Alberta Linguistic Association (To appear in *The Canadian Journal of Romance Linguistics*).

Crothers, J. (1971). 'On the abstractness controversy'. *Project on Linguistic Analysis.* Phonology Laboratory, Department of Linguistics, University of California, Berkeley. No. 12 (February), pp. CR1–29.

Čukovskij, K. (1961). *Ot Dvux do Pjati.* Moskva: Gosudarstvennoe Izdatel'-stvo Detskoj Literatury.

Dale, P.S. (1972). *Langauge Development: Structure and Function*. Hinsdale, Ill.: Dryden Press.

Darden, B. J., Bailey, C-J. N. & Davison, A. (eds.) (1968). *Papers from the Fourth Regional Meeting of the Chicago Linguistic Society*. Department of Linguistics, University of Chicago.

Darley, F. L. (ed.) (1967). *Brain Mechanisms Underlying Speech and Language*. New York and London: Grune and Stratton.

Deese, J. (1970). *Psycholinguistics*. Boston: Allyn & Bacon.

Deese, J. & Hulse, S. H. (1967). *The Psychology of Learning*. New York: McGraw-Hill.

Denes, P. (1955). 'Effect of duration on the perception of voicing', *The Journal of the Acoustical Society of America*, **27**, 761–4.

Denes, P. B. & Pinson, E. N. (1963). *The Speech Chain: The Physics and Biology of Spoken Language*. Baltimore; Md.: Bell Telephone Laboratories.

Derwing, B. L. (1965). 'On the English Interpretation of the Russian Word'. Unpublished M.A. thesis, Indiana University.

  (1970). 'Transformational Grammar and Language Acquisition'. Unpublished Ph.D. dissertation, Indiana University.

Dingwall, W. O. (1971). *A Survey of Linguistic Science*. Linguistics Program, University of Maryland.

Dunkel, H. B. (1948). *Second-Language Learning*. Boston: Ginn & Co.

Einstein, A. (1934). *Essays in Science*. New York: Philosophical Library.

Emig, J. A., Fleming, J. T. & Popp, H. M. (1966). *Language and Learning*. New York: Harcourt, Brace & World.

Engel, W. von Raffler- (1970). 'The LAD, our underlying unconscious, and more on "felt sets" ', *Language Sciences*, no. 13, pp. 15–18.

English, H. B. & English, A. C. (1958). *A Comprehensive Dictionary of Psychological and Psychoanalytical Terms*. New York: Longmans, Green.

Ervin, S. M. (1964). 'Imitation and structural change in children's language'. In Lenneberg (1964), pp. 163–89.

Fagan, W. T. (1969). 'An Investigation into the Relationship between Reading Difficulty and the Number and Types of Sentence Transformations'. Unpublished Ph.D. dissertation, University of Alberta.

Faust, G. P. (1970). Review of Chomsky (1965a). *General Linguistics* (State College, Pa.: Pennsylvania State University Press), **10**, 43–7.

Feigl, H. & Maxwell, G. (eds.) (1961). *Current Issues in the Philosophy of Science*. New York: Holt, Rinehart & Winston.

Feyerabend, P. K. (1968). 'How to be a good empiricist – a plea for tolerance in matters epistemological'. In Nidditch (1968), pp. 12–39.

Fodor, J. A. (1966). 'How to learn to talk: some simple ways'. In Smith & Miller (1966), pp. 105–22.

  (1968). 'Functional explanation in psychology'. In Brodbeck (1968), pp. 223–38.

  (1971). 'Current approaches to syntax recognition.' In Horton & Jenkins (1971), pp. 120–39.

Fodor, J. A. & Garrett, M. (1966). 'Some reflections on competence and performance'. In Lyons & Wales (1966), pp. 135–54.

Fodor, J. A. & Katz, J. J. (1964). *The Structure of Language: Readings in the Philosophy of Language*. Englewood Cliffs, N.J.: Prentice-Hall.

Foster, J. M. (1966). 'Some Phonological Rules of Modern Standard Ukrainian'. Unpublished Ph.D. dissertation, University of Illinois.

Francis, W. N. (1958). *The Structure of American English*. New York: Ronald Press.

Fries, C. C. & Pike, K. L. (1949). 'Coexistent phonemic systems', *Language*, **25**, 29–50.

Fromkin, V. A. (1968). 'Speculations on performance models', *Journal of Linguistics*, **4**, 47–68.

(1971). 'The non-anomalous nature of anomalous utterances', *Language*, **47**, 27–52.

Fudge, E. C. (1967). 'The nature of phonological primes', *Journal of Linguistics*, **3**, 1–36.

(1970). 'Phonology'. In Lyons (1970), pp. 76–95.

Garvin, P. L. (1953). Review of Jakobson *et al.* (1952), *Language*, **29**, 472–81.

Ginsburg, H. & Opper, S. (1969). *Piaget's Theory of Intellectual Development: An Introduction*. Englewood Cliffs, N.J.: Prentice-Hall.

Gleason, H. A., Jr (1961). *An Introduction to Descriptive Linguistics*. New York: Holt, Rinehart and Winston.

(1964). 'The organization of language: a stratificational view'. In Stuart (1964), pp. 75–95.

Goodman, N. (1969). 'The emperor's new ideas'. In Hook (1969), pp. 138–42.

Gough, P. B. (1966). 'The verification of sentences: the effects of delay of evidence and sentence length', *Journal of Verbal Learning and Verbal Behavior*, **5**, 492–6.

Greenberg, J. H. (1957). *Essays in Linguistics*. Chicago: University of Chicago Press.

(ed.) (1963). *Universals of Language*. Cambridge, Mass.: MIT Press.

Greenberg, J. H. & Jenkins, J. J. (1964). 'Studies in the psychological correlates of the sound system of American English', *Word*, **20**, 157–77.

Hale, K. (1971). 'Deep-surface canonical disparities in relation to analysis and change: an Australian example'. Unpublished MS.

Halle, M. (1954). 'The strategy of phonemics', *Word*, **10**, 197–209.

(1959). *The Sound Pattern of Russian*. The Hague: Mouton.

(1961). 'On the role of simplicity in linguistic descriptions'. In Jakobson (1961b), pp. 89–94.

(1962). 'Phonology in generative grammar', *Word*, **18**, 54–72. Reprinted in Fodor and Katz (1964), pp. 334–52. (Page references to the latter.)

(1963). 'O pravilax russkogo sprjaženija'. In *American Contributions to the Fifth International Congress of Slavists*. The Hague: Mouton, pp. 113–32.

(1964). 'On the bases of phonology'. In Fodor and Katz (1964), pp. 324–33.

(1971). 'Research objectives'. *Quarterly Progress Report* no. 100, Research Laboratory of Electronics, MIT, pp. 177–8.

Halle, M. & Stevens, K. N. (1964). 'Speech recognition: a model and a program for research'. In Fodor & Katz (1964), pp. 604-12.

Hanson, N. R. (1958). *Patterns of Discovery*. Cambridge: Cambridge University Press. (Page references to the 1969 paperback edition.)

(1961). 'Is there a logic of scientific discovery?' In Feigl & Maxwell (1961), pp. 20-35.

Harman, G. (1967). 'Psychological aspects of the theory of syntax', *Journal of Philosophy*, **64**, 75-87.

Harris, J. W. (1970). 'A note on Spanish plural formation', *Language*, **46**, 928-30.

Harris, P. R. (1970). 'On the Interpretation of Generative Grammars'. Unpublished M.Sc. thesis, University of Alberta.

(1971). 'What is a generative grammar: II'. Unpublished paper distributed at the annual meeting of the Canadian Linguistic Association, St John's, Newfoundland.

Harris, Z. S. (1951). *Methods in Structural Linguistics*. Chicago: University of Chicago Press.

(1957). 'Co-occurrence and transformation in linguistic structure', *Language*, **33**, 283-340.

Hayes, J. R. (ed.) (1970). *Cognition and the Development of Language*. New York: Wiley.

Hempel, C. G. (1966). *Philosophy of Natural Science*. Englewood Cliffs, N.J.: Prentice-Hall.

(1968). 'Explanation in science and in history'. In Nidditch (1968), pp. 54-79.

Hempel, C. G. & Oppenheim, P. (1948). 'The logic of explanation', *Philosophy of Science*, **15**, 135-46, 152-7. Reprinted in part in Krimerman (1969), pp. 54-68. (Page references to the latter.)

Hildebrand, J. H. (1957). *Science in the Making*. New York: Columbia University Press. (Page references to the 1962 paperback edition.)

Hilgard, E. R. & Bower, G. H. (1966). *Theories of Learning*. New York: Appleton-Century-Crofts.

Hill, A. A. (1955). 'Linguistics since Bloomfield', *Quarterly Journal of Speech*, **41**, 253-60.

(1961). 'Grammaticality', *Word*, **17**, 1-10.

(ed.) (1962). *Third Texas Conference on Problems of Linguistic Analysis in English*. Austin: University of Texas.

(1967). 'The current relevance of Bloch's postulates', *Language*, **43**, 203-7.

Hiż, H. (1967). 'Methodological aspects of the theory of syntax', *Journal of Philosophy*, **64**, pp. 67-74.

Hjelmslev, L. (1961). *Prolegomena to a Theory of Language*. Translated by F. J. Whitfield. Madison: University of Wisconsin Press.

Hockett, C. F. (1942). 'A system of descriptive phonology', *Language*, **18**, 3-21. Reprinted in Joos (1963), pp. 97-108. (Page references to the latter.)

(1948). 'A note on "structure"', *International Journal of American Linguistics*, **14**, 269–71. Reprinted in Joos (1963), pp. 279–80. (Page references to the latter.)

(1949). 'Two fundamental problems in phonemics', *Studies in Linguistics*, **7**, 29–51.

(1950). 'Peiping morphophonemics,' *Language*, **26**, 63–85.

(1954). 'Two models of grammatical description', *Word*, **10**, 210–31. Reprinted in Joos (1963), pp. 386–99. (Page references to the latter.)

(1958). *A Course in Modern Linguistics*. New York: Macmillan.

(1961). 'Grammar for the hearer'. In Jakobson (1961b), pp. 220–36.

(1963). 'The problem of universals in language'. In Greenberg (1963), pp. 1–22.

(1968a). Review of Lamb (1966a). *International Journal of American Linguistics*, **34**, 145–53.

(1968b). *The State of the Art*. The Hague: Mouton.

Holden, K. T. (1972). 'Loan Words and Phonological Systems.' Unpublished Ph.D. dissertation, University of Texas, Austin.

Holton, G. & Roller, D. H. D. (1958). *Foundations of Modern Physical Science*. Reading, Mass.: Addison-Wesley.

Hook, S. (ed.) (1969). *Language and Philosophy*. New York: New York University Press.

Hörmann, H. (1971). *Psycholinguistics: An Introduction to Research and Theory*. Translated by H. H. Stern. New York: Springer-Verlag.

Horton, D. L. & Jenkins, J. J. (eds.) (1971). *Perception of Language*. Columbus, Ohio: Merrill.

Householder, F. W., Jr (1952). Review of Harris (1951). *International Journal of American Linguistics*, **18**, 260–8.

(1961). 'On linguistic terms'. In Saporta (1961), pp. 15–25.

(1965). 'On some recent claims in phonological theory', *Journal of Linguistics*, **1**, 13–34.

(1966). 'Phonological theory: a brief comment', *Journal of Linguistics*, **2**, 99–100.

(1967). 'Distinctive features and phonetic features'. In *To Honor Roman Jakobson*, vol. II (The Hague: Mouton), pp. 941–4.

(1968). 'The ultimate goals', *Language Sciences*, no. 1, pp. 7–11.

(1971). Review of Langendoen (1969). *Language*, **47**, 453–65.

Howells, T. H. (1945). 'The obsolete dogmas of heredity', *Psychological Review*, **52**, 23–34.

Hyman, L. M. (1970). 'How concrete is phonology', *Language*, **46**, 58–76.

Hyman, R. (1964). *The Nature of Psychological Inquiry*. Englewood Cliffs, N.J.: Prentice-Hall.

Jacobs, R. A. & Rosenbaum, P. S. (1970). *Readings in English Transformational Grammar*. Waltham, Mass.: Ginn & Co.

Jakobovits, L. A. (1969). 'The psycholinguists: whither now?' Review of Miller (1967). *Contemporary Psychology*, **14**, 156–7.

Jakobovits, L. A. & Miron, M. S. (1967). *Readings in the Psychology of Language*. Englewood Cliffs, N.J.: Prentice-Hall.

Jakobson, R. (1948). 'Russian conjugation', *Word*, **4**, 155–67.

(1961a). 'Linguistics and communication theory'. In Jakobson (1961b), pp. 245–53.

(ed.) (1961b). *Structure of Language and its Mathematical Aspects. Proceedings of Symposia in Applied Mathematics*, vol. XII, Providence, R.I.: American Mathematical Society.

Jakobson, R., Fant, C. G. M. & Halle, M. (1952). *Preliminaries to Speech Analysis: The Distinctive Features and Their Correlates*. Cambridge, Mass.: MIT Press.

Jakobson, R. & Halle, M. (1956). *Fundamentals of Language*. The Hague: Mouton.

Jakobson, R. & Kawamoto, S. (eds.) (1970). *Studies in General and Oriental Linguistics: Presented to Shirô Hattori on the Occasion of His Sixtieth Birthday*. Tokyo: TEC.

Joos, M. (ed.) (1963). *Readings in Linguistics*. New York: ACLS.

Jungk, R. (1958). *Brighter than a Thousand Suns: A Personal History of the Atomic Scientists*. New York: Harcourt, Brace & Co.

Katz, J. J. (1964). 'Mentalism in linguistics', *Language*, **40**, 124–37.

(1966). *The Philosophy of Language*. New York: Harper & Row.

Katz, J. J. & Fodor, J. A. (1963). 'The structure of a semantic theory', *Language* **39**, 170–210.

Katz, J. J. & Postal, P. M. (1964). *An Integrated Theory of Linguistic Descriptions*. Cambridge, Mass.: MIT Press.

King, R. D. (1969). *Historical Linguistics and Generative Grammar*. Englewood Cliffs, N.J.: Prentice-Hall.

Kiparsky, P. (1968a). 'How abstract is phonology'. Unpublished MS. Reproduced by the Indiana University Linguistics Club.

(1968b). 'Linguistic universals and linguistic change'. In Bach & Harms (1968), pp. 170–202.

(1970). 'Historical linguistics'. In Lyons (1970), pp. 302–15.

Koch, S. (ed.) (1963). *Psychology: A Study of a Science*. vol. VI. *Investigations of Man as Socius: Their Place in Psychology and the Social Sciences*. New York: McGraw-Hill.

Koestler, A. (1964). *The Act of Creation*. London: Hutchinson.

(1967). *The Ghost in the Machine*. London: Hutchinson.

Kohler, K. J. (1970). Review of Chomsky & Halle (1968). *Lingua*, **26**, 73–95.

Koutsoudas, A. (1966). *Writing Transformational Grammars: An Introduction*. New York: McGraw-Hill.

(1972). 'The strict order fallacy', *Language*, **48**, 88–96.

Koutsoudas, A., Sanders, G. & Noll, C. (1971). 'On the application of phonological rules'. Unpublished MS. Reproduced by the Indiana University Linguistics Club.

Kreidler, C. W. (ed.) (1965). *Report of the Sixteenth Annual Round Table Meeting on Linguistics and Language Studies, Monograph Series on*

Languages and Linguistics, no. 18. Washington, D.C.: Georgetown University Press.

Krimerman, L. I. (1969). *The Nature and Scope of Social Science: A Critical Anthology.* New York: Appleton-Century-Crofts.

Kuhn, T. S. (1962). *The Structure of Scientific Revolutions.* Chicago: University of Chicago Press.

Lackowski, P. (1968). Review of Katz (1966). *Language*, **44**, 606–16.

Lakoff, G. (1965). *On the Nature of Syntactic Irregularity.* Cambridge, Mass.: The Computation Laboratory, Harvard University. Report NSF-16.

(1969). Review of Hockett (1968b), *Foundations of Language*, **5**, 118–27.

(1970). *Irregularity in Syntax.* New York: Holt, Rinehart & Winston. (= Lakoff, 1965)

Lamb, S. M. (1964). 'On alternation, transformation, realization, and stratification'. In Stuart (1964), pp. 105–22.

(1966a). *Outline of Stratificational Grammar.* Washington, D.C.: Georgetown University Press.

(1966b). 'Prolegomena to a theory of phonology', *Language*, **42**, 536–73.

Langacker, R. W. (1967). *Language and Its Structure: Some Fundamental Linguistic Concepts.* New York: Harcourt, Brace and World.

Langendoen, D.T. (1969). *The Study of Syntax: The Generative-Transformational Approach to the Structure of American English.* New York: Holt, Rinehart & Winston.

Leech, G. N. (1968). 'Some assumptions in the metatheory of linguistics', *Linguistics*, no. 39, pp. 87–102.

Lees, R. B. (1957). Review of Chomsky (1957b), *Language*, **33**, 375–408.

(1965a). 'On the testability of linguistic predicates', *Linguistics*, no. 12, pp. 37–48.

(1965b). 'Two views of linguistic research', *Linguistics*, no. 11, pp. 21–29.

Lehmann, W. P. & Malkiel, Y. (1968). *Directions for Historical Linguistics.* Austin: University of Texas Press.

Lenneberg, E. H. (ed.) (1964). *New Directions in the Study of Language.* Cambridge, Mass.: MIT Press.

(1966). 'The natural history of language'. In Smith and Miller (1966), pp. 219–52.

(1967). *Biological Foundations of Language.* New York: Wiley.

Levin, M. I. (1969). 'On presenting the Russian verb', *The Slavic and East European Journal*, **13**, 229–41.

Lightner, T. M. (1965). 'Segmental Phonology of Modern Standard Russian'. Unpublished Ph.D. dissertation, MIT.

(1966a). 'Ob al'ternacii e∼o v sovremennom russkom literaturnom jazyke', *Voprosy Jazykoznanija*, **15**, 64–80.

(1966b). 'On the phonology of the Old Church Slavonic conjugation', *International Journal of Slavic Linguistics and Poetics*, **10**, 1–29.

(1967). 'On the phonology of Russian conjugation', *Linguistics*, no. 35, pp. 35–55.

Longacre, R. E. (1964). *Grammar Discovery Procedures: A Field Manual.* The Hague: Mouton.

Lotz, J. (1950). 'Speech and language', *The Journal of the Acoustical Society of America*, **22**, 712–17.

Luce, R., Bush, R. & Galanter, E. (1963). *Handbook of Mathematical Psychology*. vol. II. New York: Wiley & Sons.

Lunt, H. G. (1959). *Old Church Slavonic Glossary.* Department of Slavic Languages and Literatures, Harvard University.

Luria, A. R. & Vinogradova, O. S. (1959). 'An objective investigation of the dynamics of semantic systems', *British Journal of Psychology*, **50**, 89–105.

Lynkowsky, P. E. (1970). 'Ukrainian Diminutives in -OK'. Unpublished M.A. thesis, University of Alberta.

Lyons, J. (1966). Review of Chomsky (1965a). *Philosophical Quarterly*, **16**, 393–5.

  (1968). *Introduction to Theoretical Linguistics.* Cambridge: Cambridge University Press.

  (ed.) (1970). *New Horizons in Linguistics.* Penguin Books.

Lyons, J. & Wales, R. J. (eds.) (1966). *Psycholinguistics Papers.* Edinburgh: Edinburgh University Press.

Maclay, H. & Sleator, M. D. (1960). 'Responses to language: judgments of grammaticalness', *International Journal of American Linguistics*, **26**, 275–82.

Macnamara, J. (1972). 'Cognitive basis of language learning in infants', *Psychological Review*, **79**, 1–13.

Maher, J. P. (1969). 'The paradox of creation and tradition in grammar: sound pattern of a palimpsest', *Language Sciences*, no. 7, pp. 15–24.

Malone, J. L. (1970). 'In defense of non-uniqueness of phonological representation', *Language*, **46**, 328–35.

Mandelbaum, D. G. (1968). *Selected Writings of Edward Sapir in Language, Culture and Personality.* Berkeley and Los Angeles: University of California Press.

Martinet, A. (1964). *Elements of General Linguistics.* Translated by E. Palmer. London: Faber & Faber.

Matthews, P. H. (1967). Review of Chomsky (1965a). *Journal of Linguistics*, **3**, 119–52.

Matthews, W. K. (1960). *Russian Historical Grammar.* London: Athlone Press.

McCarthy, D. (1954). 'Language development in children'. In Carmichael (1954), pp. 492–630.

McCawley, J. D. (1967a). 'Le rôle d'un système de traits phonologiques dans une théorie du langage', *Langages*, **8**, 112–23.

  (1967b). 'Sapir's phonologic representation', *International Journal of American Linguistics*, **33**, 106–11.

  (1968a). 'Can you count pluses and minuses before you can count?' Unpublished MS.

(1968b). 'Lexical insertion in a transformational grammar without deep structure'. In Darden *et al.* (1968), pp. 71–80.

(1968c). *The Phonological Component of a Grammar of Japanese.* The Hague: Mouton.

(1968d). Review of Sebeok (1966). *Language,* **44,** 556–93.

(1968e). 'The role of semantics in a grammar'. In Bach & Harms (1968), pp. 124–69.

McNeill, D. (1966a). 'The creation of language by children'. In Lyons & Wales (1966), pp. 99–115.

(1966b). 'Developmental psycholinguistics'. In Smith & Miller (1966), pp. 15–84.

(1970a). *The Acquisition of Language: The Study of Developmental Psycholinguistics.* New York: Harper & Row.

(1970b). 'The development of language'. In Mussen (1970), pp. 1061–161.

Mehta, V. (1971). 'Onward and upward with the arts: John is easy to please', *The New Yorker,* **47,** No. 12 (8 May 1971), 44–87.

Menyuk, P. (1969). *Sentences Children Use.* Cambridge, Mass.: MIT Press.

Micklesen, L. R. (1971). Review of Hockett (1968b). *General Linguistics* (State College, Pa.: Pennsylvania State University Press), **11,** 28–31.

Miller, G. A. (1951). *Language and Communication.* New York: McGraw-Hill.

(1967). *The Psychology of Communication: Seven Essays.* New York: Basic Books.

Miller, G. A. & Chomsky, N. (1963). 'Finitary models of language users'. In Luce *et al.* (1963), pp. 419–91.

Miller, G. A. & Nicely, P. E. (1955). 'An analysis of perceptual confusions among some English consonants', *The Journal of the Acoustical Society of America,* **27,** 338–52.

Mussen, P. H. (ed.) (1960). *Handbook of Research Methods in Child Development.* New York: Wiley.

(ed.) (1970). *Carmichael's Manual of Child Psychology.* Third edition, vol. 1. New York: Wiley.

Nagel, E. (1961). *The Structure of Science: Problems in the Logic of Scientific Explanation.* New York: Harcourt, Brace & World.

Nagel, E., Suppes, P. & Tarski, A. (eds.) (1962). *Logic, Methodology and Philosophy of Science.* Stanford, Calif.: Stanford University Press.

Nida, E. A. (1949). *Morphology: The Descriptive Analysis of Words.* Second edition. Ann Arbor: University of Michigan Press.

Nidditch, P. H. (ed.) (1968). *The Philosophy of Science.* London: Oxford University Press.

O'Brien, R. J. (ed.) (1971). *Report of the Twenty-Second Annual Round Table Meeting on Linguistics and Language Studies, Monograph Series on Language and Linguistics,* no. 24. Washington, D.C.: Georgetown University Press.

Olmsted, D. L. (1955). Review of the 1954 edition of Osgood & Sebeok (1965). *Language,* **31,** 46–59.

Osgood, C. E. & Jenkins, J. J. (1965). 'Diachronic psycholinguistics'. In Osgood & Sebeok (1965), pp. 126–35.

Osgood, C. E. & Sebeok, T. A. (eds.) (1965). *Psycholinguistics: A Survey of Theory and Research Problems.* With Diebold, R., Jr. *A Survey of Psycholinguistic Research, 1954–1964.* Bloomington: Indiana University Press.

Paul, H. (1891). *Principles of the History of Language.* Translated by H. A. Strong. London: Longmans, Green.

Peizer, D. B. & Olmsted, D. L. (1969). 'Modules of grammar acquisition', *Language,* **45,** 60–96.

Perlmutter, D. M. (1970). 'Surface structure constraints in syntax', *Linguistic Inquiry,* **1,** 187–255.

Peters, P. S. (1970). 'Why are there so many "universal" bases?' *Papers in Linguistics,* **2,** 27–43.

Peters, P. S. & Ritchie, R. W. (1969). 'A note on the universal base hypothesis', *Journal of Linguistics,* **5,** 150–2.

Pike, E. V. (1970). Review of Postal (1968), *Lingua,* **25,** 30–46.

Pike, K. L. (1947a). 'Grammatical prerequisites to phonemic analysis', *Word,* **3,** 155–72.

(1947b). *Phonemics: A Technique for Reducing Languages to Writing.* Ann Arbor: University of Michigan Press.

(1952). 'More on grammatical prerequisites', *Word,* **8,** 106–21.

Plath, W. J. (ed.) (1968). *Specification and Utilization of a Transformational Grammar.* Yorktown Heights, N.Y.: IBM Corporation.

Platt, J. (1964). 'Strong inference', *Science,* **146:3642,** 347–53.

Popper, K. R. (1965). *The Logic of Scientific Discovery.* New York: Harper & Row.

(1969). 'The hypothetical-deductive method and the unity of social and natural science'. In Krimerman (1969), pp. 47–53.

Postal, P. M. (1964). *Constituent Structure: A Study of Contemporary Models of Syntactic Description.* Supplement to vol. xxx of *International Journal of American Linguistics.* The Hague: Mouton.

(1966). Review of Martinet (1964). *Foundations of Language,* **2,** 151–86.

(1968). *Aspects of Phonological Theory.* New York: Harper & Row.

Postman, N. & Weingartner, C. (1966). *Linguistics: A Revolution in Teaching.* New York: Dell.

Prideaux, G. D. (1970a). 'On the selection problem', *Papers in Linguistics,* **2,** 238–66.

(1970b). *The Syntax of Japanese Honorifics.* The Hague: Mouton.

(1971a). 'On the notion "linguistically significant generalization" ', *Lingua,* **26,** 337–47.

(1971b). 'An excluded generalization'. Paper read at the annual meeting of the Canadian Linguistic Association, St John's, Newfoundland. (To appear in *Festschrift for A. A. Hill.*)

(forthcoming). 'Surface structure resolution of structural ambiguity'.

338   Bibliography

Putnam, H. (1967). 'The "innateness hypothesis" and explanatory models in linguistics', *Synthèse*, **17**, 12–22.

Read, C. (1971). 'Pre-school children's knowledge of English phonology', *Harvard Educational Review*, **41**, 1–34.

Reich, P. A. (1969). 'The finiteness of natural language', *Language*, **45**, 831-43.

Ringen, C. (1971). 'On arguments for rule ordering'. Unpublished MS. Reproduced by the Indiana University Linguistics Club.

Rivers, W. (1964). *The Psychologist and the Foreign-Language Teacher.* Chicago: University of Chicago Press.

Roberts, P. (1964). *English Syntax.* New York: Harcourt, Brace & World.

Robins, R. H. (1966). *General Linguistics: An Introductory Survey.* Bloomington: Indiana University Press.

Rosenbaum, P. S. (1966). 'On the role of linguistics in the teaching of English'. In Emig *et al.* (1966), pp. 176–94.

Ross, J. R. (1967). 'Constraints on Variables in Syntax'. Unpublished Ph.D. dissertation, MIT.

Rothblatt, B. (ed.) (1968). *Changing Perspectives on Man.* Chicago: University of Chicago Press.

Salmon, W. C. (1967). *The Foundations of Scientific Inference.* Pittsburgh: University of Pittsburgh Press.

Sanders, G. A. (1967). 'Some General Grammatical Processes in English'. Unpublished Ph.D. dissertation, Indiana University.

(1970). 'On the natural domain of grammar', *Linguistics*, no. 63, pp. 51–123.

Sapir, E. (1921). *Language.* New York: Harcourt, Brace & World.

(1933). 'La Realité psychologique des phonèmes', *Journal de Psychologie Normale et Pathologique*, **30**, 247–65. Reprinted in English as 'The psychological reality of phonemes' in Mandelbaum (1968), pp. 46–60. (Page references to the latter.)

Saporta, S. (1961). *Psycholinguistics: A Book of Readings.* New York: Holt, Rinehart & Winston.

(1965). Review of Koch (1963). *Language*, **41**, 95–100.

Saussure, F. de (1959). *Course in General Linguistics.* Translated by W. Baskin. New York: Philosophical Library.

Schachter, P. (1969). 'Natural assimilation rules in Akan', *International Journal of American Linguistics*, **35**, 342–55.

Schane, S. A. (1968). *French Phonology and Morphology.* Cambridge, Mass.: MIT Press.

(1971). 'The phoneme revisited', *Language*, **47**, 503–21.

Schlesinger, I. M. (1967). 'A note on the relationship between psychological and linguistic theories', *Foundations of Language*, **3**, 397–402.

(1971). 'Production of utterances and language acquisition'. In Slobin (1971b), pp. 63–101.

Schwarcz, R. M. (1967). 'Steps toward a model of linguistic performance: a preliminary sketch', *Mechanical Translation and Computational Linguistics*, **10**, 39–52.

Scriven, M. (1969a). 'The comprehension theorem'. Unpublished MS.

(1969b). 'The covering law position: a critique and an alternative analysis'. In Krimerman (1969), pp. 94–116.

Searle, J. R. (1970). *Speech Acts: An Essay in the Philosophy of Language.* Cambridge: Cambridge University Press.

Sebeok, T. A. (ed.) (1966). *Current Trends in Linguistics*, vol. III. *Theoretical Foundations.* The Hague: Mouton.

Seuren, P. A. M. (1969). Review of Koutsoudas (1966), *Journal of Linguistics*, **5**, 188–9.

Shipley, E. F., Smith, C. S. & Gleitman, L. R. (1969). 'A study in the acquisition of language', *Language*, **45**, 322–42.

Sigurd, B. (1970). 'The phonemic principle and transformational grammar', *Language Sciences*, no. 11, pp. 15–18.

Skinner, B. F. (1957). *Verbal Behavior.* New York: Appleton-Century-Crofts.

Sklar, R. (1968). 'Chomsky's revolution in linguistics', *The Nation*, **207**, 213–7.

Sledd, J. H. (1962). 'Prufrock among the syntacticians'. In Hill (1962), pp. 1–15.

Slobin, D. I. (1966). 'Comments on "developmental psycholinguistics" '. In Smith & Miller (1966), pp. 85–91.

(1971a). 'Developmental psycholinguistics'. In Dingwall (1971), pp. 298–400.

(ed.) (1971b). *The Ontogenesis of Grammar.* New York: Academic Press.

(1971c). *Psycholinguistics.* Glenview, Ill.: Scott, Foresman.

Smith, C. S. (1970). 'An experimental approach to children's linguistic competence'. In Hayes (1970), pp. 109–35.

Smith, F. & Miller, G. A. (1966). *The Genesis of Language: A Psycholinguistic Approach.* Cambridge, Mass.: MIT Press.

Stankiewicz, E. (1966). 'Slavic morphophonemics in its typological and diachronic aspects'. In Sebeok (1966), pp. 495–520.

Stanley, R. (1967). 'Redundancy rules in phonology', *Language*, **43**, 393–436.

Steinberg, D. D. (1970a). 'Psychological aspects of Chomsky's competence-performance distinction'. In *Working Papers in Linguistics*. Department of Linguistics, University of Hawaii. vol. II, no. 2 (February–March), pp. 180–92.

(1970b). 'Some psycholinguistic implications of Chomsky's doctrine of notational variants'. In *Working Papers in Linguistics*. Department of Linguistics, University of Hawaii. vol. II, no. 3 (April), pp. 256–9.

Steiner, G. (1967). *Language and Silence.* New York: Atheneum.

Stockwell, R. P. & Macaulay, R. K. S. (eds.) (1972). *Linguistic Change and Generative Theory. Essays from the UCLA Conference on Historical Linguistics in the Perspective of Transformational Theory 1969.* Bloomington and London: Indiana University Press.

Stuart, C. I. J. M. (ed.) (1964). *Report of the Fifteenth Annual (First International) Round Table Meeting on Linguistics and Language Studies, Monograph Series on Language and Linguistics*, no. 17. Washington, D.C.: Georgetown University Press.

(1969). 'On the empirical foundations of linguistic description'. In *Actes du Xᵉ Congrès International des Linguistes* (Bucharest: Éditions de l'Académie de la République Socialiste de Roumanie), pp. 393–400.

Sturtevant, E. H. (1947). *An Introduction to Linguistic Science*. New Haven: Yale University Press. (Page references to the 1960 paperback edition.)

Swadesh, M. (1934). 'The phonemic principle', *Language*, **10**, 117–29. Reprinted in Joos (1963), pp. 32–7. (Page references to the latter.)

Swadesh, M. & Voegelin, C. F. (1939). 'A problem in phonological alternation', *Language*, **15**, 1–10. Reprinted in Joos (1963), pp. 88–92. (Page references to the latter.)

Teeter, K. V. (1964). 'Descriptive linguistics in America: triviality vs. irrelevance', *Word*, **20**, 197–206.

(1966). 'A note on uniqueness', *Language*, **42**, 475–8.

(1969). 'Leonard Bloomfield's linguistics', *Language Sciences*, no. 7, pp. 1–6.

Thorne, J. P. (1965). Review of Postal (1964). *Journal of Linguistics*, **1**, 73–6.

Toulmin, S. (1963). *Foresight and Understanding*. New York: Harper & Row.

(1967). 'The evolutionary development of natural science', *American Scientist*, **55**, 456–71.

Townsend, C. E. (1968). *Russian Word-Formation*. New York: McGraw-Hill.

Trager, G. L. (1934). 'The phonemes of Russian', *Language*, **10**, 334–44.

Trubetzkoy, N. S. (1964). *Études Phonologiques Dediées a la Mémoire de M. le Prince Trubetzkoy*. University, Alabama: University of Alabama Press.

(1969). *Principles of Phonology*. Translated by C. A. M. Baltaxe. Berkeley and Los Angeles: University of California Press.

Turner, M. B. (1967). *Philosophy and the Science of Behavior*. New York: Appleton-Century-Crofts.

Twaddell, W. F. (1935). 'On defining the phoneme'. *Language Monograph*, no. 16. Reprinted in Joos (1963), pp. 55–79. (Page references to the latter.)

Wang, W. S-Y. (1968). 'Vowel features, paired variables, and the English vowel shift', *Language*, **44**, 695–708.

Warnock, G. J. (1958). *English Philosophy since 1900*. Oxford: Oxford University Press.

Watt, W. C. (1970). 'On two hypotheses concerning psycholinguistics'. In Hayes (1970), pp. 137–220.

Weinreich, U., Labov, W. & Herzog, M. I. (1968). 'Empirical foundations for a theory of language change'. In Lehmann & Malkiel (1968), pp. 95–188.

Weksel, W. (1965). Review of Bellugi & Brown (1964). *Language*, **41**, 692–709.

White, L. A. (1949). *The Science of Culture: A Study of Man and Civilization*. New York: Ferrar, Straus.

Whitney, W. D. (1889). *Sanskrit Grammar*. Cambridge, Mass.: Harvard University Press.

Wiest, W. M. (1967). 'Some recent criticisms of behaviorism and learning theory', *Psychological Bulletin*, **67**, 214–25.

Woodworth, E. D. & DiPietro, R. J. (eds.) (1963). *Report of the Thirteenth Annual Round Table Meeting on Linguistics and Language Studies, Monograph Series on Language and Linguistics*, no. 15. Washington, D.C.: Georgetown University Press.

Yngve, V. H. (1969). 'On achieving agreement in linguistics'. In Binnick *et al.* (1969), pp. 455–62.

Ziff, P. (1960). *Semantic Analysis*. Ithaca, N.Y.: Cornell University Press.

Zimmer, K. E. (1964). *Affixal Negation in English and Other Languages: An Investigation of Restricted Productivity*. Supplement to *Word*, vol. xx, no. 2. Monograph No. 5.

Zwicky, A. M. (1970). 'The free-ride principle and two rules of complete assimilation in English'. In *Papers from the Sixth Regional Meeting of the Chicago Linguistic Society* (Chicago: Chicago Linguistic Society), pp. 579–88.

Index

abstraction, *see* idealization

abstractness, 247*n*, 310; of deep structures, 70, 157*n*, 158–9, 212; of lexical representations, 100–1, 103ff, 108, 126–8, 134, 135, 140*n*, 143–53, 159, 190, 192ff, 212

adequacy: descriptive, 42*n*, 109, 141–2; explanatory, 61–2; observational, 42*n*, 156

Agnew, N. M. & Pyke, S. W., 248

Allport, G. W., 154

alternatives, method of, 16–20, 23–4, 221, 234–6

ambiguity, 160–1, 163*n*, 166–7

analogy, 34, 35, 126, 147*n*, 309–13

analysis by synthesis, 271–2

Anastasi, A., 64

anomaly, 160–1

arbitrariness, 37, 43, 79, 132, 135*n*, 155, 159, 185, 195, 199, 245, 247, 276, 285, 295, 297, 302, 305

assumptions, 3, 5, 20, 74, 78, 80, 83, 132, 198–9, 206*n*, 218

autonomy of linguistics, 301

axiomatization: of empirical issues, 78, 121–2, 132, 138–40, 159–60, 195, 246, 286*n*, 292; of sentences, 285, 294–5

Bach, E., 88, 225–6, 228, 247

Benjamin, A. C., 139, 239

Berko, J., 313–14

Bever, T. G., 261*n*, 285–6

bidirectionality, 268–9

Bloch, B., 182–3

Bloch, B. & Trager, G., 29*n*, 30*n*, 31, 177, 301*n*, 302*n*

Bloomfield, L., 27–8, 34, 35, 116, 120*n*, 126*n*, 144*n*, 301, 309

Botha, R. P., 45, 46

Braithwaite, R. B., 226, 237

Brown, R., 56, 219*n*

Campbell, R. & Wales, R., 267

Cattell, R. B., 227

Caws, P., 11, 13, 15, 38, 77*n*, 130, 226, 227, 230, 231, 232, 234, 237–8, 240, 246, 248

Chafe, W. L., 45, 60, 103, 118*n*, 161, 164, 165, 208, 212, 268*n*

Chambers, J. K., 165

Chao, Y-R., 30*n*, 34, 35

Chase, R. A., 220

Chomsky, N.
his influence, 3–4, 9, 25–6,
on abstractness, 89*n*, 108, 126–7, 145*n*, 148, 159
on analogy, 34–5, 310
on competence *v.* performance, 29–30, 33, 251, 258, 259–60, 265, 267, 270–1, 275, 277, 294
on descriptive adequacy, 42, 109–10
on discovery procedures, 37, 57ff
on evaluation procedures, 57–8, 62, 117, 138–9, 141, 142, 155, 246
on explanation, 39, 41*n*, 65*n*, 101*n*, 130, 134*n*
on explanatory adequacy, 61–2, 62*n*, 242
on foundations, 28*n*, 78, 132*n*, 228, 236, 239, 246, 250, 259, 286*n*, 288, 290
on habits, 35, 202*n*
on idealization, 34, 120
on innateness, 43*n*, 50, 53, 56
on knowledge, 251, 254–5
on language acquisition, 48–9, 50ff, 54*n*, 55–6, 67ff, 78, 82, 89*n*, 117, 123, 125*n*, 202*n*, 218, 277
on language change, 117–18
on linguistic creativity, 34, 67, 264, 266, 278
on linguistic intuition, 42, 130, 253
on linguistic performance, 33–4, 282, 298, 311*n*
on linguistic universals, 38–9, 45–6, 53, 66*n*, 78, 143
on mentalism, 43*n*, 47, 250
on methodology, 32–3, 41, 297*n*, 315
on the nature of language, 29–30, 30*n*, 33
on the phoneme, 171, 187